HELEN GABRIEL

TEACHING TECHNIQUES

A HANDBOOK FOR HEALTH PROFESSIONALS

TEACHING TECHNIQUES

A HANDBOOK FOR HEALTH PROFESSIONALS

Richard P. Foley, Ph.D.
Associate Professor of
  Health Professions Education
Center for Educational Development
University of Illinois
  at the Medical Center, Chicago

Jonathan Smilansky, Ph.D.
Assistant Professor of Education
Hebrew University
Formerly of the Center
  for Educational Development
University of Illinois
  at the Medical Center, Chicago

McGRAW-HILL BOOK COMPANY
New York   St. Louis   San Francisco
Auckland   Bogotá   Hamburg
London   Madrid
Mexico   Montreal   New Delhi
Panama   Paris   São Paulo
Singapore   Sydney   Tokyo   Toronto

TEACHING TECHNIQUES
A Handbook for Health Professionals

Copyright © 1980 by McGraw-Hill, Inc.
All rights reserved.
Printed in the United States of America.

4 5 6 7 8 9 0 D O D O 8 9 8

This book was set in Press Roman by Allen Wayne Technical Corp.
The editors were Laura A. Dysart and Henry C. De Leo;
the designer was Nicholas Krenitsky;
the production supervisor was Nancy Parisotti.
R. R. Donnelley & Sons Company was printer and binder.

Library of Congress Cataloging in Publication Data

Foley, Richard P.
    Teaching techniques.

    Bibliography: p.
    Includes index.
    1. Medicine—Study and teaching.
2. Paramedical education. 3. Teaching.
I. Smilansky, Jonathan, joint author.
II. Title.
R834.F64   610'.7'1   79-25237
ISBN 0-07-021420-4

To our teachers at the University of Chicago,
who taught us theories,
and
to Patricia Mueller and Norman Litowitz,
who helped us put these theories into practice

CONTENTS

Preface   ix

1 THE LECTURE   1

2 THE USE OF QUESTIONS   15

3 GROUP DISCUSSION   27

4 PROMOTING CLINICAL PROBLEM SOLVING   47

5 SKILL LESSONS   71

6 INSTRUCTIONAL DESIGN   93

CONCLUSION   137

APPENDIX A
Self-Assessment Questionnaires on Teaching   139

APPENDIX B
Posttest: Classifying Questions   147

APPENDIX C
Instructional Media: Overview and Annotated Bibliography   149

APPENDIX D
Evaluation: Overview and Annotated Bibliography   157

APPENDIX E
Annotated Bibliography   165

APPENDIX F
References   173

APPENDIX G
List of Planning Guides, Checklists, Questionnaires, and Self-Tests   175

Index   177

PREFACE

For the past several years we have been collaborating to improve the teaching skills of health professionals. Our work began in the Center for Educational Development, University of Illinois at the Medical Center in Chicago. Since the late sixties, the Center has been in the forefront, nationally and internationally, in educational development and research for the health professions. Much of this effort has focused on developing and testing innovative approaches to curricula and evaluation. These activities led to the introduction of a new integrated curriculum for the College of Medicine in Chicago, and three satellite institutions in Peoria, Rockford, and Urbana. A model, comprehensive examination plan was instituted throughout the system to continuously assess student performance in all phases of the curriculum.

Upon joining the Center, we observed the need to augment these efforts by providing assistance to individuals on the firing line: the instructors responsible for day-to-day teaching. Knowing that most health professions faculty had little or no training in teaching methods, we believed they would have difficulties implementing a new curriculum and utilizing the student achievement data they received.

To assess the need for initiating programs to improve instruction, a survey was conducted (Page, Foley et al., 1975) among University of Illinois faculty in the Colleges of Dentistry, Medicine, Nursing, and Pharmacy; and the Schools of Associated Medical Sciences and Public Health. Most of more than 1000 respondents had no formal education in instruction, yet 75 percent expressed interest in receiving some form of assistance, primarily through short-term (2- to 4-hour) programs. Subsequently, a series of ongoing workshops was implemented to address the various needs and interests expressed in the survey.

Direct experience and evaluation of these programs (Smilansky, Taylor, and Foley, 1976) led to the development of more in-depth workshops to assist health professionals improve instructional methods in such areas as lecturing, group discussion, and laboratory teaching. We experimented with a variety of formats to achieve the greatest impact upon teaching practices. One of the more effective approaches involved working with the faculty of an entire department over an extended period of time (Foley, Smilansky et al., 1976). To complement our work with faculty groups we developed self-instructional programs for verbal questioning techniques (Risley and Foley, 1976), lecturing skills (Foley et al., 1976), and the use of a simulation in clinical instruction (Smilansky et al., 1976). Through the use of videotapes and written materials, these packages enable health professionals to improve their teaching skills on their own time and at a comfortable pace.

In addition to our work at the University of Illinois, we have consulted with numerous organizations and institutions, resulting in direct, individual contact with more than 1500 participants from nearly all branches of the health sciences. We have consulted with the American Dietetic Association, American Medical Association, American Medical Record Association, American Podiatric Association, American Psychiatric Association, American Public Health Association, American Society of Plastic and Reconstructive Surgeons, and the Medical Library Association. We have conducted workshops on teaching techniques from coast to coast with dentists, dieticians, medical record personnel, medical social workers, nurses, occupational therapists, pharmacists, physical therapists, and physicians.

In adapting our program to the specific needs of these varied groups, a number of concepts and techniques emerged for improving instruction which are useful in almost every setting. For instance, as a result of observing hundreds of professionals deliver lectures, we developed a brief checklist of effective lecturing behaviors that has proved extremely beneficial in upgrading the organization and delivery skills of most participants attending our programs. We have designed equally useful materials and approaches for other areas of instruction and course planning.

At this point in our professional lives, it seemed appropriate to reflect upon our experiences, draw from our published work, and compile our material. The result of this effort is this handbook, which outlines an integrated and systematic approach for improving instruction in the health professions.

This book is intended for health professionals in any discipline responsible for teaching in a classroom, laboratory, clinical, field, or continuing education setting. It is as applicable for experienced teachers as for those about to enter the field. The first five chapters focus on teaching techniques. Each chapter includes planning guides and suggestions for improving the delivery of instruction. Examples are provided from a variety of health disciplines to illustrate the broad application of the principles and techniques discussed. Chapter 6 describes a systematic process for putting together a course. The preceding chapters on teaching skills should provide the basis for making informed decisions for organizing a larger unit of instruction such as a course, a 4-week clinical experience, or a workshop.

An overview of evaluation and an annotated bibliography of references on how to write multiple-choice tests, construct student feedback sheets, or evaluate your total course are included. A comparable section will guide you in the selection, use, and location of readily available instructional media. Also provided is a comprehensive annotated bibliography of other useful books and articles related to improving instruction.

Personally, we do not believe in the adage "teachers are born, not made," but rather attribute the wide variance in teaching ability among health professionals to the fact that very few have received formal experience in education. As with any field, mastery in teaching requires knowledgeable, careful planning and continuous practice. Becoming familiar and comfortable with the most widely-used, traditional teaching techniques should, over time, free you to experiment with new ways to improve student learning and make teaching a very enjoyable professional endeavor.

As educators, our feelings about improving instruction are best summarized by one of the foremost contributors to the field of education in this century, Benjamin Bloom (1972).

During the past fifty years there has been much research on teacher characteristics and their relation to student learning. This research was intended to improve the selection of teachers for particular teaching positions. One could summarize most of this research with the simple statement that the characteristics of teachers have little relation to the learning of their pupils.

More recently, some researchers have taken the position that it is the *teaching*, not the *teacher*, that is the key to the learning of students. That is, it is not what teachers are *like* but what they *do* in interacting with their students in the classroom that determines what students learn and how they feel about the learning and about themselves. This point of view has led to some of the most fundamental research about the nature of teaching, the role of the teacher in the classroom, and the kinds of learning materials that are useful in promoting particular kinds of learning (p. 340).

In writing this book, we are grateful to Wynn Scott for providing opportunities to test many of our ideas at George Washington University, School of Medicine and Health Sciences. The contributions of Barbara Barzansky, Robert Davis, Betty Horton, Dorthea Juul, Betty Risley, Nancy Runkle, and Larry Solomon greatly enriched the scope of our work. Anne Jenkins and Nancy Autrey were fastidious typists. Rhonda Goldberg was always there to listen, encourage and provoke. Tom Loesch's editorial head and hand pared and polished our writing. And we are forever indebted to Becky Lerfelt for her patience and understanding.

Richard P. Foley
Jonathan Smilansky

In a lecture given by a brilliant scholar with an outstanding topic and a highly competent audience, ten percent of the audience displayed signs of inattention within fifteen minutes. After eighteen minutes one-third of the audience and ten percent of the platform guests were fidgeting. At 35 minutes everyone was inattentive; at 45 minutes trance was more noticeable than fidgeting; and at 47 minutes some were asleep and at least one was reading. A casual check twenty-four hours later revealed that the audience recalled only insignificant details, and these were generally wrong. (Frost, 1965, pp. 282-283)

THE LECTURE[1]

As inevitable as this experience has been for all of us at some time, the lecture remains the predominant mode of instruction in all health profession fields. This one-way method for communicating factual information is utilized extensively not only in basic science programs but also in clinical settings such as grand rounds, seminars, and patient management conferences.

Research has shown, however, that an average of 80 percent of information delivered in lecture form is forgotten within 8 weeks. With such findings, why do we continue to lecture? As a mode of instruction, lecturing has a number of advantages. It is economical in terms of instructor-student ratio, space requirements, and, often, the preparation required. Also, to change the basis of a curriculum which has traditionally relied on the lecture would be a complex process requiring new resources of personnel and material as well as knowledge of a good alternative. Finally, there are rewards for individuals who use this form of teaching: the lecture highlights the teacher as the central content authority. Who can deny the gratification that results when an audience applauds an especially effective presentation?

Since it is likely that the lecture will remain a principal mode of instruction in the health professions, the aims of this chapter are to review the purposes of the lecture, to discuss methods for increasing effectiveness of organization and for improving delivery skills, and to introduce a number of techniques which can result in a more creative presentation.

WHEN TO USE THE LECTURE

In deciding whether or not to lecture it is important to recognize which objectives can best be achieved through this method. In general, lectures are an effective tool for helping students acquire information and are less useful for teaching problem-solving skills or for changing student attitudes. For the purpose of providing information, the lecture cannot be replaced by a reading list alone. Not all students are motivated to read a

---

[1]A portion of this chapter was adapted from R. Foley, J. Smilansky, F. Bughman, and A. Sajid, *Learning Package Designed to Improve Lecture Skills,* Audio Visual Concepts, Inc., Chicago, 1976.

great deal of material on their own. An effective lecturer can emphasize key ideas and can synthesize a large amount of information from multiple sources, which many students are unable to do. Finally, the lecturer can provide up-to-date information that may not be available in published sources.

If you decide that the lecture is appropriate for what you want to achieve, the first step in planning is to consider the student. Often planning focuses on how much content can be conveyed in a specified period of time rather than on what a student can gain from listening. The focus of a lecture should be on student performance: what should students be able to think, do, believe, or discuss at the end of your lecture that they could not before it? For example, lecturers in an anatomy series frequently include a tremendous amount of content which consists primarily of terminology and information about various body systems. It is often unclear in these lectures whether students are expected to remember all of the terms and descriptions provided or if the information is to be used as a basis for explaining the basic principles underlying body functioning. Deciding in advance what students should be expected to learn will affect the selection and organization of the content.

After determining what students should learn, it is necessary to have some notion of what they already know about a subject. Frequently students attend a series of uncoordinated and isolated lectures which may be either repetitious or too sophisticated. Since pretests are usually time-consuming, it will be useful to discuss your goals with colleagues and former students prior to planning your lectures.

In specifying your goals it is necessary to consider the following questions:

1. Does the audience really need to learn or know about the subject matter being presented?

2. Is the content appropriate for the audience given the time available?

3. Do you want to be informative, persuasive, or thought-provoking?

PLANNING CONTENT ORGANIZATION

In planning the content of your lecture include an <u>introduction</u>, a <u>body</u>, and a <u>conclusion</u>.

The Introduction

Many lecturers begin with opening statements such as, "Today we will discuss diabetes mellitus," and proceed immediately with the body of the lecture. As the lecturer continues, the audience is never certain what points will be covered or in what order. A frequent result is that when time is up, students begin leaving while the instructor is hurriedly covering final points. This problem can be rectified.

An effective introduction to a lecture should clearly delineate the specific topics to be covered and give their order. For a lecture on diabetes mellitus a more careful opening might be as follows: Today we will discuss possible factors which cause diabetes mellitus, the chief signs and symptoms of untreated diabetes, and the role of insulin in controlling the disease. As a result of this lecture you should be able to recognize cases in which diabetes is clearly indicated and discuss relevant courses of treatment.

Another component of an effective introduction is a clear specification of the relevance of the material to be covered. We all have wondered at times how some of the basic science information being presented would be helpful in actual practice. It is not enough to say that something is important; it is necessary to show why. Beginning with clinical examples or data that demonstrate the need for learning the information is one device to capture audience attention. For example, if the introduction to a lecture on electrofluid balances includes its significance in determining intravenous (IV) schedules, there is a greater chance that students will remain attentive.

Opening with a series of questions that students should be able to answer at the end or presenting a clinical case that sets the stage for analyzing a problem are other ways to make an introduction more interesting.

Finally, establishing ground rules for audience participation is useful. You might do this by making a statement such as, I will address any questions which relate to issues of clarification at any point during the lecture. However, I have reserved 10 minutes at the end of my talk to discuss general questions or concerns that you may have about the material. Without knowing such ground rules in advance students may divert the thrust of the speech by introducing involved comments and questions at the wrong time or may remain mute when they do not understand a key idea.

Initial impressions are formed on the basis of your opening remarks, particularly when you address an audience for the first time. Introductory statements should be carefully planned, as they will influence attention during the delivery and retention following it.

The Body

A well-shaped introduction will provide you with the framework needed for elaborating your content. In planning the main portion of your presentation, a number of considerations should be kept in mind.

Relating the Body to the Introduction   One frequent fault made in delivering a lecture is to overstep the boundaries established in the introduction. This can occur when a lecturer introduces topics to which the audience has not been alerted. Similarly, an inordinate amount of digression on a single topic may create an imbalance. Returning to the example of the diabetes lecture, given earlier, if the lecturer spends only 10 minutes on the definition, causes, and treatment routes and devotes the balance of the hour to some interesting clinical cases observed in practice, the main body of the lecture is not appropriately related to the purposes specified in the introduction. If the purpose had been to review briefly the causes, characteristics, and treatments of the disease and to explore in depth five unusual cases, the body of the lecture would be consistent with the introduction.

Although poor planning is most often the cause of this imbalance, it can also occur as a result of lecturers' enthusiasm or their knowledge of the subject matter. One idea or example touches off another, and before they know it these lecturers have diverted both themselves and their audiences from the concerns at hand. To prevent this, outlines of the content with approximate time notations for each topic should be developed. This provides a guide for planning and will assist in keeping you on the right track during the actual delivery.

Clarification   A lecturer must remain sensitive to the audience's needs, especially when delivering new or complex concepts. Most health professionals are learning a new language during training, and failure to clarify technical terms or overuse of jargon will result in confusion. The daily language of the professional may be incomprehensible to a beginning student.

Much of what we teach involves abstractions that demand concrete examples in order to be understood. The use of clear-cut examples from clinical experience is one means of clarifying an idea. When balloons can be used to demonstrate the effects of pressure in the lungs, use them. Pictures, videotapes, and simple verbal descriptions will increase the students' ability to incorporate a concept. Since students differ in ability to understand material because of varying backgrounds and capabilities, two or three different examples can be used to illustrate a main idea in order to ensure comprehension.

In addition to clarifying terms and using examples, it is important to emphasize key ideas; simple repetition and labeling can accomplish this. Often a central idea is mentioned only once with the expectation that students will remember and understand it. What we fail to recognize is that students are generally bombarded with a tremendous amount of new information in a variety of courses, and they may be struggling with what is old hat to the instructor.

Providing a short glossary of terms, a handout emphasizing main points, and direct references for more in-depth explanations are a few ways to clarify material. Slides, overhead transparencies, drawings on the chalkboard, and brief demonstrations will not only break a monotonous pace but can further enhance understanding. In summary, an idea can be powerfully conveyed when opportunities to hear, see, and touch stimuli which reinforce it are provided.

Change of Pace   Research has demonstrated that after 20 minutes of listening to a speaker, audience attention drops dramatically. Since most lectures run from 15 minutes to an hour, this relatively short attention span must be considered in planning.

An effective lecturer will make clear transitions from one topic to the next, providing some breathing space for the listeners, as well as alerting them to where they are in the content outline. Such transitions are ideal after the completion of a given objective or goal. A good transition might be, I have just discussed the chief signs and symptoms of untreated diabetes, including excessive urination, sugar in the urine, high blood sugar, and loss of weight. We will now proceed with three clinical examples that demonstrate the effect of insulin treatment on these symptoms. In this example the student is provided with a brief review of the objective covered, a summary of key points to be remembered, and a description of the upcoming segment of the talk.

In addition to effective transitions, the astute lecturer will maintain audience interest by periodically changing the pace of the lecture. The best tragedies include some comic relief; the same rule of thumb applies to lectures. The use of humor, brief demonstrations, movies, slides, videotapes, and the introduction of patients can all function as pace breakers. In each of these instances, however, the technique used should be weighed in terms of its appropriateness to the purposes of the presentation. An interesting patient or a clever joke can revitalize your audience, but may also prove distracting if they are unrelated to the topic or take an undue amount of time. While we encourage you to diversify your presentation as much as possible, this cautionary note is in order: there is no faster way to lose your credibility than to have a joke fall flat, or to have a patient discuss data which you have not heard before, or to waste 15 minutes trying to get a movie projector to work. Therefore, a critical component of incorporating change-of-pace techniques is to test them before using them.

The Conclusion

A conclusion is critical in influencing which portions of the lecture will be recalled, particularly in light of the retention loss inherent in the lecture mode. A good conclusion should relate back to the introductory statement of purpose. If the lecture opened with a series of questions, a conclusion should specify how they were addressed. If specific objectives were delineated, the conclusion should review and summarize them. A good conclusion will tie the introduction and body of the lecture together in a fashion similar to an abstract of a scientific paper.

In addition to summarizing the lecture, the conclusion can further stimulate student thought or action. A series of challenging questions, references to pertinent readings, or a discussion of methods for applying the material are likely to increase learning. If a lecture is one of a series, it is particularly useful to place it in context of what has come before and what will follow. Again, outlines of approximate time notations should be developed. Concluding with statements such as, "Even though our time is up, I have a few more things to say," or, "Although we have some time left, I have nothing more to add today," create the image of an unprepared speaker, especially when such statements are delivered in an apologetic manner.

In summary, the key steps in planning your lecture are as follows: tell the audience what you're going to tell them (introduction), tell them (body), and tell them what you've told them (conclusion). Organized repetition will increase the probability of your audience's retention.

DELIVERY SKILLS

Summaries of research on teaching effectiveness consistently cite factors such as warmth, enthusiasm, and motivation as characteristics of the effective instructor. These traits are as important in the lecture as in teaching situations which involve more direct interaction with the students. Suggesting that a lecturer be warmer or more enthusiastic legitimately raises the question, How? These are personality characteristics, and there are no magical formulas for making an individual enthusiastic. On the other hand, our experience in observing hundreds of lectures is that these qualities often exist but are not exhibited by a person speaking to a group. We often work with individuals who give a lifeless lecture and afterward, when discussing their presentation with us, are humorous, articulate, and self-assured. The problem is often the discrepancy between the personality we observe at the lecture platform and the personality away from it. The purpose of this section is to share our observations and offer suggestions which have proved beneficial to the majority of persons with whom we have worked to narrow this gap.

Use of Voice

The most effective lecturers talk to an audience of 500 as if they were talking to a single person. Too often a stage, lectern, and lecture notes result in an overly stylized or formal presentation, and by distancing the speaker from the audience make the speech less interesting. Several tips are helpful in overcoming this problem. Having a complete script of your speech at the lectern usually precludes your moving away from it and talking informally to your audience. Alternatively, using a content outline which specifies only major topics and key facts will maintain the flow and organization of your presentation and at the same time will facilitate a more conversational manner of speaking, which will improve contact with listeners.

Varying the pitch and force of your voice can also affect the presentation. Key points you want your audience to remember can be identified by shifting the tone of your voice when they are described. Lecturers vary in degree of ability to exhibit animation comfortably. Within this range of comfort, however, plan shifts where you raise and lower your voice, pause, or vary the speed of your delivery to emphasize ideas you want your audience to remember.

A final suggestion regarding the use of voice relates to the pace of your speech. Depending upon the content of the lecture and your audience, speaking too quickly or too slowly can be detrimental. If you are lecturing to beginning students and describe the Krebs cycle as quickly as you give biographical information about Pasteur, you will undoubtedly leave most of them perplexed. One cannot prescribe a suitable rate of speech for each topic. Listening to your talk on audiotape or videotape or checking with a few students after delivery will put you in touch with the appropriateness of your pace.

Body Movement

We have observed many instructors standing motionless behind a lectern which covers three-quarters of the body, with their eyes glued to the set of notes in front of them or to a slide on the screen behind them. This posture is guaranteed to make 95 percent of your audience daydream, sleep, or feel angry.

In conversation with a single person there tends to be a sense of distance if eye contact is not established. This is true for a large-group setting as well, and the competent speaker should keep eye contact with the audience. It is important to direct your eyes to various individuals and locations in the room and to scan the audience in order to draw in individuals on the periphery as well as those in front of you. At the beginning of your talk you may find it useful to identify a few friendly faces in various parts of the room and subsequently to look at and talk to them as if on a one-to-one basis. Also consider the use of appropriate facial expressions. As much as possible, attempt some variability in expression. The overly animated individual may be as ineffective as the person who never moves a muscle, and appropriate changes are usually indications of a relaxed presenter. The best way of assessing this quality is to videotape and view your presentation.

We have found that the effective lecturer moves purposefully rather than remaining stuck to the lectern, pacing from one end of the stage to the other, or standing midstage with hands in pockets. If your tendency is to hide behind a lectern, try moving toward a screen to point out details on a slide, or periodically approach your audience for emphasis. Alternatively, setting up a table to provide anchoring points may be appropriate if you need to restrain unnecessary movement.

Delivery skills constitute your general stage presence as an instructor. As with any good actor, being comfortable in your role, cognizant of your style and its effect upon others, and capable of alternative behaviors can enrich your lecturing repertoire. Various techniques are available to make you conscious of your voice, pace, eye contact, and other body movements as aids in communicating. Peer observations, videotapes, audiotapes, student evaluations, and other feedback mechanisms can assist you in this type of self-assessment. After identifying your strengths and areas needing improvement, focus on a manageable number of changes which you would like to make. In our experience we have found an initial tendency for individuals to focus on personal mannerisms such as a high voice or hands in the pockets as major faults in lecturing. Most often, however, audience feedback suggests that these mannerisms do not interfere with comprehension or interest. Focusing on minor details may, in fact, prevent recognizing more important delivery elements such as moving away from the lectern and maintaining eye contact. Our best advice is to practice and to use the suggested sources of feedback.

USE OF AUDIOVISUAL AIDS

This segment will present suggestions regarding the use of the most common audiovisual lecture aids: the chalkboard, overhead projector, and slides. A list of references which discuss the value and use of these and other instructional media will be found in Appendix C.

Appropriate audiovisual aids enhance even the most talented lecturer's presentation. Besides providing a change of pace, media used effectively can amplify main ideas, as the visual stimuli enrich what the audience is hearing from the speaker. In addition, certain content is best conveyed visually. It would be ludicrous to describe verbally the findings on an x-ray without showing it. Similar complex material can be simplified by using a diagram, flowchart, or picture. When using these aids, the suggestions which follow are useful.

The Chalkboard

This has been the most consistently used teaching aid. It is inexpensive, simple to use, and requires little advance preparation. Although very useful in some settings, the chalkboard is least effective in lectures to large groups. We have all observed the lecturer who faces the chalkboard writing ferociously and illegibly with one hand while erasing with the other, with students learning more about the lecturer's posterior than the subject at hand. As with every other element of your lecture, preplanning is the key to being effective. If you have the time and resources, avoid the chalkboard and use other aids to clarify your message. If you do use it, consider these suggestions:

1. Drawings, charts, and written information should be placed on the board prior to the presentation. The time saved during delivery helps you maintain eye contact with the audience and ensures the accuracy of details such as labeling, spelling, and relative object size. If board work is done beforehand, you can judge what the student in the last row will be able to see.

2. Shading and the use of colored chalk can provide depth and reality to a drawing and focus attention on its particular aspects.

3. Keep your diagrams simple and accurate. The most artistic drawings cannot replace a good slide and may confuse rather than clarify.

Overheads

Transparencies for overhead projectors can be prepared in advance, or you can write on blank transparencies with a felt pen during the lecture. Both project a clearer and larger image than the chalkboard, and enable you more easily to face the students. Certain problems can occur while using transparencies. Too much information may make them illegible, and standing in their way can block all or part of the image. There are minor complexities in placing the transparencies right side up, refocusing when changing them, and remembering to turn the bulb on and off. These drawbacks are minimal, however, when weighed against the difficulty of producing slides.

Slides

Well-produced slides project the clearest and most accurate image. Slides can be changed with ease and accuracy and permit the lecturer to face the audience and move about. In our observations, however, we have noted misuses. Some instructors present a slide show in a darkened room that creates an atmosphere not unlike the one you endure when seeing slides of your neighbor's last vacation. There are instances when too much information appears on a slide or the contrast is not strong enough to produce a clear image. Occasionally instructors do not organize slides ahead, and valuable time is lost looking for a missing slide or turning slides right side up.

Four points should be kept in mind when using instructional media. They should be carefully incorporated into the verbal presentation since they illustrate and clarify particular ideas rather than provide the major focus. If you talk for the first half hour and show slides the second, you are probably not giving an effective presentation. Media should be used only when they enhance understanding of the subject matter. When selecting an aid, decide what it will add to your verbal presentation. In describing the structure of a cell, a diagram indicating its morphology will clarify what would otherwise be a complicated and abstract verbal description. Audiovisual aids should be easily visible and audible. A list of all possible causes of acute bacterial pneumonia should not be placed on a single slide. Lists can be better viewed and remembered if presented on a handout.

Finally, remember Murphy's law: If anything can go wrong, it will. Consider each lecture as a performance, and like a competent stage manager check every prop or special effect that will be used prior to curtain call. Is your slide projector working and focused? Have you previewed your series of slides for order and relevance? Have you practiced raising and lowering the screen? Have you threaded the tape recorder and adjusted the volume on the monitor? Attention to detail and preplanning will differentiate the professional from the amateur.

THE INTERACTIVE LECTURE

Lecturing is typically a one-way method of communication; you talk, and hopefully the audience listens. Yet most will agree that the active participation of the learner is essential for understanding and retaining information. Among the major teaching methods they are exposed to, students are generally the most passive during a lecture. To overcome the inherent passivity in this format, the creative speaker must employ numerous techniques to break the barrier with the audience in order to establish a two-way system of communication. Three approaches are suggested here.

The lecturer can interact with individual members of the audience. Questions can be directed to the audience at large or to an individual. Expecting students to answer in front of a large group can provoke anxiety, but if the question is reasonable and relevant, this technique can keep your audience alert and facilitate comprehension of the material.

When asking questions that require a group rather than an individual response, the audience can answer by raising their hands: "How many of you have seen a case of anorexia nervosa?" This question can provide data which can be incorporated into the lecture. Depending upon student response, it might be followed by, "How many of you have seen a case that involved young women?" and "Did any involve men?" This technique makes it possible for the audience to characterize the typical patient population of the disease. Decide in advance the questions you want to ask, their relevance to the lecture, and how you want students to respond. Give care to designing questions the audience is capable of answering, and which will facilitate interest and comprehension rather than fill time or digress from the topic.

Another way to increase student involvement is to devise short tasks individuals can complete at their seats. This requires a good handout. You can provide a topical outline of your lecture with appropriate spaces for note taking under each heading. A more elaborate version can include problems or questions to be answered at appropriate intervals throughout the presentation. Students might be asked to apply a formula that was just described in the lecture, solve a problem, or respond to multiple-choice questions about the material. These suggestions are not intended to evaluate student comprehension as much as to increase audience involvement. It is worthwhile developing tasks such as these since, as has been mentioned, audience attention drops dramatically after 20 minutes of listening.

A final suggestion is to isolate periods in the lecture during which students work in pairs to address a task. For example, a brief case description could be provided for which students are asked to select appropriate laboratory tests or plan a course of management. In a large lecture hall, students can work with the person sitting next to them. Students can work in small groups in rooms where seats can be moved. Whatever the setting, tasks should be brief and instructions delineated clearly in the handout to save time.

One must be continuously aware of the passive role the lecture format imposes on an audience. Planned interventions stimulate more student involvement and allow opportunities to apply the information provided.

EVALUATING YOUR LECTURE SKILLS

So far this chapter has presented information regarding techniques for improving your lecture presentation. Self-assessment questionnaires are included in Appendix A if you are interested in evaluating your perceptions of yourself as a lecturer. The following section provides tools helpful in identifying areas of strength as well as those needing improvement. It is intended to help you collect as much data as possible in order to make informed decisions about those lecture skills you need to improve.

Recording and Assessing Your Lecture

Research has demonstrated that one of the central elements in improving skills is to observe yourself in the actual performance of a task. The availability of portable videotape equipment makes it possible for you to see how you come across to others.

If you have not been videotaped before, you will probably feel some anxiety about this process. Experience indicates, however, that after awhile the lecturer tends to forget the camera, and the advantages gained from seeing yourself outweigh any initial discomfort you may feel.

After preparing your lecture, follow the procedures outlined below to review and assess your performance.

1. Select for videotaping an upcoming lecture that you will deliver to your students or colleagues. The lecture should be between 15 and 60 minutes.

2. Employ your usual presentation, i.e., avoid adding new features just because you are being recorded on videotape.

3. Contact the media service in your institution and request portable video recording equipment. Also make arrangements for someone to operate the equipment for you. Often such arrangements need to be made at least 2 weeks in advance.

4. Record a complete presentation rather than selected segments of your lecture.

5. Review and assess your taped lecture by utilizing the rating scale on the following pages. You may want to ask a colleague to do this with you to receive additional feedback.

CHECKLIST FOR RATING YOUR LECTURE

Date: _____   Presentation: _____

Listed below are 22 statements intended to serve as guides for rating lecture presentations. After observing a lecture, please respond to each statement by checking the category that most closely corresponds to your observations.

Name: _____   Rater: _____

	NOT DONE	ONLY PARTIALLY OR RARELY DONE	COMPLETELY OR USUALLY DONE	NOT APPLICABLE OR CAN'T RECALL
SKILL IN ORGANIZING LECTURE MATERIAL				
Specifies purposes of the lecture in introduction.	☐	☐	☐	☐
Sets general ground rules for audience participation.	☐	☐	☐	☐
Relates the main body of information to the introductory purposes.	☐	☐	☐	☐
Makes clear transitions between different segments of the lecture.	☐	☐	☐	☐
Uses clear, relevant examples to illustrate main ideas.	☐	☐	☐	☐
Clarifies technical terminology.	☐	☐	☐	☐
Periodically summarizes most important points or ideas of the lecture.	☐	☐	☐	☐
Develops a conclusion related to the purposes and body of the lecture.	☐	☐	☐	☐

	NOT DONE	ONLY PAR-TIALLY OR RARELY DONE	COMPLETELY OR USUALLY DONE	NOT APPLI-CABLE OR CAN'T RECALL
Cites appropriate authorities to support statements.	☐	☐	☐	☐
Presents divergent viewpoints for contrast and comparison.	☐	☐	☐	☐
Separates facts from opinions.	☐	☐	☐	☐

SKILL IN USE OF VOICE AND BODY MOVEMENTS IN DELIVERING A LECTURE

	NOT DONE	ONLY PAR-TIALLY OR RARELY DONE	COMPLETELY OR USUALLY DONE	NOT APPLI-CABLE OR CAN'T RECALL
Speaks at a volume suitable for audience (not too soft or too loud).	☐	☐	☐	☐
Speaks at a suitable pace for presentation.	☐	☐	☐	☐
Varies rate, pitch, and force of voice for emphasis.	☐	☐	☐	☐
Speaks in a conversational manner (not formal or stylized).	☐	☐	☐	☐
Uses eye contact (scans total audience).	☐	☐	☐	☐
Uses a variety of facial expressions (not deadpan).	☐	☐	☐	☐
Uses hands and arms appropriately (not hand waving, but for emphasis).	☐	☐	☐	☐
Moves purposefully (not pacing or sticking to lectern, but moves for emphasis).	☐	☐	☐	☐

	NOT DONE	ONLY PAR- TIALLY OR RARELY DONE	COMPLETELY OR USUALLY DONE	NOT APPLI- CABLE OR CAN'T RECALL

SKILL IN THE USE OF AUDIOVISUAL AIDS

	NOT DONE	ONLY PAR- TIALLY OR RARELY DONE	COMPLETELY OR USUALLY DONE	NOT APPLI- CABLE OR CAN'T RECALL
Coordinates audiovis- ual aids with verbal presentation.	☐	☐	☐	☐
Uses audiovisual aids to enhance under- standing of the sub- ject matter.	☐	☐	☐	☐
Uses audiovisual aids which are easily visible or audible.	☐	☐	☐	☐

Use this form to write strengths and weaknesses which you see in your videotaped lecture:

Strengths: _____

_____

_____

_____

_____

_____

_____

_____

Weaknesses: _____

_____

_____

_____

_____

_____

_____

PLANNING YOUR NEXT LECTURE

We hope you now have a clearer perspective about your strengths and weaknesses as a lecturer as well as some vehicles for improvement. The annotated bibliography at the end of the book provides references if you are interested in further information on lecturing.

The best advice we can give at this point is to practice. The rating scale should serve as a guide to guarantee that the many components of an effective lecture have been addressed. The scale can be used for self-analysis of other videotaped lectures and can be given to students, colleagues, or educational specialists for additional feedback. The key to improving your lectures is to become aware of how you come across to others and to identify specific behaviors that can be improved.

THE USE OF QUESTIONS

Since Socrates, the notion has been with us that questions are essential in challenging students to think creatively and in stimulating further inquiry, yet few contemporary classroom instructors are aware of or have been educated to the subtleties of effective questioning. In 1912, Rommiet Stevens published a report derived from 4 years of observational analysis of teachers' verbal behavior in secondary school classrooms. It revealed that teachers talked an average of 64 percent of the time, and 80 percent of total classroom talk was asking, answering, or reacting to questions. Rarely did these questions call for more than rote memory or superficial comprehension. Fifty years later an extensive review by Hoetker and Ahlbrand (1963) showed essentially the same findings.

Although these studies dealt with secondary school settings, similar findings are reported in higher education. Spears (1950) revealed in his observational analysis of graduate classes that recitation of textbook facts was still the representative method of teaching in schools of education throughout the United States. Within health professions, Foley (1979) analyzed 17 hours of videotaped clerkship instruction of medical students. Findings were consistent with those already cited. For example, in both the teaching and working rounds medical students talked only 5 percent of the time. When students were asked to participate, they were primarily asked questions requiring only simple recall, usually concerning data in the patient's chart. Few cases were observed in which higher order questions which would have provoked students to think were asked. It appears setting does not influence the questioning pattern. Instructors in elementary schools and at the university level continue to do most of the talking, and recitation as an instructional technique persists.

This pattern has serious implications for the education of health professionals. The knowledge explosion does exist, and it is folly to expect today's health professional to be cognizant of, much less be able to memorize, the ever-increasing body of knowledge needed to solve medical problems. Even if it were possible, the practice of health science goes beyond knowing facts. Health professionals must be good problem solvers. They must interpret and synthesize data, formulate alternative treatment routes, and evaluate the effects of a selected action. The question raised here is whether instructors teach students to engage in these processes. They do not if they themselves do most of the talking, and students are questioned primarily at the memory and simple comprehension levels.

An instructor who delivers basic content to students or who questions their knowledge of factual information is not a poor teacher, since these are essential components in training a health professional. The issues are appropriateness and degree. A lecture (largely teacher talk) may be a useful vehicle for presenting basic information to students, and a review of their knowledge of essential facts and concepts might best be accomplished through low-level questioning. On the other hand, if seminars

and conferences are largely conducted as lecture and recitation sessions, an opportunity for students to engage in critical thinking is lost. Therefore, the appropriate use of questions and choice of their levels depends upon the goals desired in a particular setting.

It has been shown that teachers do most of the talking, and often it is erroneously assumed that students are learning in the process. However, most research on the lecture method (teacher talk) demonstrates that an average of 80 percent of the information delivered is forgotten. Bloom's 1953 study of the relative impact of lectures and discussions in promoting problem-solving thought among undergraduates revealed that all the discussion sections, save one, promoted more thinking of this type than any of the lectures studied. One must question who is doing most of the learning, the teacher or the student, if instructors do most of the talking in a student's education. Similarly, if students are rarely asked questions which challenge them to interpret, synthesize, and assess data, the result may be health professionals who are good medical dictionaries rather than skilled practitioners.

Since questioning is a natural process, many assume that it takes no preparation or practice. However, questions can be effective and useful when thoughtfully developed or ineffective and stifling when developed carelessly. Training educators to be more sensitive to the role questions play in teaching has resulted in less teacher talk, greater use of higher order questions, and increased skill in developing effective questions. The self-instructional program that follows will introduce basic categories of questions with the level of thinking required to answer each. The first step in learning to use questions effectively is to become familiar with each type. Work through the chapter carefully, taking time to do each of the self-check exercises.

SELF-INSTRUCTIONAL PROGRAM IN QUESTIONING TECHNIQUES

Questioning is a stimulus to interaction. Instructors ask questions to review content, verify understanding, and assess readiness, ability, and skills. Students generally ask questions to clarify understanding and to review content. The kinds of questions teachers ask, the way they ask them, and teacher reactions to student responses determine to a great extent the instructional environment existing in the classroom. More importantly, the teacher's skill in asking questions and the types of questions used greatly affect the quantity and quality of student thinking.

Effective questioning skills can be developed through an understanding of the types and levels of questions, their possible uses, and practice in developing appropriate questions. This process begins by recognizing the various types of questions. Questions can be classified by their range of acceptable responses and the level of thinking a student uses in making the response. Upon completion of the program in this chapter you will be able to do the following:

1.   When given a series of questions, be able to identify each as *open* or *closed*.

2.   When given examples of open and closed questions, be able to identify the level of thinking required to answer each.

Closed Questions

Closed questions include those which have only one of a small range of possible correct answers. The answers can be predicted, require limited thought of a student, and can be answered with a single word or phrase. They are used to test recall and student ability to recognize factual information. These are examples of closed questions:

1.   Does passively acquired immunity require antigenic stimulation?

2.   Is the deltoid classified as a smooth or a striated muscle?

3.   How many chambers does the human heart have?

4.   What enzyme(s) acts on lactose?

5.   What is the relationship between the liver and the gallbladder?

Each of these has a narrow range of correct responses. Questions 1 through 4 can be answered using a single word. The fifth requires more thought in giving a response, but still there is a narrow range of appropriate answers. Closed questions are efficient in terms of time (i.e., several questions can be asked and answered quickly), and can be used effectively to review previously studied material, to assess readiness to continue, or to verify data. The use of closed questions may be a first step in concept development.

Recognition of Closed Questions   If you identify the question as closed, put a *C* in the blank before it.

_____ **A.**   What organelle carries out cell respiration?

_____ **B.**   What is meant by the term *nonverbal cue* ?

_____ **C.**   What do you consider to be ethical conduct in the use of placebos?

_____ **D.**   Can the vagus nerve be cut without causing death?

_____ **E.**   How might allied health personnel justify their services in a hospital?

You should have identified A, B, and D as closed questions.
Question A requires a one-word answer – the name of the organelle.
Question B requires the definition of nonverbal cues.
Question D is worded so that it requires only a yes or no answer.
If you did not correctly identify A, B, and D as closed questions, you may want to read the explanatory section again.
Questions C and E require higher level thinking and permit a greater diversity of answers. If you had difficulty with these, the differentiation should become clearer as you proceed.

Two Categories of Closed Questions   Within this classification there are two specific categories: *memory* questions and *convergent* questions.

Memory Questions   Memory questions are the narrowest form of closed questions and require the lowest level of thinking. They do not require any use of knowledge other than the repetition of what has been learned. Answers are usually one word or definitions, repeated by rote. The questions test only memory, not understanding. Several examples follow.

1. Does saliva have an enzyme component? (Yes or no.)

2. Is systolic pressure written above or below the line? Is *Neisseria meningitidis* gram positive or negative? (Cue: the answers are within the questions.)

3. Where is norepinephrine produced? What is Avogadro's number? (Recall.)

4. What organ produces insulin? What are the spaces between the myelin sheaths called? (Name.)

5. What is a virus? What does *endogenous* mean? (Define.)

All these questions have simple, rote memory answers. If these questions were asked of several students, the correct answers would be very similar. Memory questions can be appropriately and effectively used for the rapid review of facts, and also to establish that a student has basic background information needed for use in interpretation, application, and problem solving.

To be sure that you can identify memory questions, read each question below and label the memory questions by placing an *M* in the space provided.

_____ A. What does the term *calorie* mean?

_____ B. How is high blood pressure related to a cerebrovascular accident (stroke)?

_____ C. What is the vector of malaria?

_____ D. Is the biceps femoris a smooth or a striated muscle?

_____ E. What kind of information can be elicited in an interview?

You should have identified A, C, and D as memory questions.

Question A asks the student to *define* calorie.

In Question C the student is to *name* the vector of malaria.

For Question D the answer is in the question.

Questions B and E are asked at a higher level than simple memory. A student must apply knowledge rather than recall information. This type of question will be clarified as you continue.

Convergent Questions   Convergent questions fall within the general classification of closed questions. While they require a more complex thinking process than memory questions, answers are still limited and predictable. Convergent questions require students to recall background information, then to translate, interpret, rephrase, reorganize, explain, or apply that information. This type of questioning is useful in the further development of concepts and helps a teacher assess student understanding of the material or the concept being developed. Examples of convergent questions follow.

1. What are the circular clusters in the upper right hand corner of this slide? (Observe.)

2. Why is influenza more common in winter months than at other times of the year? (Explain.)

3. How does a nerve impulse cross a synapse? (Describe.)

4. How is muscle contraction affected by curare? (State relationships.)

5. How is a mitochondrion similar to a virus? How does the action of DNA differ from that of RNA? (Compare and contrast.)

While these questions have limited right responses, there are different ways to phrase or organize the response. The sense of an appropriate answer is predictable but not the wording. Students must *use* knowledge to develop an answer in their own words. Thus, this type of question increases the freedom of student response even though there is still a limited right answer. Convergent questions often begin with the words *how* and *why*, although careless wording can convert a how or why question into a memory question.

To be sure that you can distinguish between the two groups of closed questions, read each of the following and mark memory questions with an *M* and convergent questions with a *C*.

_____ A. How does gonorrhea differ from syphilis?

_____ B. How does a normal child develop between the ages of 24 months and 4 years?

_____ C. Why are children encouraged to clean deciduous teeth?

_____ D. Does gastric juice turn litmus paper red or blue?

_____ E. In what ways does salt intake affect body weight?

Questions A, B, C, and E are convergent questions; Question D is a memory question.

In Question A, the respondent is asked to *contrast* the two diseases.

Question B calls for a *description*.

Question C is phrased so that it calls for an *explanation*.

In Question D the respondent uses simple recall of a learned fact. (The question contains the answer and therefore is a *cue*-type question.)

Question E requires the respondent to state a *relationship*.

If you had difficulty in identifying these questions, you may want to review the pertinent discussion before going on.

Review Closed questions are narrow in scope, have predictable answers and require low-level thinking. The two types are these:

Memory: say yes or no, cue, recall, name, and define.

Convergent: describe, explain, state relationships, compare, and contrast.

While closed questions can be appropriate, their uses are limited. Closed questions tend to be overused in the classroom and thus retard high-level student thinking. If an objective of instruction is to encourage problem solving, consistently asking closed questions may hinder its being met; instead the focus should be on questions which encourage students to think at a higher level. High-level thinking is developed through the use of open questions.

Open Questions

Open questions are directed toward problem solving, evaluation, or judgment. Rather than having one correct, predictable answer, they allow a range of appropriate responses. The level of thinking required is more complex because several thought processes may be demanded, and students must have background information that can be recalled. This information must then be processed in order to hypothesize, predict, or interpret data; identify variables and assumptions; infer, criticize, justify; and defend or make reasoned judgments. Open questions may also ask a student to suggest a course of action, such as choosing a treatment or stating appropriate goals.

Open questions motivate students to think more deeply and critically than closed questions. Students can freely formulate answers, rather than guessing what the instructor wants as an answer. These are examples of open questions:

1. A patient is given a course of treatment. What might be the reasons it does not have the expected effect?

2. How might a patient react if an interview is interrupted several times?

3. Why do you think Medicare should or should not cover all allied health services?

4. Given the following data, what activities would you suggest for this patient?

5. How would you set up an experiment to test the effects and side effects of a newly discovered antibiotic?

These questions clearly call for a higher level of thinking than closed questions. A student must organize background information, then reformulate it to develop a response. In each case there is a wide variety of possible answers.

To test your ability to recognize open questions, read each of the following. Place an *O* before those which are open, an *M* if they are memory, and a *C* if they are convergent.

_____ **A.** What is meant by the term *synergist*?

_____ **B.** In what ways can *Diplococcus pneumonia* be described?

_____ **C.** If a person's diet consists of beans, white rice, brown bread, and boiled green vegetables, what physical signs and symptoms might you expect to occur?

_____ **D.** An experimental animal weighing 150 g is given 195 mg (0.78-mL injection) of urethan and after 2 hours it dies. What might be the cause of death?

_____ **E.** What did you think of the article in **Science** on the investigation of children with an XYY karyotype?

You should have identified C, D, and E as open questions. A is a memory question and B is a convergent question dealing with description.

Question C requires the student to analyze the components of the diet and *predict* the consequences.

Question D requires a knowledge of the proper drug dosage and its effects; and then asks the student to *hypothesize* regarding the unexpected death.

Question E calls for the student to give a personal *evaluation* of the article and its investigation.

Two Categories of Open Questions Within this classification, there are two specific categories: *process* questions and *evaluation* questions.

Process Questions Process questions are directed toward a problem-solving or scientific method. They may relate to any of the stages in the problem-solving process, which usually includes these elements:

1. Identify the problem.

2. State hypotheses which might be tested.

3. Predict possible outcomes.

4. Design an experiment.

5. Identify variables.

6. Identify assumptions.

7. Collect data.

8. Interpret data.

9. Make inferences.

10. Suggest a course of action.

Developing and phrasing process questions requires more thought of the instructor, just as answering them requires higher level thinking of the student. Examples of process questions follow.

1. What might be the reasons a person cannot lift her right arm? (Hypothesize.)

2. How could you test the hypothesis that bile contributes to the digestion of fats? (Design.)

3. What might these data mean? (Interpret data.)

4. What questions could you ask to assess an adolescent's status regarding Havighurst's developmental tasks? (Collect data.)

5. You notice that a patient grimaces, holds his breath, and forms a fist any time his younger sister's name is mentioned. What inferences might you make? (Infer.)

6. After gathering these data, what treatment might you suggest? (Choose course of action.)

These questions allow some original, reflective thinking by a student, and there is more than one way to answer them. Each requires a student to perform one process in a sequence used for solving a problem. Generally, the full sequence is followed once a problem has been stated, though it is difficult to classify process questions without knowing the context in which they are asked. Try it, however, by reviewing these questions. For those you identify as process, put a *P* in the blank; an *M* for memory; and a *C* for convergent.

_____ A. What part of a cell contains DNA?

_____ B. What might happen if the body is invaded by tubercle bacilli?

_____ C. How could you find out if a patient is apprehensive about release from the hospital?

_____ D. What variables must be controlled when testing basal metabolism?

_____ E. How does a muscle contract?

Question A calls for a name and is a *memory* question.

While Question B may look like a convergent question, it is much more open than that. The student must consider all possibilities and predict all possible consequences of this event. This is a *process* question.

Question C asks the student what data should be collected and how to collect those data; this is a *process* question.

Question D is also a *process* question. In setting up a basal metabolism test, the student must be able to identify variables to be controlled if the test is to be an accurate measure.

The student is expected to explain or describe muscle contraction, making Question E a *convergent* question.

Evaluation Questions Evaluation questions are the most open of all questions, and a student is free to take any position that can be defended. These questions are sometimes referred to as *affective* questions because they involve opinion and judgment. This is the highest level of questioning because it includes all other levels. In responding to an evaluation question a student must organize knowledge, formulate an opinion based on the scientific processes, and take a self-selected stand which can be defended. In making the defense it is necessary to use evidence and to organize it in a logical, convincing way. Since evaluation questions can be asked in a closed or open mode, they are sometimes difficult to recognize. However, even a closed question which asks for an opinion is evaluative. Evaluation questions ask students how they feel or think about something, and may ask for a rationale. Examples of evaluative questions follow.

1. What do you think contributed most to the control of infectious diseases?

2. Do you agree with your classmate's conclusion?

3. Which do you think is the more effective means of eliciting information: a structured or an unstructured interview?

4. How can you justify your conclusion?

5. Would you rather practice in a large, city hospital or in a rural area?

All of these questions ask for an opinion or require defense or justification of the position taken. There is one caution: where criteria are clearly established or the student has a fixed guide to judge by, a question would be memory or convergent. An evaluation question must clearly give a student the freedom to select any position and defend it.

Read the following questions, and identify them using the symbols *M, C, P,* or *E.*

_____ **A.** What might be the reasons a person does not seek medical help?

_____ **B.** How does the release of epinephrine into the blood change respiration?

_____ **C.** Is $180°$ a normal range of motion for shoulder abduction?

_____ **D.** Do you think a person suffering from a terminal illness should be told?

_____ **E.** How would you defend the position that the family should or should not sit in on a consultation with a psychiatric patient?

Question A is a process question. The student is presented with a problem and is asked for possible reasons; that is, to state as many hypotheses as possible.

You should have identified Question B as a convergent question. It is asking for the relationship between epinephrine and respiration.

Question C is a memory question of the yes or no type; this question should have been easy to identify.

Question D is an evaluation question. Identifying it might have caused some problem because it is asked in the yes or no mode; however, it does ask for an opinion. This type of evaluation question often precedes further discussion when the student is asked to defend a position.

Question E is another evaluation question; this one asks the student to take a position and defend it.

Review

1. Closed questions

    a. Memory: yes/no, prompt, recall, name, define.

   b. Convergent: observe, explain, describe, state relationships, compare, contrast.

2.   Open questions

   a. Process: identify problems, state hypotheses, predict, design experiments, identify variables, identify assumptions, collect data, interpret data, make inferences, suggest courses of action.

   b. Evaluation: judge, defend a position, justify a value.

You have been given examples and have read a discussion of four categories of questions: memory, convergent, process, and evaluation. If you have questions about any of these, the following chart summarizes the salient points thus far. For a more thorough review of these concepts, complete the test in Appendix B.

TYPES OF QUESTIONS	DESCRIPTION AND THINKING INVOLVED IN ANSWERING	APPROPRIATE USES
Closed		
Memory	Verbatim responses. Recall of facts, definitions.	Basic background information. Facts needed to build upon later. Verification of basic facts. Quick review of presented material.
Convergent	Predictable answers. Use of facts to translate, re-phrase, reorganize basic material.	Check understanding of basic facts. Part of process of concept development. Understanding of relationships.
Open		
Process	Wide range of appropriate responses. Elements of problem solving. Analysis and synthesis of data.	Problem solving. Scientific inquiry.
Evaluation	Independent judgment based on analysis and synthesis of data.	Express values. Defend a position.

The purpose of this self-instructional program has been to familiarize you with the array of questions that can be asked to evaluate student knowledge and to stimulate thinking in the classroom. Using the categories of question classification presented in this chapter is one practical method for labeling their various types; and while other classification systems are available, all share the assumption that different kinds of questions create different levels of student thinking. The way an instructor phrases and sequences questions also influences the nature and effectiveness of the verbal exchange. Additional hints and an elaboration of these issues will be helpful when you consider the role questions can play in your own teaching.

PHRASING QUESTIONS

Phrasing is a central component of effective questioning. The guidelines outlined here may be useful in the preparation of questions you intend to ask.

1. Grammatical arrangement influences clarity. Questions should be complete sentences, economical in length, and should consist of words chosen with lucidity and conciseness in mind.

2. Questions which contain too much data are often confusing and should be avoided. The following are examples.

    a. What are some factors which contribute to the spread of tuberculosis, and how can it be controlled?

    b. During an interview, how can patients be led to answer questions honestly, and what elements might contribute to their not doing so?

    c. Do you think, based on what you read about environmental factors, that any or all of them could influence the normal development of a human being during the life cycle, and which ones would you say they are?

3. Refrain from asking obvious questions which give too much guidance to the answer, or those which contain the response and only require agreement. Three such questions are illustrated below.

    a. The biceps is a flexor, isn't it?

    b. When a culture does not stain with gram stain, we call it gram _____ ?

    c. Is blood in the carotid artery oxygenated or not oxygenated?

4. Avoid ambiguous questions; especially ones containing the words **what about**, **how about**, and **all about**. Questions such as, "How about viruses?", "What about the legal aspects?", or "Tell all you can about the digestion of fats," are too broad and do not encourage students to focus their thinking.

5. Avoid questions that result in a "yes" or "no" response, since a yes/no question is usually followed by Why? or When?, and two questions are used when one would be more economical. It may be useful to remember that yes/no questions result when questions begin with such auxiliary verbs as **is, could, would, can, does, do,** and **have.**

SEQUENCING AND LEVEL OF QUESTIONS

Surely the majority of instructors are interested in offering stimulating education to their students, but much teaching is extemporaneous, and not enough thought goes into its preparation. This is especially true with questioning. To test this assumption, ask yourself how much time you spend thinking about a series of well-thought-out, logical questions before meeting with your students. Our experience in working with health professions educators has shown this rarely occurs.

Our first suggestion is to draft a list of key questions you want to ask before each class. The sequence of questions you plan should be consistent with your goals for a particular lesson. If your objective is to test a student's knowledge of specific information, as in being able to list possible side effects of penicillin, a closed question would be appropriate. If your goal is to cultivate analytic thinking in students, open-ended questions requiring them to form opinions or solve problems must be constructed.

Having determined the sort of thinking you expect from students, a sequence of appropriate questions must be devised. Sequencing questions can be complex and requires practice. Suppose you began a class by asking this evaluative question, "In your opinion, how ethical is it to administer a placebo?" You could begin a discussion by asking this open-ended question, but you might discover later that some students do not know the meaning of a placebo and the first question should have been the closed question, "What is the definition of a placebo?"

Other closed questions, such as "What are the side effects of administering a placebo?" may also be necessary before asking the more thought-provoking evaluative question. Each student brings a different frame of reference into the classroom based on the sum of that person's knowledge, values, and previous experience. Thinking through this sequencing process and listing various questions appropriate to all expected levels of thinking provides you with a framework for assessing student readiness to answer particular questions.

One cannot be prescriptive in sequencing. A planned sequence of questions is always an experiment in which you need to anticipate possible student responses. However, if time is spent planning questions and speculating about possible responses, it is more likely that you will be able to stimulate student thinking in a logical and economical manner.

Phrasing and sequencing the levels of questions you will be using plays a central role in supervising students, promoting problem solving in clinical settings, and in facilitating an effective group discussion, the topic of the next chapter.

This chapter was adapted from E. Risley and R. Foley, *Verbal Questioning Techniques,* Audio Visual Concepts, Inc., Chicago, 1976.

GROUP DISCUSSION

In a summary of research on instruction, McKeachie (1971, p. 7) writes, "Other things being equal, small groups are probably more effective than large, discussions than lectures, and student-centered discussions more effective than instructor-centered discussions for goals of retention, application, problem solving, attitude change and motivation for future learning." This statement suggests the value of incorporating small-group discussions and, in particular, student-centered discussions into one's teaching.

In health professions education, group discussions are frequently used to enhance student understanding of basic content or cognitive material, and are referred to as *discussion sections*, *tutorials*, *review* or *recitation sections*, and various other labels. Whatever it is called, a group generally has an instructor whose role is to clarify previously encountered content and to discuss the clinical application or implications of cognitive material. Discussion groups follow lectures, movies, videotapes, demonstrations, laboratory work, readings, and other formats in which basic material has been presented.

A major advantage of discussion sections is their relatively high instructor-student ratio when compared with lectures. This means there is greater opportunity for active student participation, which makes it possible for the skillful instructor to determine problems individual students are facing and assist them in understanding the material gained from lectures or readings. If planned carefully, the small-group setting also allows students to learn from each other and trains them to view peers as resources to draw upon in future learning situations.

The primary disadvantage of this mode of teaching is that more faculty time and facilities are needed than for the lecture format, at unjustifiable expense if discussions are poorly conducted. Frequently, discussion sections commence with the instructor asking a global question such as, "What didn't you understand about today's lecture?" A few students ask questions, and the instructor is prompted to redeliver segments of the lecture in question, assuming that simply by hearing it again students will understand what they did not learn before. Another pattern is for discussion sessions to be dominated by a small group of students secure in their knowledge and adept at seducing the instructor to discuss topics of their own personal interest, leaving the balance of students bored, frustrated, and still unhelped. The frequency of these occurrences can be attributed both to a lack of thoughtful planning by instructors and to their not knowing the skills required to manage an effective small-group session aimed at promoting student comprehension. Considering the value of group discussion as a method of instruction, close attention is due to the text that follows; it should assist you to improve your skills in planning and delivery.

Among the most important considerations in planning discussion sections is the instructor's ability to use questions effectively. Questions are essential for conducting

a well-organized and productive session that can stimulate student thought. Before proceeding with this chapter, you should have completed Chapter 2, The Use of Questions.

PLANNING DISCUSSION SECTIONS

This section focuses on planning two different types of discussion sections frequently used in health professions education. The first, referred to as the *review section*, has as its primary goal improving student understanding of material previously presented. The second type, called the *application section*, assists students to apply basic science information to clinical problems.

In planning either type of session, it is important to maintain uniformity if more than one discussion section is offered. Instructors of all sections should meet before and during a course to reach agreement about expected student performance and the specific material to be covered. In general, sessions should be coordinated to ensure that students receive fairly similar experiences. If this is not done, students will hear of discrepancies between sections, and will feel cheated if they miss something important provided in another group or are assigned work not required of their peers. It should be mandatory to focus on similar content in all sections if the discussion group deals with material which will be tested in examinations. Since the goals of review and application sections are different, planning for each will be dealt with separately.

Planning a Review Section

The first step in planning a review section is to identify what students already know. Then strategies should be developed to provide students with whatever information they need. The instructor should also prepare for activities which expand upon cognitive material covered in lectures or readings, for it is possible that after the core subjects have been sufficiently clarified in the review, time will be available to utilize the session for additional learning.

Identifying Student Comprehension A number of techniques can be used to determine whether students have understood the material received prior to the review session.

Posttest If time is available, a brief posttest can be administered to students to identify knowledge gaps. The test could be developed by the group of section leaders in conjunction with the lecturer and administered at the end of a lecture, could be given to students as a "take home" in preparation for the review session, or could be given at the beginning of the discussion period. It might be a brief multiple-choice test or an essay based on solving a problem which requires knowledge of the content presented in the lecture or readings. A key can be provided to students to score their answers.

After the test has been scored, one option is to have the group of students determine collectively what they know and do not know. Alternatively, the instructor can review the test item by item, asking the group of students to agree on an answer to each question. This approach is generally preferable to the first, since the instructor can determine the reasoning behind a student's answer and probe for knowledge of related content.

Questions designed for the test need to be keyed to the subtopics, or objectives, of the specific content presented. After reviewing the test, a summary should be provided by the instructor or students to specify areas in which further work is needed. The posttest is also an excellent way of providing feedback to the lecturer as to whether students understood the presentation. The following illustration of test items, keyed to topics, could be used after a lecture on the cardiovascular system:

CARDIOVASCULAR SYSTEM POSTTEST
Embryology, congenital defects, histology, physiology

LECTURE	SUBTOPIC	QUESTION
Embryology of the heart	Partitioning of the heart	1. The membranous interventricular septum is formed from _____ .
	Embryonic origin of adult structures	2. The sinus venarum in the adult heart is derived from the embryonic. a. Aortic sac b. Bulbus cords c. Right ventricle d. Sinus venosus e. Truncus arteriosus
Histology of the heart	Cardiac muscle	3. The element of the intercalated disc that facilitates simultaneous contraction of cardiac muscle fibers is the: a. Fascia adherens b. Gap junction c. Macula adherens (desmosome)
		4. Discuss the role of the t-tubule in cardiac muscle contraction.

Twenty Questions Instead of the instructor designing questions in advance, students can generate them for the group to answer. The purpose of twenty questions is to see who can ask the most difficult, relevant, or thought-provoking questions based on the content just read or received in lectures. Each student can spend a few minutes alone at the beginning of the session preparing questions. An alternative is to have students bring questions to class. The instructor begins the game by asking a question. The student who knows the answer gets to ask the group one of his or her questions. The session continues until the instructor and students can think of no additional questions to ask. Unanswered questions are noted and categorized according to themes or objectives as a way of summarizing material students were unsure of, and can be listed on the chalkboard throughout the game. The entire group can then review the questions, identify topics or concepts that were unclear, and either continue with a group discussion to address these questions, or determine how to locate the information needed to answer them.

Asking Students Another method is the obvious one of asking students what they do not understand. Some students may be hesitant, however, to acknowledge what they don't know. Rather than asking the group outright, students can be requested to list specific information or topics that were unclear on a sheet of paper. These items should then be written on the board and organized into logical groupings for additional discussion. Another slant involves each student listing questions or concerns on paper, with pairs or trios of students attempting to address each other's questions. At the end of a specified time, each small group records on the board or poster sheets the questions they could and could not answer. This helps the whole group know the topics on which there were unanswered questions.

Strategies for Providing Information A few suggestions have been made about how to find out what students do and do not know following a large-group presentation or after their independent work. In each situation described, the group was left with unanswered questions or topics to be reviewed. The needed information or review may be provided in several ways: through other students, material resources, or the group instructor.

Student Resources Students enter a review section with varying degrees of knowledge about the topic. If well-thought-out diagnostic procedures have been employed, each student should be able to assess areas of proficiency and areas where further learning is required. Instead of always focusing on the instructor, students should learn to use their classmates as sources of information. Educational research in a variety of settings has demonstrated the effectiveness of peer tutoring in providing remedial assistance. It has been shown to be economical, productive, and generally accepted by students. Both the tutors and those being tutored appear to benefit greatly from this process.

One way to use peer tutoring is to have students select three or four fellow students and work together to solve their unanswered questions. You may want to make these groups competitive by giving each group time to prepare its members as fully as possible about the material under discussion, and during the last 15 minutes administering another written test on the same material, comparing team scores. Another option is an oral testing situation similar to television quiz shows. While the competitive version of tutoring can be fun and involving, it should be used judiciously and observed closely so it does not intimidate less capable students or create an atmosphere in which students are afraid to admit their mistakes.

Material Resources It should not be too difficult for the discussion leader to gather copies of lecture outlines, scripts of the lectures (if they exist), and audio- or videotapes of the presentations. These materials, in conjunction with copies of the related readings and relevant slides, can be made available to students during the discussion section.

In this way, after appraising for themselves their comprehension of the material, it will be possible for students to use the available resources to address their individual deficiencies. If a large number of resources is needed for the review section, students should be provided with a written guide that specifies where they can find the material relevant to each topic or objective presented. Group instructors can save time by meeting to identify and categorize the resources.

If the deficiencies identified by students are minor, it is probably best to have them do the remedial work on their own. On the other hand, if a substantial portion of the lecture content has not been understood by most students, working alone could prove frustrating. In this case the astute instructor can assign teams of students to work on different elements of the content for a specified period of time after which each team can present its findings to the group at large. Some time should be allowed to synthesize the teamwork and answer any remaining questions.

Teacher As Resource   In most review sections, the teacher is the major source of information. We have reserved the subject of the instructor until last, since we feel that in professional education it is essential that students develop skill in using each other as well as auxiliary resource materials to gain knowledge. In our opinion, the best use of the instructor is to structure learning opportunities which, early in a student's education, foster autonomy and cooperation with colleagues rather than dependency on the teacher as the only legitimate source of knowledge.

While valuing this viewpoint, there are times during discussions when an instructor needs to provide information to students. There are cases in which the lecture is so poor that most students leave baffled. As a result, there is little merit in employing your preplanned activities to identify student knowledge, and you may need to present the information again. Program changes are in order if this becomes the rule rather than the exception; otherwise the course will deteriorate, and valuable review sections will be used to duplicate inadequate lectures. More likely, there will be certain questions which students were unable to answer after working together or studying material. At this point, provide students with the needed information or direct them to resources where it can be located.

If it becomes apparent during the first few minutes of a review session that there are only a few minor questions which need to be addressed, then using the entire period for them is unwarranted. When students understand the content of the lectures and readings, the time available for the review section provides an opportunity to assist students to apply known material to clinical or research-based problems. The next section centers on planning a discussion section for application purposes.

Planning an Application Section

So far, the group discussion sections of which we have been speaking would occur only in a health-professions student's curriculum. In this portion of their education, students are generally amassing a tremendous amount of basic science information, and need to be assisted in retaining and understanding this content. They are just beginning to grapple with the ways in which this content relates to the clinical or research-based material they will be dealing with as professionals.

Early in the curriculum, discussion sections can help students apply basic science content to clinical material. Lectures, laboratories, and texts provide opportunities for encountering clinical material, but students are generally dealing with limited stimuli, such as autopsy specimens, slides, radiographs, or specific aspects of a clinical case. At this point, they are usually not dealing with the whole patient or disease entity. Discussion sections can be used to let students engage in the initial clinical application of basic science material. For example, after lectures on congenital defects of the cardiovascular system, students could see actual heart specimens to identify certain defects and then discuss their signs and symptoms, without, however, being required to collect detailed histories, interpret laboratory findings, and conduct physical examinations to diagnose and plan a course of treatment.

Using discussion sections to promote the application of cognitive material requires thorough preplanning. The selection of clinical material should be carefully weighed to maximize the opportunities for integration with basic science content. An instructor needs to decide in advance which concepts students should be expected to internalize. This is particularly important when a number of discussion section leaders are involved; all of them must meet to determine the relevant aspects of the clinical material being covered. Dissimilarity between discussion sections will only lead to student frustration. Once the concepts and materials for discussion have been selected, there are a variety of ways to conduct the group discussion. We will illustrate two separate approaches.

Application Through Instructor Questioning This type of session stresses the integration of facts and principles from a variety of disciplines. The first step in planning is to determine what tasks students must be able to do or what conclusions they are expected to reach based on the clinical material chosen. For example, if the topic of the discussion were "The effects of a myocardial infarction upon heart function," the selected clinical material might include a histological microscope slide or a 35-mm photomicrograph of tissue from the region of a myocardial infarction, showing both normal (cardiac muscle) and affected (connective tissue) areas. In this case, the instructor's objectives might be to have students realize that because the properties of connective tissue (i.e., it cannot contract) differ from those of cardiac muscle (i.e., it can contract), the result of a myocardial infarction is that heart function diminishes because there is less tissue present to contract and, therefore, less force available in contraction. Another conclusion could be that cardiac muscle cannot regenerate, since it heals by scarring (connective tissue formation). Given these points as expected outcomes, the instructor needs to determine in advance the sequence of questions to ask in order to facilitate students' problem-solving efforts.

In planning this small-group activity, the essential ingredient is to have students, rather than the instructor, do the talking. The instructor's role should be to ask questions in a logical order which guides students' thinking. Unless a sequence of questions has been considered and even scripted in advance, there is a likelihood the session will proceed somewhat aimlessly. Ambiguous questions, or ones which are too elementary or sophisticated, can lead to student silence, forcing the instructor to lecture.

As you will recall from Chapter 2, there are three issues to consider when planning questions. First is the level of student thinking required to answer the question (e.g., factual recall of facts or the integration of ideas). The second is the order in which questions will be asked: perhaps first a clarification of factual information, next a discussion of the meaning of these facts, and then, what actions they imply. Finally, it is important to have well-phrased questions; that is, questions which do not contain the answers or which ask five questions at once.

To continue the example of the discussion on myocardial infarction, the instructor could have scripted in advance the following sequence of questions, all referring to the specimen:

1. What tissue is this?

2. What are its properties?

3. How often is it found here?

4. Why is it here now?

5. How will the presence of this type of tissue affect heart function?

Several principles guided this sequence of questions. The closed questions which begin the discussion check for student knowledge of the factual information needed to address the more advanced questions. Also, starting a discussion with simpler questions usually gets students to participate more readily than beginning with difficult ones. The sequence builds logically from basic information, leading students to the final questions which are the primary purpose of the discussion. The questions are also carefully phrased to preclude cueing, and they are not ambiguous.

In summary, when you are conducting an application section by asking questions in a group discussion, it is important to specify the purpose of the session, choose relevant clinical material, and write in advance a logical sequence of questions.

Application Through the Use of Task-Oriented Groups Another method for using a group discussion section to promote the application of cognitive material is planning a sequence of tasks that will lead students to achieve the expected goals. In this case, the instructor plays a less active role than when asking questions, since the tasks are done by the students. Determining the purposes of the session, selecting the clinical content, and outlining student tasks, however, still requires careful thought.

A discussion section on the topic "Embryology and congenital defects of the cardiovascular system" could be planned using task-oriented groups. The purposes of the session could be to enable students to (1) diagnose certain defects, (2) discuss at what point during embryonic development the defects occurred and the possible reasons for their occurrence, (3) list the implications of the defects for blood oxygen levels in the chambers of the heart and in various vessels, and (4) discuss signs, symptoms, and prognosis of specific defects.

Given these goals, the instructor needs to select appropriate clinical materials that would facilitate student achievement. Suppose in this instance a number of autopsy specimens of pediatric hearts are given to the students along with written summaries of the related case histories. With the goals and materials now in mind, an instructor could script a series of questions and conduct a group discussion as previously described. On the other hand, activities could be structured to help students achieve the same objectives individually or in small groups.

One option is for the instructor to assign students to groups of three, giving each trio a heart specimen and the respective case history. All trios are then given a list of questions they should be able to answer based on the clinical material. For each objective on the list below, these sample questions could be asked:

OBJECTIVES	QUESTIONS
1. Diagnose certain defects.	1. What abnormality(ies) is present in this specimen?
2. Describe at what stage during embryonic development the defects occurred and possible reasons for their occurrence.	2. During what stage of cardiovascular system development would the defect have occurred?
	3. Speculate about the other events happening at this time.
	4. In the case of multiple defects, what common factor can be identified as a possible cause(s)?
	5. Trace the circulation through the heart and great vessels and identify any irregularities.

Students are given these questions and allotted about a half hour to answer them individually in writing. This task is followed by an additional 15 minutes of work in the trio to compare and synthesize individual work. Collective small-group responses are recorded on a board or flip chart, and each group then reviews the work of the other teams. Up to this point, the instructor's role has been largely administrative — assigning tasks and observing student work. Now the instructor may reassemble the entire body of students and conduct a group discussion around the following sequence of questions:

OBJECTIVES	QUESTIONS
3. List the implications of the defects for blood oxygen levels in the chambers of the heart and in various fetal vessels.	6. What are the implications of the shunts identified for blood oxygen levels in the individual?
	7. What possible signs and symptoms might be manifested in this case (e.g., cyanosis)?
4. Describe signs, symptoms, and prognosis of specific defects.	

In reviewing this sequence of activities, note that Questions 1 to 5 given to the triads were related to the first two objectives of the session. Questions 6 and 7, addressed to the general group, related to Objectives 3 and 4. This example suggests one path for using task-oriented groups to facilitate student application of cognitive material. An instructor can design other tasks which would have similar results.

The advantages of the task-oriented group are that students are engaged in problem solving on their own and use each other as resources rather than immediately relying on the instructor to guide their thinking.

Leading a group discussion through instructor questioning has the advantage of making students active participants. However, even in the questioning situation there is a tendency for many students to look for cues in the instructor's behavior which will indicate "the right answer." The advantage of the task-oriented group is that the instructor's judgment of student responses comes after students have relied on their own intellectual capabilities and those of their classmates to address the problem. This pattern more closely reflects how they will need to function as professionals in the field.

This chapter has, so far, dealt with a number of techniques for planning discussion sections which will promote greater understanding and application of basic content. The following checklist, enumerating several important considerations, should assist you when planning for discussion groups of this nature.

CHECKLIST FOR PLANNING A DISCUSSION SECTION

1.   What specific objectives do I want students to achieve as a result of this session?

2.   What methods will I use to diagnose student comprehension of the material to be covered?

3.   What activities will students engage in to ensure attainment of the objectives?

4. Have I made provisions for utilizing additional time which might be available once my planned objectives have been attained?

5. What materials will I need for this session?

6. How will I conclude this session?

7. What overview, instructions, and assignments will I give students for the upcoming session?

DELIVERY SKILLS

Without advance planning, the probability is high that your discussion will not be organized or meaningful, and it may result in unnecessary silences or aimless student chattering. The best-planned discussion, however, may be a failure in practice if you have not learned the delivery skills needed to guide student learning efficiently and effectively. The balance of this chapter concerns techniques we have found helpful to professionals interested in improving their skills in leading group discussions.

Organizing the Setting

Be present before students arrive to make certain the setting is appropriately organized. If you plan to have students talk to each other during the class, chairs should not be arranged in rows as if for a lecture. Remember that where you sit in the arrangement of a circle or series of semicircles will affect the nature of the interaction between you and the students. If you expect students to work in small groups on assigned tasks, moveable chairs and ample room must be available so the conversation of one group does not interfere with that of another. If the room is not large enough, try to reserve a second one for small-group activities. A cramped room can crowd a good discussion: use the hallways or meet outside, if necessary. Although this is obvious, consider room temperature. Open a window in a hot room before students must ask you to do so. Complain if you are faced with poor lighting or filthy chalkboards. Such annoyances can generally be rectified if you are willing to spend the energy.

Space is one consideration; materials are another. Prior to class, you may want to make a list of the materials and equipment you will need. One aspect of good teaching involves setting the stage. Be there to check out the small details before students arrive. If you intend to use a chalkboard, you know that chalk will be necessary, and it is a waste of valuable time to be scouting for it during the class period. If you plan to have a number of student groups present ideas to the group at large, provide flip charts and magic markers; these work very well in such situations. Masking tape is necessary if you want work posted on the board or walls. Overhead projectors, videotapes, and other equipment require pretesting.

The Introduction

Any discussion section should start with an introduction which includes a statement of the goals to be accomplished. While the goals may be stated verbally, it is generally preferable to present them in writing, using a handout, transparency, flip chart, or chalkboard. Ideally, you should be able to specify in the list of goals what you expect students to know or do at the end of the meeting. In addition to a statement of expected performance, students should be given an overview of the activities planned for the session. An outline of activities on the board can provide you and the students with the necessary bridges for making transitions from one activity to the next.

During the introduction, let participants know the ground rules for the discussion. You may decide that everyone is expected to contribute during the class. If so, say it. If you are using task-oriented groups, you might tell students that they can ask for clarification of instructions on procedural issues but should hold content questions until the group discussion period. If your sequence is tightly timed, ground rules will aid you in keeping to your original schedule.

As a final point, when dealing with a new group of students, it is useful to open the session with an activity through which they can get to know each other. This is especially important in a discussion section where they will be drawing upon each other for information and assistance. Having students introduce themselves to the group at large is generally less effective (it takes time, and who can remember all those names?) than arranging activities which require them to interact at some point with everyone in the class.

Guiding the Discussion

After an appropriate introduction, you can proceed to the body of the discussion. Even if you employ small-group activities, there will usually be some portion of the session in which you take the lead. During these periods, remember to retain your role as a leader who guides student thinking. A series of prepared, carefully thought-out questions should help restrict tendencies to want to provide information.

Clarifying Student Responses Knowing ahead of time the special questions you want to ask is one element of an effective discussion. These only provide a framework, however, for guiding the general direction of the session you will need additional questions depending upon the level of student responses. For example, following a question you will usually need to have a student clarify or explain the reasoning behind an answer. A student could also give an ambiguous response with several thoughts interspersed within it or might misuse terminology. In this situation empathic instructors might attempt to rescue the student by paraphrasing what they thought they heard the student say. These attempts are reflected in phrases such as, "What I think you're trying to say is," or, "You probably meant *meiosis*, not *mitosis*." The problem with assistance like this is that when you provide the needed clarification, the student misses an opportunity to unravel knotty thinking, and neither of you is sure if the student had the necessary knowledge to respond. Instead, ask a student to clarify a response by using phrases such as, "You seem to be saying a number of different things, could you state your ideas separately?", "What do you mean by mitosis?", "Could you rephrase your comment in simpler terms?", or "What more would you want to add?"

On the other hand, a student's response might be clear and correct but still leave you in doubt of his or her degree of knowledge. For example, a student might choose the correct laboratory test to run for a given case. It is possible, however, that this was merely a good guess or reflects only partial knowledge. The inquiring instructor should not be content with what might be a fortunate guess and will probe more deeply with questions such as, "On what basis would you order that laboratory test?", or "What other tests would you run to guarantee you are accurate in your conclusion?" Often a simple Why? suffices. Other probing comments like, "What are you assuming by that response?", or, "What is the basis for believing that is true?" push students to justify their answers. How many times have we heard a student refer to the instructor who "really made me think"? Asking questions which test the reasoning behind responses creates a climate in which students learn to justify their thinking, resulting in a richer exploration of the topic.

Facilitating Student-to-Student Interaction   Also important in conducting an effective discussion is the pattern of interaction between the instructor and the student. Even when the instructor is a good facilitator in discussions and asks questions effectively, there is still the potential danger of teacher dominance. A pattern to avoid is one in which instructors initiate all the questions and constantly react to student responses with a statement or question of their own. This sequence creates a monotonous pattern of instructors asking all the questions and the students always directing their responses back to the teacher.

Fostering student-to-student interaction will be the goal of an instructor who is conscious of good group processes. This can be done by asking one student to comment on another's response. Questions can be addressed to the group at large, and the instructor can remain silent, placing responsibility for advancing the discussion on the students. With effort, an environment can be created during a discussion section in which students freely agree or disagree with one another, probe each other for the reasoning behind a response, and turn to the instructor for the needed knowledge only as a last resort.

There are significant advantages in having students share the responsibility for maintaining the flow and pace of the discussion. Developing a student's ability to ask good questions of others has value beyond learning in the classroom. Asking precise questions of others should make students more aware of asking precise questions of themselves when they are functioning alone. Learning how to probe a colleague's thinking in the classroom can prove useful when interviewing patients in clinical settings. Finally, the practice of asking fellow classmates for answers has the potential of making students aware of the value of using others as resources for information and support. Encouraging student-to-student interaction in the classroom may encourage the needed colleague-to-colleague interaction in future professional roles.

Getting All Students to Participate   Although silent students may be understanding what is being discussed, by not participating they miss the opportunity to receive feedback on their thinking. The need to involve everyone in the discussion is especially important at the beginning of a discussion section, or in the first of a series of meetings. If students do not initially verbalize their thoughts, they may be even more reluctant to participate later on. Several strategies can be used to encourage total participation. Task-oriented groups, earlier described, require that students share their thinking with a small group of peers. This is generally much less threatening than speaking before the instructor and the entire class. When students have contributed something in the small group, they will usually have something to add in the larger group. Verbalizing in the small group also establishes a norm for participation early in the discussion period which should carry over to the large-group meeting.

If task-oriented groups are not used, other methods can facilitate everyone's participation. Although difficult when first meeting a large group, it is worth noting early in the discussion who is participating and who is not. If possible, pay attention to subgroups of students who are not participating. Comments such as "I haven't heard from anyone in the back of the room," should make students aware that you are conscious of who is contributing and also that general participation is expected. As time passes, you should have a better picture of those who have not contributed to the discussion and can generally involve them through a nonverbal message or direct questioning. Comments such as, "Let's hear from some who haven't talked today," further encourages the notion of involvement. Asking a question and then letting your eyes rest upon silent students for a moment or two will denote your interest in their comments. Occasionally, difficult content may be the source of a lack of participation for certain students. For a large-group discussion, you may want to design some questions which almost all students can answer. These could be simple, recall questions or ones which ask students to express their personal opinions.

As a last attempt, you may need to address questions to specific persons who have remained silent. Particularly in new groups, however, calling upon a student by name is usually threatening and may serve to depress participation. Students may spend more time worrying about when they will be called upon than on the material being discussed. Hopefully, the preceding suggestions will create an atmosphere in which there is an expectation for student participation without putting individuals on the spot.

Keeping the Discussion on Track   While there is a need to involve all students, it is as important to keep the discussion on track. Perhaps the worst distraction in a discussion is the student who talks for the sake of being heard and the instructor who allows or, worse, encourages this behavior. Often new instructors are so eager for participation that they allow a few students to monopolize the discussion and permit comments totally unrelated to the topic.

Certain teacher behaviors can promote the desired distribution of student comments, yet keep the discussion focused. Encouraging all students to talk reflects your interest in equitable participation. If, however, you see the same people raising their hands or jumping in continuously, you can state simply that at this point you would like to hear from those who have not contributed. It is possible to have a student who, despite your efforts, continues to dominate the discussion. In such an extreme case it is advisable to confront this behavior openly with a comment such as, "I've appreciated your contributions but would like to allow some other people an opportunity to talk." In this situation, however, it would be important to talk with the student after class to explain the reasoning behind your action. Let such students know you value their participation, but not at the expense of others. Without some follow-up, you could potentially change an aggressive student into a withdrawn one.

In addition to managing an equal distribution of conversation, you need to keep the entire group focused on the topic. All of us have encountered students who raise topics of personal interest which sidetrack the discussion from its proposed goals. Hopefully, you will notice these diversions before being embarrassed by a student who finally asks how the discussion is relevant to the subject matter at hand. If comments are occurring which do not relate to the established goals, say that the comments are interesting but unrelated to the specific discussion. This applies to questions as well. Even provocative ones can result in a major digression from the goals of the discussion. If you have told a student that a question or comment is not relevant, you can probably expect a few moments of silence. Politely restating an earlier question or asking another will get the discussion moving again.

Occasionally a student makes comments within the parameters of the topic but provides excessive detail or is so repetitive that too much class time is consumed. Even if you are desperate to cut this student short, use caution so that a negative tone for the balance of the period is not established. One tip is to interrupt such people by isolating something they have just said, commenting on it, and using it as a springboard to address a question to other members of the group. While you may leave such students perplexed or annoyed, you have not put them down.

Another problem that makes it difficult to keep discussions focused is the presence of students who are in some way disruptive; the sleepers, newspaper readers, knitters, and gossipers. Your response, of course, will depend upon the degree of disruption. It may be better to let sleeping students "lie" than to stop the flow of a good discussion. A number of disinterested students, on the other hand, should flag that something is wrong with your plan or its execution. This may require confronting the group with your observations and probing for the reasons behind their behavior. More typically, disruptive behavior involves a few students who are inappropriately interfering with other students' learning. Here your responsibility is to stop the disruption. You might halt the discussion and simply stare the clique down, or comment that their behavior is interfering with you and the rest of the group. After taking such action, however, you will need to reinitiate the discussion by restating a previous question, asking a new one, or providing some form of summarization.

Summarizing the Discussion An effective discussion should have periodic summaries prior to a transition to the next goal or topic. During these periods, it would be useful to return to the stated objectives and clarify how the group is progressing in accordance with the plan. Writing key points that have been made in the discussion on a chalkboard or flip chart is a useful way of summarization and facilitating student memory. Ask students to provide the needed summary when appropriate, using a statement such as this one: "I would like you to summarize the major issues, conclusions, or conflicts that have emerged so far." This will encourage students to reflect upon and capsulize what has been discussed. Student summaries also provide opportunities for you to assess student learning and give feedback if needed.

Your responsibilities as a discussion leader involve more than knowledge of the content. Many of the ideas discussed in this chapter involve group management techniques which an effective leader uses in any group situation. Clear parallels exist between running a group discussion section and chairing a committee or faculty meeting. As a knowledgeable leader, you need to make certain the meeting begins and ends on time, major points are addressed, everyone has had an opportunity to speak, and that the flow of the discussion is related to the purposes for coming together.

The Conclusion

The topic during a group discussion may be so compelling and everyone so engaged that you suddenly realize the time is up and people need to leave. Although climactic, this kind of ending can leave students without a clear picture of what was achieved during the discussion. Do not forget that the session began with purposes, and there should be some opportunity to reflect upon the degree to which they have been met.

A conclusion can range from a simple restatement of the goals to the administering of a short task or test to measure student learning. An effective conclusion should involve a review of what students were expected to gain from the discussion, what has actually been done, and what will come next. Although the conclusion can be provided by the instructor, a better indicator of student learning may be to ask them to summarize key points from the meeting and draw conclusions. The group can be asked an open-ended question: "As a result of today's discussion, what do you feel are the most important considerations in delivering effective patient care?" After a student or two volunteers, others can be asked to refine previous statements or contribute additional points. As points emerge, writing them on the board further clarifies important conclusions and may bring forth ideas which were missed during the discussion.

If the discussion is part of a series of group meetings, conclude the class by reviewing upcoming assignments, and give an overview of the goals and activities for the next meeting. The level of organization displayed by an instructor has been demonstrated to be one of the most important factors in effective university teaching. Providing a useful summary of the day's discussion and an overview of the upcoming meeting will reflect your careful preplanning.

General Instructor Behaviors

Thus far, the suggestions discussed regarding an effective delivery have related specifically to the introduction, body, and conclusion of the discussion section. Throughout a discussion, though, certain kinds of behavior can enhance your teaching effectiveness.

Unlike lecturing, small-group teaching is characterized by the large degree of potential teacher-to-student and student-to-student interaction in a less formal atmosphere. For students to feel free to participate, a comfortable environment must be created. The level of tension in a given group will, in part, be related to how relaxed you are as a teacher, and your level of comfort will be in part related to the amount of preplanning you have done. Clear ideas of how you want the session to proceed should give you a sense of direction and, consequently, of comfort. If you find yourself feeling tense about an upcoming discussion, the following suggestions may be helpful. As mentioned earlier, the physical arrangement of a room can facilitate participation. Chairs placed in a large circle, in small clusters, or around a table indicate that interaction is expected. If you have checked the materials needed prior to the class, you can interact with students as they enter the room by introducing yourself, finding out who they are, or even discussing the weather. This will let students know that you are a person, not just an authority figure, and will give you the opportunity to know some of the students more personally.

During the session, a degree of comfort can be maintained by sitting with the group, occasionally shifting location rather than always sitting in the "teacher's chair," keeping eye contact with students, listening attentively, and maintaining a relaxed posture. These actions should reduce the potential distance between you and the students and facilitate mutual active involvement.

Even when remembering these considerations, you can be sure the discussion will come to an early death if you or other individuals are disrespectful of anyone's contributions. Accepting all responses as correct or important is wrong, and always responding to students with comments such as, "This is a good point, but. . .," may come across as a subtle form of disregard. On the other hand, what needs to be made clear to students is that their personalities or intelligence are not in question when they give an inaccurate response. It is very easy to follow an incorrect response with a sequence of probing questions which can lead the student to an appropriate answer. If you feel additional probing might be too threatening to a particular student, move the discussion away from the person in focus by bringing in other students. A group discussion leader should work at developing strategies which sensitively draw out the best thinking a student has to offer. Only a very few thrive on the competitiveness of a threatening environment.

EVALUATING YOUR PERFORMANCE AS A DISCUSSION LEADER

The checklist that follows summarizes behaviors which in our opinion characterize the leader of an effective discussion section. Using this form and the checklist for planning a discussion should help improve your skills in this area. It may be beneficial to have a colleague observe one of your classes, and use the checklist as a basis for discussing your performance. Students could complete the form at the end of the session to give you their opinions. You might videotape one of your sessions and use the checklist for self-assessment. The discussion checklist, as with those provided elsewhere in the text, is not definitive, and should be adapted according to the objectives you have planned for a given session. Add other items you would like to see exhibited in your group discussions. We urge you, however, to use these forms as a starting point for reflecting upon your present group discussion practices.

CHECKLIST FOR EVALUATING A DISCUSSION SECTION

Date: _____

Listed on this sheet are statements to be used for rating group discussion sessions. Please respond to each statement by checking the category that most closely corresponds to your observation.

Instructor: _____   Rater: _____

	RARELY OR NOT DONE	PARTIALLY OR SOME-TIMES	COMPLETELY OR USUALLY DONE	NOT APPLI-CABLE OR CAN'T RECALL
ORGANIZING THE SETTING				
1. Organizes the room to facilitate student interaction.	☐	☐	☐	☐
2. Ensures all materials (books, audiovisuals) are available and workable.	☐	☐	☐	☐
THE INTRODUCTION				
3. States goals for the teaching session.	☐	☐	☐	☐
4. Presents an outline of planned activities.	☐	☐	☐	☐
5. States ground rules for audience participation.	☐	☐	☐	☐
6. Structures an activity which facilitates students' getting to know each other.	☐	☐	☐	☐
GUIDING THE DISCUSSION				
7. Asks questions rather than continuously providing information.	☐	☐	☐	☐

	RARELY OR NOT DONE	PARTIALLY OR SOME-TIMES	COMPLETELY OR USUALLY DONE	NOT APPLI-CABLE OR CAN'T RECALL
8. Asks students to clarify or explain the reasoning behind their comments.	☐	☐	☐	☐
9. Facilitates student-to-student interaction.	☐	☐	☐	☐
10. Facilitates participation of all students.	☐	☐	☐	☐
11. Keeps the discussion moving toward stated goals.	☐	☐	☐	☐
12. Paces discussion (does not drag out or hurry over major ideas).	☐	☐	☐	☐
13. Uses audiovisual aids, x-rays, specimens, chalk-boards to further promote understanding of materials.	☐	☐	☐	☐
14. Summarizes important points or asks students to do so.	☐	☐	☐	☐

THE CONCLUSION

15. Develops a conclusion or asks students to do so based on the goals of the discussion section.	☐	☐	☐	☐

	RARELY OR NOT DONE	PARTIALLY OR SOME- TIMES	COMPLETELY OR USUALLY DONE	NOT APPLI- CABLE OR CAN'T RECALL
16. Relates topic to upcoming teaching sessions.	☐	☐	☐	☐

GENERAL INSTRUCTOR BEHAVIORS

17. Teaches in a re- laxed and enthu- siastic manner.	☐	☐	☐	☐
18. Deals with stu- dents' opinions respectfully.	☐	☐	☐	☐

In evaluating this discussion section, which item rated above indicates the **best** aspect of the instructor's behavior?   Item # _____.

Which item rated indicates the **worst** aspect of your instructor's behavior?

Item # _____.

Comments: _____

_____

_____

_____

_____

_____

_____

_____

PROMOTING CLINICAL PROBLEM SOLVING[1]

Much of health professions education is conducted in clinical settings to teach students how to manage patients. This instruction generally occurs in clinics, in ward rounds, at nursing stations, in patient conferences, and at case presentations. Teaching in these sessions should consist of helping students learn how to collect data, interpret and synthesize their findings, formulate alternative management plans, and evaluate the effects of the action taken. In brief, the goal should be teaching clinical problem solving.

If students are to learn how to manage problems, they should be actively engaged in the higher-level mental operations involved in this process. An active student role means that the instructor must create an environment in which the students are expected to solve problems and receive feedback on their efforts. This chapter begins with strategies for planning clinical teaching endeavors which promote problem solving. A section follows in which the interaction between students and the instructor around an actual clinical case is examined. Methods for developing simulations and role-play experiences to challenge student thought are discussed last. The examples used are drawn mostly from medicine. The techniques are applicable to any health discipline.

PLANNING CLINICAL EXPERIENCES

No richer experiences are potentially available in a student's education than those in the clinical setting. Here a student can synthesize and apply the enormous amount of content previously learned. This potential, however, places immense responsibility on clinical instructors. Compared with lectures, laboratories, and group discussions, it is usually more difficult to determine what should be taught and to prepare lessons in advance. Much of the content is dictated by the clinical cases available and the definite battle of priorities existing between patient management and clinical instruction. As some clinicians point out, "How can we take time to teach students how to solve problems when a patient's mental or physical welfare is at stake?" Even if the cases for study were readily available and an instructor could devote all energies to teaching, fostering a student's clinical thinking ability remains among the most complex activities in education.

Instruction in a clinical environment requires forethought and planning, yet clinical teaching is usually impromptu. Students may see an overabundance of routine or of rare cases and not be sufficiently challenged to hone their abilities to manage the

[1]Portions of this chapter were adapted from J. Smilansky, N. Runkle, R. Foley, and L. Solomon, *Instructor Plays Patient – Using Simulation for Case Presentation,* AudioVisual Concepts, Inc., Chicago, 1976, and E. Risley and R. Foley, *Verbal Questioning Techniques,* AudioVisual Concepts, Inc., Chicago, 1976.

wide array of problems they will confront in practice. We have found—whether it be pharmacists working with students during a practicum, a pedodontics faculty responsible for 125 students, or an emergency medicine staff supervising 4 residents— that the faculty responsible do not meet to consider what they expect students to achieve as a result of 5 weeks, a quarter, or 3 years of clinical education. In the few curricula where we found explicitly stated clinical goals, faculty rarely worked collectively to ensure that students achieved the goals, nor did they evaluate student performance accordingly. For the most part clinical instruction tends to be a hit-or-miss proposition without regard to the planning and delivery of instruction, or the evaluation of student learning.

Faculty responsible for planning clinical experiences must first determine the essential knowledge, attitudes, and skills they expect students to exhibit upon completion of a course or rotation. Designing instructional activities which are consistent with these goals is next. If one goal in a pedodontic rotation for dental students is to be able to work effectively with children from various socioeconomic groups, practice with a variety of children must be built into the experience. If in an emergency medicine department educating residents to administer new programs in other settings is important, the resident needs sufficient opportunities and related supervision to be able to do so.

Expected student outcomes for an entire clinical experience need to be *as* explicit, if not more so, as for a series of lectures and group discussions. It is important to restate that the goals and related instruction of clinical experiences should not be based on currently available cases. Objectives should be based on what the faculty feels students should be minimally accomplished in upon completing this portion of their education. Once these expectations are clear, it will be possible to locate the needed resources.

Means for judging whether a student has met established objectives should also be planned in advance. Evaluation is too frequently the result of faculty impressions, notebook notations, vague rating scales, or letters of recommendation compiled by department heads. We cannot afford to remain naive about the contributions of educators in this area. Tested systems for measuring student performance can be found in the evaluation references listed in the annotated bibliography in Appendix D.

PLANNING A SINGLE LESSON

Every clinical teaching session must also be planned in advance and related to the master instruction plan. If students are expected to manage a variety of diseases in infants, it is the instructor's responsibility to determine how a particular teaching session will aid in achieving that goal. For example, an immediate objective of a teaching round could be for students to diagnose various kinds of seizures in infants. While other issues may emerge, the focus of the round should remain on seizures and how the topic fits into the broader goal of managing early childhood complications.

After determining the purpose of a given class, select the resources you will need to teach it. The session might involve the examination of a single patient, several patients, preselected charts, or a combination. Review former patient charts and written cases, or develop simulated cases as a backup if an actual case is unavailable or unsuitable. Resources must be selected in advance to avoid random and anecdotal discussions of the cases on hand.

A sequence of activities needs to be developed which will help students achieve the lesson goals. Each sequence should have an introduction, body, and conclusion. The introduction should specify the purposes of the session, how the activities planned will aid students to learn what is expected, and provisions for students to raise questions about the plan. Time could also be allocated for assessing student comprehension of any previously assigned reading materials.

Decide what formats you will use for a specific class. Students may examine a patient individually and then as a group discuss the diagnosis and management. You may decide to delay your comments until the students conclude their efforts and then probe for the rationale behind their decisions. An alternative would be to assign them a set of readings about various types of childhood seizures. After a theoretical discussion, students could then examine a specific patient, make a diagnosis, and plan a course of treatment. You may choose to question students throughout the process or only after they have reached some conclusions about the case. Thought should be given to how the session will proceed. Consider generating in advance a sequence of logical questions to help you guide student thinking throughout the lesson.

Concluding a clinical teaching session can be done in several ways. You can summarize the original purposes and main points of the day's meeting, then allow reactions to the case by asking students what they felt was gained from the session. For the example used here, students could be asked to summarize the characteristics of different seizures in infants. You could also reiterate questions under consideration for the next meeting and suggest references, other patients to observe, or staff with whom students might consult in the interim. Although the conclusion need not be as structured as in the lecture, students should leave a clinical encounter clear about its accomplishments and future direction. Upcoming assignments can be as simple as asking students to remain knowledgeable of developments in the case just seen or to familiarize themselves with the chart of another. Students will see their need to expend effort in preparation if your planning is apparent.

Even with careful planning, goals for student learning can be formulated which are difficult to accomplish in practice. No one, for example, would dispute the precept that health professions students should be competent problem solvers. Teaching in a manner that supports this goal, however, is infinitely more difficult than acknowledging its importance.

PROMOTING CLINICAL PROBLEM SOLVING THROUGH QUESTIONS

The importance of questions and suggestions for using them effectively have been discussed in preceding chapters. The way you use, select, phrase, and sequence questions in clinical settings affects how well you provoke thinking in your students.

For some time we had been interested in the effective use of questions in clinical teaching. In a study of a pediatric clerkship for medical students (Foley, 1979) teaching rounds, working rounds, grand rounds, lectures, patient management conferences, and journal clubs were videotaped and analyzed. In all settings there was a strong tendency for instructors to supply factual information rather than conduct higher-level discussions involving analysis, problem solving, and application of clinical data. Only 17 percent of the total interaction was devoted to questioning students. The overwhelming majority of these questions required low-level responses (81 percent), for the most part relating to factual data about a case for which students were responsible. Few questions required students to discuss their reasoning, propose alternatives, or suggest implications for action; that is, to verbalize their problem-solving efforts.

The teaching rounds we observed were illustrative. We found that 95 percent of the average discussion occurred between the physician and resident in charge. Medical students for whom the teaching rounds were conducted spoke only 5 percent of the time. Only 18 percent of the interaction during these rounds was devoted to asking questions, and 75 percent of these were closed or low-level.

After hundreds of less systematic observations in other clinical settings—nursing stations, dentists' chairs, laboratory benches, bedsides, and offices—we have found a general tendency for the instructor, not the student, to solve most clinical problems. The instructor talks most of the time while students passively observe the expert. Unquestionably, many health professions students are competent to solve clinical problems upon graduation. The question is whether this competence is a result of the teaching they receive or their innate abilities.

Asking open-ended questions is a central aspect of promoting student reasoning. Sequencing questions is another. The problem-solving process used here includes these steps:

1. Explicate what is known and formulate tentative hypotheses.

2. Gather further data.

3. Interpret data by the following means:
   a. Organize it.
   b. Select groups of data related to the problem.
   c. Identify various relationships which may exist.
   d. State hypotheses to explain the data.

4. Test the hypotheses as follows:
   a. Gather further data.
   b. Plan experimentation.
   c. Initiate a treatment.

After testing the hypotheses, additional information has been acquired, and the process above resumes with an explication of what is now known, an assessment of the need for further data, and so on to check the results of the hypothesis testing. While time and the nature of the patient's problem may alter the implementation or order of this process, it is important for students to understand and be conscious of it when solving problems.

To demonstrate more effective use of questions, we have selected a clinical case which could be discussed during a teaching round. An attending physician, residents, medical students, student nurses, and a pharmacy major will discuss the case of a 15-month-old infant, John Jones. The topic is management of seizures based on the following information:

Case: 15-month-old white male; mother very upset

Chief complaint: "Fever and jerking."

Present illness: He seemed well yesterday, acted "normal" and ate as usual; he didn't sleep well last night, kept waking up and crying; hasn't eaten much at all today; he seemed "feverish" (she didn't take his temperature), and then about 30 minutes ago he had a jerking spell; his arms and legs jerked for about a minute and his eyes rolled up; he seemed unconscious afterwards and she got "really scared"; he's awake now; but not back to his "old self."

Past history: No previous spells like the one today. Psychomotor development normal by history. No significant prior illness or injuries; no known allergies. Antenatal, perinatal, and neonatal histories are unremarkable. Immunizations complete as recommended, last one (1 month ago) was triple (measles, mumps, rubella).

Systems review: No vomiting, diarrhea, or other problems in past few days or recently except a little "runny" nose. Otherwise, patient is within the normal range.

Family history: One paternal grandparent dead of cancer; a maternal grandparent and aunt have diabetes; mother recalls that her brother had convulsions as a baby, "but he outgrew them." Otherwise, patient is within the normal range.

The nurse obtained the following data: weight 25 lb; temperature 104.2°F; respiration 32/minute; heart rate 110/minute.

Your examination reveals a somewhat sleepy, but easily aroused and then irritable, 15-month-old who moves all extremities equally. Examination of the eyes reveals apparently full extraocular movement with equal pupils which react normally to light. Adequate funduscopy was not feasible, though attempted. There is some cloudy rhinorrhea; the left tympanic membrane (TM) is red and mildly bulging, the right TM is slightly infected. Throat is normal and the neck seems supple, though any exam maneuver increases the boy's irritability. Lungs are clear; heart sounds are normal; abdomen soft with no organomegaly; skin revealed two small café-au-lait spots; extremities seem normal. A quick neurological exam reveals no gross abnormalities.

The physician begins the teaching round with this introduction: "Today I've planned for us to discuss the identification and management of seizures in infants. We've all seen the child and the record so there is no need to recite the data on the chart. I see my role as asking what you would do in this case, why, and how you would deal with the potential consequences of your actions. I will try to avoid stating what I would do since ultimately you have to solve the kind of case we have in front of us. I hope you will ask questions of each other and try to work together to understand this problem."

A dialogue ensues. Note the nature of the questions and corresponding student responses.

Instructor: (Question 1) I'd like to begin by asking the nursing students what data in the history seem important or relevant to you for the decisions you have to make right now.

Nursing student A: First of all I think the important thing was the seizure that he had.

Instructor: (Question 2) Can you elaborate on why you think this was a seizure?

Nursing student A: The fact that he was jerking his arms and legs, his eyes rolled back, he was feverish, he seemed to be unconscious at the time, and afterwards he was awake but not his regular self, sounds like a postictal state.

Instructor: (Question 3) I'd like to ask the medical students if you think the fever is of importance here?

Medical student B: Well, seizures frequently occur in children of this age after a febrile illness or after a fever reaching a high level.

Instructor: (Question 4) Would your approach to thinking about this case be any different if the fever were not present, but the seizure described had occurred?

Medical student B: Definitely.

Instructor: (Question 5) Can you tell me in what way your thinking might be different?

Medical student B: Well, if there was no fever to precipitate it, then I could not assume that this is a seizure caused by febrile illness. I would still work the patient up for other causes of seizures to make sure I wasn't missing anything, like a meningitis. I would consider doing a spinal tap on the patient and would get an electroencephalogram.

Instructor: (Question 6) I'd like to ask one of the residents, suppose John Jones were 7 years old instead of 15 months. Would this alter your thinking about the case?

Resident A: Well, in 7-year-olds febrile seizures are less likely to occur, and I would start looking toward meningitis and familial types of seizure disorders which frequently start appearing around that age.

Instructor: (Question 7) What would your approach be if the mother had described a seizure that was occurring on only one side of the body?

Resident A: As I understand it, febrile seizures are of the grand mal type. If it was more of a focal seizure, I would not think of it as febrile and would consider other causes.

Using Open-Ended Questions

This brief scenario was designed to demonstrate the use of questions and is not a complete script of the examination of the case. The instructor first asks a process question requesting students to identify data from the history that would be important in diagnosing and managing the case. A question of this nature lets the instructor know whether the students can distinguish the data in the history which are relevant. The discussion could have begun with a more leading question: "What kind of seizure do you think he had?" To answer, students would still have had to reason, but the instructor would have already identified the presence of a seizure. The student should make this determination, even if it seems obvious from the chief complaint. Suppose one or more students had not recognized the apparent problem. The instructor would have to weigh the merits of providing the diagnosis instead of asking them to study the case and related reading material more fully before continuing.

Many instructors argue that questioning consumes too much time in clinical settings in which patients need to be managed. On the contrary, unless immediate management is at stake, why spend time lecturing students who, in this instance, cannot recognize a seizure—or in other cases cannot sort out relevant details from the history, physical, or laboratory findings. Providing information, particularly factual, does not create in students the expectation that they are responsible for their own learning and ultimately for solving clinical problems.

We need to admit to ourselves and our students that much is unknown in solving health problems. Focusing on what is known is only one aspect of scientific investigation. Inquiry is at the heart of learning more about what is unknown. The value and economy of using open-ended questions, which do not reveal an answer, should be considered seriously if a goal of clinical education is promoting higher-level student thinking.

Probing

When the nursing student states that the child had a seizure, the instructor immediately asks for the reasons for this opinion. If instructors hear a correct response, particularly a diagnosis, they often move to management issues or another patient. Here the instructor probes for reasoning, forcing the student to justify answers. This tactic allows the instructor to verify the accuracy of the student's thinking. The fourth question asks whether the student's approach would be different if the fever were not present. "Definitely," says medical student B. Rather than letting this reply suffice, an additional probing question is asked to determine in what way the student's strategy would be different. A guess can be accurate. A simple Why? to an answer not only ensures the legitimacy of the student's reasoning, but creates an expectation that the student should be able to defend it.

Using Hypothetical or Speculative Questions

Depending upon the length of their clinical experience, students in our example might not have had the opportunity to see a 7-year-old with febrile seizures. Question 6 capitalizes upon the present case to explore another clinical possibility. To answer it, students need to relate their knowledge of febrile seizures to another age group. If they had been unable to answer, the instructor could have rephrased the question to, "What does anyone know about seizure disorders that first appear around the age of 7?" If blank stares continue, the instructor has the option of providing the information. A time-saving approach that should arouse greater responsibility for solving the problem would be to ask the students to research this area before they see John Jones again, when it would be a topic under discussion.

Similarly, students are asked to speculate as to whether their approach would be different if the seizure were occurring on only one side of the body. This open question pushes students to consider both the difference between focal and grand mal seizures and their relationship to febrile episodes. Hypothetical questions like these help students learn how to differentiate between and generalize about the various types of seizures that occur in children. Again, if students cannot address these questions, they might be encouraged to study them for the next meeting. How refreshing it would be for students to leave a teaching session with questions to contemplate rather than answers fed on the spot. Do not forget the figures for loss of retention after lectures. While not entirely parallel, often clinical teaching sessions around actual cases are no more than brief lectures; yet most of us remember how to approach a problem longer when we solve it ourselves than when we are told how.

Discussion of John Jones continues. Notice the character of these questions and student responses.

Instructor: (Question 8) Let's move on to the data available from the physical examination. What data have relevance for the decisions you have to make?

Medical student B: The fact that the patient had rhinorrhea and a left bulging tympanic membrane gives us a cause for the fever. We have an infectious process present and don't see anything in the physical exam like nuchal rigidity or meningeal signs. The neurological exam seemed to be normal.

Instructor: (Question 9) What is your understanding of the significance of nuchal rigidity or its absence in this age range?

Medical student B: I have no idea.

Instructor: (Question 10) Can anyone else address this question?

Resident A: In 15-month-old children you may not see nuchal rigidity in meningitis, which is why I would do a spinal tap to rule it out.

Instructor: (Question 11) That seems to lead us to what further data based on the history or physical you would want to acquire at this time?

A discussion about the laboratory findings ensues, and the next question is as follows:

Instructor: (Question 12) What long-range plans for management and additional data might you consider for this child?

Students engage in discussion.

Instructor: (Question 13) Put yourself in the mother's position and try to consider what questions she might ask you that haven't been addressed so far.

Nursing student B: I think I would address myself to whether he would have seizures again, since that is probably her major concern.

Instructor: (Question 14) What other concerns might she have?

Nursing student B: I'm not sure.

Instructor: (Question 15) What management suggestions for the mother might assist in preventing further febrile seizures?

Nursing student B: Okay, I would tell her that if the child is ill in any way to take his temperature immediately. Bring his fever down quickly with acetaminophen or a sponge bath. The sponge bath would be a very easy thing to do first.

More discussion ensues.

Instructor: (Question 16) Could one of you discuss any possible relationship between febrile seizures and subsequent seizures not associated with fever?

Medical student A: I don't think preventing a febrile seizure at this point would prevent seizures later on.

Instructor: (Question 17) What would you do if there were data to suggest that the greater the number of febrile seizures, the greater the likelihood of nonfebrile seizures later?

Medical student A: Ah, then I would start the patient immediately on phenobarbital if those data were substantiated.

Instructor: (Question 18) Perhaps you could respond to this last comment.

Pharmacy student: Phenobarbital is a barbiturate, and one of its side effects is possible respiratory problems. Depending upon the dose, children can become lethargic initially. Yet it does work in most kinds of seizure disorders.

Sequencing Questions in a Logical Order

There is a coherent order to the line of questioning in both excerpts. Explored first are data from the history and then the findings from the physical examination and laboratory tests. Immediate and long-range management questions are addressed next. While there are other logical ways of ordering the questions, this example follows a scientific path for solving a clinical case. Competent practitioners, particularly in routine cases, can quickly sort out relevant details from the history and physical to determine appropriate laboratory tests, radiographs, or other data which should be collected. When teaching, though, instructors tend to forget that students have not had the benefit of practice and need to learn the processes of logical problem solving. Unless they are privy to the reasoning behind the clinician's thinking and learn to examine their own, they may remain in the background, watch the expert solve the problem, and lose the richness of thought that led to its solution.

Excerpts from the Jones case reflect this process. The sequence of questions includes the following:

1. Data from history (explication of what is known): Question 1.

2. Clarification of these data and their possible implications (interpretation of data): Questions 2 to 7.

3. Data from the physical examination report (explication of what is known): Question 8.

4. Clarification of these data and their possible implications (interpretation of data): Question 9.

5. Plans for management and need for additional data (testing the hypotheses): Questions 11 to 15.

6. Prevention aspects of management: Questions 16 to 18.

This is an orderly sequence consistent with one problem-solving process. Other series of questions could be designed. If you are concerned with the sequencing of questions, most students will probably learn to solve problems in a systematic and logical manner.

Phrasing

The questions asked by this instructor were clearly and efficiently stated. Only a few were phrased in a way which could be answered by a simple yes or no. The questions are relatively brief but demand a good deal of student thought, and they do not combine a number of ideas or questions in one. To phrase questions like this requires practice. Audiotape your next teaching session to examine how the questions were stated and analyze student responses as well. This evaluation should make you keener of phrasing the next time you teach.

Adjusting Levels of Questions to Student Ability and Interest

This script of questions was obviously contrived to demonstrate a method to involve *various* levels of health professions students from several disciplines. Often student nurses, medical students, and other health professions who attend a teaching round are ignored. Knowing that such educational practices occur in clinical settings, should we wonder why it is so difficult to create health care teams among practitioners?

To make everyone attending a clinical teaching session feel involved and responsible for the case under discussion, speculate about questions appropriate to the range of students' specialities and educational levels. Some students are more withdrawn than others but in time may make valuable contributions if they are sensitively brought into a discussion with questions that help them learn rather than intimidate them. Little learning is likely to occur if students consistently remain witness to dominant individuals competitively demonstrating their brain matter.

Student-to-Student Questioning

This script includes only questions from the teacher and not dialogue among students. A model clinical interaction would reflect students questioning each other. Suggestions for assisting this interaction are presented in the group discussion chapter. Before students feel confident to ask intelligent questions of each other, however, most will need to see questions used skillfully by their mentors. As instructors many of us tend to emulate our former teachers, so for the instructor to ask questions first is a means of helping students to ask intelligent questions of each other. When students are excited by their own ability to ask questions and solve problems effectively, they may be more prepared to share this enjoyment with each other.

General Issues in Questioning

Being sensitive to and competent to manage patients is the essence of quality practice in the health professions. Nowhere is the notion of a role model more apparent or important than when students see you, their instructor, work with a patient. At the bedside, clinic, office or pharmacy, the students' role should be made clear to the patient. The way you interact with students in front of the patient not only affects the student but also the person under care. To be pleasant to the patient but abrupt and annoyed with a student can only raise questions in both parties' minds. The extent to which you allow students to engage in problem solving with the patient present must be judged by the appropriateness of the situation and is dependent upon your feelings, the personality of the patient, and the students involved.

Another important issue involves reinforcement of student thinking or accomplishments. In our opinion, reinforcement is important for learning, but one should be wary of its overuse in the problem-solving process. If a student's line of thinking is continuously reinforced by the instructor's approval or disapproval, the effect may be similar to placing pieces of cheese in a rat's maze. There was no standard reinforcement in the dialogue between the instructor and students in the John Jones case. Never does "Yes, that's good" or "No, that's wrong" come from the instructor. Instead, the reinforcement evolves from the teacher's pattern of questioning. When the nursing student is stumped about additional things the mother might ask, the instructor neither provides suggestions nor says "That's O.K.," but handles the question in a more indirect manner. Instead, the teacher asks, "What management suggestions for the mother might assist her in preventing further febrile seizures?" While a more leading question, the student is neither placated nor demeaned, but asked to think further. The teacher's question becomes the reinforcer as to whether the student is pursuing an appropriate line of reasoning.

Suppose that after sufficient probing, the students' thinking was incorrect; they arrived at an incorrect diagnosis or mismanaged the patient. Though time may have been spent pursuing an inaccurate path, these students may remember their errors in solving this particular case forever. As long as the patient is not in jeopardy, time can be set aside following a case discussion for students and instructors to examine any incorrect thinking and determine what information is needed to solve the problem. If instructors can remain open and admit what they do not know, then mutual problem solving will be encouraged. In clinical settings where students are practicing on patients, there is even more cause to let the student reason before acting.

In practice we are in situations where we must make decisions on our own. No one may be available to reinforce a correct or an incorrect decision. Hopefully our educational training will have instilled enough confidence in us to be able to solve problems independently when necessary. Providing feedback at appropriate intervals should aid this development. Continuous reinforcement of student thinking at each stage of the problem-solving process may only result in teacher solutions.

The rating scale that follows is a guide for you to consider when promoting problem solving through questions.

PROMOTING PROBLEM SOLVING THROUGH QUESTIONS

Date: _____

Instructor: _____   Rater: _____

These statements are to be used for rating a lesson designed to teach clinical problem solving through the use of questions. After observing the lesson, please respond to each statement by checking the category that most closely corresponds to your observation.

ORGANIZATION AND DELIVERY SKILLS	RARELY OR NOT DONE	PARTIALLY OR SOME-TIMES	COMPLETELY OR USUALLY DONE	NOT APPLI-CABLE/ CAN'T RECALL
INTRODUCTION				
1. Specifies goals of the teaching session.	☐	☐	☐	☐
2. Sets ground rules for student participation.	☐	☐	☐	☐
THE BODY				
3. Asks predominantly open-ended questions rather than those requiring factual recall.	☐	☐	☐	☐
4. When appropriate, probes for additional data, reasoning, possible actions.	☐	☐	☐	☐
5. Asks hypothetical, speculative "what if" questions.	☐	☐	☐	☐
6. Gives students adequate time to think about and answer questions without interrupting with another question or with the answer.	☐	☐	☐	☐

ORGANIZATION AND DELIVERY SKILLS	RARELY OR NOT DONE	PARTIALLY OR SOME-TIMES	COMPLETELY OR USUALLY DONE	NOT APPLI-CABLE/ CAN'T RECALL
7. Encourages students to try and answer their own questions or those asked by others.	☐	☐	☐	☐
8. Sequences questions in a logical order such as this: a. History, physical, lab, management, follow-up.	☐	☐	☐	☐
b. What would you do? Why? What does it mean? What if?	☐	☐	☐	☐
9. Uses appropriate phrasing. a. Asks clear and concise questions rather than using long and ambiguous ones that combine a number of issues.	☐	☐	☐	☐
b. Avoids repetitive questions.	☐	☐	☐	☐
10. Adjusts level of questions and difficulty of required answers to students' ability.	☐	☐	☐	☐
11. Creates an atmosphere in which students ask each other questions.	☐	☐	☐	☐

ORGANIZATION AND DELIVERY SKILLS	RARELY OR NOT DONE	PARTIALLY OR SOMETIMES	COMPLETELY OR USUALLY DONE	NOT APPLICABLE/ CAN'T RECALL

CONCLUSION

12. Develops a conclusion including key points.	☐	☐	☐	☐
13. Directs and encourages students to further their understanding of the topic.	☐	☐	☐	☐

OTHER CONSIDERATIONS

14. Interacts with patients appropriately.	☐	☐	☐	☐
15. Teaches in a relaxed, open, non-threatening manner.	☐	☐	☐	☐
16. Uses AV aids (x-rays, patient record, chalkboard) to enhance understanding and promote problem solving.	☐	☐	☐	☐
17. Gives students concrete feedback about their performance at appropriate intervals.	☐	☐	☐	☐

18. Overall, what percentage of the time was the instructor talking? (Check the appropriate space.) ☐ 0% ☐ 20% ☐ 40% ☐ 60% ☐ 80% ☐ 100%

In evaluating this teaching session, which of the items above indicate the **best** aspect of the instructor's behavior? Item # _____

Which item indicates the **least effective** aspect of the instructor's behavior? Item # _____

Comments: _____

_____

_____

_____

_____

_____

_____

_____

PROMOTING PROBLEM SOLVING THROUGH SIMULATIONS AND ROLE PLAY

The preceding section dealt with using questions to promote solving the clinical problems of actual patients or case material. Students could be interviewing patients, extracting teeth, planning a diet, analyzing a blood sample, or conducting physical therapy on a myocardial infarction patient —all involving hands-on experience with an individual. In a clinical setting where the patient population is limited, the cases too common or too unusual, or when student practice may be potentially harmful to a patient's welfare, simulated experiences can be devised which mirror real clinical encounters. The balance of this chapter will be devoted to developing students' problem-solving abilities through techniques that do not involve patients: computer-assisted instruction, written simulations, and a role-play situation called "Instructor Plays Patient."

Computer-Assisted Instruction

A health professions student can sit in front of a computer terminal and, by typing letters on a keyboard, face realistic decision-making situations more complex than those possible with simulations on paper. Students can type questions, receive responses to their answers, and be given an immediate evaluation of their progress with the case. Portions of a computer simulation are presented here to provide you with a sense of the process. It was prepared as one of a series of case studies in coagulation, using the computer system PLATO. After selecting the program, the following information would appear on the computer screen:

title

CASE STUDIES IN COAGULATION

CASE 1

Content provided by
Franz Rodriguez-Erdmann, M.D., FACP
Abraham Lincoln School of Medicine

Programmed by
William Bonetti
Center for Educational Development
University of Illinois at the Medical Center

Copyright © 1976
The Board of Trustees of the University of Illinois

Press NEXT

intro

INTRODUCTION

The purpose of this lesson is to review and quiz you about your basic lab knowledge in the workup and management of a patient.

Consider yourself the primary physician in the case that follows. Throughout this case you will be presented with information and then asked questions regarding what your actions will be. Please be succinct with your answers. If PLATO does not understand your answer then try rephrasing it. Help is always available after you have made two or more incorrect attempts at a question. The answer will also be available at that time by pressing ANS . Separate multiple answers with commas (,). Pressing SHIFT DATA will always return you to the catalog.

Press NEXT to continue

warning

This lesson is experimental at this time. Because each question allows you to enter answers in your own words, we must think of all of your possible responses ahead of time. If PLATO does not understand your answer, it is due to the fact that we did not anticipate it as a possible response to that question. Try rephrasing your answer. You might try changing the word order or deleting any unnecessary words from your response. If PLATO does not understand one of your abbreviations, then try spelling it out.

All unanticipated responses will be stored so that we can constantly improve the lesson and give more replies to more and different types of responses in the future.

Press NEXT to continue

open

A 19-year-old man was admitted in the early morning to the emergency room because he had been involved in a street fight the night before. He stated that he felt well until midnight when he noticed that some areas, where he had been hit, were swollen and very tender. He also noted "something" in his right eye, and a few hours later he felt a sharp pain in his right eye.

[When you have a multiple answer separate different parts of your answer with commas (,).]

What will you do?

>

In this instance the student decided to type "Perform an examination." Notice the response that is flashed to the student on the screen.

What will you do?

> Perform an examination.
   uuuuuuu

Sorry, but I do not understand your statement. Try rephrasing it please.

indicates words that I do not understand.
uuuu

        Press NEXT to type in more answers.

If the student had stated, "Examine the patient," the computer would respond. It does not take long for a student to learn the appropriate wording since hints can be supplied by the computer after a couple of attempts. In this instance the student thinks again and types in "Take a history." The immediate response on the screen:

What will you do?

> Take a history.

Correct. And what should you do in conjunction with a history?

The student chooses to examine the patient as well and the following information is provided.

explq1

The patient tells you that he is a bleeder. He states that although he has never hemorrhaged badly, he has developed some large bruises in the past; for example, when he fell from his bike when he was 8 years old. At age 10 he bled after a tonsillectomy. At that time his doctor told him that he had von Willebrand's disease.

The patient has never been evaluated in a large hospital nor is he aware of any family history of bleeding. He has taken no medications for the last 2 months.

        Press NEXT to continue.

q2

The physical examination revealed some tender, fresh ecchymoses in both arms and in the right thigh. The right eye has blood in the anterior chamber.

What do you do now?

>

The student proceeds to suggest that laboratory tests should be ordered and the computer response is

Exactly, but which lab tests do you feel are indicated for this case?

The student then requests certain laboratory results and is told whether they are appropriate, incorrect, or insufficient to make a diagnosis. Since coagulation is the topic of this simulation, it emphasizes laboratory interpretations. During the process of logically selecting and eliminating certain lab tests and results, the student is eventually supplied with the results understood to be essential and is asked by PLATO to make a diagnosis. When the student has made a correct diagnosis the following response is brought to the screen:

You have now completed the lesson.

Please feel free to comment on the lesson by pressing SHIFT-TERM and typing "comment" at the "What term? >" phrase which appears at the bottom of the screen.

The number of people who have finished this lesson is 130.

Press SHIFT-DATA to return to the Medical Catalog.

Written Simulations

Paper simulations comparable to the computer example can also be constructed. A brief vignette of the patient and chief complaint are presented to the student in written format. The student is then asked to make a series of decisions regarding the appropriate history to collect, relevant physical examination data, a diagnosis, and a course of treatment. Written simulations can be developed in which the student's decision affects what follows next in the program. The alternatives and consequences of a decision are presented in print, with correct and incorrect information revealed through the use of opaque tape, a card which is removed to reveal the information, or chemically, as with the currently popular latent image format.

Sophisticated paper simulations can be developed. Teams of individuals can construct them, predict possible responses and consequences, and build many nuances into the case. Many simulations are available commercially. Written simulations are excellent for teaching supplements and can be used for diagnostic and evaluation purposes (Appendix D) and also as stimuli for group discussions. They can be transferred to a computer format.

Instructor Plays Patient

A primary method for teaching clinical problem solving to students is the case presentation or conference. In contrast to more didactic techniques, these teaching sessions present students with actual clinical cases around which students can test their problem-solving abilities. Engel (1971, p. 20) criticizes the typical case presentation

As a mechanism whereby the teacher may effectively supervise or evaluate the quality of the student's interaction with his patient and the methods he used to collect and evaluate clinical information, the case presentation has decided limitations. This is particularly so when rounds are conducted without the patient's being seen, the material being presented being used merely as a springboard for discussion of a disease or basic principles. Such a lack of attention to the patient on rounds can have the unfortunate consequence of reducing in the eyes of the student the individuality of the patient and his particular problems and of minimizing the value of the information that derives directly from the patient in the course of interview and observation. It encourages callous attitudes as well as the deplorable tendency to overemphasize the laboratory work-up.

Engel proceeds to offer an alternative approach which involves more interaction with the patient and discussion of the problem-solving elements involved in the case.

While there are advantages to Engel's proposal any approach involving live patients has its limitations as well. Patients may be unavailable when an instructor wants to discuss a given clinical problem, and those who are accessible may have cases too sophisticated for a beginning student's analysis. Working with the patients at hand also does not allow students to experiment with alternative courses of action or confront their mistakes as readily. When patients are present, students may be intimidated by the reality of the situation.

"Instructor Plays Patient" is an alternative technique which has these advantages: students have the opportunity to experience a variety of clinical cases, the instructor can vary the complexity of the case, opportunities are provided for students in which they can collect data, suggest alternative hypotheses, recommend treatment plans, and review the consequences of their actions; and situations are constructed which are real enough to explore interpersonal issues between a student and patient without high risk to either party.

In "Instructor Plays Patient" the instructor plays the role of a patient seeking care. The instructor creates the case in advance and, in addition to playing the patient, can provide physical examination data and the results of laboratory tests to students, who act as practitioners.

The following example, in which this technique was used with a group of 4 third-year medical students in a dermatology clerkship, will illustrate the method. Before the session began, students were shown slides of the patient's condition. These were used to make the situation more realistic and present symptoms students might typically see when this patient entered the office, clinic, or hospital. Time was provided for students to view the slides carefully. They were told they could return to them at any point during the class.

The slides were reviewed, and the instructor began the class: "Good morning. My name is Mrs. Hannah Brown. You've got to help me! Do something for me! Please!" The students, acting as physicians, began to collect data and quickly learned that she was 39 years old and suffering from extremely sore hands and feet. The session continues, and the physicians (students) elicit further history from Mrs. Brown with questions: "How long have you had this problem? What type of work do you do? Have you used any medication for this problem?" As the interview proceeds, the patient (instructor) interjects additional pertinent information about herself. It becomes quickly evident that Mrs. Brown's work has intensified her concern with her problem. She is employed as a cleaning lady in an office building and has to use her hands and be on her feet constantly.

After extracting a certain amount of history, the students were interested in physical examination findings. The instructor switched roles and functioned as an intern giving results to physician inquiries but did not provide any interpretation of the findings. For example, a student asked, "Was scaling apparent on her hands?" The intern (instructor) replied, "You may want to review the slides again." Laboratory results can also be requested by students. The instructor provides these data without interpretation. If the instructor has prepared a case, replicating a situation with an actual patient, the response to some requests may be that certain laboratory tests were not conducted or would take a few days to do. Later in the session students can suggest that particular tests be conducted.

While interviewing Mrs. Brown, the students are confronted with a variety of psychosocial issues similar to those they would encounter in an actual situation. At one point Mrs. Brown was told by one of the students that he wanted to "ascertain" the basis of her problem. Mrs. Brown seemed satisfied and the interview continued, but two or three questions later she suddenly said, "What's ascertain?" The instructor, playing Mrs. Brown, used that opportunity to alert students to the patient's level of verbal comprehension.

Another psychosocial issue arose when the "physicians" lost sight of the patient's major complaint. They discovered a number of problems with this patient, such as episodes of menorrhagia, a positive serological test for syphilis, and a complete blood count which indicated chronic anemia. As a result of these findings, the students continued to inquire about them without explaining to Mrs. Brown the relationship between these problems and her perception of her ailment. She finally became extremely agitated about the situation and said, "Please, you're very nice, but I came here for some help with my hands and feet." The instructor's use of this plea served to illustrate the importance of keeping in mind the patient's perception of the problem.

In "Instructor Plays Patient," students are encouraged to call a "time out" to consult with each other. They may want to discuss additional data from the history which should be collected, decide on the significance of certain physical and laboratory findings, or discuss a management plan. Depending upon the time available, the instructor, if students have not done so, asks them to decide on a course of management. In Mrs. Brown's case, three of the four students ordered biopsies, all suggested that compresses be applied to her hands and feet 3 to 4 times a day, and she was sent home with a prescription for an ointment to allay her discomfort.

In some cases, as a result of faulty management, the instructor can play the patient on a followup visit with additional complications, and the role play continues. This was not the case with Mrs. Brown, and the last portion of the 1-hour class was devoted to a discussion of the strengths and weaknesses demonstrated by students during the problem-solving session. The instructor pointed out to individuals and to the group in general "clues" the patient had given them that they had failed to pick up, such as her symptoms of flushing, irritability, and temper.

"Instructor Plays Patient," using cases such as the one described, are used weekly with medical students during the dermatology clerkship we observed. Other cases included a homosexual with syphilis, an elderly man with skin cancer, and a young woman fearful of cancer. Cases such as these were designed to illustrate issues one would confront when dealing with cases involving psychological or social concerns in addition to the medical complaint.

Cases can be developed by any health professions instructor working with students who need to solve patient problems. Choosing cases should be considered carefully. They should be developed on the basis of what you want students to accomplish in establishing a relationship with the patient and in terms of the factual material to be covered. In general the case should be relatively uncomplicated since correct diagnosis is not the only goal of this technique. Psychosocial issues should be an integral part of the cases so students can develop an awareness of their importance in dealing with a patient. These issues, however, should be designed so that they do not result in unnecessarily long distractions or digressions. After a case is chosen, a definition of basic demographic characteristics needs to be selected and memorized. As instructor you should be as comfortable with the "character" of the patient as possible.

While you are role-playing, it is important not to abandon your role as teacher. As the role play ensues, watch for emerging leaders in the group, attempt to involve the quieter students, and encourage time out for discussion when students' need for some direction becomes apparent. Try to remain aware of what is said by whom, taking notes if necessary, in order to be able to provide specific feedback to students in the wrap-up session. If possible, students should be on the same educational level.

Through this method an instructor can teach elements which are not specifically included in the curriculum or do not lend themselves to "book treatment." This alternative provides an opportunity for you to learn about student thought processes as they act and interact in situations similar to those in which they will soon find themselves.

It is generally best to use this method with no more than five or six students. If the class is larger, other students can observe the process. We have found observers tend to become very involved, and can be included if they take notes as to what they would have done, and contribute comments in the wrap-up session. Following is a set of suggested procedures for presenting a case and a grid to assist you in developing it.

Procedures for Presenting a Case

At the Beginning of the Session

1. The instructor explains to students the rules of the game:

    a. The purpose of exercise is described.
    b. Instructor will play patient, lab technician, or other appropriate roles. (Laboratory results can be provided verbally. Actual lab results can be brought, such as radiographs, slides, or written test results.)
    c. No interpretation of the data will be provided.
    d. Students will play the particular health professional and relate to the instructor as the patient.

   e. Students can take time out to consult among themselves.

   f. Students can take divergent paths in their approaches to case management.

   g. Each student will be required to choose a specific course of management.

   h. At the conclusion of the session, there will be a wrap-up discussion of the case and students' management of it.

   i. Instructor should emphasize that this is a learning experience and will not be used to evaluate students.

   j. Ask for student questions regarding the process.

2.   In introducing the case, the instructor specifies the following:

   a. Demographic characteristics of the patient (e.g., age, sex).

   b. Setting in which students are working as health professionals (including possible limitations on getting assistance).

3.   Instructor introduces the case as a patient would present a problem (e.g., uses language consistent with patient background; uses first person in description).

Throughout the Session

4.   When acting the role of the patient, the instructor does the following:

   a. Uses appropriate language (consistent with patient's background, level of education; use of first person in descriptions).

   b. Understands and reacts to students' questions and comments the way the patient would.

5.   The patient's case selected for this exercise should have these characteristics:

   a. A complaint which is not too complicated.

   b. A complaint that allows a combination of physical and psychosocial factors.

6.   When acting the role of the individual doing the physical examination or collecting laboratory results, you as instructor should:

   a. Give data only upon request.

   b. Give *no* interpretation of the data.

   c. Consider the time necessary for completing a procedure (for example, lab results that take several days cannot be provided).

7.   When switching to your role as teacher, remember these points:

   a. Do not allow one student to dominate the exercise.

   b. Attempt to draw out all students.

   c. Encourage students to take divergent paths in managing the case.

   d. Use the role as patient or laboratory technician to "lead" students back to the main path rather than allowing them to wander off to side issues.

   e. Remind students that time out is allowed, and do not interfere with their taking time out for consultation among themselves.

   f. Require each student individually to make a commitment to a course of management.

At the End of the Session

8.   Ask students to comment on the case and their management of it.

9. You or the students should summarize the major issues.

10. Allow the students to point out their own strengths and weaknesses.

11. Point out factors students have missed, such as these:

    a. Incorrect or less effective courses of management.
    b. Strengths or weaknesses in isolating important elements of the case.
    c. Strengths and weaknesses in their interaction with the patient, such as language, tone, level of explanation.

12. Provide feedback to students which is constructive, encouraging, and not demeaning.

SAMPLE CASE FORM

Patient's Name _____

DEMOGRAPHIC INFORMATION	HISTORY	PHYSICAL EXAM RESULTS	LABORATORY TEST RESULTS	PSYCHOSOCIAL ISSUES	IDEAL MANAGEMENT

SKILL LESSONS[1]

The term *skill* is applied to a variety of tasks. The manipulation of symbols as in language or thought has been referred to as a skill. This chapter concentrates on *skill* defined as the mental and motor activity required to execute manual tasks. Health professionals must be competent to perform a multitude of "hands-on" or psychomotor skills. These require the practitioner to combine knowledge of the procedure, dexterity in handling the instruments and body parts involved, and the ability to adapt the skill to a specific patient or setting. Drawing blood, performing a gastric bypass, curettage, and emergency patient relocation are representative.

How one intellectually processes information from the environment and transforms it to motor movement is a topic of controversy and study. Research in this area is not unlike studies of problem solving which explore how an individual assembles memorized information and observed data to produce new inferences. Here, we will deal with conclusions that have generally been agreed upon by investigators who have examined the development and improvement of skills through training programs. Many of these findings have been applicable in our work with health professionals.

Some students are innately gifted in their ability to perform manual tasks. Other conceptually bright students have two left hands when they attempt the same procedure. Teaching a skill is not simple, and many instructors experience great frustration when students who had no difficulty learning cognitive material cannot manage the most basic manual task. It would be easy to attribute these differences to natural ability. We contend that the quality of training a student receives contributes to dexterity in performing skills. By changing the way a skill is taught, students can better master it.

In health professions settings the typical mode for skill learning has been the "see one, do one" approach. After observing the instructor demonstrate a procedure in a laboratory, clinic, or classroom, students are sent to practice by themselves. They are usually not provided with a clear picture of the precise steps involved in the procedure or with time for the supervised practice that guarantees they are performing it in the correct manner and sequence. The assumption underlying the "see one, do one" strategy is that after watching someone perform a skill, the observer will have the knowledge needed to repeat the process. This is akin to a piano instructor playing "The Minute Waltz" for a beginner and then saying, "Now, try it yourself."

Students may eventually learn a skill through years of trial and error in professional practice. We believe that students can and should learn to perform skills cor-

[1]The use of examples for IV therapy were adapted from Mary O'Leary, Myra C. Beniger, Charles Kanakis, Jr., and Dianne Kehl, *Intravenous Therapy Program: Color Videotape and Study Guides,* AudioVisual Concepts, Inc., Chicago, Ill., 1979.

rectly during their formal education. If more scrutiny is given to teaching and testing mastery of required skills in performance situations, then the likelihood of error in actual practice will be reduced. The approach presented here offers a systematic model for teaching students to master even the most complex psychomotor skills.

To conduct an effective skill lesson the bulk of your effort should be spent designing the lesson and preparing the needed materials. Delivery of a lesson requires careful execution of the lesson plan. Basic educational principles which should be applicable for teaching any psychomotor skill will be demonstrated by examining the instruction of intravenous (IV) therapy.

PREPARING A SKILL LESSON

The approach for teaching skills suggested here involves four elements: (1) Analyze and separate the skill into its component parts and determine which aspects of the skill are the most difficult to perform. (2) Provide students with a model of the skill they are expected to perform, demonstrated effectively and in its entirety. (3) Make provisions for students to practice until the expected behavior is mastered. (4) Provide adequate supervision and an evaluation of final performance. These elements can be incorporated into a lesson in various ways, depending upon the content, available resources, student population, and your inventiveness.

Skill Analysis

Prior to teaching any skill, it must be analyzed and separated into its component parts. Skills can usually be divided into a prescribed sequence of activities which are requisite for performing the task appropriately. We have encountered many health professions students who bitterly complain that they learned a procedure from one instructor and are then told by another within the same department that what they learned was incorrect. Students are then required to learn how to perform the technique again. Within the field of dentistry, for example, we hear of regional philosophies or approaches to defend varying dental practices. These claims are not unique to dentistry. However, we often ask health professionals with differing approaches to work collectively to define the essential steps involved in a technique. Almost always, more congruities emerge than differences. What is eminently clear, however, is that instructors generally have not spent time determining the commonalities inherent in their views of the components of a skill.

When specifying the behaviors that constitute a skill, it is useful to establish its broad components first. IV therapy, for example, could be said to include the following:

1. Advance preparation

2. Initiation

3. Maintenance

4. Termination

Each component can then be divided into its required procedural steps. Advance preparation for IV therapy might entail these steps:

GENERAL COMPONENT	PROCEDURAL STEPS
Advance preparation	1. Check physician's order.
	2. Assemble equipment.
	3. Identify patient.
	4. Explain procedure to patient.
	5. Secure proper lighting.
	6. Prepare equipment.

Although no hard-set rule exists as to how specifically steps should be written, extremely broad terms above such as "Assemble equipment" or "Prepare equipment" tell students little about the details needed to perform these steps of the process. They can be more fully delineated into substeps as shown in this example:

SKILL: STEEL OR SCALP-VEIN NEEDLE INITIATION

STEPS	CONTENT DESCRIPTION (SUBSTEPS)
ADVANCE PREPARATION	
1. Check physician's order.	
2. Assemble equipment.	☐ IV solution
	☐ IV administration set
	☐ Labels
	☐ Two scalp-vein needles
	☐ Sterile barriers
	☐ Iodophorm solution
	☐ Tourniquet
	☐ Emesis basin with medicinal soap
	☐ 4- X 4-in sterile dressings
	☐ 2- X 2-in sterile dressings
	☐ Adhesive tape
	☐ Colored marking tape
	☐ IV pole
	☐ Ball-point pen

STEPS	CONTENT DESCRIPTION (SUBSTEPS)
3. Identify patient.	☐ Check arm band and/or ask patient his/her name.
4. Explain procedure to the patient.	☐ Inform patient what you are going to do, and try to alleviate fears by asking patient if he/she has any questions.
	☐ Explain to the patient any limitations of movements.
5. Secure proper lighting.	
6. Prepare equipment.	☐ Tear open the IV bag container using the slit at the top.
	☐ Dry the bag with a paper towel. (If more moisture appears, there may be a leak in the bag, and it is contaminated.)
	☐ Inspect the fluid and container for any particulate matter.
	☐ Check for leaks and/or punctures. (If any problem, disconnect bag.)
	☐ Check expiration date on bag.
	☐ Lay the bag on a flat surface with the label side facing down.
	☐ Remove the seal from the bag.
	☐ Connect the administration set to the bag.
	☐ Hang the bottle or bag of fluid from the IV stand.
	☐ Either connect the needle to the administration set now or wait until after venipuncture.
	☐ Fill the tubing with fluid to remove any air in the tubing.
	☐ Protect the end of the tubing from contamination.
	Fill in information on the IV label:
	☐ The number of the IV ☐ The type and amount of solution

STEPS	CONTENT DESCRIPTION (SUBSTEPS)
6. Prepare equipment (continued)	☐ The number of drops per minute ☐ The number of hours the solution is to run ☐ The date and time started ☐ The time it should be finished ☐ Any medications added ☐ Your initials

The content description beside the second step, "Assemble equipment," becomes a checklist of materials the student needs in order to perform the procedure. The fourth step, "Explain procedure to patient," is defined more explicitly to remind students of important behaviors such as being sensitive to the patient's concerns. While this may seem obvious, it is often neglected in practice. The sixth step, "Prepare equipment," details a series of substeps which to the veteran are automatic but to the new student require thought and repetition.

Defining the steps in the advance preparation component of IV therapy is followed by determining those involved in initiation. These steps (continued from the above table) might be distinguished as important:

7. Select vein site.

8. Thoroughly wash and dry hands.

9. Place sterile barrier under site.

10. Apply tourniquet.

11. Cleanse infusion site.

12. Anchor vein.

13. Insert needle.

14. Check bloodstream.

15. Release tourniquet.

16. Connect needle to administration set.

17. Check for signs of swelling and hematoma.

18. Open flow clamp.

19. Check for signs of swelling.

20. Anchor needle.

21. Apply dressing and tape.

22. Loop tubing and secure with tape.

23. Regulate flow.

24. Instruct patient.

25. Record procedure.

These steps could be further refined into substeps as was done with the advance preparation component. Alternatively, Steps 12 to 16 could have been combined and simply labeled "Perform venipuncture." The level of specificity you establish is important and should reflect your estimation of the degree of exactness your students will need to perform a given step. Step 7, "Select vein site," for example, may be precise enough, yet it does not address certain factors such as when feet and ankle veins should be used. These and other factors could be amplified at this point in a substep column. While such considerations can be found in books or other references, your noting them in written format as factors to be remembered is likely to result in greater student retention of their importance.

When dividing a skill into its component parts, anticipate those steps which students may find most difficult to perform or potential obstacles they might encounter. A good driver anticipates problems on an icy street or foggy night. The more effort you spend determining circumstances students will need to deal with in performing a procedure, the more apt they will be to expect and attend to them in practice. Problem areas can be flagged on the checklist or raised in discussion. For instance, what should be done if a patient's IV bag backs up?

Time should also be built into your plan for questions students can be expected to raise about the steps of the skill. Some of these may be points not included on the checklist. Issues of clarification are sure to arise such as, "Which is the cephalic vein?" or fears such as, "What do I do if the patient refuses to let me insert the needle?"

Prior to instruction, carefully weigh which content is necessary for understanding and implementing the skill. Unfortunately, many skill courses are oriented to knowledge of cognitive material and sacrifice measurement of actual performance. Conversely, a course should not focus solely on the mechanical aspects of learning. As a general rule, it is wise to choose issues which are relevant to performance in professional practice. Knowledge of legal ramifications when administering an IV would be vital for executing this procedure. On the other hand, extraneous information – knowledge for knowledge's sake – should not determine the focus of the course content or examinations. There is no clear-cut relationship between knowledge of cognitive content and the ability to perform manual skills.

Depending upon the length of a course, there may not be enough time to cover all the content you consider important for implementing a procedure. This is especially true if a large proportion of class time is needed to practice the skill. Periodic assessment of students' knowledge of requisite cognitive content associated with the skill is then appropriate. Some of this information can be acquired by students on their own time. In-class and take-home examinations related to additional reading materials or lectures can also be designed in advance to test whether a student is knowledgeable of content as well as adept at technique.

Another consideration when analyzing a skill is which activities will help students adapt the skill to various patients or settings. A careful task analysis of the skill results in a detailed outline of the mechanics necessary to perform the technique. A professional analysis of the skill is needed as well. Students minimally should be conscious of the variety of professional situations they will most likely encounter when performing a procedure. How does initiation of IV therapy differ when working with very young, geriatric, or comatose patients? In what way does the loss of an extremity alter the procedure? Such issues can be addressed through distribution of written materials, discussions of case studies in class, or videotaped examples. Observation or, depending upon the skill, actual practice in different settings and with a variety of patients would be most desirable.

In summary, any skill should be divided into the discrete steps which underlie it. Areas in which students are most likely to encounter difficulties should be noted, and attention given to the professional situations in which they may need to apply a procedure. The goals of the skill unit or lesson should be explicitly stated. The course objectives and the written checklist of steps necessary to perform a skill should be distributed to students before they see the operation demonstrated.

Selecting Performance Models

"Rather than strictly following the old guideline of practice makes perfect, it might be more important to instill in memory a perfect standard." (Posner, 1973, p. 824.) Before practice of a skill begins, provide students with a complete template or cognitive map of the technique you expect them to perform. Even with a lengthy surgical procedure, they need to see a picture of the entire operation prior to drill. With IV therapy, a student should understand the components that make up the procedure: advance preparation, initiation, maintenance, and termination.

The skill students are to learn must be correctly demonstrated. If you learned to swim or type incorrectly, you know how hard it is to reverse old habits once ingrained. Decide how you will present a demonstration of the skill being accurately executed in advance of the course.

Usually students observe instructors demonstrating a skill live. Often, however, this tactic makes it difficult for all students to see each step being exhibited. The possibilities of an instructor forgetting an aspect of the procedure, or more likely demonstrating it too quickly, are also problems associated with the mode of direct presentation. This is especially true when a skill is introduced for the first time. Although live demonstration seems to be practical and efficient, alternatives are available which can rectify the potential difficulties inherent in this format.

Films or videotapes which provide an almost perfect template of a procedure are often commercially available. If not, they can be produced by an instructor. These models provide students the chance to observe a procedure performed without error and review the medium throughout the unit of instruction. Videotapes, in particular, can be easily stopped for purposes of discussion. They can be played back to review difficult areas and, when studied prior to class, free more time for discussion and skill practice.

Media departments exist in most institutions. With reasonable notice and relatively little effort, portable videotape equipment in black and white or color can be used to tape an instructor demonstrating and discussing a procedure. Through close-ups, precise, procedural operations can be captured and used repeatedly during a course and for years to come. Although more expensive and time-consuming, quality color videotaped demonstrations can be produced in studios.

A video cassette of the IV process, for example, can be constructed so that the equipment needed and each step of the procedure can be seen and labeled. A videotape demonstrating how to rectify complications which could arise during IV therapy, such as pulmonary edema or an embolism, can be available for students to view independently, again releasing more class time for skill exercise. The effort and expense spent seeking commercially available media or producing them yourself should be weighed against that expended giving the same live demonstrations or lectures repeatedly.

A television camera can also serve as the eye for an entire class during the demonstration of a skill. Through magnification techniques, an instructor can perform detailed procedures on objects as small as a fractured tooth, which can be enlarged and transmitted to as many as 100 students. If enough real objects, models, and instruments are available, individuals can practice simultaneously with the instructor.

Although less authentic than videotapes or films, slide-sound programs can be created to illustrate the components of a skill. A series of slides, synchronized with an audiotape, is advanced by students at their own rate to thoroughly review each step. Study questions about the procedure can be easily built into the program. Especially when accompanied by an instructional guide, slide-sound programs can supply logistic information such as the positioning or use of equipment. Besides providing early demonstration of a skill, they can be used by students after practice to reinforce understanding.

Whatever technique you select to present a model of performance, students should be able to observe it in conjunction with a checklist delineating each element of the skill. If you choose to demonstrate IV therapy live, each step of initiation should be done in slow motion so students have time to mentally unite the behaviors they observe with those on the checklist. Even with a simple skill, seeing it performed once is usually insufficient to understand, much less recall, the intricacies involved. Since delivering a presentation more than once consumes instructor energy and class time, we encourage you to consider the advantages of using media to demonstrate the skill. If the model is accessible, it becomes the students' responsibility to review the skill as often as necessary until they understand each step involved.

If you incorporate a film, filmstrip, or videotape into a skill lesson, preview it before the scheduled class. Take notes on the content, determine whether the entire medium or segments will be used, and calculate the class time needed for viewing. Note logical points for stopping and discussing the content. References for acquiring and developing instructional media for skill lessons are included in Appendix C.

Planning Opportunities for Practice

Anticipate before a lesson or series begins how much time will be needed and in what manner students will be able to practice the skill. Although a model of performance is essential, one must be able to practice a skill to master it. As many times as we have seen the use of an oxygen mask demonstrated on an airplane, we would probably perish if we ever needed to use it. One or two supervised trials with this simple operation would provide the skill required in an emergency.

After students are familiar with the technique to be performed and its component steps, they should be ready for practice. While it is generally agreed that interspersing practice with rest periods is preferable to massing of drill time, this must be judged in terms of the intricacy of the skill. There is controversy as to whether practice of parts of a skill is superior to practice of the whole procedure. Whether practice should occur continually on part of the skill with new parts being added successively is another topic of debate. Again, such decisions must be made after the components and complexities of the skill have been analyzed.

The amount of time available will influence which aspects of skill practice should be stressed. In teaching IV therapy, limited time may necessitate students having to learn identification and assembly of the required equipment on their own. If there is more time, this could be done during class in pairs. The steps for preparing the equipment in the content description serve as a checklist. Using this form, each student has the opportunity to practice and give feedback to a classmate. This process is likely to increase the probability that each step will be followed and committed to memory.

During study of the steps of the advance preparation stage of IV therapy, you might deem "Explain procedure to patient" worthy of more attention than other steps in this general component. If so, brief role plays could be planned for as many as 30 to 40 students working in teams of three: one playing the staff person explaining the IV process to another who plays patient. The third person can observe the interaction, utilizing the content description to see whether, for example, the practicing student remembers to ask the "patient" if he or she is comfortable or has any questions about the process. The patient could play being angry, terrified, or withdrawn while the observer takes notes on the interaction. Following the role play all three parties can discuss how this step was handled. In approximately 1 hour, each person can have the experience of articulating a patient's concerns, practicing the step, and learning through observation. If the experience is carefully planned, it will probably be remembered when performing this aspect of the therapy with actual patients.

When rehearsing the steps in any skill you should clearly specify to students if the sequence of events is critical. In some instances, such as advance preparation for an IV, it does not matter whether you "Secure proper lighting" before or after you "Assemble equipment." In contrast, the steps for initiation must be followed in a prescribed sequence and practiced accordingly. Such notations can be marked on the checklist and the logic discussed during the drill period.

In addition to working with each other, students can employ models to learn a skill gradually. Inserting a needle in an injectable training arm can be simulated countless times until the appropriate angle is learned and the insertion process mastered. Practice on models allows a student to proceed slowly, executing the skill accurately and comfortably before working with a patient. When practicing on models, one student can perform the technique while another observes, evaluates the process with the checklist, and then provides constructive feedback.

Very effective models and mock-ups have been developed for simulation purposes. Frequently employing color and texture to accent certain features, three-dimensional models, such as rubber breasts and pelvises, have been developed for teaching examination and operation methods. Many models have removable parts so that information and techniques can be better learned. Sound simulators have been developed to duplicate regular and irregular heartbeats. Mock-ups have movable parts, as do models. One mock-up of the human circulatory system has clear plastic tubing for blood vessels, a rubber hand pump for a heart, and red liquid for blood. Head and lung mock-ups are available for instruction in mouth-to-mouth resuscitation. Appendix C includes reference information on models, mock-ups, and other simulations.

The forms of practice you select for students will depend upon available space, equipment, and materials. Even if these are limited, be creative to assure that practice opportunities are sufficient. For example, if you have 12 students and only two complete IV sets, it is possible to group the class in threes to practice each part of the skill. Two groups could use the sets, while others watch a videotape or live demonstration. Other groups can work on identifying the equipment and memorizing the sequence of steps in this component. Even with limited apparatus, structure the lesson so each student receives enough practice to permit mastery of the skill.

Planning for Supervision and Evaluation

Supervision of student practice, reinforcing positive behaviors, and pinpointing areas needing improvement are essential to skill development. Using established standards a teacher can supervise student progress and determine when competence has been achieved. Direct observation, videotaped feedback, and the establishment of critical errors should aid in this process.

While students are practicing on each other or models, plan to circulate and give them feedback. Check that they are not proceeding to advanced stages of practice before mastering earlier ones. The list of written steps provides a more objective basis for feedback and should make the task easier for you and your students. Individuals who have not mastered certain steps during a period should practice on their own time. Equipment can usually be made available for use outside class, and a classmate could be recruited as a tutor. As the course progresses, those who have mastered the skill can be exempted from further practice, allowing you more time to closely monitor and correct problem areas confronting the remainder of the group.

As an adjunct to direct observation, especially when learning complex skills, the use of videotape is invaluable. Students can be videotaped while practicing the technique. Students then use the checklist to note strengths and deficiencies in their videotaped performance. The instructor or a classmate can view the tape and provide additional comments. Videotape is frequently employed to assist both beginners and pros develop and refine their skills in golf, tennis, and other sports. If such energy is being expended to improve a backhand return, it seems reasonable to consider its use with students who will be responsible for health care delivery.

The goal of a skill lesson is for students to accurately perform the complete procedure without assistance. A determination of those steps which are critical for minimally acceptable performance needs to be made. In order to assess mastery of a skill, standards should be predetermined and distributed to students at the inception of the program. The written checklist used for practicing the skill can serve to evaluate final performance. After adequate supervised practice, the instructor should be able to say, "Apply a tourniquet," and the student recall all the substeps needed to do so and accurately perform them in order. At some point the complete skill needs to be committed to memory and all steps evaluated. The following example is a checklist that could be used to assess final performance of the advance preparation and initiation phases of IV therapy.

CERTIFICATION PROCESS CHECKLIST
Initiation of IV infusions using a scalp-vein needle

Name of participant: _____ Clinical unit: _____

Written test/date passed: _____

Instructions for use: Enter a check mark in the appropriate column for each task in the checklist.

	DONE CORRECTLY	INCOMPLETE/ INCORRECT	NOT DONE	NOT APPLI- CABLE
PREPARATION SKILLS (ORDER MAY BE VARIED)				
1. Check physician's order.	☐	☐	☐	☐
2. Assemble equipment.	☐	☐	☐	☐
3. Identify patient.	☐	☐	☐	☐
4. Explain procedure to patient.	☐	☐	☐	☐
5. Secure proper lighting.	☐	☐	☐	☐
6. Prepare equipment.	☐	☐	☐	☐
PROCEDURAL SKILLS (IN SEQUENCE)				
7. Select vein.	☐	☐	☐	☐
8. Thoroughly wash and dry hands.	☐	☐	☐	☐
9. Place sterile barrier under site.	☐	☐	☐	☐
10. Apply tourniquet.	☐	☐	☐	☐
11. Cleanse infusion site.	☐	☐	☐	☐
12–16. Perform venipuncture (anchor vein, insert needle, check blood return, release tourniquet, check for swelling and/or hematoma).	☐	☐	☐	☐

	DONE CORRECTLY	INCOMPLETE/ INCORRECT	NOT DONE	NOT APPLI- CABLE
17. Connect needle to administration set.	☐	☐	☐	☐
18. Open flow clamp to infuse fluid rapidly.	☐	☐	☐	☐
19. Check for signs of swelling.	☐	☐	☐	☐
20. Anchor needle.	☐	☐	☐	☐
21. Apply dressing and tape.	☐	☐	☐	☐
22. Loop tubing and secure with tape.	☐	☐	☐	☐
23. Regulate flow.	☐	☐	☐	☐
24. Instruct patient.	☐	☐	☐	☐
25. Record procedure.	☐	☐	☐	☐

Signature of M.D./R.N. _____

A mark in the "Done correctly" category of a step implies that students are performing all of the substeps involved. Some steps may be performed only partially and checked "Incomplete." For example, when explaining the procedure to a patient, a student might forget a self-introduction. While important, it will probably not affect the overall assessment of the student's competence. Needless to say, if this student could not perform the operation required to conduct Steps 12 to 16, "Perform a venipuncture," this would constitute a critical error, and the student should not pass the procedure.

Plan in advance the options available for students who do not master the skill at the time of the final evaluation. Will testing be repeated? If so, how many times will a student be allowed to perform IV therapy before it is determined that he or she has failed? References for making such decisions are included in Appendix D.

Some manual procedures can be taught in a short while; others require much more time for students to gain the understanding and practice necessary for mastery. Time restrictions may lead an instructor to cut corners and resort to the "see one, do one" approach in order to cover all requisite skills in the allotted time. While the instructor may feel that, at least, all the steps have been reviewed, it is highly unlikely that this approach will enable students to perform efficiently or effectively. Our belief is that if adequate time is spent on preparation, it is usually possible to teach most skills thoroughly in the time available. Videotapes and other means that demonstrate correct performance and checklists of the required steps make it possible for students to work alone or with each other, outside as well as in class, until they meet the established standards. Use whatever time you have available to its fullest. A guide to assist you in this planning process follows.

Planning Guide for Teaching Skill Lessons

1. Skill analysis

    a. Do you have a written checklist that describes in adequate detail the steps required for performing the procedure?

    b. Is the list clear? Does it mirror the correct order of activities when steps are sequential? Does it denote areas in which students are likely to encounter difficulties?

    c. Are discussion opportunities provided to be sure students understand each step and its importance?

2. The model of performance

    a. How will you provide a model of performance which demonstrates accurate execution of the required skill?

    b. Does the model of performance show all necessary details? Is it designed so students can comprehend the steps in the procedure?

    c. Will there be adequate opportunities for students to observe the model?

    d. How will students be able to review portions of the model later in the lesson?

    e. Will students be able to use the checklist of steps against the model of effective performance to observe how each specific step is carried out?

3. Practice

    a. How will students practice the required skill?

    b. Is practice organized so that students can learn the skill gradually? Are there opportunities for simulated practice on models and peers prior to patient contact?

    c. Are practice sessions conducted in groups small enough for all students to be actively engaged in learning?

4. Supervision and evaluation

    a. In what ways will students assess their own performance?

    b. What opportunities will students have to receive feedback on their performance?

    c. Is final competence assessed by having each student perform the complete procedure without assistance?

    d. Will additional supervised practice be available for students having difficulties?

    e.   What activities will be designed (tests, discussions) to test knowledge not measured by performing the skill?

5.   Space and materials

    a.   What are the space requirements for the lesson?

    b.   What equipment will be necessary?

    c.   Is practice planned to ensure the best use of available space and equipment?

DELIVERY SKILLS

If you have been able to work through all the guidelines suggested for preparing a lesson, implementing it should be relatively easy. The structure for teaching the skill, the materials to be used, allotment of time, and so on will have been determined before students come to class. There are still some issues related to delivery that need consideration in order to effectively implement your lesson plan.

Advance Preparation

Before class begins, be sure that you have what is required to execute the lesson smoothly. If videotape equipment is used, check that the monitor and playback equipment have been delivered to the room. Play a short segment of the tape to be sure it has not been erased by an eager technician and that voice, brightness, and focus are properly adjusted. If you are conducting a live demonstration, be certain the necessary equipment is there and arranged so everyone can see.

    If students are to practice portions of a lesson individually or in small groups, have adequate space so one team does not disturb another. Enough sets of working equipment and an adequate number of checklists should be on hand. Bring with you a list of everything required for the lesson and, if possible, arrive at least $\frac{1}{2}$ hour before class. Locating missing pieces of equipment or attempting to start a faulty machine consumes valuable class time.

The Introduction

Whenever a new skill is being taught in a course, provide students with an overview of the goals, strategies for learning the technique, and methods for evaluation. Checklists which delineate the steps of the skill should be distributed during the first meeting. Standards for evaluating final performance should be made explicit. Give students a syllabus of what will occur during each class, noting where students will be expected to read, practice, or view media outside of class.

    At the beginning of each meeting, ask if there are questions related to the previous class or homework assignments. Explain the purposes of the day's lesson and its planned activities. A good introduction would be: "Today we will practice initiating an IV. We've observed the videotaped model of the components and steps included in IV therapy, and have reviewed in detail the list of steps comprising advance preparation, initiation, maintenance, and termination. Since we've already gone over the equipment needed, we'll watch the portion of videotape demonstrating initiation. While you watch this portion, use the checklist to see if the person on tape performs all the necessary steps. After a break you will work in groups of three during the second hour to practice locating a vein and applying a tourniquet. Don't worry if you can't do it the first time; there will be plenty of time to practice. I'll circulate and assist you if needed. Tomorrow we'll begin venipuncture, and I'll explain the activities involved then. Are there any questions?"

If you have planned a class as carefully as this, do not forget to inform students of the game plan. Explain the reasoning behind your goals and activities. During any introduction, state the ground rules for the class. Ask students to raise their hands if they are unsure of a particular point during an activity. Tell them when they can expect a coffee break.

The Body

Apart from any lectures, demonstrations, or group discussions you plan, your role during most skill lessons will largely be one of giving directions, supervising activities, and providing constructive feedback.

During practice sessions be sensitive to the pace of the class. Certain students may be dwelling too long on trivial details. Prod them to move on. Those who master a skill quickly can be supplied with additional readings, asked to help students having more difficulty, or permitted to leave. It is a waste of time for students to wait aimlessly for the class to conclude.

When providing information and feedback to students, it is important to give concrete suggestions about behaviors students can change. Saying, "I didn't like the way you treated the patient, and you need to improve in this area," does not tell a student what was wrong nor how to correct this behavior. Use comments such as, "You held the patient's hand much too tightly, were brief in answering his questions, and did not ask if he understood how to deal with complications which might arise. This manner can convey that you don't care about him, and he may be hesitant later to call you if he has problems." This statement gives students direct suggestions which they can act on. When providing feedback, allow students time to react to your comments. Create an atmosphere in which they can discuss difficulties and feel free to ask you questions.

Many skills taught to health professions students generate uncomfortable feelings. The sight of blood, performing painful procedures, or working with patients with severe conditions have psychological impact on most students. By your starting a conversation which allows students to release their feelings about a situation, you let them know that it is legitimate to feel afraid, disgusted, or sad. Tell students of difficult experiences you have had, thereby enabling them to believe you can understand their feelings.

The Conclusion

Take a few minutes to tie together each day's activities and alert students to what they can expect during the next class. When all components of the skill have been practiced, a more comprehensive conclusion is needed. An imperfect demonstration or videotape of the skill can be shown for students to criticize and test their newly acquired knowledge. Written examinations can be administered to test knowledge not covered in skill practice. Variations in individual styles which do not influence effective performance could now be discussed. Problems students encountered when attempting the skill with a different patient or in a new setting are also appropriate topics for the conclusion of a unit or course. Any concerns or questions students have after they have mastered the skill should be addressed at this time.

SUMMARY

The "see one, do one" approach to teaching psychomotor skills is overly used in the health sciences. It is typical for students to watch the instructor quickly demonstrate an entire experiment or technique which they are then expected to replicate. Unspecific guidelines, insufficient practice opportunities, as well as a lack of concrete feedback and careful supervision are often characteristic. The checklist that follows outlines the approach presented in this chapter for developing and teaching an effective skill lesson. It can be used as a guide for your planning and given to colleagues or students to provide you with feedback on the lesson.

RATING A SKILL LESSON

Date:_____

Instructor:_____   Rater:_____

These statements are to be used for rating a lesson designed to teach psychomotor skills. After observing the lesson, please respond to each statement by checking the category that most closely corresponds to your observation.

	RARELY OR NOT DONE	PARTIALLY OR SOME-TIMES	COMPLETELY OR USUALLY DONE	NOT APPLI-CABLE/ CAN'T RECALL
ADVANCE PREPARATION				
1. Arranges necessary equipment.	☐	☐	☐	☐
2. Arranges adequate student work space.	☐	☐	☐	☐
INTRODUCTION				
3. Distributes list of steps for each component (checklist of criteria for evaluation).	☐	☐	☐	☐
4. Specifies purpose(s) of the lesson.	☐	☐	☐	☐
5. Presents outline and rationale of planned activities and evaluation methods.	☐	☐	☐	☐
6. Sets ground rules for student participation and questions.	☐	☐	☐	☐
BODY				
7. Explains the equipment.	☐	☐	☐	☐

	RARELY OR NOT DONE	PARTIALLY OR SOME-TIMES	COMPLETELY OR USUALLY DONE	NOT APPLI-CABLE/ CAN'T RECALL
8. Checks for student understanding of the lesson's goal.	☐	☐	☐	☐
9. Demonstrates a complete model of the skill (by direct demon-stration or use of media).	☐	☐	☐	☐
10. Explains a proce-dure in terms of its components.	☐	☐	☐	☐

For each component:

11. Demonstrates steps in slow mo-tion or provides media for stu-dents to review steps.	☐	☐	☐	☐
12. Makes provisions for students to perform skill following check-list.	☐	☐	☐	☐
13. Provides for stu-dents to assess each other using performance checklist.	☐	☐	☐	☐
14. Rotates among students to check performance.	☐	☐	☐	☐
15. Provides for con-tinuous practice until students can perform without checklist or assistance.	☐	☐	☐	☐

	RARELY OR NOT DONE	PARTIALLY OR SOME-TIMES	COMPLETELY OR USUALLY DONE	NOT APPLI-CABLE/ CAN'T RECALL
16. Provides transitions that tie various components together.	☐	☐	☐	☐

CONCLUSION

	RARELY OR NOT DONE	PARTIALLY OR SOME-TIMES	COMPLETELY OR USUALLY DONE	NOT APPLI-CABLE/ CAN'T RECALL
17. Summarizes purposes and activities of the lesson.	☐	☐	☐	☐
18. Asks for final questions.	☐	☐	☐	☐
19. Creates testing situation where each student is evaluated performing complete process.	☐	☐	☐	☐
20. Gives students concrete feedback about their performance.	☐	☐	☐	☐
21. Allows repeated testing until mastery is achieved.	☐	☐	☐	☐

MEDIA

	RARELY OR NOT DONE	PARTIALLY OR SOME-TIMES	COMPLETELY OR USUALLY DONE	NOT APPLI-CABLE/ CAN'T RECALL
22. Uses handouts to specify steps in performing skills.	☐	☐	☐	☐
23. Uses charts, slides, videotapes, etc., to provide models and illustrate key points.	☐	☐	☐	☐

Comments:
_____

_____

_____

_____

_____

_____

_____

_____

The purpose of this chapter is to introduce a framework for designing units of instruction larger than a single class meeting, whether a half-day seminar or a 4-month course, utilizing the techniques presented in the preceding chapters. Guidelines for planning have been provided for each teaching approach discussed in this book, but a larger unit of instruction requires more extensive preparation. We have all attended conferences or continuing education programs which consisted of a series of lectures in no apparent order, or have taken courses that provided no idea of what would occur from one class to the

INSTRUC-TIONAL DESIGN

next. To avoid such occurrences a systematic plan needs to be made prior to course implementation. The process of logically organizing the teaching activities for a course or program has been labeled *instructional design.*

Planning teaching activities for any course is an experiment. In education, as in science, sound hypotheses must be formulated, data collected, the experiment conducted, and the results analyzed. Selecting relevant course goals, planning a logical sequence of learning activities for students, and determining measures for assessing student achievement and satisfaction are requisite components of any experiment with instructional design.

Before planning your course, a number of factors should be considered. Learning theorists have contributed knowledge of how, in general, people learn best that has application in the classroom. When applying general learning principles, one also has to acknowledge that each student brings to the classroom different educational experiences and personality characteristics which influence learning; these elements must be incorporated into the planning. Finally, and too often ignored, each instructor has preferences for different teaching situations. Some favor lecturing in an auditorium, while others enjoy the intimacy of working with small groups or with a single student. A discussion of important principles of learning, as well as student and teacher characteristics, precedes the description of a model for organizing teaching activities. This information, in conjunction with earlier chapters, should prepare you to make informed, logical decisions when planning a course.

PRINCIPLES OF LEARNING

It is possible to identify several principles of learning which, although not laws, generally have been accepted by most theorists as useful for planning instruction (Hilgard & Bower, 1975). In our own work, we have found several of these principles consistently applicable to the health professions. They are derived from a variety of behavioral, cognitive, and personality theories of learning and can be adapted to any teaching situation, from individual tutorials to large-group lectures. Outlined below are the seven we have found to be the most useful guides in planning a course of instruction.

The student should be provided opportunities to be an active rather than a passive learner.

Actively engaging students in the learning process has been a major theme in our discussion of every teaching method. Even regarding the lecture, we discussed techniques that can alter this very passive form of instruction and increase student participation. Our feelings concerning the importance of active student involvement have been substantiated in numerous settings when we conducted curriculum development programs for health professions faculty. In these workshops, we asked participants to describe a memorable learning experience from their professional training, early education, or any other learning situation which was of value. In all workshops the participants' own active involvement is the significant and most frequently cited factor that made these experiences memorable. The consistent identification of this factor by health professions faculty corroborates the importance educational researchers and theorists have given it for years. Consequently, one of the ultimate indications of your ingenuity as an instructor may be your ability to transform learning situations in which students receive large quantities of information passively into formats that incorporate active student participation.

The student should be provided opportunities for understanding the logic underlying teaching activities.

Students should understand what they are expected to learn in any course or session, its relevance to their future professional lives, and how the sequence of activities will enable them to learn the material. If these factors are explained and understood, learning will be more permanent and will be transferable to future situations. As an example, many health professions students, especially at the graduate level, are required to learn basic statistics. Students often have problems with this subject and legitimately question its relevance, since many of them do not plan to conduct research. They continually agonize over the need to memorize formulas, derive standard deviations, or remember different models of analysis of variance. These concerns could be allayed to an extent if the value of statistics to a clinician's future practice were clarified. Although few of us conduct experimental research, we must keep up with current developments, which requires an intelligent analysis of research reports in professional journals. In this case, the statistics instructor needs to determine the goals of the course. Is one training statisticians who must be able to derive formulas, or clinicians who need to use statistical concepts in order to understand and judge the adequacy of research findings? After this determination has been made, goals must be clarified so students can understand their relevance. Learning with understanding also implies that students should have the opportunity to help formulate goals, or at least have the option of discussing the relevance of goals set by the instructor.

Comparable examples abound in all health-related disciplines. Since the pertinence of the Krebs cycle, the molecular structure of DNA, or epidemiological statistics to future practice is often questioned by students, they typically memorize the needed facts, pass the examination, and promptly forget the material. If this climate exemplifies student encounters with a large portion of the basic science material, it is no wonder that instructors complain about students' inability to apply this content in the clinical phases of the curriculum. In short, if you want students to understand and remember certain material, explain its relevance to their future professional practice.

Once this has been accomplished, students should understand how the teaching activities you have designed will enable them to arrive at these goals. Suppose the statistics instructor's major aim is teaching students to criticize research. Teaching activities should then have students evaluating articles instead of deriving formulas if a logical relationship is to exist.

It is also essential for students to understand the relevance of the evaluation methods selected for the course. Any student will experience rage after taking an examination which focused on trivia or which covered material not taught in the course. In the beginning of any course, provide students with information about the nature of the examinations, the criteria and process for grading, and the opportunities available to improve their performance. Early clarification alerts students to what you consider essential, reduces their anxiety, and minimizes potential discontent. Once again, when dealing with advanced students it is beneficial to include their input in the determination of evaluation methods.

A learning environment may be a highly structured, content-oriented course or a flexible clinical experience. Your style of teaching may be experiential or didactic. In any case, students should understand the game plan and its rationale. This understanding provides a cognitive map which will enhance learning ability and influence retention.

The student should have the opportunity to learn through a variety of educational resources.

Preceding chapters discussed the relationship between specific teaching methods and expected educational outcomes. Research has shown that the lecture is more useful for conveying cognitive information and is less productive for teaching problem solving. Small-group discussions promote more problem solving but are less appropriate for skills development than are structured practice sessions. While conceptually one can match the merits of a given method to specific educational objectives, the real world of teaching is not so cut-and-dried.

When students are learning to scale teeth, draw blood, or insert an intravenous tube (IV), they are expected to develop a specific skill. Even with such a readily defined objective, other goals need to be considered. Decisions about scaling teeth are influenced by the degree of gum swelling, or bleeding, and the age of the patient. These and other factors must be weighed, necessitating problem solving by the student. Scaling also involves interacting with patients, requiring the development of interpersonal skills, such as understanding patient fears and how to deal with them. Therefore, within any broad goal for student learning, there is always a mixture of education expectations that calls for a blend of teaching methods.

Diversity in a student population also justifies the need for multiple educational resources. Individual differences are inherent even in the most homogeneous group of students. Some are more compulsive and need to review written materials slowly and repeatedly. Others may be less concerned with details and can gain needed information through informal study groups preceding final examinations. Some students need to discuss theoretical considerations before they can learn a new skill, while there are those who learn best by an immediate hands-on experience. Reading materials may be the most productive route for certain students, while others gain more from lectures. Being sensitive to these variances means providing a variety of methods and materials for learning. Allowing students to learn alone, providing reading materials, self-instructional packages, group discussions, or other opportunities for learning will help students master course expectations in the manner most suitable for them. One cannot plan a course which includes every type of learning experience, and it is impossible to account for all student differences. Providing as many resources as is feasible, though, increases the likelihood of students assimilating the required knowledge and skills, and creates a more exciting learning experience.

The student should be provided with models which serve as criteria for the expected performance.

The primary goal in educating health professionals is that they be able to competently perform on-the-job skills. Most learning theorists would agree that seeing the desired task executed correctly is essential before learning how to do it oneself. Restoring a Class I cavity, posturing a patient for a radiographic examination, or compounding an ointment can each be taught in a variety of ways. Regardless of methods, however, students need a visual image of the expected behavior or product. Reading, lectures, and group discussions are useful when learning the steps and vocabulary required for performance, but they cannot replace direct demonstrations. An effective demonstration will provide students with a complete model of the processes or procedures as performed in the natural setting, and an opportunity to critically examine these components. Watching the instructor, practitioners in the field, a film, a videotape, or a simulated model are ways of providing this type of experience.

Most of us had professional role models, our heroes and heroines, who contributed to our image of the competent practitioner. While valuable, education in the health professions should go beyond an emotional identification with these individuals. Students should be given concrete and systematic opportunities to observe these models and study the behaviors that constitute their effectiveness.

Until the expected level of competence is attained, students should have adequate opportunities to practice using the knowledge and skills they have learned and receive feedback on their performance.

Both the second and fourth principles discuss the need for students to have a clear picture of course goals, stated in terms of the professional functions they will be expected to perform in the field. No matter how specific the goal statement or effective the models, however, opportunities must exist for students to perform these expected behaviors. Having the necessary knowledge and observing the best clinicians does not guarantee competence, since students need practice, supervision, and feedback to determine the adequacy of their performance.

Certain elements characterize effective supervisory practices regardless of the form employed. Students must be aware of the criteria used in evaluation and have the chance to appraise their own work through some mode of self-assessment. Expert evaluation should be available as a point of comparison with students' own judgments. They should have opportunities as well to correct deficiencies until the level of mastery specified in the original criteria is reached. In general, if supervision and feedback are evaluative and not judgmental in nature, they can be used to assist students to become competent practitioners.

Students should be provided with opportunities to examine ways of adapting learned knowledge and skills based upon the characteristics of a given situation.

The steps involved in drawing blood or the behaviors that constitute an effective patient interview are influenced by a variety of factors. The age, personality, and condition of the patient are important variables. Drawing blood is a simple procedure when done with a cooperative patient and a nightmare with a screaming child; this procedure is also influenced by the number of observable veins or the presence of an IV. Similarly, an interview will differ with an old versus a young patient, or a depressed person versus the businessman coming for an annual checkup. A physical examination which can be done thoroughly in a physician's office will be performed quickly and selectively with a seriously injured person in an emergency room. Resuscitating a person at the scene of a roadside accident involves different procedures than those used in a well-equipped hospital.

In planning a teaching sequence, it is important to teach basic knowledge and skills, but students also must be able to adapt this education. When students are learning to conduct interviews, it would be next to impossible, and not necessarily desirable, to have each of them interview 10 patients. On the other hand, one patient interview is insufficient. If a variety of patients and settings is carefully selected, students can see and discuss how their behavior should vary accordingly. Each patient interview should not be viewed as a separate case, since students must learn which interviewing behaviors generally crosscut all patients and settings, and which do not. An interview with a young male child in a hospital, a geriatric female in an outpatient setting, and a middle-aged lesbian in an emergency room may provide enough material for an in-depth discussion of how to adapt an interview.

The significance of varying the characteristics of the patient and setting depends upon the skill to be taught and how much time is available. If students have only one opportunity to practice a skill, it is possible to have different students work with various types of patients in multiple settings. Individual experiences can then be discussed collectively as a basis for generalizing.

Overall, students should have learning experiences which are positive and satisfying rather than negative and frustrating.

It is unlikely that you will be able to substantially affect the motivational set students bring to their education since this is a function of personality factors and previous learning experiences. Creating a generally positive experience, on the other hand, is likely to influence the level of motivation exhibited by students in your course and perhaps their desire for future learning.

Planning your course so students have initially successful experiences is our first
suggestion. We generally continue pursuits we have been successful at and avoid areas
of failure. Our interests in swimming, dancing, art, mathematics, or chemistry have
been colored by earlier experiences of success or failure in these areas. If students experience great difficulty when beginning to learn a new subject, their investment is
likely to be minimal for the duration of the course. Students should be challenged to
struggle with new content. The struggle, though, must be one likely to lead to success
and not cause undue anxiety and frustration for the majority of the students. Initially
successful experiences in a new area will probably increase a student's tolerance for
temporary failures later on and heighten motivation to grapple with more complex
subject matter.

Learning theorists have also documented the superiority of positive over negative
reinforcement. While this is true as a general principle, it should not preclude instructors giving negative feedback when appropriate. Students can teach inaccurate conclusions in a discussion, be inattentive to information on a patient's chart, or misinterpret
laboratory data. There is nothing wrong with telling them that they have inaccurately
drawn a conclusion or performed a procedure incorrectly. Following these comments,
however, students should have opportunities to improve their performance and receive
some positive reinforcement. Moreover, in terms of the complete structure of the
course, it is important to plan activities in which more positive than negative reinforcement is provided.

We hope to educate health professionals who feel successful and enjoy their work.
Regardless of their area of practice, graduates inevitably make mistakes and encounter
occasional failure. If they have had a positive and realistic educational experience, however, they should have developed the capacity to cope with daily problems in their
individual fields and should have internalized the pleasures inherent in practicing.

Summary

These seven principles of learning have been phrased to encompass numerous ideas put
forth by different learning theorists. The order used in describing them reflects a logic
to be considered when planning instruction. We have found that creating a conceptual
framework for students followed by providing models of effective performance prior
to giving supervision and feedback is an extremely useful sequence for planning instruction and evaluating a teaching plan.

These principles are general and applicable to any teaching situation, although
all frameworks allow exceptions. The active involvement of the student has been stated
as a general principle, but there may be a special case in which a withdrawn student
would be threatened by early involvement and should be permitted to be a passive observer, at least in the early part of the course. These and other situations are exceptions,
though, and you should be able to justify why you are not incorporating these basic
principles of learning when planning a course of instruction.

These principles are intended as a guide rather than a summary of all learning
principles. A number of learning theorists suggest that learning activities be planned to
encourage students to come up with divergent, creative solutions to problems. This has
not been included here as one of the general principles, since, in our experience, much

of health professions education involves teaching knowledge and skills which require standards of correct and incorrect performance. While fostering divergent thinking should be an essential component in the overall education of any professional, we do not view this as a general principle to be applied when planning all teaching activities.

In addition to applying principles of learning when planning a course, the specific characteristics of your student population should also be considered.

STUDENT CHARACTERISTICS

The majority of health professions students are bright and motivated, since rigorous admissions procedures in most institutions ensure the selection of students who have already succeeded in school. Despite this intellectual homogeneity, a host of environmental and personality variables affect every individual's behavior, resulting in great heterogeneity among a student population within any discipline. Unfortunately, students are often taught as if these individual differences do not exist.

An elementary school teacher responsible during a year's term for 25 students 6 hours a day can ordinarily assess prior achievement and acknowledge student differences when implementing the curriculum. This luxury does not exist in higher education, where access to information about your students is greatly limited. Instructors can reasonably ask, "How can I individualize learning for 100 students to whom I lecture 3 or 4 times quarterly?" Despite such realistic limitations, it is possible to collect some information about incoming students' educational background when planning your course. Knowledge of the subject matter students have been exposed to before is essential. Catalog descriptions, a discussion with a member of the curriculum committee, talking with students' former instructors, or asking those registered in your course to complete a brief educational background questionnaire can give clues as to when a concise review of certain material will probably suffice and when more extensive presentations will be needed. Assessing prior course content still does not completely address individual differences, since students will vary in their level of knowledge and competence upon entering your course.

One way to begin to assess student ability is to delineate the knowledge and skills you feel are prerequisite for your course and design a questionnaire which will determine students' self-perceived competence in these areas. For example, if you were teaching a course to upgrade staff nurses' knowledge of diabetes mellitus you might ask them to what degree

5	4	3	2	1
Very able		Somewhat able		Unable

they feel competent to evaluate a diabetic's understanding of and compliance to a prescribed diet. A more sophisticated form of assessment is to review your outline of prerequisite knowledge and skills and then construct a pretest that evaluates student competence. Multiple-choice tests are very useful in determining what students know in terms of the factual information needed for your course. Similarly, a brief performance test at the beginning will let you know whether students can execute procedures you consider essential.

Extreme variance in knowledge and skills among your students presents problems. We speculate that pretests frequently are not used because many instructors are unsure of how to rectify the deficiencies they discover. An initial step in remediation is to inform individual students or the entire class of areas where they need more knowledge or skill. Specific reading material, self-instructional units, opportunities for peer tutoring, additional laboratory experiences, and small-group tutorials are ways to assist students. Some of these methods require little effort on your part, such as an annotated bibliography or scheduling peer tutoring seminars. Others require more investment; for instance, designing self-instructional units or conducting individual and small-group tutorials. Your available time, the size of the group, the extent of the information gap, and the willingness expressed by students to do extra work are factors which will affect the methods you select.

Information gleaned from pretests is also useful for providing advanced students with more challenging materials and experiences. Supplementing a bibliography with readings that go beyond basic course material and furnishing opportunities for additional clinical or laboratory experiences will offer these students in-depth experiences and require little additional effort on the instructor's part.

In addition to achievement differences, students vary in personality characteristics. Some are extroverted, others introverted; some demand to be told what to do, while there are those who thrive on autonomy. These characteristics influence student perceptions of a particular course and its instructor, as well as their enjoyment and achievement in the class itself. It is generally impossible to get to know each student intimately, and even if it were, how could this information be utilized in course planning? One way to gain acumen into this area is by examining the concept of students' learning preferences.

Learning Preferences

In recent years, numerous investigators have developed questionnaires that assess an individual's learning preferences. These are not personality tests, but instead provide descriptions of the types of learning situations preferred by students. Administering this kind of questionnaire to students can guide you in planning your course. Before discussing its potential uses, complete the following questionnaire yourself in order to understand the concepts involved.

REZLER LEARNING PREFERENCE INVENTORY[1]

This inventory gives you the chance to indicate those conditions or situations which most facilitate your learning. It is not a "test"; there are no right or wrong answers. The aim of the Inventory is to describe how you learn, not to evaluate your learning ability.

The Inventory has two parts. In Part I there are six sets of six words listed. In Part II there are nine items each of which contain six statements.

Instructions for answering Part I

1. Record all of your answers on the Answer Sheet for Part I on page 103.

2. Read all six words carefully in Column A and rank order them. Write 6 for the word in Column A that best promotes learning *for you*; write 5 for the word that promotes learning next best, and so on, until you write 1 for the word that promotes learning least of all. Be sure to assign a different rank to each of the six words in Column A and continue the same procedure for the remaining columns until all words are ranked.

The following example illustrates the ranking procedure:

Rank the following colors in the order in which you prefer them:

Column A

a. Yellow
b. Green
c. Blue
d. Red
e. White
f. Black

Answer sheet:

Column A

a. 6 _____
b. 3 _____
c. 4 _____
d. 5 _____
e. 2 _____
f. 1 _____

The numbers in the spaces on the sample answer sheet show that "yellow" was preferred most; "red" second; "blue" third; "green" fourth; "white" fifth; and "black" least. You are to rank the responses and mark your answers to each word in Part I (Columns A through F) in the same way.

Rank each word; please do not omit any. Be sure to assign a different rank to each of the six words in each column.

LEARNING STYLE INVENTORY

Part I

6 = Promotes learning *most for you*
5 = Promotes learning second best
4 = Promotes learning third best
3 = Promotes learning fourth best
2 = Promotes learning fifth best
1 = Promotes learning *least for you*

Column A

a. Factual
b. Teacher-directed
c. Teamwork
d. Reading
e. Self-evaluation
f. Theoretical

Column B

a. Self-instructional
b. Myself
c. Hypothetical
d. Interpersonal
e. Teacher-defined
f. Practical

Column C

a. Sharing
b. Doing
c. Guided
d. Self-initiated
e. Thinking
f. Solitary

Column D

a. Teacher-structured
b. Concrete
c. Writing
d. Group
e. Conceptual
f. Self-directed

Column E

a. Scientific
b. Assigned
c. Skill-oriented
d. Personal
e. Self-designed
f. Team-oriented

Column F

a. Individual
b. Applied
c. Supervised
d. Autonomous
e. Abstract
f. Interactive

LEARNING STYLE INVENTORY ANSWER SHEET

Part I

Column A	**Column B**	**Column C**
(26) a. _____	(32) a. _____	(38) a. _____
(27) b. _____	(33) b. _____	(39) b. _____
(28) c. _____	(34) c. _____	(40) c. _____
(29) d. _____	(35) d. _____	(41) d. _____
(30) e. _____	(36) e. _____	(42) e. _____
(31) f. _____	(37) f. _____	(43) f. _____

Column D	**Column E**	**Column F**
(44) a. _____	(50) a. _____	(56) a. _____
(45) b. _____	(51) b. _____	(57) b. _____
(46) c. _____	(52) c. _____	(58) c. _____
(47) d. _____	(53) d. _____	(59) d. _____
(48) e. _____	(54) e. _____	(60) e. _____
(49) f. _____	(55) f. _____	(61) f. _____

Instructions for answering Part II

1. Record all of your answers on the Answer Sheet for Part II on pages 106–107.

2. Read all six statements carefully in Column I and rank order them. Write 6 for the statement in Column I that best promotes learning *for you*; write 5 for the statement that promotes learning next best, and so on, until you write 1 for the statement that promotes learning least of all. Be sure to assign a different rank to each of the six statements in Column I and continue the same procedure with the remaining columns until all words are ranked.

LEARNING STYLE INVENTORY

PART II

6 = Promotes learning *most for you*
5 = Promotes learning second best
4 = Promotes learning third best
3 = Promotes learning fourth best
2 = Promotes learning fifth best
1 = Promotes learning *least for you*

1. Read the following six statements and then rank them in terms of how well they describe the teachers in whose classes you have done the best.

    a. The teacher gave many practical, concrete examples.

    b. The teacher let me set my own goals and try different approaches to reach them.

    c. The teacher encouraged me to work by myself.

    d. The teacher was friendly and outgoing.

    e. The teacher made the relationships between different schools of thought clear.

    f. The teacher made clear and definite assignments, and I knew exactly what was expected.

2. Number the following kinds of work in the order in which they would interest you.

    a. Work that would require cooperation among team members.

    b. Work with specific and practical ways of handling things.

    c. Work that would let me do things on my own.

    d. Work that would permit me to deal with ideas rather than things.

    e. Work that I could plan and organize myself.

    f. Work that would be clearly defined and specified by my supervisor.

3. Rank the following in terms of their effects on how hard you work and how much you accomplish in a class.

    a. I can set my own goals and proceed accordingly.

    b. I can address myself to a concrete, practical task.

    c. I have an opportunity to discuss or work on something with other students.

    d. I can examine different schools of thought.

    e. I understand what is expected, when work is due, and how it will be evaluated.

    f. I can accomplish most tasks by myself.

4. The evaluation of student performance is a part of nearly all courses. Rank the following in terms of how you feel about such evaluation.

 a. It should be assembled from questions provided by students.

 b. It should focus on individual performance.

 c. It should consist of a written examination dealing mainly with written concepts.

 d. It should consist of a practical examination dealing with skills.

 e. It should be consistent with clearly specified requirements.

 f. It should not interfere with good relationships between the teacher and student.

5. Rank the following in terms of their general value to you as ways to learn.

 a. Study a textbook.

 b. Engage in an internship or practicum.

 c. Prepare a class project with other students.

 d. Search for reasons to explain occurrences.

 e. Follow an outline prepared by the teacher.

 f. Prepare your own outline.

6. Rank the following in terms of how much they would attract you to an elective class.

 a. Good personal relationships between teacher and students.

 b. Clearly spelled-out standards and requirements.

 c. Emphasis on practicing skills.

 d. Emphasis on individual study.

 e. Opportunity to determine own activities.

 f. Emphasis on theoretical concepts.

7. Consider the following in terms of their general effect on how well you do in a class.

 a. I can study on my own.

 b. I can work with something tangible.

 c. I can focus on ideas and concepts.

 d. I can organize things my own way.

 e. I can work with others.

 f. I can work on clear-cut assignments.

8. Rank the following in the order in which you think teachers should possess these characteristics or skills.

    a. Getting students to set their own goals.

    b. Getting students to demonstrate concrete skills.

    c. Involving students in generating hypotheses.

    d. Preparing of self-instructional materials.

    e. Relating well to students.

    f. Planning all aspects of courses and learning activities.

9.   Rank the following in terms of how much they generally help you learn and re-member.

    a. Studying alone instead of studying with fellow students.

    b. Performing a specific task.

    c. Having a knowledgeable teacher discuss the theory upon which a practice is built.

    d. Determining your own approach and proceeding accordingly.

    e. Joining a student group to study together and share ideas.

    f. Getting an outline of the course from the teacher and a clear understanding of what will occur in the course.

LEARNING STYLE INVENTORY ANSWER SHEET

Part II

Item 1	**Item 2**	**Item 3**
(26) a. _____	(32) a. _____	(38) a. _____
(27) b. _____	(33) b. _____	(39) b. _____
(28) c. _____	(34) c. _____	(40) c. _____
(29) d. _____	(35) d. _____	(41) d. _____
(30) e. _____	(36) e. _____	(42) e. _____
(31) f. _____	(37) f. _____	(43) f. _____

Item 4	**Item 5**	**Item 6**
(44) a. _____	(50) a. _____	(56) a. _____
(45) b. _____	(51) b. _____	(57) b. _____
(46) c. _____	(52) c. _____	(58) c. _____
(47) d. _____	(53) d. _____	(59) d. _____
(48) e. _____	(54) e. _____	(60) e. _____
(49) f. _____	(55) f. _____	(61) f. _____

Item 7

(62) a. _____

(63) b. _____

(64) c. _____

(65) d. _____

(66) e. _____

(67) f. _____

Item 8

(68) a. _____

(69) b. _____

(70) c. _____

(71) d. _____

(72) e. _____

(73) f. _____

Item 9

(74) a. _____

(75) b. _____

(76) c. _____

(77) d. _____

(78) e. _____

(79) f. _____

SUMMARY SHEET

Use this page to summarize your scores. Each of the numbers in Parts I and II below
corresponds to items in the questionnaire. For each item, write the rank (from 1 to 6)
that you gave it. After filling in your ranks, total them separately for Parts I and II. At
the bottom of the page, combine the totals of both parts. To check the accuracy of
your calculations, the bottom total of the six columns should be 315.

Part I

AB	CO	TS	SS	IP	IN
(31) ___	(26) ___	(27) ___	(30) ___	(28) ___	(29) ___
(34) ___	(37) ___	(36) ___	(32) ___	(35) ___	(33) ___
(42) ___	(39) ___	(40) ___	(41) ___	(38) ___	(43) ___
(48) ___	(45) ___	(44) ___	(49) ___	(47) ___	(46) ___
(50) ___	(52) ___	(51) ___	(54) ___	(55) ___	(53) ___
(60) ___	(57) ___	(58) ___	(59) ___	(61) ___	(56) ___

Part I
subtotal: ___ +   ___ +   ___ +   ___ +   ___ +   ___ = 126

Part II

(30) ___	(26) ___	(31) ___	(27) ___	(29) ___	(28) ___
(35) ___	(33) ___	(37) ___	(36) ___	(32) ___	(34) ___
(41) ___	(39) ___	(42) ___	(38) ___	(40) ___	(43) ___
(46) ___	(47) ___	(48) ___	(44) ___	(49) ___	(45) ___
(53) ___	(51) ___	(54) ___	(55) ___	(52) ___	(50) ___
(61) ___	(58) ___	(57) ___	(60) ___	(56) ___	(59) ___
(64) ___	(63) ___	(67) ___	(65) ___	(66) ___	(62) ___
(70) ___	(69) ___	(73) ___	(68) ___	(72) ___	(71) ___
(76) ___	(75) ___	(79) ___	(77) ___	(78) ___	(74) ___

Part II
subtotal: ___ +   ___ +   ___ +   ___ +   ___ +   ___ = 189

Totals: ___ +   ___ +   ___ +   ___ +   ___ +   ___ = 315

LEARNING PREFERENCES INVENTORY

Description of categories:

Abstract (AB): preference for learning theories, general principles, concepts, and generating hypotheses.

Concrete (CO): preference for learning tangible, specific, practical tasks and skills.

Teacher-structured (TS): preference for well-organized, teacher-directed classes, with clear expectations, assignments, and goals defined by teacher.

Student-structured (SS): preference for learner-generated tasks, autonomy, and self-direction.

Interpersonal (IP): preference for learning or working with others; emphasis on harmonious relations between students and teacher and among students.

Individual (IN): preference for learning or working alone, with emphasis on self-reliance and tasks which are solitary, such as reading.

Your scores in this Inventory reflect your preferences. The range of scores on this instrument is from 15 to 90. Since there are 15 columns to answer, you might have given either a 1 or a 6 to every item in each column which implied a teacher-structured preference, resulting in a possible 15 or 90 for that category. If, for example, you scored a 78 in the first category it implies that you have a very high preference for learning abstract, conceptual material. A score of 20 would suggest that you have little interest for learning in this fashion. A score of 50 means that you do not have a specific preference for abstract learning. The same criteria can be used to interpret scores in other categories. If your scores in all categories are between 40 and 65 this implies that you are probably comfortable learning in all six of the categories described (e.g., as comfortable working alone as in a group).

As with any questionnaire, there are concerns regarding validity and reliability. Learning preference scores may reflect perceptions of how individuals would prefer to learn rather than how they learn best in actuality. We have used this questionnaire, as well as one developed by Kolb (1974), with numerous health professions faculty groups and a multitude of students. The majority of respondents concur with the data these inventories provide, indicating that the scores reflect how they learn best. While trends may prevail within a particular group, exceptions are always found. We have discovered in groups of 20 or more that wide variance exists among learning preference scores. Accordingly, you can expect a wide range of scores when using this instrument with your students.

The distribution of learning preference scores carries implications for planning instruction. Anticipated variance among student scores supports the learning principle that *students should have the opportunity to learn through a variety of educational resources.* If your course is conducted almost exclusively through group discussions, your instruction may favor students who prefer to learn interpersonally and be an anathema for those with a strong bent toward learning independently. A course taught primarily through lectures, discussions, and reading materials with concentration on theoretical issues may stimulate students oriented to abstract conceptual learning and frustrate those who need clear examples and opportunities to directly apply subject matter. Other matches and mismatches can be construed.

Many health professionals taking this questionnaire have suggested its results be used to match instruction to the learning preferences of the particular group of students. That is to say, if most students favor a teacher-structured format, the course should be designed accordingly; or if wide variance is found, students should be divided into small groups, with each group having its preferred course format. Even if it were feasible, this concept would not necessarily be desirable. Education is a lifelong process, and students will inevitably find themselves in a variety of settings which will not always be harmonious with their preferred mode of learning. As an instructor, your role is not necessarily to cater to individual preferences, but to facilitate flexibility and help students realize that they can learn in a variety of fashions. Sensitivity to individual differences mandates varying the teaching methods you use so all students will be exposed to both preferred and less familiar modes of learning.

TEACHING PREFERENCES

As with student preferences, teachers also have favored styles of instruction. Some are more comfortable with large assemblies of students, while others prefer small groups. Some lean toward teaching in a highly structured manner, whereas others view themselves as facilitators of student-structured learning. Unfortunately, teaching preference questionnaires comparable to those utilized for learning preferences were not found, and a direct correlation between teaching and learning preferences cannot necessarily be assumed. Although a person may prefer to learn in an independent manner, he or she might choose to structure group activities in a teaching situation rather than individual projects. Since we cannot provide a questionnaire on teaching preferences, you may want to consider the hypotheses used in the learning preference questionnaire in regard to your teaching. Would you rather teach students abstract conceptual materials, concrete skills, or both? Do you prefer lecturing, conducting a laboratory demonstration, leading a group discussion, or supervising individual students? Are your scores on the questionnaire reflective of the methods with which you feel most comfortable and capable in your instruction?

Preferences for various methods of instruction may be attributable to having had limited opportunities to experiment with alternative teaching strategies, since what is familiar is generally more comfortable. If you have had little experience leading group discussions, or an unsuccessful first experience in lecturing, you may be hesitant to implement these techniques in your course. This book has suggested practical strategies for improving the skillful use of a variety of teaching methods. Our belief is that with time, this input, in conjunction with practice and feedback, can help expand your repertoire of teaching skills. Experimentation with a variety of methods should create awareness of those teaching situations you enjoy most, and development of skills in basic techniques of instruction should contribute to your feelings of success as a teacher. Building this foundation of basic techniques will free you to vary your instruction by incorporating less traditional teaching methods such as simulations, games, and computer-assisted instruction.

Having reviewed principles of learning, student characteristics, your own teaching preferences, and the teaching strategies from the preceding chapters, you should now be able to apply them when planning your course. A model for integrating these considerations follows.

SEQUENCING TEACHING ACTIVITIES

The first consideration in planning a teaching unit is to specify course goals. What do you want your students to know or be able to do upon completion? Once this has been done, it would appear that the next step is to select teaching methods in accordance with these goals. As seen earlier in this chapter, however, planning teaching activities requires consideration of basic principles of learning and the background and preferences of the students and teachers involved. Resources must be taken into account for planning purposes, and the faculty-student ratio for a given course will also have impact upon the types of teaching activities that can be provided.

A process for incorporating all of these considerations in planning a unit of instruction will be presented through the use of one in-depth example. A course on teaching students basic interviewing skills has been chosen since it is a requirement in most health professions education programs. The following hypothetical setting was constructed.

Goal: Upon completing this course students should be able to conduct an initial patient interview, utilizing appropriate communication skills to collect all relevant data.

Student population: Thirty health professions students who have completed the basic science portion of the curriculum but have had no previous contact with patients.

Faculty: Five faculty members have been assigned to teach this course. One has been chosen as course coordinator, and the others are available for small-group instruction.

Time: The course meets twice weekly for 5 weeks in 2-hour sessions for a total of 20 potential contact hours.

Setting: One large classroom and five seminar rooms equipped with portable videotape equipment are available. There is adequate access to patients in hospitals and ambulatory settings.

We avoided specifying a particular group of health professions students since course organization could be very similar regardless of the discipline. This should allow you to examine the course in terms of your area of specialization. A detailed outline of one possible instructional plan for this course follows. Review the plan carefully. Following the description you will be asked to evaluate the course in terms of its adequacy in meeting its goal, adherence to principles of learning, and consideration of student characteristics and available resources.

Having reviewed this course plan, spend a few minutes jotting down those as-

SEQUENCE 1*

Goal: Upon completing this course students should be able to conduct an initial patient interview utilizing appropriate communication skills to collect all relevant data.

TOPIC	TEACHER ACTIVITIES	STUDENT ACTIVITIES	TIME	SETTING	RESOURCES
		FIRST MEETING			
Basic communication skills	Coordinator lectures on communication skills	Take notes	1 hour	Large classroom	Chalkboard Handouts of selected readings
	Coordinator shows videotape of patient interview in which poor communication skills are demonstrated.	Take notes on communication skills demonstrated on videotape.	$\frac{1}{2}$ hour	Large classroom	Playback unit Taped interview
	Coordinator leads group discussion around observation of tape.	Discuss observations of videotape.	$\frac{1}{2}$ hour	Large classroom	Chalkboard
		SECOND MEETING			
History-taking skills	Coordinator lectures on history-taking skills.	Take notes.	1 hour	Large classroom	Chalkboard Handouts of selected readings

112

	Coordinator shows videotape of patient interview in which poor history-taking skills are demonstrated.	Take notes on history-taking skills demonstrated on videotape.	$\frac{1}{2}$ hour	Large classroom	Playback unit Taped interview

THIRD MEETING

Conducting a simulated interview	Five instructors each coordinate role play with small group of six students, rotating among three pairs of students.	In pairs, one student interviews the other for 30 minutes. They then switch roles. Instructor rotates among three pairs of students.	1 hour	Five seminar rooms	None
	Five instructors each lead a group discussion around student reactions to role play. Record student reactions.	Discuss feelings and problems encountered in role play experience.	1 hour	Five seminar rooms	Chalkboards

FOURTH MEETING

Interviewing patient in hospital and ambulatory care center	Instructors assign patients to be interviewed.	Half of the class goes to hospital. Each student interviews a patient for an hour and uses other hour to write up interview. Balance of class goes to ambulatory setting for same purposes.	2 hours	Hospital and ambulatory care setting	Patients

*Read each set of activities, resources used, etc., across the page for every specified time period.

SEQUENCE 1 (Continued)

TOPIC	TEACHER ACTIVITIES	STUDENT ACTIVITIES	TIME	SETTING	RESOURCES
		FIFTH MEETING			
Interviewing patient in hospital and ambulatory care center	Instructors assign patients to be interviewed.	Same format as fourth meeting. Students who conducted patient interviews in hospital do another in ambulatory setting and vice versa.	2 hours	Hospital and ambulatory setting	Patients
		SIXTH MEETING			
Reactions to patient interviews	Five instructors lead small-group discussions on students' experiences. Facilitate discussion of reading materials assigned in first two meetings.	Discuss problems, feelings about interviews in both settings, and relevance of reading materials.	2 hours	Five seminar rooms	Chalkboards
		SEVENTH MEETING			
Conduct final patient interviews	Instructors arrange for two patients to be interviewed by small groups. Evaluate student performance on interview.	First student conducts final interview in front of group.	$\frac{1}{2}$ hour	Five seminar rooms	Patients
		Group discusses student performance.	$\frac{1}{2}$ hour		
		Second student conducts interview in front of group.	$\frac{1}{2}$ hour		

Objective	Instructor Activity	Student Activity	Time	Location	Materials
		Group discusses student performance.	$\frac{1}{2}$ hour		

EIGHTH MEETING

Objective	Instructor Activity	Student Activity	Time	Location	Materials
Conduct final patient interviews	Format is the same as seventh meeting.	Third and fourth students from each group conduct final interviews. Format is the same as seventh meeting.	2 hours	Five seminar rooms	Patients

NINTH MEETING

Objective	Instructor Activity	Student Activity	Time	Location	Materials
Conduct final patient interviews	Format is the same as seventh meeting.	Fifth and sixth students from each group conduct final interviews. Format is the same as seventh meeting.	2 hours	Five seminar rooms	Patients

TENTH MEETING

Objective	Instructor Activity	Student Activity	Time	Location	Materials
Issues in conducting effective patient interviews	Coordinator lectures on issues in effective interviewing.	Take notes.	1 hour	Large classroom	Slides Handouts
Makeup final interviews	Instructors schedule patients. Evaluate makeup interviews.	Those who failed first interview get chance to do makeup interview.	1 hour	Five seminar rooms	Patients

pects you considered good in the sequence, and any limitations. Take into account whether the sequence of activities is likely to facilitate students achieving the course goal. Evaluate the degree to which the plan follows principles of learning and make allowances for varying student characteristics.

As a basis for checking the thoroughness of your evaluation, a checklist of criteria follows which should be useful in evaluating any teaching plan. Use it to rate the teaching plan on interviewing.

CHECKLIST FOR EVALUATING A TEACHING PLAN

This checklist can be used to evaluate any sequence of teaching activities. Review the teaching plan and indicate to what degree it incorporates the items below. Indicate your ratings by checking (√) the appropriate column.

	NOT AT ALL	PAR- TIALLY	COM- PLETELY	NOT AP- PLICABLE
1. Incorporates available re- sources efficiently and ef- fectively.				
a. Instructors	☐	☐	☐	☐
b. Patients	☐	☐	☐	☐
c. Space	☐	☐	☐	☐
d. Equipment	☐	☐	☐	☐
2. Accommodates differing stu- dent characteristics.				
a. Prior knowledge and skills	☐	☐	☐	☐
b. Learning preferences	☐	☐	☐	☐
3. Provides early explanation of conceptual framework under- lying teaching activities.				
a. Course goals (competencies) and their relevance are stated.	☐	☐	☐	☐
b. Rationale for teaching ac- tivities and evaluation methods (in relation to goals) are stated.	☐	☐	☐	☐
4. Incorporates a variety of ap- propriate educational re- sources.	☐	☐	☐	☐
a. A correlation exists be- tween teaching methods and course goals.	☐	☐	☐	☐
b. A variety of teaching meth- ods and people are used.	☐	☐	☐	☐

	NOT AT ALL	PAR-TIALLY	COM-PLETELY	NOT AP-PLICABLE
5. Incorporates models as criteria for expected student performance.				
a. Includes models of correct behavior.	☐	☐	☐	☐
b. Provides criteria for analyzing student performance.	☐	☐	☐	☐
6. Provides opportunities for students to practice and receive feedback until mastery of goal is achieved.				
a. Students perform expected behaviors.	☐	☐	☐	☐
b. Opportunities for self-assessment are included.	☐	☐	☐	☐
c. Students receive expert evaluation.	☐	☐	☐	☐
d. Time is allocated to correct deficiencies.	☐	☐	☐	☐
7. Allows for adaptation of what is learned to various situations.	☐	☐	☐	☐
a. Differing patient populations are considered.	☐	☐	☐	☐
b. Alternative settings are considered.	☐	☐	☐	☐
8. Overall, provides a positive and satisfying learning experience.	☐	☐	☐	☐
a. Students experience initial success.	☐	☐	☐	☐
b. Students receive more positive than negative reinforcement.	☐	☐	☐	☐
c. After negative feedback is received, opportunities to improve performance are available.	☐	☐	☐	☐

	NOT AT ALL	PAR- TIALLY	COM- PLETELY	NOT AP- PLICABLE
9. General issues				
a. Activities are organized in a logical rather than arbitrary fashion.				
(1) The sequence moves from simple to complex material.	☐	☐	☐	☐
(2) The sequence integrates theory and practice.	☐	☐	☐	☐
(3) The sequence integrates the parts which consti- tute the complete knowledge or skill to be learned.	☐	☐	☐	☐
b. Activities include a variety of teaching techniques to avoid repetition.	☐	☐	☐	☐
c. It is reasonable to expect that the average student will be able to master the re- quired knowledge and skills.	☐	☐	☐	☐
d. Students are active learners rather than passive listeners or viewers.	☐	☐	☐	☐

Comments: _____

_____

_____

_____

_____

_____

_____

_____

ANALYSIS OF SEQUENCE 1

Now that you have completed your ratings, read our analysis of the sequence, which follows the order of the items on the checklist.

1. Incorporates Available Resources Efficiently and Effectively

The course utilizes all available instructors to teach interviewing skills. During the first two meetings, however, students are in the large classroom with the course coordinator. It would have been advantageous to use the other instructors, particularly in the discussion periods which followed the videotape, to increase the opportunity for student participation and individual attention. In the fourth and fifth sessions, when students interview patients in the hospital and ambulatory care settings, instructors are used only to assign patients. Since this was the students' first patient contact, the instructor should have been on hand to provide administrative and personal assistance as needed. The hospitals and ambulatory care centers are used effectively, and students have adequate opportunities to interview a number of patients in these two settings. A major problem was not utilizing the available videotape equipment. Students clearly could have benefited from having at least one interview recorded in the classroom, hospital, or ambulatory care center, giving them a chance to assess their own performance.

2. Accommodates Differing Student Characteristics

The student population described in the example had no prior experience with patients. It can therefore be assumed that most students would be on equal footing when interviewing patients, which does not necessitate taking prior skills in this area into account. Administering a learning preference questionnaire was not done in the sample course. In certain courses, when working with students for an extended period of time, such data could prove beneficial for you and the students. For example, if the majority of students prefer a teacher-structured setting, they may require more guidance and direct feedback to gain the feeling that they are adequately progressing toward the required goals. Also, even in a group which generally prefers more teacher structure, identification of the student-structured learner could help both of you determine projects which would allow achievement of the same goals through more independent means.

Despite the advantages of having learning preference data, it probably was not necessary to administer the questionnaire in this sample course. What is important, though, is to appraise whether the sequence accommodates the variety of learning preferences which can be expected in any group of students. This sequence provides several ways to learn interviewing skills. Concrete opportunities exist for students to interview patients individually and in groups while lectures and group discussions allow for abstract thinking. The predetermined sequence of activities provides a good deal of structure from the teachers, yet allows space for students to work with patients independently where they can structure the interview situation, perform, and experiment with their own style. This variety of approaches for learning increases the likelihood that students with varying preferences can learn through means most suited for them.

3. Provides Early Exploration of the Conceptual Framework Underlying Teaching Activities

The sample sequence does not include an introduction in which students learn of and discuss course goals, their relevance, the rationale behind the sequence of teaching activities, or the methods used to evaluate achievement. By opening with a lecture on basic communication skills, students are left in the dark as to what will occur in the course and why. This omission is not even remedied through provision of a course syllabus, since the column listing course materials shows that students only receive a list of selected readings. This inadequate introduction is a major flaw.

4. Incorporates a Variety of Appropriate Educational Resources

The course goal requires that students be able to conduct an initial patient interview, using appropriate communication skills to collect all relevant data. Although any number of teaching methods could have been used to aid in the attainment of this goal, the sample plan seems adequate in its selection of methods. Students are provided with information on communication skills and the data needed to be gathered in an interview, chances are given to practice the skills specified in the course goal, and the sequence incorporates a number of methods and settings so students can learn from patients, instructors, and each other.

5. Incorporates Models as Criteria for Expected Student Performance

The teaching plan has several deficiencies in this area. Early in the course, students watch videotapes which demonstrate poor communication and history-taking skills as the basis for discussion of what should have been done. At no point in the sequence are students exposed to a model demonstrating effective interviewing techniques. While models of ineffective behaviors can be helpful in teaching how to evaluate performance, they do not provide a positive picture or present any standards of the effective interview. If a good interview is not observed, particularly in an introductory course, it is unlikely that students will be objective when evaluating a poor one or will have a basis for planning their own.

The sequence is especially remiss in not providing specific criteria that constitute an effective interview. Although students discuss the lecture material, videotapes, and actual interviews, there is no apparent attempt to formalize a set of criteria that can be used for planning and evaluating their own performance. A group of instructors will vary in their perceptions of the components constituting an effective interview, and no single set of behaviors will ever be appropriate for all students in all settings. However, a set of specified criteria, whether broad or highly detailed, is necessary to establish standards of acceptable and unacceptable performance. A criterion for conducting a good interview could be as general as, "The student makes the patient as comfortable as possible in the beginning of the interview." Another instructor might choose to more fully delineate this criterion by specifying, "Students introduce themselves to patients, explain their own role, assure patients' need for privacy, check for comfortable positioning, etc." Regardless of the level of specificity, it is essential to compose a list of expected behaviors which characterize effective performance. These behaviors can be presented to students by the instructor at the beginning of the course or can be derived as a result of group discussions while observing models. However general or specific, a formal set of criteria should have been made available.

6. Provides Opportunities for Practice and Feedback Until Mastery of Expected Performance Is Achieved

Opportunities for practice, self-assessment, expert evaluation, and correction of deficiencies are available in this sequence. Unfortunately, these experiences are provided late in the course, since it is not until the seventh meeting that students interview in front of their instructors and peers. The fifth and sixth student in each small group conduct their interview 1 week before the course concludes, leaving little opportunity for remediation. A better plan would allow for early observation of students while they perform an interview so they could receive specific feedback on their strengths and weaknesses, and have time to practice and correct deficiencies.

7. Allows for Adaptation of What Is Learned to Various Situations

In teaching a clinical process, it is frequently important to help students become aware of how their performance needs to be adapted when working with different patients in different settings. The sequence is excellent in this respect. Each student interviews a total of three patients in an ambulatory, hospital, and classroom setting. The effect of interviewing patients with different characteristics is further stressed when students watch their peers conduct interviews in the latter portion of the course.

8. Provides an Overall Positive and Satisfying Learning Experience

A well-designed course, and in particular one which focuses on introducing basic clinical skills, should incorporate initially successful experiences for students in order to increase their motivation. Early positive experiences provide a backlog of success which can sustain students when they are confronted with failures. In this sequence students receive feedback on their performance late in the course, precluding early successful experiences and chances to correct deficiencies, factors likely to increase anxiety about the final interviews. Lack of feedback also means that students receive little reinforcement of good aspects in their performances, which does not address the need for a positive balance in the ratio of reinforcement. The course does provide an opportunity for students to utilize feedback concerning their deficiencies as a basis for improvement during the last makeup session. This is inadequate, however, since even the most proficient student needs improvement in some area, and a second test interview is given only to those who fail the first.

9. General Issues

a. Activities Are Organized in a Logical Rather Than an Arbitrary Fashion It is not easy to evaluate the rationale behind a teaching plan, since we assume instructors designing any plan have organized the content and teaching activities in a manner they consider logical. To preclude judgments based upon personal preferences, however, certain criteria that are generally applicable for assessing the logical organization of a teaching plan should be specified. In our work we have discovered three criteria which have proven useful for this assessment.

Obvious, but often forgotten, is that teaching should be structured so students learn simple content before grappling with complicated concepts and skills. Students learning mathematics, for example, need to learn addition and subtraction before multiplication and division. This notion applies equally to learning in the health fields. In teaching interviewing skills, the sequence incorporates this criterion by having students practice their interviews with each other prior to interviewing patients in the hospital and ambulatory setting. The role play for the first interview is an appropriate task, since students are interviewing healthy rather than ill individuals in a situation which is fairly low risk.

Another criterion for judging the logic of a teaching sequence concerns the integration of theory and practice. If students are expected to perform a task, solve problems, or assess situations, they need opportunities for practice early in the course. In the sample sequence, students receive the bulk of information, readings, lectures, and discussions in the first few meetings, and all practical interviewing experience is conducted at the end of the course. This separation of theory and practice, even in a 5-week course, makes it difficult to incorporate the information given on interviewing. Since opportunities to apply this knowledge occur later in the sequence, students must strain to recall theoretical material presented much earlier and judge its applicability. A more logical sequence would have students conducting interviews close to the time they learn the conceptual material.

A third criterion for judging the logic of sequencing teaching activities is the need to integrate the many parts which comprise the necessary knowledge and skills to be taught. In a course on patient interviewing, the instruction of communication skills (e.g., asking questions, maintaining eye contact, putting patients at ease) should be integrated with the teaching of interview content (e.g., family history, chief complaint, history of medication). To conduct an interview a student must appropriately utilize communication skills to collect relevant data, requiring the integration of these two components. In the sample sequence these are taught separately. A logical approach to integrate content and process could have been accomplished by having students examine a short, uncomplicated interview in order to determine how communication skills are utilized in the collection of vital data. The observation of a simple interview, such as one with a healthy person, before hearing the lectures would have given students a chance to see the interrelationship of communication skills and data collection.

b. Activities include Variations of Teaching Techniques to Avoid Repetition Variety is the spice of life, and an effective teaching sequence should not make students repeat activities over an extended period of time. In this respect, the sequence is deficient. When teaching communication skills in the course's first session, students listen to a lecture, watch a videotape, and discuss both. The same format is immediately repeated for the topic of history-taking skills. This duplication could have been avoided by alternating teaching strategies. Similarly, three consecutive class meetings are devoted to small groups watching students conducting their final interviews and receiving feedback. This activity is repeated 6 times. More creative approaches could have been employed to achieve the same goals.

c. It Is Reasonable to Expect That the Average Student Will Be Able to Master the Required Knowledge and Skills While it is difficult to conclusively judge to what degree an instructional sequence assists students in achieving course goals, the sample course is not especially promising in this respect. The lack of specified criteria and only one supervised interview make it doubtful that students will be able to conduct an effective interview. Achievement on a final examination and follow-up observations in the field are utlimately the only objective means of evaluating accomplishment. Sequencing activities, particularly when planning a new course, is always experimental since data on student achievement are unavilable until the course is underway. It is probable, though, that a course plan incorporating the considerations outlined in this chapter will successfully realize the expected results. Appraisal of student performance early in the course, done through some form of diagnostic evaluation, will reveal to the instructor whether the plan is progressing as expected. This information should alert you to students needing assistance and, in more extreme cases, flag the need to restructure portions of the course. None of these considerations are attended to in the sample interviewing sequence.

d. Students Are Active Learners Rather Than Passive Listeners or Viewers We have included the active involvement of students in learning as the last item on the checklist for evaluating a teaching plan since the degree of inclusion or exclusion of this criterion influences our overall impression of any instructional plan. While students are involved in group discussions and later conduct actual interviews in the sample sequence, the instructor dominates initial meetings, diminishing student participation. This structure is weak in our view. Since this final checklist item is extremely important, we rated it partially done.

Despite the criticisms regarding this course, we do not want to imply that it is a poorly constructed teaching plan. Several points on the checklist were adequately addressed and others, while incomplete, were at least included. However, a sequence can be designed that adequately and comprehensively incorporates all the items on the checklist. Therefore, a second plan for teaching the same content is presented next.

SEQUENCE 2*

Goal: Upon completing this course students should be able to conduct an initial patient interview utilizing appropriate communication skills to collect all relevant data.

TOPIC	TEACHER ACTIVITIES	STUDENT ACTIVITIES	TIME	SETTING	RESOURCES
		FIRST MEETING			
Introduction	Coordinator distributes syllabus. Describes relevance of course goals, related teaching activities, and evaluation methods.	Students listen and ask questions.	$\frac{1}{2}$ hour	Large classroom	Syllabus
Interviewing skills	Coordinator shows videotape of interview with cooperative patient to demonstrate effective interviewing skills.	Students watch interview and individually write what they consider effective and ineffective behaviors.	$\frac{1}{2}$ hour	Large classroom	Playback unit Taped interview
	Five instructors facilitate discussions with small groups of six students each.	Students in each group discuss degree of agreement. Reach consensus as to effective behaviors of the interviewer. Record final list on poster sheets	$\frac{3}{4}$ hour	Large classroom	Poster sheets Magic markers

*Read each set of activities, resources used, etc., across the page for every specified time period.

125

SEQUENCE 2 (Continued)

TOPIC	TEACHER ACTIVITIES	STUDENT ACTIVITIES	TIME	SETTING	RESOURCES
	Instructors collect poster sheets and assign reading materials.	Listen and ask questions.	$\frac{1}{4}$ hour	Large class-room	Selected readings on how to conduct an effective interview
	Summarize activities, answer questions, and discuss next class activities.				
SECOND MEETING					
Interviewing skills	Instructors meet with same small groups and facilitate further discussion.	Discuss and add or change behaviors listed on poster sheets, based on new information from assigned readings.	$\frac{1}{2}$ hour	Large class-room	Poster sheets Magic markers
	Coordinator leads group discussion and records lists on chalkboard.	Each group presents its list. Class as whole discusses common and differing items to reach greater consensus.	$\frac{3}{4}$ hour	Large class-room	Chalkboard Course checklist of effective interviewer behaviors
	Distributes interviewer behavior checklist and compares with students' list.	Class uses student list to modify course checklist.			
	Coordinator shows video-taped segment of ineffective interview.	Watch and use modified course checklist to rate tape.	$\frac{3}{4}$ hour	Large class-	Playback unit Taped interview

THIRD MEETING

Topic	Instructor Activity	Procedure	Time	Location	Materials
Conducting a simulated interview	Instructors meet with small groups and set ground rules for providing constructive feedback.	Three students meet. One student interviews the second, the third student observes using checklist. The student interview is videotaped.	$\frac{1}{3}$ hour	Seminar rooms	Copies of new, modified checklist of effective interviewer behaviors
	Explain role-play procedures and videotaping process.	Students switch roles within the trio and repeat above process.	$\frac{1}{3}$ hour		Videotape recording and playback system
	Rate student interviews using checklist.	Students switch roles and repeat process.	$\frac{1}{3}$ hour		
		First group leaves, and second group goes through same procedures.	1 hour		Playback units
		Prior to next session, each student schedules time to rate own videotape using checklist.			

FOURTH MEETING

Topic	Instructor Activity	Procedure	Time	Location	Materials
Individual supervision and further information on interviewing skills	Instructors meet with their students individually to discuss interview, compare ratings, and identify areas needing improvement.	Student discusses self-assessment of videotape and makes recommendations for improvement.	$\frac{1}{3}$ hour for each student	Five seminar rooms	

SEQUENCE 2 (Continued)

TOPIC	TEACHER ACTIVITIES	STUDENT ACTIVITIES	TIME	SETTING	RESOURCES
		Before or after meeting with instructor, students have ***option*** of working independently on the following:		Large class-room used as resource center	Reading materials Self-instructional package with videotape
		Self-instructional pack-age on methods of dealing with uncoop-erative patients			
		Selected reading mate-rials on interviewing various kinds of pa-tients (e.g., dying pa-tients)			
		FIFTH MEETING			
Conduct a patient in-terview	Instructors assign patients to students.	Teams of two students go to hospital or ambulatory center.	2 hours	Ambulatory care center or hospital	Patients and in-terview checklists
		Each student conducts in-terview with two patients while other observes.			

Topic	Instructor activity	Student activity	Time	Setting	Materials
		Team discusses each other's reactions, feelings, strengths, and areas in need of improvement.			

SIXTH MEETING

Topic	Instructor activity	Student activity	Time	Setting	Materials
Issues in interviewing	Instructors give instructions.	Students from different seminars meet in groups of six to discuss experiences to date, prioritize areas in which they need additional help. One student in each group records consensus.	$\frac{1}{2}$ hour	Large classroom	
	Instructors assist in identifying problem areas. Suggest additional resources to address needs.	Students reassemble. Identify key problem areas. Ask questions.	$\frac{1}{2}$ hour	Large classroom	
	Coordinator conducts interview with patient.	Students observe instructor interview. Give ratings on checklist.	$\frac{1}{2}$ hour	Large classroom	Preselected patient with complicated history or personality
	Coordinator pools student ratings. Facilitates discussion of own strengths and weaknesses among students.	Students discuss interview and ask questions.	$\frac{1}{2}$ hour	Large classroom	

SEQUENCE 2 (Continued)

TOPIC	TEACHER ACTIVITIES	STUDENT ACTIVITIES	TIME	SETTING	RESOURCES
		SEVENTH MEETING			
Conducting a patient interview	Instructors arrange patient interview in hospital and ambulatory setting. Provide feedback after student interviews.	In teams of three, students go to hospital with instructor. Each conducts $\frac{1}{2}$-hour interview and receives feedback from instructor and peers.	2 hours	Hospital	Patients and checklists
		The other team of three goes to ambulatory care setting. Each conducts $\frac{1}{2}$-hour interview which is videotaped. Group observes each tape and provides feedback.	2 hours	Ambulatory care center	Patients Checklists Videotape equipment
		EIGHTH MEETING			
Same format as previous meeting. Teams of three switch locations and activities.					
		NINTH MEETING			
Conducting final patient interview	Instructors arrange schedule of patient and videotape equipment.	Student conducts a patient interview which is videotaped.	$\frac{1}{2}-\frac{3}{4}$ hour (student's time)	Ambulatory care center or hospital	Patients Videotape equipment

		½ hour per student	Five seminar rooms	Videotape Checklists Final evaluation forms
Instructors view and rate final videotape.	Rates own tape using checklist.			
Write formal evaluation according to checklist.	Receives instructor evaluation.			
Instructor schedules time to meet with students individually if necessary and schedules makeup interviews for those who failed to meet competency requirements.	Can meet to discuss instructor evaluation.			

TENTH MEETING

			1 hour	Large classroom	Additional readings
Summary lecture	Coordinator summarizes purposes of course, logic of activities, and general student progress.	Evaluate 10-week experience.			
	Discusses application in field and provides additional resources.				
	Distributes course evaluation forms.				

SEQUENCE 2 (Continued)

TOPIC	TEACHER ACTIVITIES	STUDENT ACTIVITIES	TIME	SETTING	RESOURCES
	Depending upon performance in ninth meeting, instructors meet with students who failed on final evaluation to review videotape and assign final grade.		$\frac{1}{2}$–1 hour (if needed)	Five seminar rooms	Patients Videotape equipment Checklists Evaluation forms

EVALUATION OF SEQUENCE 2

When we applied the checklist "Evaluating a Teaching Plan" to the first sequence, a number of deficiencies were noted and corrected in the second plan. We suggest you apply the checklist to the second sequence before reading our assessment. Discussion of the revised plan for teaching interviewing skills follows the same general order of the checklist, dealing only with those areas we felt were inadequately addressed in the first sequence.

1. Incorporates Available Resources Efficiently and Effectively

The videotape equipment was used throughout the course permitting students, by means of recorded interviews, to observe and assess their evolving interviewing skills. The five course instructors were teaching in the seminars and large classroom most of the time, allotting students more individual attention. Instructors were also available to those students needing special assistance.

3. Provides Early Exploration of the Conceptual Framework Underlying Teaching Activities

The conceptual framework of the course was presented in the initial meeting. Distribution of the syllabus provided the basis for immediate discussion of course goals, discussion of activities from meeting to meeting, and evaluation methods. This discussion allowed students time to question, define, and clearly understand what they were expected to achieve. By presenting students with models of effective interviewing skills in the first meeting, a major deficiency in the first plan was rectified. The videotape was an excellent way for students to identify components and criteria of the effective interview, and furnished standards of assessment for their own performance. These criteria also formed the basis for a final course evaluation. The ineffective interview was not shown until the second meeting, and by this time students had adequate background to criticize and discuss the tape. The coordinator's interview later in the course was useful as a review model shortly before final interviews.

6. Provides Opportunities for Practice and Feedback Until Mastery of Expected Performance Is Achieved

A most significant improvement in the new design was the chance for students to conduct a simulated interview with peers, assess their behavior via videotape, and receive instructor feedback on their performance as early as the third class meeting. Students and instructors could pinpoint strengths and weaknesses in the interviews to guide their efforts for the remainder of the course, and ample opportunities for improvement were provided before final interviews.

8. Provides an Overall Positive and Satisfying Learning Experience

The probability of having initially successful experiences was increased in this design. The first interview is with a fellow student, lessening the possibility of failure. Ordinarily, students are supportive of each other and, unlike patients, do not present illnesses which could unduly complicate a trial interview. Students are also not confronted by classmate evaluations in this interview, but first criticize their own videotaped performance, and then receive instructor feedback in a private, supervisory session.

9. General Issues

All the items within this category are more carefully thought-out in Sequence 2. The course content is fully integrated, since communication and history-taking skills are not taught separately, and theory is interspersed with practice throughout. Student activities are organized to become progressively more complex. For example, the peer interview is followed by a patient interview in which students are assisted by a friend rather than the instructor. Instructor supervision of a patient interview does not occur until the seventh class meeting, and evaluation of the student's independent performance not until the ninth. The sequence is organized so that simpler interviews precede difficult ones, and students are gradually afforded opportunities to become autonomous.

Another important alteration is that no two class meetings in this sequence have the same format. Besides offering a variety of activities, at no point during 20 hours of instruction are students put in the role of passive observers for longer than 30 minutes. This greatly encourages active student participation. As a result of the modifications in this revised teaching sequence, it is reasonable to expect that the average student will be able to conduct an initial patient interview upon completing the course.

SUMMARY CONSIDERATIONS IN INSTRUCTIONAL DESIGN

The teaching of interviewing skills has been used to illustrate a process by which a course is systematically developed. The considerations and principles discussed in this chapter are also applicable to other content areas. Instructional design involves three phases: selecting course goals, planning teaching activities, and evaluating the instructional plan.

Determining what students will be expected to do as a result of participating in your course is the first phase. While a lecture may be useful in order to provide factual information and a discussion to create certain attitudes, a course plan must be examined from the perspective of what a student should be able to *do* upon its completion. Though student performance is the obvious criterion for courses oriented to teach skills, expected competencies can be specified for any course or content area.

These competencies reflect what the student should be able to do as a professional in the field, and not all of the specific information, skills, or attitudes needed to perform them. Within the health professions, as in other fields, a tremendous amount of course content is taught without considering its relevance to actual practice. While knowledge for knowledge's sake may be justifiable to an extent, professional training should be geared toward developing a competent practitioner. In planning your course, whether basic science or clinical, consider the "end products" in terms of final professional performance.

In our work with instructional design, it has been useful to specify course competencies in terms of expected student outcomes resulting from approximately 15 to 20 hours of instruction. While this is not a set formula, it guides an instructor's thinking to plan larger units of instruction that result in integrated learning experiences leading students to acquire field-related competencies. The example of the competency for conducting a patient interview reflects the utility of this approach. The specific knowledge, skills, and interpersonal objectives which are taught in each meeting of the course build logically toward achieving the final course requirement. It is more reasonable to determine course competencies first and then design appropriate learning experiences, rather than first deciding which series of lectures or discussions will be given. Particularly when a number of instructors are responsible for the content of a course, there is a tendency to assign lectures, laboratories, and discussions in a way that often does not add up to a coherent whole. Instructors should meet before a course begins to consider, debate, and agree upon competencies, which should be the cornerstones upon which the structure for a sequence of course activities is planned and justified.

Once course competencies have been constructed, planning teaching activities follows. A blank sequencing sheet is provided at the end of this chapter to be used when outlining your course plan. The sample courses on interviewing should illustrate the value of sequencing sheets in preparing a detailed plan of action. The many considerations which affect course design necessitate such detail. To practice planning a sequence of instruction, take a course taught by you or one of your colleagues and outline it in detail on the sequencing sheets. Then apply the checklist for "Evaluating a Teaching Plan" to determine course strengths and deficiencies. If the course is not already based on competencies, using the sequencing sheets should help you define realistic goals, weed out unnecessary content and teaching activities, and add content or activities where needed. After doing this with an existing course, you should be ready to construct an exciting new program plan.

Designing a course is an experiment. After implementation, student satisfaction and achievement data will provide major indicators of its success. The experiment of instructional design is concluded with a sound course evaluation. Appendix D contains a detailed bibliography on this final phase. Course evaluations will provide data for affirming certain hunches, throwing others out, and formulating new hypotheses when redesigning the program.

Goal:

TOPIC	TEACHER ACTIVITIES	STUDENT ACTIVITIES	TIME	SETTING	RESOURCES

CONCLUSION

Health professions faculty continually question whether teaching can be improved. Interspersed with this query are the inevitable myths that "teaching is an art, not a science" and "teachers are born, not made." At times one begins to wonder if effective teaching is transmitted genetically. What is often overlooked or, perhaps, denied is that behind an artful professional in any field are years of study, training, and practice.

In contrast, the great majority of instructors hired by health sciences institutions had little or no formal education in the processes of teaching. The premise underlying this practice is that knowledge of subject matter is sufficient and that the ability to teach will magically be learned on the job. We would shudder at this assumption if it were suggested as a model for training health care practitioners.

In the discipline of teaching, as in the health sciences, there is a substantial body of knowledge — a product of years of research — which can serve as a guide for more effective educational practices. We know, for example, that employing videotape for self-assessment is a method that most teachers can use to improve their instruction. It is recognized that for the majority, understanding and retention of content increases if students are active participants in the learning process. We are assured that carefully planned group discussions better promote student problem-solving abilities than do lectures. Interested in improving teaching, investigators have asked questions and have found these and other answers. If we desire to be skillful instructors, we cannot remain innocent of the results of educational research. Each of us has the opportunity to act upon these findings.

This book is a product of concepts rooted in research which have proved helpful for most health professionals with whom we have worked. Several years of input from the people who have used them has refined the planning guides, checklists, and strategies we suggest for improving instruction. We hope you will use them when planning, executing, and evaluating your own teaching, and adapt them as well.

Even if you are an experienced instructor and generally receive favorable comments from students and colleagues, there are always means of making your teaching a more personally satisfying experience. Continuous examination of your instruction will reveal ways to diversify and refine your practices. Such an examination implies introspection, reflection, and a willingness to engage in new experiences.

With this in mind, consider these questions in regard to your own teaching.

When did you last sit down with a group of your students and discuss their reactions to your instruction?

Have you ever administered pre- and posttests to attempt measurement of what your students have learned?

Do you ever ask a colleague to watch and comment on your teaching?

Have you ever had one of your classes videotaped or audiotaped for your own review?

How often do you revise your lecture notes or redesign a class for which you have a responsibility?

When did you last read a journal article on the topic of teaching in your field?

How many faculty development programs for improving instruction have you attended?

We believe that the effective and artful instructor is more than knowledgeable, warm, and enthusiastic. He is curious. He is a student of his own teaching.

SELF-ASSESSMENT QUESTION-NAIRES

Two questionnaires are provided as a first step toward improving your lectures. The first asks that you rate yourself as a lecturer, group discussion leader, and tutor. In the second, you are asked to describe your feelings prior to, during, and after delivering a lecture.

Answer *all* questions. Following these questionnaires is a key for scoring your responses.

SELF-ASSESSMENT QUESTION-NAIRE (1)

SELF-ASSESSMENT QUESTION-NAIRES ON TEACHING

Instructions (Please Read Carefully Before Beginning)

In this questionnaire you will see three sections headed by a phrase to be judged. Beneath it are pairs of contrasting words called scales which you are to use to rate the phrase. Make your judgments on the basis of what the phrase means to you. *This is not a test. There are no right or wrong answers.*

How to Use the Scales

The phrases to be judged appear in capital letters and the scales appear below them. Suppose you were to judge the phrase *my work* on the pair of words interesting-boring:

Interesting 7 6 5 4 3 2 1 Boring

First decide whether *my work* is interesting or boring; then decide *how* interesting or boring *you feel* it is. For example, if you feel that *my work* is extremely interesting, circle between interesting and boring like this:

Interesting ⑦ 6 5 4 3 2 1 Boring

On the other hand, if you feel that it is extremely boring, circle between interesting and boring like this:

Interesting 7 6 5 4 3 2 ① Boring

However, if you feel neutral about *my work*, circle the number in the middle like this:

Interesting 7 6 5 ④ 3 2 1 Boring

The Questionnaire

Important:

1. Be sure to respond to every scale for every phrase.

2. Do not make more than one response to a given scale for a given phrase.

3. The best answers are your first impressions, so do not puzzle over items.

MYSELF AS A DISCUSSION LEADER
(e.g., in a laboratory or seminar)

1.	Organized	7 6 5 4 3 2 1	Disorganized
2.	Communicative	7 6 5 4 3 2 1	Uncommunicative
3.	Sketchy	1 2 3 4 5 6 7	Thorough
4.	Superior	7 6 5 4 3 2 1	Inferior
5.	Tense	1 2 3 4 5 6 7	Calm
6.	Articulate	7 6 5 4 3 2 1	Inarticulate
7.	Weak	1 2 3 4 5 6 7	Strong
8.	Insecure	1 2 3 4 5 6 7	Confident
9.	Prepared	7 6 5 4 3 2 1	Unprepared
10.	Coherent	7 6 5 4 3 2 1	Incoherent
11.	Unplanned	1 2 3 4 5 6 7	Planned
12.	Clear	7 6 5 4 3 2 1	Unclear

MYSELF AS A LECTURER

13.	Organized	7 6 5 4 3 2 1	Disorganized
14.	Communicative	7 6 5 4 3 2 1	Uncommunicative
15.	Sketchy	1 2 3 4 5 6 7	Thorough
16.	Superior	7 6 5 4 3 2 1	Inferior
17.	Tense	1 2 3 4 5 6 7	Calm
18.	Articulate	7 6 5 4 3 2 1	Inarticulate
19.	Weak	1 2 3 4 5 6 7	Strong
20.	Insecure	1 2 3 4 5 6 7	Confident
21.	Prepared	7 6 5 4 3 2 1	Unprepared

22.	Coherent	7 6 5 4 3 2 1	Incoherent
23.	Unplanned	1 2 3 4 5 6 7	Planned
24.	Clear	7 6 5 4 3 2 1	Unclear

MYSELF AS A TUTOR
(working with an individual student as advisor, supervisor, etc.)

25.	Organized	7 6 5 4 3 2 1	Disorganized
26.	Communicative	7 6 5 4 3 2 1	Uncommunicative
27.	Sketchy	1 2 3 4 5 6 7	Thorough
28.	Superior	7 6 5 4 3 2 1	Inferior
29.	Tense	1 2 3 4 5 6 7	Calm
30.	Articulate	7 6 5 4 3 2 1	Inarticulate
31.	Weak	1 2 3 4 5 6 7	Strong
32.	Insecure	1 2 3 4 5 6 7	Confident
33.	Prepared	7 6 5 4 3 2 1	Unprepared
34.	Coherent	7 6 5 4 3 2 1	Incoherent
35.	Unplanned	1 2 3 4 5 6 7	Planned
36.	Clear	7 6 5 4 3 2 1	Unclear

Scoring Key: Questionnaire (1)

1. Myself as a discussion leader

    a. For a total score in organization add your ratings in the rows specified:

    #1 _____

    #3 _____

    #9 _____

    #11 _____

    Total _____

    Mean score: Divide total by 4 = _____

    b. For a total score in communication add your ratings in the rows specified:

    #2 _____

    #6 _____

    #10 _____

#12 _____

Total _____

Mean score: Divide total by 4 = _____

c. For a total score in confidence add your ratings in the rows specified:

#4 _____

#5 _____

#7 _____

#8 _____

Total _____

Mean score: Divide total by 4 = _____

2. Myself as a lecturer

a. For a total score in organization add your ratings in the rows specified:

#13 _____

#15 _____

#21 _____

#23 _____

Total _____

Mean score: Divide total by 4 = _____

b. For a total score in communication add your ratings in the rows specified:

#14 _____

#18 _____

#22 _____

#24 _____

Total _____

Mean score: Divide total by 4 = _____

c. For a total score in confidence add your ratings in the rows specified:

#16 _____

#17 _____

#19 _____

#20 _____

Total _____

Mean score: Divide total by 4 = _____

3.   Myself as a tutor

   a.   For a total score in organization add your ratings in the rows specified:

   #25 _____

   #27 _____

   #33 _____

   #35 _____

   Total _____

   Mean score: Divide total by 4 = _____

   b.   For a total score in communication add your ratings in the rows specified:

   #26 _____

   #30 _____

   #34 _____

   #36 _____

   Total _____

   Mean score: Divide total by 4 = _____

   c.   For a total score in confidence add your ratings in the rows specified:

   #28 _____

   #29 _____

   #31 _____

   #32 _____

   Total _____

   Mean score: Divide total by 4 = _____

Summary Sheet: Questionnaire (1)

Complete this summary sheet by writing your mean scores in the appropriate spaces:

	DISCUSSION LEADER	LECTURER	TUTOR
Organization	_____	_____	_____
Ability to communicate	_____	_____	_____
Confidence	_____	_____	_____

Your scores are a reflection of how you perceive yourself. You will find it useful to compare your mean scores in each category to see if your confidence matches your perceived ability to communicate and degree of organization. You can also assess the teaching mode in which you are most organized, communicative, and confident.

The following key serves as a guide for interpretation:

MEAN SCORE	YOUR PERCEPTION OF YOURSELF
6.1–7.0	Extremely organized, communicative, confident
4.6–6.0	Fairly organized, communicative, confident
3.6–4.5	Average in organization, communication, confidence
2.1–3.5	Lacking in organization, communication, confidence
1.0–2.0	Very poor in organization, communication, confidence

SELF-ASSESSMENT QUESTIONNAIRE (2)

Below are 18 statements related to your feelings during the preparation and delivery and after the conclusion of a lecture. You are asked to rate yourself as to how often each statement applies to you by circling the appropriate word [for example, (5)Never].

1. Audiences seem bored when I speak.

    (5)Never   (4)Rarely   (3)Sometimes   (2)Usually   (1)Always

2. The prospect of facing an audience arouses in me feelings of apprehension.

    (5)Never   (4)Rarely   (3)Sometimes   (2)Usually   (1)Always

3. While preparing a speech I am in a constant state of anxiety.

    (5)Never   (4)Rarely   (3)Sometimes   (2)Usually   (1)Always

4. I dislike using my body and voice expressively.

    (5)Never   (4)Rarely   (3)Sometimes   (2)Usually   (1)Always

5. It is difficult for me to calmly search my mind for the right word to express my thoughts while lecturing.

    (5)Never   (4)Rarely   (3)Sometimes   (2)Usually   (1)Always

6. I am in a state of nervous tension after delivering a lecture.

    (5)Never   (4)Rarely   (3)Sometimes   (2)Usually   (1)Always

7. I lose confidence if I find the audience is not interested in my speech.

    (5)Never   (4)Rarely   (3)Sometimes   (2)Usually   (1)Always

8. At the conclusion of the lecture I feel that I have failed.

    (5)Never   (4)Rarely   (3)Sometimes   (2)Usually   (1)Always

9. I feel elated after addressing a group.

    (5) Always   (4) Usually   (3) Sometimes   (2) Rarely   (1) Never

10. I enjoy preparing my lectures.

    (5) Always   (4) Usually   (3) Sometimes   (2) Rarely   (1) Never

11. I feel relaxed and comfortable while speaking.

    (5) Always   (4) Usually   (3) Sometimes   (2) Rarely   (1) Never

12. Although I am nervous just before getting up, I soon forget my fears and enjoy the experience.

    (5) Always   (4) Usually   (3) Sometimes   (2) Rarely   (1) Never

13. I feel satisfied at the conclusion of the lecture.

    (5) Always   (4) Usually   (3) Sometimes   (2) Rarely   (1) Never

14. At the conclusion of a lecture I feel that I have had a pleasant experience.

    (5) Always   (4) Usually   (3) Sometimes   (2) Rarely   (1) Never

15. New and pertinent ideas come to me as I am planning a lecture.

    (5) Always   (4) Usually   (3) Sometimes   (2) Rarely   (1) Never

16. I feel that I can't get things organized before I lecture.

    (5) Never   (4) Rarely   (3) Sometimes   (2) Usually   (1) Always

17. I have a hard time arranging what I want to say into an organized lecture.

    (5) Never   (4) Rarely   (3) Sometimes   (2) Usually   (1) Always

18. When I finish my lecture I feel that my ideas got across well.

    (5) Always   (4) Usually   (3) Sometimes   (2) Rarely   (1) Never

Scoring Key: Questionnaire (2)

This self-assessment questionnaire provides data about how you feel while preparing and delivering and after completing your lecture. Mean scores should be calculated by adding your ratings from the questions which are indicated (write in the numbers which you circled).

1. Preparing a lecture

    #2   _____

    #3   _____

    #10 _____

    #15 _____

    #16 _____

#17 ____

Total ____

Mean score: Divide total by 6 = ____

2. Delivering a lecture

#1 ____

#4 ____

#5 ____

#7 ____

#11 ____

#12 ____

Total ____

Mean score: Divide total by 6 = ____

3. After a lecture

#6 ____

#8 ____

#9 ____

#13 ____

#14 ____

#18 ____

Total ____

Mean score: Divide total by 6 = ____

Your scores are only a reflection of how you perceive yourself. You will find it useful to compare your mean scores in each category.

The following key can serve as a general guide for interpretation:

MEAN SCORE	YOUR PERCEPTION OF YOURSELF
4.1–5.0	Very confident
3.1–4.0	Somewhat confident
2.1–3.0	Somewhat tense or unsure
1.0–2.0	Very tense or unsure

Classify teach of the following questions using these symbols:

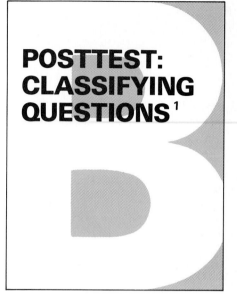

POSTTEST: CLASSIFYING QUESTIONS[1]

M = Memory

C = Convergent

P = Process

E = Evaluation

_____ 1. What physiological changes occur in a muscle when it contracts?

_____ 2. How would you justify applying or not applying a splint directly on a joint with a third-degree burn?

_____ 3. Can a person survive without a pancreas?

_____ 4. What inferences could you make if a person had normal passive range of motion?

_____ 5. What organism causes rubella?

_____ 6. How could natural selection be demonstrated in a school laboratory?

_____ 7. How is secretion different from excretion?

_____ 8. Do you think it is better that a child be exposed to and get a disease when young rather than receive passive immunity?

_____ 9. What might happen if a disease organism from space were introduced to earth?

_____ 10. What is auscultation?

_____ 11. Under what circumstances do you think a medical professional is not justified in touching a patient?

_____ 12. After reading the article, do you think the malpractice suit was justified?

_____ 13. What destroys enzymes?

_____ 14. After reading these data, what course of treatment could be recommended?

_____ 15. How does a nerve impulse travel along a myelinated nerve?

_____ 16. Why do children who lack protein develop protruding abdomens?

_____ 17. What category of questions includes memory and convergent questions?

_____ 18. What value has this self-instructional unit had for you?

[1]This posttest was developed by Betty Risley, Associate Professor of Health Professions Education, Center for Educational Development, University of Illinois at the Medical Center, Chicago.

_____ **19.** Why do students respond cautiously to open questions?

_____ **20.** What is the relationship between types of questions and thinking skills?

Answer Key

1. C	6. P	11. E	16. C
2. E	7. C	12. E	17. M
3. M	8. E	13. M	18. E
4. P	9. P	14. P	19. P
5. M	10. M	15. C	20. C

18-20 Very Good — unless all those missed were in the same category.

15-17 Good.

12-14 Shaky — better check criteria for categories again.

10-11 Poor — you might want to work through the program again.

You should have a clear understanding of *closed* and *open* questions and the level of thinking required to answer each. You should also be able to classify closed questions as either *memory* or *convergent* and open questions as *process* or *evaluative.* Do not be disturbed if you still have trouble classifying questions, as it is always difficult to do so out of context. It is sufficient if you understand the general concept of types of questions and levels of thinking.

INSTRUC- TIONAL MEDIA: OVERVIEW AND ANNOTATED BIBLIOGRAPHY[1]

In the health professions, where the most sophisticated forms of technology are put to their furthest use, it is ironic that the chalkboard and slides remain the dominant forms of media used for instruction. This book has shown how media can enrich your teaching by helping you to emphasize main points, clarify difficult concepts, and summarize content throughout a unit of instruction. Many instructors, uninformed of their potential uses, either neglect to employ media or misuse them. Laird (1974, p. 10) comments, "Perhaps the most workable ground rule for media selection is that the 'best' medium is the cheapest one which 'works.' Granted, that's not very scientific—but historically it holds up very well."

The purpose of this section is to provide a guide for media selection. The resources and references identified here, as well as those available through the media services at your institution, will direct you to materials needed for your course or assist you in producing them.

There are two basic categories of media: projected and nonprojected. Projected media are particularly needed in large-group instruction and include slides, overhead transparencies, film, and television. Nonprojected media are useful in small-group teaching and include the chalkboard, models, mock-ups, real objects, and illustrations (flip charts and displays). Audio recordings, while not visual in nature, are usually included in this category. A nonprojected medium can be used in conjunction with projected media. A real object can be placed on an overhead projector for enlargement or a live demonstration using a model or patient can be broadcast.

The first consideration in media selection is its appropriateness to your course goals. When you are teaching cognitive material involving factual information and theories, different formats and media should be used than when you are teaching a manual skill. The chart on the following pages will help you pinpoint which media are best suited to particular aspects of learning.

When planning to incorporate media into a course, determine your objectives and how they can best be achieved. What teaching method will you use? Look for portions of content or delivery that might be difficult to convey, and consider using media to assist you in such areas. It will be hard for dental students, for example, to understand the proper positioning of scaling instruments and how to use them correctly if this information is presented exclusively through a lecture. When you supply a videotape showing proper procedures, a set of the instruments to be used, and a programmed instructional package that includes diagrams, students will grasp the skill more readily.

On the other hand, instruction should not be wholly carried out through media, which are best used as supplemental aids. An entire class devoted to showing a film,

[1]This appendix was prepared by Robert Davis, Assistant Professor of Continuing Education, College of Nursing, University of Illinois at the Medical Center, Chicago.

CHOOSING INSTRUCTIONAL MEDIA

INSTRUCTIONAL MEDIUM	LEARNING OBJECTIVE*				
	LEARNING FACTS, THEORIES	LEARNING VISUAL IDENTIFICATIONS	COMPREHENDING AND APPLYING FACTS, PRINCIPLES, AND CONCEPTS	PERFORMING PERCEPTUAL MOTOR SKILLS	INFLUENCING ATTITUDES, OPINIONS, AND MOTIVATIONS
NONPROJECTED					
Drawings and illustrations	Medium	High	High	Medium	Medium
Photographic prints	Low	High	Medium	Low	Low
Chalkboard	Medium	High	Medium	Low	Low
Models and mock-ups	Low	High	Medium	High	Low
Simulators (sound and visual)	Medium	High	High	High	Low
Real objects	Low	High	Medium	High	Low
Exhibits and displays	Medium	High	Medium	Low	Medium
Programmed material	High	Low	High	Low	Medium
Printed material	High	Low	High	Low	Medium
Audio recordings	High	Low	Low	Low	Medium

PROJECTED

2- X 2-in slides	Medium	High	Medium	Medium	Low
Overhead projections	Medium	High	Medium	Low	Low
Opaque projections	Medium	High	Medium	Low	Low
Filmstrips	Medium	High	Medium	Medium	Low
Motion pictures (silent)	Medium	High	Medium	High	Medium
Motion pictures (sound)	Medium	Medium	High	High	High
Television	Medium	Medium	High	High	High

*Rating scale: High = very effective; medium = adequately effective; low = not effective.

Source: Robert Davis, *Media Handbook: A Guide to Selecting, Producing, and Using Media for Patient Education Programs,* copyright 1978 American Hospital Association.

for instance, does not allow time for discussion or other activities to ensure student comprehension. This is an error in media use, since meaningful education must include human interaction and the exchange of ideas.

Employing media that are incongruous with the content you are teaching or using them incorrectly can be more confusing than using none at all. Effective media are coordinated with the rest of your presentation, enhance understanding of content, and are easily visible and audible. They can save you time, help motivate students, add interest, and direct attention to significant portions of a lesson.

SOURCES OF EXISTING MATERIALS
Whenever possible, use materials that are already prepared and available rather than develop new ones. Existing materials distributed through educational organizations or commercial firms tend to be technically superior, and in some cases are reviewed by experts in the field to guarantee quality of content. The media services in your institution can help you obtain catalogs and order materials for preview. This should always be done to assess the adequacy of the material to meet your teaching needs.

Prepared media can be obtained from the following sources:

Commercial producers have production facilities that specialize in health science teaching materials. The organizations below can help you locate commercial suppliers of media.

American Hospital Association
Center for Health Promotion
840 North Lake Shore Drive
Chicago, Ill. 60611

Department of Health, Education, and Welfare
Bureau of Health Education
Center for Disease Control
Atlanta, Ga. 30333

National Center for Health Education
44 Montgomery Street, Suite 2424
San Francisco, Calif. 94104

Colleges and universities have media centers which produce materials for use by their facilities. Often they are available for loan, rental, or purchase directly from the institution. The major problem with these materials is that the content may be highly personal or limited in scope since they are usually prepared by a single faculty member. Call the media or resource center or specific departments to determine what materials are available from a university or college.

Teaching hospitals and those affiliated with universities generally have *hospital media centers* with production facilities and staff that prepare materials "in-house."

The American Hospital Association, American Medical Association, American Dental Association, and American Society of Plastic and Reconstructive Surgeons represent only a few of the *professional organizations* that have materials available for rental or purchase. If your society or organization does not produce or distribute materials, it should be able to direct you to media suppliers in your specialty.

Voluntary agencies such as the American Heart Association, American Diabetes Association, American Cancer Society, American Lung Association, Arthritis Foundation, and the National Foundation—March of Dimes can be called upon for materials which are often free of charge.

A wide variety of materials are available from *special interest groups* like the American National Red Cross and National Dairy Council.

Local and state departments of public health have media available for loan. *Law enforcement departments* have materials on drug abuse. *Departments of aging and consumer protection*, along with other government agencies, can also be contacted.

Industries often prepare media about the products they sell. Pharmaceutical companies, equipment companies, food processors, and baby product manufacturers are particularly good sources for materials.

The following books are useful guides for locating and previewing existing media resources.

Audio-Visual Equipment Directory, 1979–1980, 25th ed., National Audio-Visual Association, Inc., Fairfax, Virginia.

A fully illustrated audiovisual buyer's guide giving specifications for more than 1,500 products and the location of nearby dealers. This directory lists available equipment as well.

Laird, D., *A User's Look at the Audio-Visual World,* 2d ed., National Audio-Visual Association, Inc., Fairfax, Virginia, 1974.

A buyer's guide for selecting, purchasing, and maintaining media. Included is a short description of 17 forms of media and a brief list of the advantages and disadvantages of each.

PREPARING MATERIALS

After previewing existing materials you may find that what is available does not suit your instructional needs. Certain content might not be covered, or the presentation could be inadequate. This gap would lead you to develop your own media resources. Although production is often an expensive and time-consuming process, it may be the only way to obtain materials that meet your requirements. Usually, the process is done in close cooperation with the media services staff in your institution. They will be able to provide technical expertise and assistance in organizing the content.

The following annotated bibliography can help you become a more educated producer of instructional media. The texts included will tell you what can be done with media and enable you to communicate more clearly with media service staff. As a result, you will be able to produce media that match your needs more closely.

General Texts on Instructional Media

Brown, J. W., R. B. Lewis, and F. W. Harcleroad, *A-V Instruction: Technology, Media and Message,* McGraw-Hill, New York, 1973.

Dale, E., *Audiovisual Methods in Teaching,* McGraw-Hill, New York, 1973.

Erickson, C., and D. Curl, *Fundamentals of Teaching with Audiovisual Technology,* 2d ed., Macmillan, New York, 1972.

These are basic texts surveying all aspects of teaching with instructional media. Each covers types of media and their characteristics, planning and production, and examples of media in use. Examples cited in these texts do not relate directly to health professions teaching, but the principles are applicable.

Television

Mattingly, G., and W. Smith, *Introducing the Single-Camera VTR System, A Layman's Guide to Videotape Recording,* Scribner, New York, 1973.

A basic look at the technical aspects of single-camera videotaping from planning to actual taping of simple productions. This manual discusses the basic components of the television system: the camera, the videotape recorder (VTR), and audio system. Selecting and purchasing a videotape recording system, planning, and simple production techniques are described in terms understandable to the layman.

Planning, Preparation, and Use of Media

American Hospital Association, *Selecting Media for Patient Education,* videotape, 10 minutes, American Hospital Association, Chicago, 1978.

Through dramatization the viewer is shown the process of selecting and planning media for patient education programs. The patient education coordinator describes the activities as various committees meet and make decisions about the use of media.

Davis, R., *Media Handbook: A Guide to Selecting, Producing, and Using Media for Patient Education Programs,* American Hospital Association, Chicago, 1978.

This handbook presents guidelines for the selection, production, and use of media for staff and patient education. An eight-step planning process is described in clear, understandable language. "How-to" illustrations are featured. This handbook should be helpful to beginners and to those more experienced with media.

Davis, R., and L. Solomon, Planning teaching slides, *Archives of Dermatology,* 106: 317–318, 1972.

This article is written for anyone preparing slides themselves or using them in their teaching. Production planning guidelines as well as presentation techniques are summarized.

Gerlach, V., and D. Ely, *Teaching and Media: A Systematic Approach,* Prentice-Hall, Englewood Cliffs, N.J., 1971.

This book takes the reader through the design of instruction, emphasizing instructional media. Each chapter begins with a statement of objectives for that section, teaching examples are cited, and the reader is asked questions related to the content.

Kemp, J., *Planning and Producing Audiovisual Materials,* 3d ed., Thomas Y. Crowell, New York, 1975.

Minor, E., and H. Frye, *Techniques for Producing Visual Instructional Media,* 2d ed., McGraw-Hill, New York, 1977.

These are the best books currently available for instructors wishing to prepare their own teaching materials. Both describe methods of planning and producing materials in a simplified, step-by-step manner. Design and preparation of overhead transparencies, slides, displays, and many other types of audio and visual materials are presented. Kemp takes a broader look at media production including story boarding and audio production. Minor and Frye concentrate on visual materials. These two books are musts for education or media libraries.

Rowe, M., D. Curl, H. Frye, J. Kemp, and W. Veenendall, *The Message Is You: Guidelines for Preparing Presentations,* Association for Educational Communications and Technology, Washington, D.C., 1971.

This is a short, fun book, loaded with information on planning and making deliveries with visual materials. The procedures and guidelines are appropriate for anyone giving presentations in front of groups.

INTRODUCTION

Ideally, evaluation plans are formulated during the course development phase so that the effectiveness of a unit of instruction can be determined while it is in progress or after it is completed. The information most often desired concerns student achievement such as their retention of cognitive knowledge or abilities to adequately execute a skill. You may also be interested in assessing the quality of your instruction as well as other outcomes of your program.

EVALUATION: OVERVIEW AND ANNOTATED BIBLIOGRAPHY[1]

The purposes of this summary section are to briefly describe the components of the evaluation process and to identify resources that will assist you in collecting and utilizing relevant data. Although the selection is by no means exhaustive, the references included were chosen both for their usefulness to health professions educators and because they provide access to other resources.

THE EVALUATION PROCESS

The role of evaluation in education has been schematized as follows.

Evaluation data give us clues about the adequacy of the design and implementation of an educational program and should be taken into account when planning revisions. Popham (1975, p. 13) states:

Systematic educational evaluation . . . is a formal effort to affix the worth of things in education, such as programs, products, or goals. The reason we evaluate is to enable educators to make better decisions. Evaluation is an unashamedly practical undertaking. Evaluators want to improve education.

Different approaches to evaluation have been developed and are described in detail in some of the texts listed at the end of this section. Generally, a systematic approach to evaluation should include the following steps:

1. Specify the purpose.

2. Determine what is to be measured.

[1]This appendix was prepared by Dorthea Juul, M. Ed., Instructor of Health Professions Education, Center for Educational Development, University of Illinois at the Medical Center, Chicago.

3. Select appropriate data collection techniques.

4. Collect the data.

5. Summarize the results.

6. Make a judgment of worth.

Specifying the Purpose

The first step in the evaluation process is to determine those questions you want answered. As in a research project, the formulation of questions is a crucial stage because the inquiries being made shape the evaluation. If more questions are generated than resources permit investigating, you will have to decide which have the most value and eliminate the rest.

Two types of evaluation are used: *formative* and *summative.* The purpose of formative evaluation is to provide continuous feedback to students and faculty in order to enhance student mastery of course goals, and possibly to modify current program structure. Summative evaluation focuses on more final go/no-go decisions that determine if a student passes a course or if a program should be offered again. Has this student met the necessary requirements for receiving a professional degree? Should the introductory anatomy sequence continue to be offered as it has in the past?

Determining What Is to Be Measured

After the general purpose of the evaluation is identified, the next step is to define more specifically what is to be measured. Depending on the goals established, evaluation may focus on the educational *process* or its *products.* Both areas may be of interest.

Process refers to what happens to students in a course. Are the instructional methods and materials selected consistent with the course goals? Product refers to outcomes such as determining what students have learned as a result of the course. The measurement of cognitive knowledge by written tests is often the major focus of evaluation. There may be other student outcomes that should be assessed, however, such as psychomotor skills, habits, and attitudes. The effects of health professions instruction on patient care might also be of concern, as well as effects on the faculty and the institution.

An analysis of the congruence between process (what happens to students) and product (what they achieve) is especially important for the remediation of educational shortcomings. Suppose students score poorly when their performance of certain skills is measured. An evaluation of the adequacy of the teaching program might show that students were not given enough opportunities to practice these skills during the course. Therefore, the problem becomes one of changing the course rather than continuing to penalize the students.

Selecting Appropriate Data Collection Techniques

This step of the evaluation process may require a great deal of time since written or oral tests, rating scales, and questionnaires often have to be developed. Consultation with an evaluation specialist may be helpful in assisting you with this process. Standardized instruments suitable for your needs may already be available. Another resource is colleagues in your own or other institutions who have struggled through the developmental phase and are willing to share what they have produced.

In selecting evaluation instruments, two of the most important criteria are *validity* and *reliability*. In order to determine whether or not an instrument is valid, one must ask if it measures what it is intended to measure. For example, what assurance is there that a student who passes a paper-and-pencil test about injection techniques could perform the task on a patient? Without further evidence that there is a direct correspondence between the two, the written examination cannot be considered a valid measure of the behavior. Reliability refers to the accuracy or reproducibility of the measurement results. If the ratings of two observers who watch the same student perform a physical examination are quite different, then the estimate of the student's ability is not reliable. The variation in the ratings may be due to a poorly defined scale, inadequately trained raters, or both. Some of the references included in this section contain descriptions of different types of validity and reliability and how they are established.

A current, widely discussed issue in measurement is *norm-referenced* versus *criterion-referenced* tests. Norm-referenced tests are constructed to discriminate among examinees. The grade a student receives on a test is determined by how well the rest of the group does. In a class of 500 the top 100 students might get an A, the next 100 a B, and so on, regardless of the actual number of questions those students got right. Grading in this manner leads to the possibility that a given score might be considered adequate one year with a less able group of students and inadequate with a more able group the next. Most standardized tests, such as the National Boards, are constructed and their results interpreted in a norm-referenced manner with the assumption that one group of examinees does not differ significantly from another.

The main purpose of criterion-referenced tests is not to compare students with each other but to determine to what extent each examinee has mastered predetermined criteria. Tests are constructed to adequately sample a particular area of knowledge or behavior rather than to maximize differences among examinees. An examinee's performance is not affected by how well or how poorly the rest of the group does, but by how well the student has demonstrated mastery of the content tested.

One of the benefits of the criterion-referenced testing movement has been the requirement of a clear statement of what students should have achieved at the end of an instructional sequence. Obviously the evaluator's task is facilitated by the existence of such objectives. Many of the selected references have extensive coverage of the development of these instruments and also present a number of options for testing various objectives.

Collecting Data and Summarizing Results

After instruments have been developed, it is desirable to pilot-test them so their validity and reliability can be checked and any flaws corrected. You might decide a test question should be deleted because it is poorly worded or it has no correct answer. Examinees must be given clear directions and adequate time to complete the required tasks. If observational techniques are being used, raters should be trained to use the instruments properly.

After data collection, the results must be carefully reviewed even if pilot testing was done. The findings should then be summarized in a way that facilitates answering the original evaluation questions. The audience for whom the report is intended is another consideration. Feedback to students usually requires a different format than information for instructors and administrators.

Making a Judgment of Worth

The approach to evaluation outlined here views the evaluator's task as making a judgment of worth or helping the appropriate decision makers to do so. Holzemer (1976, p. 107) states:

There is a popular myth that objective criteria exist "somewhere out there" and that it is the evaluator's responsibility to discover that "truth." In fact, criteria are not objective. They are usually established by individuals with authority or by a committee of individuals.

Although the task may be difficult, it is the evaluator's responsibility to make assessments and to clearly indicate the criteria and supporting data used in making them.

SUMMARY

We cannot assess the effectiveness of educational programs in the health professions unless we systematically collect and analyze data. Those of you new to evaluation should now have a general idea of the components of this process. The following materials are included to provide more concrete guidance.

The first part contains general works in the field of education, and the second materials specifically developed for health professions educators. References addressing special evaluation topics are included last.

General References on Evaluation

Bloom, B. S. (ed.), *Taxonomy of Educational Objectives. Handbook I: Cognitive Domain,* McKay, New York, 1956.

Krathwohl, D. R., B. S. Bloom, and B. B. Masia, *Taxonomy of Educational Objectives. Handbook II: Affective Domain,* McKay, New York, 1964.

Schema for classifying cognitive and affective objectives are presented in these two handbooks. The cognitive taxonomy is based on the notion that different tasks require different mental processes. For example, recall of a particular fact may be all that is necessary to correctly answer one test question whereas another question requires interpretation of data to arrive at the right answer. The affective taxonomy is based on the different states in the development of attitudes and interests. Both handbooks give examples of test items for the different objectives.

Tyler, R. W., *Basic Principles of Curriculum and Instruction,* University of Chicago, Chicago, 1950.

This small book is a classic work in education, and Tyler is often referred to as the originator of the contemporary evaluation movement. Chapter 4 is entitled "How Can the Effectiveness of Learning Experiences Be Evaluated?" and succinctly covers many of the issues surrounding evaluation.

Popham, W. J., *Educational Evaluation,* Prentice-Hall, Englewood Cliffs, N.J., 1975.

Popham gives a comprehensive introduction to evaluation and is enjoyable to read. He covers different evaluation models, measurement alternatives, analyzing and reporting data, and has a chapter on teacher evaluation.

Worthen, B. R., and J. R. Sanders (eds.), *Educational Evaluation: Theory and Practice,* Wadsworth, Belmont, Calif., 1973.

A collection of key original works on evaluation by such authors as Scriven, Stake, and Stufflebeam is included as well as chapters by the authors on the state of the art of evaluation, evaluation as disciplined inquiry, and the future of evaluation.

Bloom, B. S., J. T. Hastings, and G. F. Madaus, *Handbook on Formative and Summative Evaluation of Student Learning,* McGraw-Hill, New York, 1971.

Gronlund, N. E., *Measurement and Evaluation in Teaching,* 3d ed., Macmillan, New York, 1976.

These are two of the many books available on the construction of multiple-choice tests, rating scales, and other evaluation instruments. They were selected because of their comprehensiveness and practicality.

General References on Evaluation in Health Professions Education

Morgan, M. K., and D. M. Irby, *Evaluating Clinical Competence in the Health Professions,* Mosby, St. Louis, 1978.

Rezler, A. G., and B. J. Stevens (eds.), *The Nurse Evaluator in Education and Service,* McGraw-Hill, New York, 1978.

Although the second book was written primarily for nurses, both cover a broad spectrum of evaluation topics of concern to health professionals. Special features include a section in the Morgan and Irby book with examples of evaluation models from different health professions disciplines, such as dentistry. The Rezler and Stevens book has a section on evaluation in the service setting.

Ford, C. W., and M. K. Morgan (eds.), *Teaching in the Health Professions,* Mosby, St. Louis, 1976.

Holcomb, J. D., and A. E. Garner, *Improving Teaching in Medical Schools: A Practical Handbook,* Charles C Thomas, Springfield, Ill., 1973.

Knopke, H. J., and N. L. Diekelmann, *Approaches to Teaching in the Health Sciences,* Addison-Wesley, Reading, Mass., 1978.

Miller, G. E. (ed.), *Teaching and Learning in Medical School,* Harvard University Press, Cambridge, Mass., 1962.

The main purpose of these works is to discuss teaching in health professions education, but all have a section devoted to evaluation. The Ford and Morgan and the Miller books cover evaluation topics more extensively than the other two. Holcomb and Garner devote a chapter to the methods of evaluating and improving instruction, and Knopke and Diekelmann include an annotated bibliography.

Charvat, J., C. McGuire, and V. Parsons, *A Review of the Nature and Uses of Examinations in Medical Education,* The World Health Organization, Geneva, Switzerland, 1968.

Development of Educational Programmes for the Health Professions, The World Health Organization, Geneva, Switzerland, 1973.

Miller, G. E., and T. Fulop (eds.), *Educational Strategies for the Health Professions,* The World Health Organization, Geneva, Switzerland, 1974.

All of the articles in Charvat, McGuire, and Parsons relate to evaluation. Two relevant articles in the second reference are "Diagnostic Examinations in Medical Education" and "The Assessment of Attitudes." The third has articles on "Simulation in Instruction and Evaluation in Medicine," "Examinations and Decision-Making," and "Evaluation of Teachers and Teaching Effectiveness."

Special Topics
Many of these topics are also covered by references in the first two sections.

Program Evaluation
Holzemer, W. L., A protocol for program evaluation, *Journal of Medical Education,* 51(2):101–108, 1976.

Holzemer outlines a straightforward approach to program evaluation and includes an example from a medical school clerkship.

Teacher Evaluation
French-Lazovik, G., *Evaluation of College Teaching,* Association of American Colleges, Washington, D.C., 1975.

Kulik, J. A., and W. J. McKeachie, The evaluation of teachers in higher education, in F. N. Kerlinger (ed.), *Review of Research in Education 3,* F. E. Peacock, Itasca, Ill., 1975.

McNeil, J. D., and W. J. Popham, The assessment of teacher competence, in R. M. W. Travers (ed.), *Second Handbook of Research on Teaching,* Rand McNally, Chicago, 1973.

Miller, R. I., *Evaluating Faculty Performance,* Jossey-Bass, San Francisco, 1972.

Pi Lambda Theta, *The Evaluation of Teaching,* Banta, Washington, D.C., 1967.

Faculty evaluation is an area in which a great deal of information is available. Both practical and more research-oriented references are included here.

Simulations
Barrows, H. S., *Simulated Patients (Programmed Patients),* Charles C Thomas, Springfield, Ill., 1971.

McGuire, C. H., L. M. Solomon, and P. G. Bashook, *Construction and Use of Written Simulations,* The Psychological Corporation, New York, 1976.

Barrows' book discusses the use of "actors" to simulate patients. The second book is a step-by-step guide to the development of written simulations, also known as patient management problems.

Oral Examinations
Levine, H. G., and C. H. McGuire, The validity and reliability of oral examinations in assessing cognitive skills in medicine, *Journal of Educational Measurement,* 7(2):63–74, 1970.

Pokorny, A. D., and S. H. Frazier, Jr., An evaluation of oral examinations, *Journal of Medical Education,* 41:28–40, 1966.

Both articles discuss the use of oral examinations in the medical setting.

Other
Barro, A. R., Survey and evaluation of approaches to physician performance measurement, *Journal of Medical Education,* 48:1051–1093, 1973.

Barro critically appraises different measurement techniques being used in medicine.

GENERAL TEXTS FOR IMPROVING INSTRUCTION IN HIGHER EDUCATION

ANNOTATED BIBLIOGRAPHY

Eble, K. E., *The Craft of Teaching,* Jossey-Bass, San Francisco, 1976.

A beautifully written book that offers honest and humane suggestions for dealing with difficult situations which can arise in the classroom such as cheating, classes that fall flat, or plagiarism. Eble discusses how to create the right classroom atmosphere and provides helpful suggestions on matters such as lectures, discussions, seminars, tutorials, and advising. The book is particularly inspirational for a beginning teacher confronting university politics.

Kozma, R. B., L. W. Belle, and G. W. Williams, *Instructional Techniques in Higher Education,* Educational Technology Publications, Englewood Cliffs, N.J., 1978.

This is one of the more concrete books available on teaching methods in higher education. It was written for instructors and is well documented, with an emphasis on teachers who also conduct research. Discussions of lectures, content, media, and evaluation, related checklists, and the Grasha-Reichman "Student Learning Styles Questionnaire" are included. The authors examine the various techniques available and discuss their application to different content areas such as psychomotor skills and art history. A model for making decisions about instructional methods is also developed.

McKeachie, W. J., *Teaching Tips: A Guidebook for the Beginning College Teacher,* Heath, Lexington, Mass., 1978.

Although written for a general university audience, this book is applicable for improving teaching in the health professions also, as its many editions testify. It is particularly useful in providing an excellent background of educational research findings regarding the value of the lecture versus group discussion, programmed instruction, and other instructional methods.

GENERAL TEXTS FOR IMPROVING INSTRUCTION IN HEALTH PROFESSIONS EDUCATION

Ford, C. W. (ed.), *Clinical Education for the Allied Health Professions,* Mosby, St. Louis, 1978.

Ford, C. W., and M. K. Morgan (eds.), *Teaching in the Health Professions,* Mosby, St. Louis, 1976.

Both texts consist of chapters written by different authors. Many of the individual contributions on topics such as microteaching, legal considerations in clinical affiliation agreements, and research design are useful. There is an attempt, however, to cover so many areas that one is left a bit confused as to how to implement these considerations.

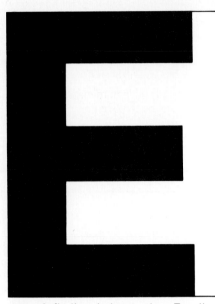

Holcomb, D. J., and A. E. Gardner, *Improving Teaching in Medical Schools,* Charles C Thomas, Springfield, Ill., 1973.

The book focuses on traditional techniques such as the lecture, group discussion, and independent study in medical school teaching. The text is bereft of health-related examples and a bit excessive in its use of educational jargon.

Knopke, H. J., and N. L. Diekelmann, *Approaches to Teaching in the Health Sciences,* Addison-Wesley, Reading, Mass., 1978.

A well-documented book of educational research findings in instruction. Excellent annotated bibliographies are presented at the end of each section. The discussion of innovative techniques such as simulation games, learning packages, and personalized instruction is useful, but the book is extremely heavy to wade through.

Miller G. E., et al., *Teaching and Learning in Medical School,* Harvard University Press, Cambridge, Mass., 1962.

This classic text in the field of medical education covers numerous topics from student selection, to the use of various instructional techniques, to grading techniques. It is provocative and delightful to read.

THE LECTURE

Bruce, D. L., E. Brunner, J. Breihan, and R. Menges, A public speaking course for foreign medical graduates, *Anesthesiology,* 4(4):380–388, 1974.

A brief study involving foreign medical graduates who participated in an intensive communications skills course. Performance criteria, audio- and videotapes, and group and self-evaluations were used.

Foley, R., J. Smilansky, E. Bughman, and A. Sajid, A departmental approach for improving lecture skills of medical teachers, *Medical Education,* 10:369–373, 1976.

Concepts in this article are applied to a medical teaching staff in a single department. The program includes videotaping faculty lectures, written feedback, and formal training sessions. It also serves as a pilot for a self-instructional program for faculty development.

Gregory, I. D., A new look at the lecture method, *British Journal of Educational Technology,* 6(1):55–62, 1975.

An assessment of the strengths and weaknesses of the lecture method, including helpful step-by-step suggestions for an effective presentation.

McLeish, J., *The Lecture Method,* Cambridge Institute of Education, Cambridge, England, 1968.

A classic monograph of research studies on student retention of lecture material, student attitudes toward the lecture, and discussion of improving the lecture.

Staton, T. F., *How to Instruct Successfully: Modern Teaching Methods in Adult Education,* McGraw-Hill, New York, 1960.

This book has a good chapter on specific advantages and applications of the lecture method. It provides a guide for planning a lecture with a focus on learner outcomes and activities.

Verner, C., and G. Dickinson, The lecture, an analysis and review of research, *Adult Education,* Winter 1967, pp. 85–100.

A concise presentation on appropriate uses of the lecture to enhance learning. Research results are summarized relative to lecture factors, such as length, delivery, intelligibility, learner response, and format. Comparisons of the lecture to other teaching methods are included.

THE USE OF QUESTIONS

Hoetker, J., and W. P. Ahlbrand, Jr., *The Persistence of the Recitation,* Central Midwestern Regional Educational Laboratory, St. Ann, Mo., Occasional Paper Series No. 3, 1968.

An excellent summary and list of references reviewing observational studies of teacher questioning behavior. As the title implies, most studies examined during the last 50 years show instructors, from elementary through higher education, doing most of the talking and asking largely low-level, factual questions.

Payne, S. L., *The Art of Asking Questions,* Princeton University Press, Princeton, N.J., 1951.

An extensive review of considerations to use when asking questions. The importance of asking questions, of phrasing them well, and of the selection of words are discussed. A bit cute, but loaded with examples and concrete suggestions.

Sanders, N. M., *Classroom Questions: What Kinds?* Harper & Row, New York, 1966.

Sanders redefines and simplifies Benjamin Bloom's taxonomy of educational objectives and categories of thinking and relates them to the use of questions. He urges that imaginative questions be asked to stimulate students to employ ideas rather than only remember them. The definitions used are helpful. One drawback is that all examples are taken from history and social studies.

GROUP DISCUSSION

Bloom, B. S., Thought-processes in lectures and discussions, *Journal of General Education,* 7:160–169, 1954.

A description of one of the classic studies documenting the value of group discussions over lectures for promoting student problem-solving efforts.

Eaton, S., G. Davis, and P. Benner, Discussion stoppers in teaching, *Nursing Outlook,* 25(9):578–583, 1977.

A concrete article describing 11 examples of teacher behaviors, such as judgmental responses and cutting students off, that "stop" discussion in the classroom. If they can identify and modify their discussion-stopping behaviors, the authors contend, then instructors can improve their abilities to stimulate classroom discussions.

Olmstead, J. A., *Small-Group Instruction: Theory and Practice,* Human Resources Research Organization, Alexandria, Va., 1974.

A very explicit analysis of the state-of-the-art of small-group discussion. Explicit guidelines are provided for the use of such methods as the Harvard case discussion, buzz sessions, and committee problem solving. Chapter 2 is particularly useful for its discussion of group forces that affect learning, establishing a conducive climate for learning in small groups, and the influence of group norms.

Robinson, E., Community dentistry: Developmental discussion approach, *Community Dentistry Oral Epidemiology,* 5:273–277, 1977.

An excellent paper which discusses an approach to teaching a course in community dentistry based on the "developmental discussion" method of problem solving. With this technique the teacher breaks problems into parts for groups of students to work on simultaneously. This paper modifies the concept to develop a course designed to have students work on tasks in a group situation. The result is active student participation related to the assigned task, which is often not solvable. Instead, relationships, applications, and analysis of facts emerge. The paper provides specifics on course procedures, course topics, task procedures, and student and course evaluation.

CLINICAL PROBLEM SOLVING

Barrows, H. S., *Simulated Patients (Programmed Patients),* Charles C Thomas, Springfield, Ill., 1971.

This is a classic book on the use of patient simulations. The uniqueness of Barrows' method is that he uses actors to play patients, creating a more realistic situation for teaching clinical problem solving.

Barrows, H. S., and R. M. Tamblyn, *Problem-Based Learning in Health Sciences Education,* U.S. Department of Health, Education, and Welfare, Public Health Service, National Institutes of Health, National Library of Medicine, National Medical Audiovisual Center, Washington, D.C., 1979.

Excellent monograph, relevant for any health science discipline, which describes a definition of problem-based learning, the clinical reasoning process and its evaluation, and suggestions for enhancing student problem-solving efforts.

Cogan, M. L., *Clinical Supervision,* Houghton Mifflin, Boston, 1973.

Deals in general with planning clinical teaching activities but focuses to a large extent on problems related to clinical supervision.

Donabedian, D., Computer-taught epidemiology, *Nursing Outlook,* 24(12):749–751, 1976.

This paper presents a computer-taught exercise in a public health issue. Specific learning objectives are built into planned interaction between the student and computer. A description of the situation is given, the student interacts with the computer by responding to related questions, and receives feedback on correct and incorrect answers. Besides allowing students to actively solve a problem and assess their own performance with immediate feedback, the instructor can also evaluate student problem-solving ability.

Ellis, A. B., *The Use and Misuse of Computers in Education,* McGraw-Hill, New York, 1974.

The many uses of computers for educational purposes are clearly described in this book, as is the development of system software. Potential values and drawbacks for using computer-assisted instruction within a course or department are considered. A helpful appendix is also included.

Elstein, A., L. Schulman, and S. Sprafka, *Medical Problem-Solving,* Harvard University Press, Cambridge, Mass., 1978.

The book centers on a study of how physicians make accurate diagnoses but is also richly researched in the general areas of problem solving, judgment, and decision making. Current theories of problem solving are explored. The concluding chapter provides an excellent summary of the book and the implications of problem solving for medical education.

Lincoln, R., J. Layton, and H. Holdman, Using simulated patients to teach assessment, *Nursing Outlook,* May 1978, pp. 316–320.

This article supports the use of the simulated patient to provide students with opportunities to learn and practice assessment skills. The simulated experience was developed in a four-stage sequence: observation of a videotaped model demonstrating assessment, supervised practice with peers, practice with a simulated patient, and assessment of real patients. The specifics of each stage are described and student feedback of the experience is documented.

McGuire, C. H., L. M. Solomon, and P. G. Bashook, *Construction and Use of Written Simulations,* The Psychological Corporation, New York, 1976.

This book is the authoritative guide for the design and implementation of written simulations. The clear and logical presentation should enable the reader to construct his own. This book has been the springboard for the development of texts on simulations in a variety of specialties.

SKILL LESSONS

Johnson, S. R., and R. B. Johnson, *Developing Individualized Instructional Material,*
Westinghouse Learning Press, Palo Alto, Calif., 1970.

This is a short but valuable book for those wishing to develop materials for individualized instruction. The principles and techniques discussed are especially applicable for building learning packages and teaching psychomotor skills.

Posner, M. I., and S. W. Keele, Skill learning, in R. M. W. Travers (ed.), *Second Handbook of Research on Teaching,* Rand McNally, Chicago, 1973.

This is a stimulating and informative chapter on skill-related research. *Skill* is defined on several levels, but the authors discuss the topic primarily as the integration of motor and mental activities. Attention is given to task analysis and information processing. A skill can be analyzed with respect to the demands of time and those of attention. The authors contend that while all skills demand time, it is the degree of attention required that will determine how a skill can be taught most effectively. The chapter is wonderfully documented.

Singer, R. N., To err or not to err: A question for the instruction of psychomotor skills, *Review of Educational Research,* 47(3):479–498, 1977.

This article opens with a discussion of instructional techniques that range from discovery to heavily guided and structured approaches. The author describes studies on the relationship between learning retention and the instructional method chosen, discussing and supporting research on unique learning processes and outcomes of skills teaching. The primary focus is on open skills (when behaviors must be adapted to a specific situation) as opposed to closed-loop, self-paced tasks (performed under predictable conditions). Practical implications, conditions, and parameters are identified. Extensive references are included.

INSTRUCTIONAL DESIGN

Hilgard, E. R., and G. H. Bower, *Theories of Learning,* 4th ed., Prentice-Hall, Englewood Cliffs, N.J., 1975.

This is an explicit, easy-to-read book that discusses a variety of theories of learning. Comparisons between associationist, cognitive, and other major approaches are detailed and weighed in a systematic manner. The last chapter is particularly useful in its considerations of theories of learning as applied to instruction.

Hyman, R., *Ways of Teaching,* Lippincott, Philadelphia, 1970.

Specifically, read Chap. 3, "Perspectives on the Choice of Method," pp. 53–65. It opens with an excellent examination of the interest in and concerns regarding how to teach from ancient times to the present. The author comments on elements common to different instructional methods, discusses steps and phases in the flow of teaching, and determines criteria for the selection of an appropriate teaching method.

Segall, A. J., H. Vanderschmidt, R. Burglass, and T. Frostman, *Systematic Course Design for the Health Fields,* Wiley, New York, 1975.

Intended for professionals with teaching responsibilities but no educational background, this is a guide for designing a course, units within a course, or an entire curriculum. How instructional objectives are derived, a series of self-instructional cases, and methods of performance analysis and evaluation are included. This book is applicable to any of the health fields.

Spady, W. G., Competency-based education: A bandwagon in search of a definition, *Educational Researcher,* January 1977, pp. 9–14.

An analysis of competency-based education which delineates and discusses its six critical elements—outcomes, time, instruction, measurement, certification, and program adaptability. Each element is clearly described and the structure of the overall concept is supported.

Tyler, R. W., *Basic Principles of Curriculum and Instruction,* University of Chicago Press, Chicago, 1950.

This book is brief, but a hallmark in the field of curriculum and instruction. Fundamental issues are raised about the relationships among planning, implementing, and evaluating instruction.

REFERENCES

Bloom, B. S., Thought-processes in lectures and discussions, *Journal of General Education,* 7:160–169, 1954.

Bloom, B. S., Innocence in education, *School Review,* May 1972, pp. 333–352.

Engel, G. L., The deficiencies of the case presentation as a method of clinical teaching, another approach, *The New England Journal of Medicine,* 284(1):20–28, 1971.

Foley, R., J. Smilansky, E. Bughman, and A. Sajid, A departmental approach for improving lecture skills of medical teachers, *Medical Education,* 10:369–373, 1976.

Foley, R., J. Smilansky, E. Bughman, and A. Sajid, *Learning Package Designed to Improve Lecture Skills,* Audio-Visual Concepts, Inc., Chicago, 1976.

Foley, R., J. Smilansky, and A. Yonke, Teacher-student interaction in a medical clerkship, *Journal of Medical Education,* 54:622–626, 1979.

Frost, H. G., Observations on a great occasion, *Adult Education* (U.K.), 37:282–283, 1965.

Hilgard, E. R., and G. H. Bower, *Theories of Learning,* 4th ed., Prentice-Hall, Englewood Cliffs, N.J., 1975.

Hoetker, J., and W. P. Ahlbrand, Jr., *The Persistence of the Recitation,* Central Midwestern Regional Educational Laboratory, St. Ann, Mo., Occasional Paper Series, No. 3, 1968.

Holzemer, W. L., A protocol for program evaluation, *Journal of Medical Education,* 51(2):101–108, 1976.

Kolb, D., On management and the learning process, in D. Kolb, I. Rubin, and J. McIntyre (eds.), *Organizational Psychology: A Book of Readings,* 2d ed., Prentice-Hall, Inc., Englewood Cliffs, N.J., 1974.

Laird, D., *A User's Look at the Audio-Visual World,* 2d ed., National Audio-Visual Association, Inc., Fairfax, Virginia, 1974.

McKeachie, W. J., "Research on college teaching," *Memo to the Faculty,* No. 44, Center for Research on Learning and Teaching, University of Michigan, Ann Arbor, May, 1971.

Page, G., R. Foley, and D. Pochyly, A survey of interests in teacher training of health science faculty, *British Journal of Medical Education,* 9(3):182–187, 1975.

Popham, W. J., *Educational Evaluation,* Prentice-Hall, Englewood Cliffs, N.J., 1975.

Posner, M. I., and S. W. Keele, Skill learning, in R. M. W. Travers, *Second Handbook of Research on Teaching,* Rand McNally, Chicago, 1973, pp. 805–831.

Risley, E., and R. Foley, *Verbal Questioning Techniques,* Audio-Visual Concepts, Inc., Chicago, 1976.

Smilansky, J., N. Runkle, L. Solomon, and R. Foley, *Instructor Plays Patient: Using Simulation for Case Presentation,* Audio-Visual Concepts, Inc., Chicago, 1976.

Smilansky, J., J. Taylor, and R. Foley, Planning, implementing and evaluating faculty development programs: A case study, *Faculty Development and Evaluation in Higher Education,* 4(1):11–16, 1978.

Spears, H., *The School for Today,* American Book, New York, 1950.

Stevens, R., *The Question as a Measure of Efficiency in Instruction: A Critical Study of Class-Room Practice,* Contributions to Education, Teachers College, Columbia University, New York, 1912.

LIST OF PLANNING GUIDES, CHECKLISTS, QUESTION-NAIRES, AND SELF-TESTS

		Pages
1.	Checklist for Rating Lectures	11–13
2.	Self-Assessment Questionnaires on Evaluating Your Teaching	139–146
3.	Posttest for Classifying Types of Questions	147–148
4.	Checklist for Planning a Discussion Section	35–36
5.	Checklist for Rating a Group Discussion Leader	43–45
6.	Checklist for Promoting Problem Solving Through Questions	58–61
7.	Procedures for Planning the "Instructor Plays Patient" Technique	67–70
8.	Planning Guide for Teaching Skill Lessons	84–85
9.	Checklist for Rating a Skill Lesson	88–91
10.	Rezler Learning Preference Inventory	101–109
11.	Checklist for Evaluating a Teaching Plan	117–119
12.	Sequencing Sheet for Planning Instruction	136
13.	Chart for Choosing Instructional Media	150–151

INDEX

Active learners, passive versus, 94
Adaptation of learned knowledge, providing for, 97
Advance preparation for skill lessons, 85
Affective questions (*see* Evaluation questions)
Ahlbrand, W. P., Jr., 15
Application sections, 27, 28
  planning, 31–35
Assessment (*see* Evaluation)
Attention span, duration of lecture and, 1, 4
Audiovisual aids:
  for discussion sections, 37
  for lectures, 7–8
    checklist for evaluating, 13
  for skill lessons, 77–78, 84
    for supervision of skill lessons, 80

Bloom, B. S., 16
Body:
  of lectures, 3–4
  of skill lessons, 86
Body movement while lecturing, 6–7
  checklist for evaluating, 12
Bower, G. H., 93

Chalkboards for lectures, 7–8
Change-of-pace technique for lectures, 4–5
Clarification:
  while lecturing, 4
  of students' responses in discussion sections, 37–38
Clinical experiences, planning, 47–48
Clinical problem-solving promotion, 47–70
  planning, 47–49
    with clinical experiences, 47–48
    with single lesson, 48–49
  with questions, 49–61
    checklist on, 58–61
    and general issues in questioning, 56–61
    hypothetical or speculative questions, 53–55
    open-ended questions, 50, 52–53
    phrasing and level of questions, 56
    probing questions, 53
    sequencing of questions, 50, 55–56
    student-to-student questioning, 56
  through role play, 64–70
    procedures for presenting a case, 67–70
  through simulation, 61–64
Closed questions, 17–20
  in application sections, 33
  categories of, 18–19
  convergent questions as, 18–19, 22
  memory questions as, 18
  place of, in sequencing of questions, 26
  recognizing, 17
  review on, 20
Competence, practice opportunities to attain expected level of, 96–97

Components of skills, 72–77
Computers, clinical problem-solving promotion with assistance of, 61–64
Conclusions:
  of discussions, 41
  of lectures, 5
  of skill lessons, 86–87
Conferences, 16
Content of lectures, planning organization of, 2–5
Convergent questions, 18–19, 22
Courses (*see* Instructional design; *specific instructional modes*)

Delivery skills:
  for discussion sections, 36–42
  for lectures, 5–7
  for skill lessons, 85–87
Discussion sections (tutorials), 27–45
  application sections as, 27, 28
    planning, 31–35
  delivery skills needed for, 36–42
  and evaluating performance as discussion leader, 42–45
    checklist for, 43–45
  planning, 27–36
    checklist for, 35–36
  review sections as, 27–31
    planning, 28–31
Duration of lectures, attention span and, 1, 4

Educational resources:
  learning with multiple, 95–96
  (*See also specific educational resources*)
Effective teaching (*see* Teaching effectiveness)
Engel, George L., 65
Evaluation:
  of lecture skills, 10–13
    checklist for, 13

Evaluation:
  of performance as discussion leader, 42–45
    checklist for, 43–45
  of skill lessons, 80–85
    checklist for, 82–84
    checklist for rating of, 88–91
  of teaching plan, 120–124, 133–134
    checklist for, 117–119
Evaluation questions (affective questions):
  as open questions, 22–23
  place of, in sequencing of questions, 26
Expected student performance:
  performance models as criteria for, 96
  practice opportunities to help achieve, 96–97

Feedback on student performance, 96–97
Frost, H. G., 1

Group discussions (*see* Discussion sections)
Guidance of discussion, 37
  by keeping discussion on the track, 39–40

Hilgard, E. L., 93
Hoetker, J., 15
Hypothetical questions in clinical problem-
  solving promotion, 53–55

Information, strategies for providing, in review sections, 30–32
Instructional design, 93–135
  defined, 93
  principles of learning and, 93–99
    active versus passive learning and, 94
    and adaptation of skills to given situa-
      tions, 97
    positive versus negative learning experi-
      ences and, 97–98
    practice opportunities and, 96–97
    and providing performance models, 96
    understanding logic underlying teaching
      activities, 94–95
    use of multiple educational resources,
      95–96
  sequencing teaching activities in, 111–132
    checklist for evaluation of plan, 117–119
    plan for, 112–115, 125–132
    plan analysis, 120–124, 133–134
  student characteristics and, 99–110
    learning preferences and, 100–110
  summary considerations in, 134–135
  teaching preferences and, 110–111
Instructors:
  as information resources, 31
  recommended behaviors for, in group dis-
    cussions, 41–42

Instructors:
  verbal behavior of, 15, 16
  (*See also* Teaching effectiveness; Teaching
    preferences; *specific instructional modes*)
Interaction:
  interactive lectures, 9–10
  questioning as stimulus to, 16
  student-to-student, in discussion sections,
    38–39
Interviewing skills (*see* Instructional design,
  sequencing teaching activities in)
Introduction:
  to discussion sections, 37
  to lectures, 2–3
    relating lecture body to, 3–4
  to skill lessons, 85–86

Knowledge:
  adapting, to given situations, 97
  student, instructional design and, 99–100
Knowledge explosion, 15
Kolb, D., 109

Learners, active versus passive, 94
Learning, principles of (*see* Instructional
  design, principles of learning and)
Learning preferences, instructional design
  and, 100–110
Learning Preferences Inventory, 109
Lectures, 1–14
  audiovisual aids used in, 7–8
  delivery skills needed for, 5–7
  discussion sections compared with, 27
  evaluating one's skills as lecturer, 10–13
    checklist for, 11–13
  impact of, 16
  interactive, 9–10
  overheads used in, 8–9
  planning content organization of, 2–5
  planning next, 14
  usefulness of, 15
  when to use, 1–2
Level of questions, 25–26
  in clinical problem-solving promotion, 56

McKeachie, W. J., 27
Manual tasks (*see* Skill lessons)
Materials and equipment:
  for discussion sections, 37
  for providing information in review sec-
    tions, 30–31
  for skill lessons, 85
  (*See also specific types of materials and
    equipment, for example:* Audiovisual
    aids)
Memory questions as closed questions, 18

Models of performance:
  importance of, 96
  in skill lessons, 77–78, 84
Multiple educational resources:
  learning with, 95–96
  (*See also specific educational resources*)
Murphy's law, 8

Negative learning experiences, positive versus,
  97–98

Open questions, 20–23
  categories of, 21–23
  in clinical problem-solving promotion, 50,
    52–53
Overheads, use of, in lectures, 8–9

Pace of speech in lectures, 6
Passive learners, active versus, 94
Performance:
  models of: importance of, 96
    in skill lessons, 77–78, 84
  (*See also* Evaluation; Student performance)
Phrasing of questions, 25
  in clinical problem-solving promotion, 56
Planning:
  of application sections, 31–35
  in clinical problem-solving promotion:
    planning clinical experiences, 47–48
    planning of single lesson, 48–49
  course, and positive learning experience, 98
  of lectures: body content, 2–5
    next lecture, 14
  of review sections, 28–31
  of skill lessons, 72–80
PLATO (computer system), 61
Positive learning experience, negative versus,
  97–98
Posner, Michael I., 77
Posttests, review section, 28–29
Practice opportunities:
  and attaining expected level of competence,
    96–97
  clinical experience as, 47–48
  in skill lessons, 78–80, 84
Preparation, advance, for skill lessons, 85
Preparation skills, 74–75
  checklist for evaluating, 82
Pretests, function of, 99–100
Probing questions in clinical problem-solving
  promotion, 53
Problem solving (*see* Clinical problem-solving
  promotion)
Procedural skills, 75
  checklist for evaluation of, 82–83
Process questions as open questions, 21–22

Questions, 15–26
  in application sections, 32–33
  in discussion sections, 27–28
  level of, 25–26
    in clinical problem-solving promotion, 56
  phrasing of, 25
    in clinical problem-solving promotion, 56
  promoting clinical problem-solving through
      (*see* Clinical problem-solving promotion,
      with questions)
  in review section posttests, 29
  self-instructional program in questioning
      techniques, 16–24
  sequencing of, 25–26
    in application sections, 33
    in clinical problem-solving promotion, 50,
      55–56
  for task-oriented groups in application sec-
      tions, 34–35
  twenty, to ask students, in review sections,
      29–30
  (*See also* Closed questions; Open questions)

Recordings of lectures for assessment purposes, 10
Remembering lecture material, 1, 16
Review sections, 27–31
  planning, 28–31
Rezler Learning Preference Inventory,
  101–108
Role play, clinical problem-solving promotion with, 64–70
  procedures for presenting a case, 67–70

Self-instructional program in questioning
  techniques, 16–24
Seminars, 15–16
Sequencing:
  of questions, 25–26
    in application sections, 33
    in clinical problem-solving promotion, 50,
      55–56
  of teaching activities, 111–132
    checklist for evaluation of plan, 117–119
    plan for, 112–115, 125–132
    plan analysis, 120–124, 133–134
Setting and space:
  for discussion sections, 36–37
  for skill lessons, 85
Simulation:
  clinical problem-solving promotion through,
    61–64
  skill practice with models of, 79–80
Single lesson, planning of, for clinical problem-
    solving promotion, 48–49
Skill lessons, 71–91
  delivery skills needed for, 85–87
  planning, 72–80

Skill lessons:
  planning: checklist for evaluation of,
      82–84
    guide for, 84–85
    with performance models, 77–78, 84
    with practice opportunities, 78–80, 84
    skill analysis in, 72–77, 84
    for supervision and evaluation, 80–85
  rating checklist for, 88–91
  skill, defined, 71
Skills:
  components of, 72–77
  delivery: for discussion sections, 36–42
    for lectures, 5–7
    for skill lessons, 85–87
  evaluating one's, as lecturer, 10–13
    checklist for, 11–13
  student, instructional design and, 99–100
  (*See also* Skill lessons)
Slides for lectures, 8–9
Small-group discussions, effectiveness of, 27
Socrates, 15
Spears, Harold, 15
Speculative questions in clinical problem-
    solving promotion, 53–55
Stevens, Rommiet, 15
Student ability and comprehension:
  adjusting level of questions to, in clinical
      problem-solving promotion, 56
  identifying, in review sections, 28
Student characteristics, instructional design
    and, 99–100
  learning preferences as, 100–110
Student participation in discussion sections, 39
Student performance:
  expected: performance models as criteria
      for, 96
    practice opportunities to help achieve,
      96–97

Student performance:
  focus of lectures on, 2
Student responses, clarifying, in discussion
    sections, 37–38
Student-to-student interaction, facilitating, in
    discussion sections, 38–39
Student-to-student questioning in clinical
    problem-solving promotion, 56
Students (*see specific instructional modes;
    entries beginning with term:* student)
Summaries of discussions, 40–41
Supervision of skill lessons, 80–81,
    84–85

Task-oriented groups, application sections
    using, 33–35
Teachers (*see* Instructors)
Teaching effectiveness:
  guide to, 138–139
  increasing, in group discussions, 41–43
Teaching preferences, instructional design
    and, 110–111
Tests:
  posttests, review section, 28–29
  pretests, function of, 99–100
Transitions in lectures, 4–5
Tutorials (*see* Discussion sections)

Verbal behavior of instructors, 15, 16
Voice use in lectures, 6
  checklist for evaluating, 12

Written simulation, clinical problem-solving
    promotion with, 64

ROLAND N. STROMBERG
University of Wisconsin, Milwaukee

After Everything
Western Intellectual History Since 1945

St. Martin's Press • New York

Library of Congress Catalog Card Number: 74-24980
Copyright © 1975 by St. Martin's Press, Inc.
All Rights Reserved.
Manufactured in the United States of America.
For information, write: St. Martin's Press, Inc.,
175 Fifth Avenue, New York, N.Y. 10010

1 2 3 4 5 6 7 8 9 10 11 12 13 14 15   88 87 86 85 84 83 82 81 80 79 78 77 76 75

To Frances and Hilary
who encouraged me

Preface

This book is an account of the main themes of Western thought since 1945. Ideas, of course, are not neatly confined to chronological eras; they seem fond of reappearing mysteriously from age to age, like so many Cheshire cats, and the historian writing an account of recent thought is tempted to range far back to show that the novelties of today are only slightly different versions of very old ideas or developments of ancient lines of thought. In the 1960s the "death of God" was much discussed; but when Friedrich Nietzsche spoke of it in 1882, he certainly knew that speculation about the decline of traditional religious belief was already very old. The women's liberation movement, thought by a few votaries to date from c. 1968, is in fact a new phase of a venerable movement that had been carried forward in the nineteenth century by Socialists and suffragettes.

The existence of antecedents does not mean that ideas cannot be put to new uses and take on new life; they can and do. The historian's traditional work of showing connections between present and past is not intended to expose claims of newness but to give us perspective and improve our understanding. And this process of illumination is applied to ideas of every kind. Several historians have supported the thesis that the nineteenth century invented all the ideas and ideologies that the twentieth has tried out; they have made a particularly strong case to show that "modernism" in the widest sense was born between 1880 and 1900.

One might easily go further. Underneath the innumerable epiphenomena of contemporary history, there is good reason to believe that we are still living in the epoch opened by the French Revolution—an age only very inadequately described by the terms "capitalism" and "bourgeois society," though they get at a part of it, a complex age characterized in at least some of its aspects by Henry Maine's discerned shift "from status to contract," by Auguste Comte's positivism and Age of Facts, by Thomas Carlyle's Mechanical Age and Maurice Barrès' "deracination." The age is also marked by democracy and legal equality, by urbanization and political aggregation, and by the increase of power and loss of individuality. (Of this last, Alexis de Tocqueville and John Stuart Mill complained bitterly more than a century ago, and we are still complaining today.) This modern epoch has seen the destruction of "traditional society" and the emergence of what Wyndham Lewis called Cosmic Man. It has been corroded, according to Walter Lippmann, by the "acids of modernity," by intellectualism and scepticism; with its social simplicity, it has lost its religious faith and thus succumbed to "anomie." It has forced art to the margins of society and "rationalized" everything. At the same time it has created, by reaction, a defiant individualism, a romantic egoism and Promethean intellectual pride, which is the response of outraged human nature to the ravages of this strange modernism. Intellectual processes at work today have been going on for nearly two centuries, though their pace may have constantly accelerated.

He who would write a history of contemporary ideas accordingly finds himself tempted again and again to go far behind the present. But in this book, the temptation has generally been resisted. The manifold inheritance of today is taken as given; it is studied as it manifests itself in the minds of living and thinking people. Now, as always, people live in a world of ideas; they think no matter what they are doing, and their thoughts draw on the store of ideas supplied by the intellectual culture around them. Unhappily, the intellectual culture of the modern world is exceptionally bewildering; society is compartmentalized, information accumulates at a startling rate, and hugeness, fragmentation, and disunity characterize the times. This book is intended to orient, not to announce profound or original discoveries; its task is the humble but useful one of showing the interconnections between numerous strains of contemporary thought, in order to help the reader understand better the large and confusing world in which we live.

The book is an account of the main themes of modern Western thought; but just as ideas are not limited to chronological eras, they are not limited by geographical boundaries. The intellectual culture of today is nearly global. The contemporary consciousness of people from most walks of urban life is a good deal alike, whether they live in Zagreb, Paris, London, Buenos Aires, or New York—or, for that matter, in Singapore, Seoul, Tokyo, Casablanca, Dakar, or Tel-Aviv. Jean-Paul Sartre, though unmistakably a Frenchman, learned much from German, Danish, and Russian thinkers; his works have appeared in scores of languages, and his ideas are familiar from Warsaw to San Francisco, from Rio de Janeiro to New Delhi.

The prevailing climate of intellectual opinion is international, and ideas spread almost instantaneously to remote places through the marvels of modern communications, yet the leading producer of ideas in the modern period has probably still been Europe. The book's European focus may help to correct a tendency in some Americans to exaggerate the uniqueness of what is happening in their own country. The role of the United States as a producer and not merely a consumer of ideas, styles, and fashions in art and thought has been growing, however, to match its power and wealth, and I wish to dedicate my book to the cosmic culture of the future in which the Americas will join the Old World in complete cultural partnership.

R.N.S.

Contents

1 Moods of the Postwar Years   1

Retreat from Ideologies   1
Existentialism   10
Analytical Philosophy   20
The Novelist as Philosopher   26

2 The Conservative Fifties   31

Political Quietism   31
Uncommitted Art   36
Trends in Political Thought   43
The Return to Religion   49
Varieties of Conservatism   52

3 The Radical Sixties   55

Toward a New Politics   55
Ideologists of the New Left   62
New Left and Old   73
Conservative Counterreaction   83

4 The Disease of Modernism   87

Neophilia   87
The Modernist Neurasthenia   89
After Modernism   94
Some Recent Themes   100
The Pornographic Revolution   106
Some Consequences of Neophilia   115

5 The Overburdened Mind   119

Intellectual Fragmentation   119
Attempts at Synthesis   123
Consequences of Fragmentation   128
Assaults on the Heritage   131

6 The Other Culture: Science and Scientism   145

Humanist Versus Scientist   145
Attacks on Science   148
The Attraction to Science   155
The Clash of Cultures   160
Attempts at Mediation   166
The Behavioral Sciences   169
Psychology   175
The Age of Computers   180
The Case for Scientific Reason   183

7 Dissolutions   189

The Communist Schism   189
The Christian-Communist Dialogue   201
Secular Christianity   205
Other Dissolutions   208

8 Reconstruction   217

A Rage to Order   217
Neoclassicism   220
Structuralism   226

9 Conclusion: The Malaise of Our Age   235

Sources   249

Index   265

After Everything

Western Intellectual History Since 1945

The drama of Europe is a spiritual drama, a drama of the mind.

Georges Bernanos

In the raw, existence is always one damned thing after another, and each of the damned things is simultaneously Thurber and Michelangelo, simultaneously Mickey Spillane and Maxwell and Thomas à Kempis.

Aldous Huxley

I propose to evoke for you the disorder in which we live.

Paul Valéry

1

Moods of the Postwar Years

Retreat from Ideologies

Already in the aftermath of the First World War, thoughtful people had the feeling that all gods were dead, all faiths overturned. Ezra Pound called Western civilization "an old bitch gone in the teeth," while Dadaists tried to find the ultimate gesture of contempt and despair, and historian Oswald Spengler, in oracular terms, pronounced the collapse of the West. This was not only because the war had been so terrible. It was also because of an ensuing sense of weariness and decadence.

Thousands of years of thought, and the ruin of many systems, lay behind contemporary Western civilization, reaching all the way back to the age of Greece and Rome. Most particularly, since the French Revolution had overturned the old social order and Romanticism had announced a fundamental revolution against traditional standards in thought and style, nearly two centuries of intellectual ferment had brought to that civilization a succession of styles and moods, a dozen major ideologies or substitute religions, and, in the end, a radical scepticism. The dominant intellectual currents of the nineteenth century—Darwinism, Marxism, Freudianism, scientific positivism—each worked in its own way to undermine the certainty of rational concepts or to challenge beliefs in an objective world order. These concepts became rationalizations, tools or weapons in the power struggle between men and groups, or instincts, myths. Already before 1914 representative avant-garde thinkers assumed that men live by myths.

In a fashionable book of the 1920s, *The Modern Temper,* Joseph Wood Krutch (an American) observed gloomily that "the world

1

may be rejuvenated in one way or another, but we will not. Skepticism has entered too deeply into our souls ever to be replaced by faith," though some "young barbarians" mercifully ignorant of the great tradition might be capable of faith. Yet the "young barbarians" would only begin the same weary trek over again; in time they too would lose their innocence and become jaded worldlings.

But hope is hard to kill in the modern West. After hardly more than ten years of fashionable despair, it rose again. During the 1930s sophisticated Western intellectuals suspended their reason and turned, as an act of faith, to embrace the strong young barbarian god of Russian Communism. Or, in lesser numbers, they accepted the deliberate atavism of Italian Fascism or German National Socialism. No one who experienced this phase of thought or has studied it closely can regard it as other than the most remarkable of chapters in the spiritual history of man. But within a few years these desperate gambles of faith also failed.

There were few Fascists or Nazis left after the collapse of Hitler's grisly empire of death and the lynching of Benito Mussolini by furious Italians at the end of the Second World War. The world rejoiced at having rid itself of the most monstrous of all historic tyrannies. Few people outside Germany any longer remembered that for many Germans Nazism had been a high ideal, a glorious crusade or that between the wars Fascism had blossomed all over the Western world, seducing some of the most brilliant individuals in all countries and becoming a significant political factor in France, Belgium, Austria, and Rumania, as well as Italy and Germany. The war made the word *Fascism* simply a synonym for evil and the suppression of what it stood for was well worth the appalling cost. There was no doubt about its demise. Those who saw its shadow here and there in the postwar years only testified to the terror it had once inspired: liberals would see Fascists under the bed as conservatives saw Communists. *Fascism* stuck in all vocabularies as an epithet. Not for nearly twenty years was it possible even for scholars to approach it dispassionately, asking exactly what Fascism was as an intellectual and social phenomenon.

In German and Italian intellectual and cultural life, the years of Nazism and Fascism and the war constituted an enormous hiatus, a period of limbo which interrupted that life and formed a gulf between past and present. Much that seemed extraordinary in these countries after the war can be related to this loss of continuity, which left them out of step, requiring a forced march to catch up or payment of dues to causes obsolete in other countries. Their sensitive spirits suffered even more from a burden of guilt. Bertolt Brecht's pronouncement that after Auschwitz (and Hiroshima) there simply could be no poetry, though too extreme to be accepted, was all too understandable. After a period of numb semisilence Germans returned to the subject of Nazism; curiously, the 1960s produced a more intense discussion of that horror than did the immediate postwar years. Rolf Hochhuth's bitterly controversial play blaming the papacy (*The Deputy*, 1963) was an example; on a different level, so were the truly great novels wrenched from the mediation of suffering and guilt by Günter Grass and Heinrich Böll. It took several years for German literature, choked into strangled silence by the awful iniquity, to find its voice.

The most significant postwar development in the West was probably the tendency to share the blame for these evils with Germany and Italy. Hatred of Nazism during the war had taken the form of a self-righteous projection by the Allies of all evil onto the Germans. Long a "problem," the German people and their nation had become a disease; demonic forces had descended on the region between the Alps and the Baltic. The corruption was traced far back in German history and even considered as a racial taint. Victorious American soldiers, entering this tainted land, were issued orders not to speak to or render any kindness to Germans. Faced with the horror of cities levelled by bombs and stinking of death, the Allies' general reaction was that the Germans deserved what they got. Few in the Allied lands during the war thought that blasting priceless German antiquities into rubble was any loss to Western civilization. No one doubted that Hitler had deliberately begun a war of aggression in order to enslave his neighbors and eventually conquer the world. The only debate about the German Question—and it was a lively one—concerned what particular manner of sickness or insanity had invaded the Teutonic body. The poison might variously be traced to Arminius, Barbarossa, Luther, Hegel, or Nietzsche; to Frederick the Great or Otto von Bismarck or Kaiser Wilhelm II; to an innate slavishness or a wild cruel streak; to a stolid medievalism or a technocratic modernism—contradictions were overlooked in the rush to vilify a people who had succumbed to Hitlerism, brought on the terrible war, slaughtered the Jews, and stoked the gas chambers of Dachau and Auschwitz with human bodies.

Unfortunately, the assumption that the Germans were totally blameworthy carried within it seeds of its own destruction. Some observers were bound to point out that the Allies had done their share of mischief, terror-bombing cities, murdering survivors of torpedoed merchant ships, imprisoning and massacring Poles, and almost casually dropping the atom bomb on defenseless Japanese civilians. Apart from the facts, there was the inherent implausibility of God having chosen to concentrate all evil in one people—"A little particular of Providence," as Charles Dickens might have said. And there were the frightful gaffes committed by those analysts of German history and culture who protested too much and proved too much—and forgot too much. They made Luther and Nietzsche into what they were not, they twisted Bismarck and Wilhelm out of all recognition, they forgot Kant and Goethe. They even failed abysmally to understand Adolf Hitler. The historical myths of World War II, nourished on hysteria and hatred, fell one by one in the postwar years, as the myths of war always do. The demythologizing is still going on.

The evil remained; there was nothing to do but share the blame. Georges Bernanos with his impassioned eloquence described Hitlerism as "the sin of a world so profoundly corrupted that the peoples corrupt each other," adding that "the last service rendered by the German people to the old civilization they formerly honored is to show to each nation, as in a monstrous mirror, the image of that which it perhaps already is without knowing it and which it will surely be tomorrow" (*La Liberté pour quoi faire?*). In *The Age of Anxiety* (1947), the major English poet W. H. Auden, once the briskly optimistic socialist ("lone flyer, birdman, my bully boy!"), now found deep depravity in the human marrow. Hitler is in all of us. The seeds of total corruption are everywhere. Karl Barth's 1919 theology was better known and better understood in 1949. The novels of Graham Greene and François Mauriac spread a similar message among Catholics. One misses much of the authentic postwar mood if one fails to understand how the monstrous guilt of the Nazis was transmuted into a sense of the general guilt of the human race. (The self-righteous Nuremberg trials of 1946, which punished the German leaders for crimes against humanity, tailed off in severe doubts about whether the victors, in a war waged with maximum inhumanity on both sides, had the moral authority to pass such judgment. The presumptuous Allied plans to civilize and educate the Germans ended in embarrassed laughter.)

Communism died much harder than Fascism. But that god had failed for most Western intellectuals of the between-the-wars generation by the later 1940s. Those intellectuals had watched Stalinism destroy all that was free and creative in Russia, watched the ghastly farce of the great Purge trials, known about the slave-labor prison camps even if they did not yet suspect the full dimensions of that horror. (It was widely believed that if Stalin had slain his thousands, this came nowhere near equalling Hitler's millions; only later was it learned that the Russian slaughter was even greater.) The fellow-travelling intellectuals of the 1930s had lost their faith largely as a result of seeing moral obliquity in the Party. The calculated Machiavellianism of Communism emerged from a crude application of Marx's crude evolutionary ethics: only success counts and whatever serves the Revolution (that is, the Communist Party of the USSR) is justified. In the name of this *reductio ad absurdum* of historicism, Stalin's henchmen were prepared to cut down Spanish anarchists, murder Trotsky, collaborate with the Nazis, and reverse themselves on a moment's notice. Many sometime friends of the Party were disillusioned in the Spanish Civil War, where all the glorious idealism of the People's War against Fascism ended in a cynical Stalinist power play. Many more never forgot that between August 1939 and June 1941 Stalin and Hitler were allies, as Communists followed orders to go easy on Nazism and blast democracy, whose cause they thus deserted at a critical moment.

True, most of this was forgotten during the war of 1941–1945 when, as ally of the West, Soviet Russia bravely bore the brunt of the German offensive and heroically overcame staggering losses to rally and defeat Hitler. Stalin became a hero, and it was said that not only his draconian measures but also his devious diplomacy stood vindicated by the results. As a war measure the Western press deliberately played down criticism of Communism and encouraged the most favorable image of Stalin's regime.[1] In any case normal sympathies for a beleaguered ally had the natural effect of discouraging criticism. During the war Communists in many countries of

Europe earned admiration by their courage in fighting against Nazism in the movements of resistance, such as the French underground, the Partisans of Yugoslavia, the anti-Fascists in Italy, and the Greek resistance to German occupation. In these heroic actions they cooperated with non-Communists, forging friendships which lasted into the postwar years.

Nevertheless, the end of the war saw the beginning of a swing away from Communism. The generation of the 1930s, now grown to maturity, functioned as the natural leaders of the intellectual world in these years, c. 1945–1960. Their disenchantment predated the war's conclusion. They had hoped for a "rejuvenation" of civilization, a "progress toward a new community of belief," as David Daiches wrote in the 1930s. They discovered that Communist Party membership inhibited their creativity and destroyed their self-respect. They concluded with Simone Weil that "the revolution is the opiate of the people" or with Raymond Aron that it is *The Opium of the Intellectuals* (1957).

If there were some who, like Jean-Paul Sartre, felt that Marxism might be rescued from the hands of Stalin, the movement away from Communism included many more. Simone Weil and Arthur Koestler and George Orwell; Harold Laski and Ignazio Silone and Albert Camus—such people could scarcely be accused of lacking courage or faith or a social conscience. They were of the Left, they had fought in the ranks, they had dedicated their lives to the working class. Mlle. Weil, "wasted by chagrin," died during the war, an apparent suicide by starvation; her spirit lived on in a very special way in postwar France. In *Darkness at Noon* and his autobiographical books, Koestler probed the nightmare morality of the Communist with uncanny skill. In 1946 his *The Yogi and the Commissar* found the crude externalism of the social revolutionary to be just as wrong as the subjective passivity of the Oriental sage; only a combination of the two could save the world. That every revolution leads to a new tyranny, Silone discovered in a life of suffering, though he might have read it long since in the academic writings of his fellow Italian, Vilfredo Pareto. As Yeats wrote in "The Great Day,"

> Hurrah for revolution and more cannon-shot!
> A beggar upon horseback lashes a beggar on foot.
> Hurrah for revolution, and cannon come again!
> The beggars have changed places, but the lash goes on.

It remained for the postwar years, culminating in 1956 (and repeated in 1968), to show that the beggars who had become masters of the Kremlin were now interested only in the lash and would use it against further revolutions.

It nevertheless took a good deal of intellectual energy to dispel the attraction of the opium of Communism for intellectuals, and it never quite disappeared. The idea had been deeply planted that somehow, though it did wrong, Communism meant good. "In communism I see hope. It does many things which I think evil, but I know that it intends good"—the words of E. M. Forster (*Abinger Harvest,* 1936) were representative of their time and milieu. Arnold J. Toynbee, in his system of spiritual labelling, put Communism closer to the saving truth than any other error; though violent and "futuristic," it had ecumenical qualities and could turn into transfiguring *agape* more easily than other spiritual deviations. In a similar manner Reinhold Niebuhr had seen the Communists as basically misguided Children of Light rather than Children of Darkness. (Even today, a Christian interested in the "dialogue" with Communism asserts that "Communism, unlike Fascism, cannot simply be equated with evil."[2]) Though he later changed his mind, in 1945 the French philosopher Maurice Merleau-Ponty, like Sartre, argued that the Soviet Union should be granted an indulgence not accorded to other tyrannical states (*Humanism and Terror*). Sartre held that "as a result of tragic political and historical circumstances Marxism has been paralyzed, petrified," but remains nevertheless the inevitable mental framework of our age. That, somehow, the Left may be forgiven for the sins that condemn the Right remained almost a dogma of the modern intellectual.

In a remarkable way Jean-Paul Sartre, the high priest of Existentialism, clung to a simple faith in Communism which rested on a faith that it represented the future: the proletariat is always right, because it is on the side of History; the Communists are always right, because they speak for the proletariat. The man whose ethic extolled absolute integrity and who made "bad faith" the cardinal sin was willing to lie—as Sartre did about alleged American germ warfare in Korea—to support the cause of the Party. The moral of Sartre's play *Dirty Hands* apparently was that you can justifiably dirty your hands in the cause of the Party. Sartre had defended Stalinism even during the Nazi-Soviet pact. But in 1956 the Soviet invasion of Hungary lifted the scales from his eyes.

Yet Sartre himself, paradoxically—and nothing, surely, is more characteristic of our times—struck mortal blows at Marxism. He brilliantly refuted its materialism and its worship of a god of History, ridiculed its naive nineteenth-century scientism, ripped it apart as "system." No historical reason or any other kind of reason subsists in the absurd world of Existentialism. The two things, classical Marxism and Existentialism, were utterly irreconcilable. "One cannot be at the same time the heir of Hegel-Marx and the heir of Kierkegaard," as Raymond Aron put it.[3] The Communists, to Sartre's dismay, persisted in regarding him with contempt, though he continued to court them. He belonged, in their book, with other degenerate excretions of a dying bourgeois culture—he who so hated the "bourgeoisie." A liberated, nondogmatic, very loose form of Marxism, emerging more prominently in the sixties than the fifties, was to be an intellectual feature of the postwar years. It often amounted to little more than the sense of a changing, flowing, "dialectical" world, a truism almost anyone could accept. (The real Marx, students of the newly available early writings found, was in fact such a dialectical, nondogmatic thinker; Engels and Lenin had perverted him.)

With that special combination of pragmatic hardheadedness, independence, and ordinary decency that marked his personality, George Orwell perhaps more than any other writer set himself to deflate the mythology of Communism. He saw simply that it made men lie and kill. This interesting British writer was one of the leaders of a rebellion against abstract things which swept the postwar world. "An intellectual hatred is the worst": men will murder millions in the name of a slogan when they would shrink from taking a single real human life. In one of Orwell's typical pieces (November, 1945), he told how a Belgian who hated "Germany" and demanded its destruction saw one dead German on the approaches to Stuttgart and changed his whole attitude. The false imagination, as another Englishman said, can hate whole races and classes; the true imagination cannot hate a single human being. The true awfulness of the Nazi destruction of the Jews, or operation "Final Solution," was, as its historians discovered, its impersonality: conceived as an idea, passed down through the faceless channels of bureaucracy, it ground out genocide virtually without any individual having to involve his personal emotions in the task.

Orwell also saw through the dreadful myth of History—of a "redemptive historicity," of "Time, the Refreshing River" in the words of W. H. Auden's poem. It was an insight he shared with Albert Camus. Even Kingsley Martin, the humane and civilized editor of the eminent British journal *New Statesman*, could argue that a few million deaths are a small price to pay for the advance of events towards their inevitably benevolent consummation—an argument as old as Robespierre. The Viennese-British philosopher Karl R. Popper dedicated a profound and subtle book, *The Poverty of Historicism*, to those millions of human beings who had been sacrificed to the moloch of Historical Inevitability. Orwell in his less subtle way saw this quite clearly. "Crime follows crime, one ruling class replaces another, the Tower of Babel rises and falls, but .one mustn't resist the process—indeed, one must be ready to applaud any piece of scoundrelism that comes off—because in some mystical way, in the sight of God, or perhaps in the sight of Marx, this is Progress." The modern mind with all its sophistication had been gulled by a childish idea: that "each age is better than the one that went before."

A searching critique of Marxism went on in the postwar decades, exposing its errors, finding it an irrational dogma—a bastard religion rather than a science, and a peculiarly narrow and intolerant one at that. Those who had been its dupes in the 1930s led off in parading its exposures. *The God That Failed,* a collection of essays by notable ex-Communists, became a classic. Most of the contributors admitted they had been looking for a faith. "I came to it not so much through consciousness of the political and economic situation as through despair," wrote Edward Upward, who came out of it only in 1954.[4] Koestler stressed "the intellectual comfort and relief found in escaping from a tragic predicament into a closed system of beliefs that left no room for hesitation and doubt." (See also Harold Laski's frankly irrationalist *Faith, Reason, and Civilization,* 1944.) The appeal of such blessed relief from thinking and from doubt continued to be felt. There was a rereival of Marxism, in somewhat different dress, in the 1960s. The Western intellectual continued to be fascinated as well as repelled by it. But for the moment, it was a spent force.

A rebellion against all "ideologies" proceeded during the years following World War II. Judith N. Shklar's *After Utopia: The*

Decline of Political Faith and Daniel Bell's *The End of Ideology: On the Exhaustion of Political Ideas in the Fifties* were fashionable books. Realism prevailed in politics. It was discovered that underneath the sloganizing, Communism and capitalism were much alike: the managers or Organization Men rule in both systems, both in Max Weber's conceptualization are bureaucratic-rational by nature, and Industrial Society is much the same whoever happens to own the machines. It was found that international relations are governed by the balance of power, and that much harm had been done by pretending otherwise. There was, in general, much preoccupation with power, the stark reality that underlies all human affairs. Bertrand de Jouvenel wrote a treatise about it (*Du Pouvoir*). He also worried about it; the dominant fact of modern history is its fostering, under whatever ideological banner, of the omnivorous and omnipotent State, against which the individual is helpless. The nightmare vision of the total state rooting out the last remnants of individual privacy and converting men into robot-slaves drove the Swedish writer Karin Boye to suicide after her terrible novel *Kallocain.* Franz Kafka at last came into his own; Orwell's *1984*, his last testament, was almost *the* serious book of the post-1945 decade. Reconsidering his own *Brave New World*, Aldous Huxley found things even worse than he had expected in 1932. "I do not think the danger before us is anarchy," Edwyn Bevan wrote to Arnold J. Toynbee, "but despotism, the loss of spiritual freedom, the totalitarian state, perhaps a universal world totalitarian state." [5] Neither in 1939 nor in 1949 was the world totalitarian state an entirely unreasonable fear. The great countries of Germany and Russia had each been captured by a small, fanatical sect and then easily dominated by its use of the vast power modern technology and communications provide. Orwell's picture of perpetual war between huge power conglomerates mirrored the Cold War.

Existentialism

What is one to think and do when all possible beliefs are gone? Existentialism, the philosophy that burst upon the world right after the war, was an ultimate scepticism that, drawing on all the scepticisms rising in the West for more than a century, saw the world as totally absurd and man's unique consciousness as something thrown absurdly into the chaos. "One thrives on the mere fact that one exists," a character in Gabriel Celaya's novel *Los buenos negocios* (1965) says. "And there is nothing beyond . . . no need for more." D. H. Lawrence was the English novelist who found ultimate value in life itself, in particular in the forked flame of sexual passion, and forced this conception on readers by the power of his art. This philosophy stemmed above all from Nietzsche. Life for life's sake remains when other values have dissolved, or when men's sophisticated self-awareness reaches a stage where they see the mythical element in all ideals.

"Nothing beyond . . . no need for more" were the slogans of popular Existentialism, which was, like Romanticism before it, a fusion of many and sometimes logically inconsistent ideas. Its story has many odd byways. It burst on the awareness of the world in postwar Paris, where it seemed, if one read popular magazines, to be a fad of café society. The Existentialism of *Aux Deux Magots* was, however, soon traced to the lair of Jean-Paul Sartre, a most formidable figure when flanked by his friends Simone de Beauvoir and Albert Camus. They made the journal *Les Temps Modernes* the leading vehicle of serious avant-garde thought. Novelist, dramatist, editor, critic, dialectician, the brilliant and incredibly energetic Sartre, the Existentialist fountainhead, is a modern prodigy fit to be ranked with Descartes, Voltaire, Rousseau, and Bergson, but more versatile than any of them. He is one of some half-dozen intellectual marvels of the post-1945 generation.

Yet it soon appeared that Sartre was primarily a popularizer. His teacher was the difficult German philosopher Martin Heidegger, author of *Being and Time* (1927), behind whom stood other obscure German philosophers, reaching back to Hegel at the beginning of the nineteenth century. Sartre's philosophical masterwork, *Being and Nothingness* (1943; English translation 1956), which struck the educated world as fascinatingly strange, turned out to be based so closely on an early work of Hegel, *The Phenomenology of the Spirit* (1807), as at times to border on plagiarism (though in significant respects it came to different conclusions).

This seemed strange, since it was popularly supposed that Existentialism emerged from the French Resistance against German rule during the war, a product somehow of the stark realities and grim choices forced on men who chose to fight tyranny against hopeless odds. And Heidegger once stood very close to the Nazis. It is also strange that *opposition* to Hegel supposedly inspired the original Existentialist, Sören Kierkegaard. (He had interpreted Hegel as the author of an abstract, determinist system, probably a misconstrual but a common one.)

Kierkegaard's revival itself made a strange story. It began, after the name of Kierkegaard had been obscure for more than half a century, in Germany in 1909, spread to France and England in the 1930s, and continued to swell ("The number of books about him shows no sign of diminishing," a review of numerous recent publications observed in 1969). Kierkegaard's influence was first made manifest after World War I in the exciting "crisis" theology of Karl Barth, the Lutheran pastor who snatched Kierkegaardian fire to light a brand intended to destroy the idea of divine assurance of secular progress. Like Kierkegaard, Barth was of course a Christian; but Sartre was an atheist, and the philosopher Karl Jaspers somewhere in between. Analytically viewed, the ancestry of Existentialism is enormously complex, no doubt, and in one way or another can be traced far back. Anthologies of literature appeared, bearing titles such as *The Existential Imagination,* in which the adjective apparently means only "serious," or "concerned with urgent situations." Like M. Jourdain talking prose, Shakespeare and Pascal were Existentialists without knowing it, as were Tertullian, William of Ockham, Martin Luther, and the Marquis de Sade.

The ferment of ideas, which works so slowly, is always interesting. The exact moment of existential crystallization was clearly 1927–1931, the moment of Heidegger's *Being and Time* and Jaspers' *Existence.* But both men drew on the "phenomenological" philosopher Edmund Husserl, who first used that term in 1900; Husserl in turn went back to Hegel's *Phenomenology of the Spirit.* This book preceded Hegel's once much more famous discovery that there is reason in history, and it was long condemned for hopelessly mixing up philosophy, psychology, and history in a vast and formless mess. But such integration of all existence into a unity now became appealing.

In this connection the remarkable career of Karl Jaspers is worth comment: he began as a student of medicine, getting his M.D. in 1909, and proceeded from that to psychology and psychiatry and thence to philosophy, where his 1931 classic overcame strong prejudices on the part of his fellow philosophers against such an academic gadabout. And of course Jaspers was also a historian—of ideas and culture. He continued to pour out books until his death in 1969, quite unlike Heidegger, who lapsed into virtual silence, broken only by gnomic utterances (so far as concerns published work). Jaspers regarded the sociologist-historian Max Weber as the greatest mind of the century.

The point is that Existentialists all affirmed the wholeness of the human spirit against the compartmentalization and specialization that has dehumanized it in the modern world. Against all the odds they tried to restore thinking, feeling, and acting man as a unity, a unity assailed from a dozen directions in today's technological, bureaucratic society, which converts people into a congeries of functions and objects.

So the basic drive that created Existentialism out of all those bits and pieces from the past was a protest against mass society. Between the wars it was related to the disgusted total alienation from society of those who, like T. S. Eliot, felt they had been born out of date in a half-savage country, where the women come and go, talking of Michelangelo, in a cultural Wasteland. And it continued to maintain that relationship; no one could be more bitterly alienated than Jean-Paul Sartre. But the Second World War and its experiences also entered into the mood of the post-1945 Existentialism of Sartre and Camus.

This was a special mood which supplanted the ideological commitments of the 1930s and the war. It was a product of their exhaustion and of the alarming prospects of a world emerging from hell without faith. It was Sartre and Camus in post-1945 Paris; it was a generation for whom they spoke. To say that it was a disenchanted generation is to miss the point; it was beyond disenchantment. The survivors of World War I could be disenchanted; those of World War II had to be something else. They were naturally appalled by the most ghastly slaughter in history, and they could not but be dismayed at what seemed the likely continuance of strife. At the same time they had found the experiences of the war and the Resistance exciting, with "boundary situations" bringing one up against rock-bottom choices. Those who went through the worst horrors of the war often testified to the exhilarating effect of

facing simple and ultimate questions—of stripping away the irrele-
vancies and getting to essentials. After such thrills, it was hard to
return to normal existence. The revulsion from bourgeois existence
that artists and writers naturally felt was doubled and redoubled.
But new gestures were needed. The myths of the thirties were as
dead as the attitudes of the twenties.

From an unlikely mixture of Heidegger and the Maquis, stirred in
his own bitter, sharp, alienated, metaphysical brain, Sartre con-
cocted the new outlook. In 1957 a pool that asked a sample of those
French men and women born between 1927 and 1939 to designate
the one writer who most forcefully "struck the mind of people of
your age" revealed that by far the largest vote, 20 percent, went to
Sartre—of those casting ballots, about 33 percent. This is a remarkable ascendancy in view of the huge arena of contemporary intellectual life. (No one else got more than 1 or 2 percent.) Sartre became
almost equally famous in other countries, as did Camus—the
literature in English is of course enormous.[6] The world once again
followed Parisian fashions in philosophy. Sartre was another
Voltaire. Existentialism was soon an international byword.

Life is gratuitous and contingent, absurd, without apparent
meaning. We are here, in brief, as on a darkling plain. (Matthew
Arnold, Existentialist?) It dawns on us that the ignorant armies
make no sense, and yet we find ourselves fighting. Despair, loneliness, the sense of absurdity and nausea depart when we choose and
act. Driven to the last ditch, the existent person throws away his
props and acts authentically. He creates value and endows the
universe with meaning. The full realization of his complete and
terrible freedom, of the fact that he even has no "nature" but must
create one, that he is a radically different kind of being from
anything else—really a kind of nothingness which can penetrate
being—that he has no essence but is a protean Becoming—
overwhelms him at first, as does his frightening responsibility, a
total responsibility for himself and for his actions. No one can tell
him what he must do, there is no rational way of discovering his
duty, yet act he must. In choosing and acting he makes himself and
makes his world. If he feels crushed by this prospect, he can reflect
that there is no honest alternative save the cowardly path of suicide
and that he is a creature of too great dignity to make that choice.

These items of the Existentialist decalogue are by now platitudes.

They were thrilling in their time, and they still exert their influence. Our bewildered age has at least been serious. "The contemporary gods are chthonic, splanchnic and desperately serious."[7] The remark occurs in a review of a book about Anatole France, reminding us that that great Olympian—in recent times very much out of fashion—was quite aware of the absurdity of mankind, but was not thrown into spasms of gloom thereby. The world is a comedy to those who think, a tragedy to those who feel, Horace Walpole once observed. The implications are perhaps unflattering to the modern mind. To laugh at the ridiculousness of it all is one of the things contemporary Existentialist man seemed unwilling, or unable, to do. The existential mood looked back to prophets who were almost humorless; to apocalyptic and deeply religious thinkers; to those who peered into the mysterious heart of things, who detested glibness and intellectuality, and who like Pascal "can approve only of those who seek in anguish." It owed something not only to Nietzsche and Dostoyevsky, the anguished atheists, but to the Jungian and Freudian searches for the dark depths beneath (even though Existentialist psychology denied the formal existence of such a thing as the "unconscious"), and to the Phenomenological philosophers. And it was much indebted to the religious quest of all the great modern seers, Martin Buber, Nicholas Berdyaev, Karl Barth, Rudolf Bultmann. The Existentialist gods do not laugh, they cry.

In Sartre's case, there was bitter pessimism as well as seriousness. The message of personal authenticity, responsibility, freedom, and "commitment" is not so far from traditional religion, and many of the Existentialists were deeply religious. But the Sartrean strain was poisoned by the ontology of Nothingness. There can be no God since by definition mental being or being-for-itself can have no general form. Nor can there be any really satisfying relationships with other people. We must treat other people as objects, there being no possible points of contact between one *pour-soi* soul and another. The very existence of other people produces falsity and guilt. "Hell is other people." We see others as types; of course, insofar as we are inauthentic personalities, we see ourselves as types. The Kantian imperative is impossible; I cannot treat other people as ends, I *must* treat them as means. I try to manipulate and use them, not just in the crude way of practical exploitation but in psychological ways, in the very nature of my dealings with them. They must be to me objectified and essentially nonhuman things, simply roles and functions.

Even love becomes a self-defeating project, a study in frustration, because it is a desperate attempt at the impossible: lovers try to ensnare each other's free consciousness, to unite *pour-sois,* but this cannot be done, and so an angry disappointment is the result. Sartrean love is a battle between two hypnotists in a closed room. "A game of mirrors," as Sartre put it, a battle to maintain the illusion that two *pour-sois* can make contact as such.[8] Thwarted by the attempt to fuse in pure being, each lover makes an object of the other, struggles against being made an object of, tries to enslave the other and reduce him/her to total dependence, tries to escape this trap. It rang all too true. Sartre's play *No Exit* may be the most fascinating psychological drama ever written. There is no way out of the human dilemma, which consists of being face to face with another person!

Karl Jaspers also stressed that *Existence,* the world of inward or subjective being, of consciousness making itself through choices and projects, is radically different from the kind of being possessed by the phenomenal world; this view is reminiscent of Kant, Jaspers' acknowledged master in philosophy. Possibly the contribution of Existentialism was to drive home this point, pounding it so deeply into our minds that no one could ever hereafter doubt it, and to insist that we think about the consequences. It is part of the subjectivist trend of modern times, which might be described as the growing awareness that truth is not something which the human mind discovers but which it creates.

Jaspers joined other Existentialists in holding, contrary to Sartre, that in certain heightened moments and "boundary situations" we can have intimations of transcendence. Living authentically may bring this reward of knowing contact with Being itself. The issue between religious and atheistic Existentialists was at bottom not very great. Gloomily or with some glimmering of hope, one should be faithful to the inner conscience and seek to be "authentic." One also should accept one's responsibility and make choices. Fence-sitting is abhorrent to the Existentialist. The danger he runs is that there may be a loss of concern for objective truth, for careful sifting of evidence; choices become arbitrary and personal, thinking autistic and irrational. And of course almost any specific doctrine and action is consistent with what is, as Sartre came to realize, only a method. Existentialism invites one to choose, in sincerity and integrity; to "blow on the coals of the heart" (Archibald MacLeish). It does not on principle prescribe what to choose.

The leading debate within the camp of the French Existentialists in the early 1950s made this clear. By temperament radical and bitter, Sartre chose Communism, though he intermittently scolded the Soviet Union for its bloody crimes and was a Communist beyond all pales of party orthodoxy, one who would not have lasted two days in any Communist-ruled country. Albert Camus, as well as Maurice Merleau-Ponty, was typical of his decade in being increasingly inclined in the post-1945 years toward a moderate or even conservative political outlook. Both participated in Orwellism. A deep suspicion of abstract ideas and ideologies goes well with Existentialism. It was Camus who declared "the end of ideologies" and preached in his widely read novels the moral that people slaughter and torture and hate each other because they substitute empty names for living realities and think in abstract, rather than human, terms. One cannot kill a real man, but one can cheerfully consign to death whole races of capitalists, socialists, heretics. Camus's existential hero-rebel was a moderate, opposed to fanaticism, concerned to minimize violence. Rejecting Communism, Camus broke with Sartre on this issue, finding it very strange that his friend should embrace Marxism, the very epitome of a creed that spoke in generalities and encouraged intellectual hatred.

No one influenced popular Existentialism more than the Algerian-born Camus, a glamorous figure whose vivid novels bore a clear fréight of metaphysical meaning but bore it even more gracefully than Sartre's rather didactic plays and novels, though it was a lighter burden. He moved from the sense of the absurd, of the dehumanized man in a meaningless world, revealed in *The Stranger,* to the exultation of sheer life triumphing over despair, to the essential happiness of Sisyphus who defied the gods and then outwitted them. The terrible punishment they devised was really a blessing—what would Sisyphus have had to do if he ever *did* get the stone to the top? At times the message of Camus seemed as old as the Epicurean—gather rosebuds while you may. Enjoy the sun and the sex and let the rest go. Camus could face the awkward consequences of his naive humanism—man simply creating values by asserting them—quite naively; What could he say to his German friend who had "chosen" Nazism, except that he, Camus, chose differently? And where does that leave us? But no one communicated to the young the simple message of popular Existentialism as well as Camus: Choose, commit yourself, be your own man, be aware of your dignity. And do not injure others. That no one has a right to inflict suffering and death on others in the service of the god of History, any more than in the service of any other god, was a conviction Camus shared with Orwell that led him to anti-Communism.

The more academic cousin of Existentialism was Phenomenology. Consciousness as it is in its raw, primeval state, before it has conceptualized and verbalized and thus drawn a screen of words across its face—what is it? Popular Existentialism described it as a kind of protean nothingness, a "hole in being"; one cannot conceptualize consciousness, which exists only if it has an object, and which devours objects. Is there any way of getting at it to see if it has a structure? Not to Sartre, evidently. "Consciousness is a great emptiness: a wind blowing towards objects." Sartre began around 1937 by being stimulated by, yet driven to criticize, the philosopher Edmund Husserl's "Phenomenological" school; he agreed with the Husserlian concept of "intentionality" as the root quality of consciousness but rejected Husserl's assumption that there is an Ego, a Self, lying behind this consciousness. Sartre's radical pessimism dissolved the ego into the world of objects, refused to accept any metaphysical unity, and left us with just so many great emptinesses immersed in a sea of objects.

Others nevertheless thought it profitable to work at the investigation of "basic structures of consciousness." Most followers of Husserl were at one with Sartre in rejecting the Idealist metaphysics, or at least reserving judgment; they simply described the modes of conscious intentionality. These are presumably nonrational categories of the understanding, like Rudolf Otto's Idea of the Holy[9]; intangible sentiments, like Jungian archetypes, lying at the base of the mind before rational thought begins.

The founder of Phenomenology was a brilliant thinker and remarkable intellectual personality, fit to rank with the greatest among the pioneers of contemporary intellectual culture. In his youth Husserl, like Wittgenstein and Jaspers, was interested in the sciences (astronomy, physics, mathematics) as well as in psychology and philosophy. The Nazis muzzled him and got him dismissed from his professorship. He died in 1938 at seventy-nine, almost exactly the same age as Freud. His influence was much slower to develop than Freud's, but in the end it may prove even more powerful and enduring. The bulk of his work survived almost by accident. How the great Phenomenologist's body of unpublished manuscripts was rescued from the Nazis and hidden in a Belgian convent during the war is one of the many remarkable adventure stories of intellectual history. Today the Husserl Archives are in Louvain.

As Husserl himself boasted, the revolutionary quality of his thought makes Lenin's look mid-Victorian and Freud's conservative. "Phenomenology is an empiricism more adequate than that of Locke, more sceptical than that of Hume, and more radical than that of William James." The appeal of this radical subjectivism, this attempt to get behind every verbalization and conceptualization to the raw, absolutely unconditioned state of pure experience (by "bracketing" or suspending everything else) extended across the superficialities of mere religion and ideology: the custodian of the works of the Jewish-born father of Phenomenology is a Franciscan priest, H. L. van Breda; his most influential disciple was the Marxist Sartre; his growing army of followers has included mystics and scientists—Husserl himself was something of both.

If it is possible to describe the preconceptual as Phenomenological philosophers thought, then we have finally probed to the very bottom of mental activity. Could there be any further philosophy? Phenomenology announced that "the day of systems is over." The phenomenal world (life world) of consciousness is a world of concrete objects, infinitely rich, unable to be embraced in any system because of its "ambiguities and confusions" (John Wild). Phenomenology leaves us with a taste of reality in specific situations, but with no sense of unity or order.

The Phenomenological trend in thought was related to the probing after psychological reality that marked the high intellectual scholarship of Sigmund Freud, Carl Jung, and Max Weber at the beginning of the century and went on remorselessly thereafter. When we get to the bottom of the mind, we find ourselves back at the beginning, before the Greeks invented "rational" or conceptual thought, operating with "mythopoeic" modes—concrete, eidetic images existing in disorderly fashion. The whole path of reason from Socrates on was evidently a wrong one, ultimately barren. We have lived through the long Age of Reason and are now to reenter the mind of pre-Socratic man. Such was the implication of much Existentialist and Phenomenological thought.

Analytical Philosophy

If Existentialism was an obvious "After Everything" position, so too was its rival among the philosophies, the school of Linguistic Analysis. It is true that the latter's lineage was quite different, and that the two groups often seemed completely hostile to each other. At international conclaves of philosophers, French, German, and Italian Existentialists stared uncomprehendingly at Anglo-Austrian-Scandinavian Analysts. They represented something like C. P. Snow's Two Cultures, humanists versus scientists. The literary-prophetic-religious background of the Existentialists seemed sheer bombast and empty noise to many in the other camp, schooled to subject each utterance to the severest scrutiny to determine whether it really meant anything or was so much hot air, while the Existentialists found pedantry and littleness of soul among these professional nitpickers. The Linguistic school had its roots in places sharply rationalistic, scientific, "anally" analytical: in Bertrand Russell, in Viennese Logical Positivism, in the Oxford movement of the 1930s led by A. J. Ayer, whose specialty was showing that all the utterances of priests and prophets were mere sound and fury.

Yet a deeply significant change came over the Analytical school after 1945. Nothing was more revealing of the changed atmosphere of the 1950s than this new course. It softened the earlier dogmatism with a greater scepticism, a more sophisticated sense of the manifold horizons of thought. In the 1930s Logical Postivism was a brash young upstart, matching the revolutionary mood of that decade with its exuberantly announced "revolution in philosophy," which would render all metaphysics obsolete by showing that every meaningful statement could be reduced to statements about sense-data. A. J. Ayer, *enfant terrible* of the movement, has recalled how his 1936 manifesto *Language, Truth and Logic* "outraged the old men" of philosophy and had a *succès de scandale* throughout the intellectual community. Two decades later, almost no one except Ayer wished to be called a Logical Positivist. Logical Positivism had failed to carry out its plan. High hopes were dashed. Criticism had turned up insuperable difficulties. "Like most endearingly simple views," Mary Scrutton wrote of Logical Positivism, "it is full of ambiguities; like most dashingly sceptical manifestos it asks us to swallow premises much more staggering than its opponents'." [10]

Retaining a continuity with the earlier phase in virtue of the same interest in clarifying statements—the linguistic dimension—the Analytical school now, in the 1950s, changed strikingly in some ways. The continuity as well as the change was mirrored in the remarkable fact that the same philosopher appeared to be responsible for both phases—Wittgenstein I and Wittgenstein II. Ludwig Wittgenstein, an Austrian who shuttled between Austria and England, an offshoot both of the Viennese school and of the Cambridge of G. E. Moore and Bertrand Russell, was the extraordinary person who had virtually launched the Analytical school with his 1921 *Tractatus Logico-Philosophicus*. But subsequently Wittgenstein, a person given to formidable silences between intervals of producing rare and gnomic books, shifted his ground—a shift so subtle that it went almost unperceived at first and yet so profound that it altered the very premises of the neopositivist school. For he reached a position of absolute scepticism that considered "the desire to understand the world an outdated folly," because the world of language is utterly divorced from the world of fact—there is an impenetrable veil. Thus Wittgenstein in his later works landed man in an absurdity as hopeless as the Existentialists' and left him apparently with only the option of making up myths (language-games) knowing they must be myths. So, at least, the average man who approached this high and austere philosophy was likely to conclude.

But though the later Wittgenstein (see especially the posthumously published *Philosophical Investigations*, 1953) seemed far removed from the early one in respect of his confidence in rational inquiry to get at truth, it is likely that the germs of his shift were already in the *Tractatus* and that this book was misunderstood, as he later claimed. He delivered the new gospel in some lectures of the 1930s. But he did not publish it, and an A. J. Ayer-minded philosophical community was not prepared to receive it in the 1930s. The basic doctrine of Logical Positivism had been that statements are testable by empirical reality and that no assertion has any real meaning unless it is or can be reduced to a statement so testable. The spirit of this philosophy was antimetaphysical, astringent, yet confident that clarity of expression and scientific methodology could restore thought to a sound foundation. This mode of philosophizing admonished us to watch our language, and it was sure that if we did we would get to truth by eliminating error and confusion. Still fascinated by language, the later Wittgenstein concluded that there is no discoverable reality outside language. We live in a world of words; the world of facts is something as different and alien as Karl Barth's hidden God.

There is no doubt about the importance of the language dimension for modern man. Wittgenstein was a true prophet. Contemporary "structuralist" linguistics conforms to his vision. There is an emblematic story about Fritz Mauthner, who in 1873, as a law student at the University of Prague, experienced a shattering intellectual revelation akin to that of Augustine in the garden in Milan, Descartes in the Bavarian stove, or Rousseau on the road to Vincennes. Mauthner's overpowering idea was that we are prisoners of our language. (See his *Prager Jugendjahre,* recently reprinted.) Coming down to us from the past freighted with all kinds of strange meanings, language is an irrational structure that we cannot get outside of; we are forced to think largely as it directs. "There's a cool web of language winds us in," as a modern poet (Robert Graves) wrote. This insight stunned Mauthner into silence for a time and then launched him on a career in linguistic studies. Rather than try vainly to think, we had better scrutinize the structure which thinks us. A large slice of contemporary cognitive activity does just that, creating a condition surely new in man's intellectual history.

It has been claimed that the final Wittgensteinian position was something absolutely unique. It was as new and as odd a position as Existentialist absurdism and as obviously end-of-the-road. To the untrained eye it may look as if Wittgenstein was anticipated, in all that matters, by a long line of sceptics reaching back through Schopenhauer and David Hume to William of Ockham and the ancient Epicureans and Academicians. The silence to which Wittgenstein was reduced resembled that of the Greek philosopher who only wagged his head. In the absence of any rational guides, we fall back on the garden of language as it exists, a strange but priceless accumulation of the ages. Some Linguistic philosophers concentrated on gently clarifying the language of everyday life.

Wittgenstein as a person was by all accounts an austere and ascetic man of rigid integrity, who gave up professing at Oxford and was a kind of intellectual saint. Those who think of the Austrian as high priest of the rationalists and logicians, the ultimate in cold-blooded scientism, do not know the story of his life. In his youth he studied engineering and aeronautics, but he turned from this to pure philosophy after much distress and Bertrand Russell's encouragement. It is interesting to compare his early intellectual odyssey with that of Jaspers, at about the same time. Both passed from science to philosophy by way of religion or psychology. After the First World War, however, Wittgenstein fell under the influence of Leo Tolstoy's religious writings, became a simple village schoolmaster, and thought about becoming a monk. Few, it would seem, ever endured more angst than this deeply ambivalent man. So far from being the spokesman of one culture against the other, he epitomized the modern anguish in being torn apart by conflicting aspirations, intellectual and spiritual.

He does not, however, seem to have been attracted by modern literature. He is said to have enjoyed low-grade American western and detective fiction more than anything arty. He doubtless thought that virtually all contemporary thought and society were stupid and hypocritical. One gets no clear ethic from this extremely complicated thinker; but if there is any, it is very like the Existentialist injunction to be honest, sincere, and one's own man, saving at least this modicum of integrity in the worst of all possible worlds.

In his interesting book *The Theater of the Absurd,* Martin Esslin remarks that "Wittgenstein's word games have much in common with the Theater of the Absurd," which is usually thought of as strongly Existentialist. Similarities between the two philosophical groups, often assumed to be so different, abound. Both Existentialists and Linguistic philosophers saw man as deposited in a strange world from which he is altogether cut off and of which he can make no real sense, yet with the power to endow it with apparent meaning. In this dilemma both schools tended to fall back on the language of everyday life. J. L. Austin, the Oxford philosopher especially identified with this conception of philosophy's goal as elucidating the language of everyday life, may be compared to the French Existentialist and Phenomenologist Maurice Merleau-Ponty, who came to think that the aim of philosophy is to express in words what everyone knows in unformulated and half-formulated ways, to articulate tacit and everyday knowledge. An interest in "ordinary thought" was quite characteristic of the Phenomenological school. Philosophy is a method, not a creed. Here of course was a point of agreement with the Analysts. So there is really no such thing as philosophy in the sense of a message, a gospel, a body of wisdom. For that we must look somewhere else.

This abdication of the philosophers was a remarkable, some thought a dismaying or shocking, thing—a drying up of the springs of wisdom. To a world desperately in need of guidance, the philosophers, chuckling softly and drawing another glass of port in the seminar room, replied, "Sorry. Not our affair." But they could hardly be accused of arrogance, since they were determinedly bent on a course of self-extinction. According to the approved doctrine of the Analytical school—dominant in the fifties, especially in the Anglo-Saxon world—philosophy is a kindly but old-fashioned parent who takes care of the young sciences, the realms of knowledge, until they are able to fend for themselves, whereupon it retires to die or perhaps remains alive in retirement to offer occasional words of advice to the children if they get into trouble as they go about their taxing affairs. As the intellect matures, philosophy contracts, until in the end we do not need it at all. There is an echo here, of course, of Auguste Comte's belief that mankind had entered the Age of Facts, leaving behind the ages of religion and metaphysics: positivism always bore the trace of its founder. And it was destined to repeat that serious difficulty the nineteenth-century positivists had with values, which led their founder to end by inventing a new religion and his followers to struggle with the "religion of science" until they gave it up as a bad job. What are we to do about values in the age of facts?

The quality of this philosophizing was very high. "The gains and advances made [in philosophy] in the dozen years which followed the [1939–1945] war were probably as great as any which have been made in an equivalent period in the history of the subject," P. F. Strawson, a leading British philosopher, declared. The Analytical school believed a great breakthrough had been made. Through looking at language with systematic concern to clarify, to define with exactitude, to purge ambiguity and achieve precision, we can get rid of error and more nearly approach truth. (In terms of Wittgenstein II, we can at least play consistent language games and thus avoid unnecessary confusion.) And there can be no doubt that much was accomplished. The trouble with this method was simply that if we seek precision we sacrifice too much. The things that matter in life cannot be expressed with precision. "Clarity is not enough." The questions that can be answered logically and scientifically are but a small part, and not the most interesting and meaningful part, of our lives both public and private. As Immanuel Kant had long ago pointed out, the scientifically knowable is confined to the realm of the phenomenal, that is, the superficial, and if we approach the thing-in-itself, we must use other and far less exact modes of cognition. Perhaps we cannot *know* this realm at all; and yet is it not far too important to give up? Existentialists and Phenomenologists thought so: experience is anterior to words.

This debate, pitting neo-Kantians and Positivists against Idealists and Vitalists, went on in one way or another all through the nineteenth century; in the recent period it has only taken different forms. In the last analysis, the utmost efforts of the rational, clarifying mind cannot get rid of a human insistence on thinking about the unthinkable, because the unthinkable is the essential. Such was the burden of the heaviest charge laid against Analytical philosophy. To which, of course, the reply of sophisticated Analysts was that philosophy can distinguish between the cognitive and the speculative realms clearly, so that at least we know where we are, knowing how much must be metaphysical and how much can be scientifically established.

While the Anglo-Saxon Analysts, standing for common sense, clarity, and pipe-smoking reasonableness, shook wise heads over the incomprehensible roars enamating from Continental Existentialists, even in their own ranks the suspicion spread that life demands more risks than these philosophers were prepared to take. Nothing that ultimately matters is susceptible to logical proof or scientific confirmation, Nathaniel Micklem argued in *The Art of Thought*

(1970), one of many books representing a trend back toward philosophy as everything from which the Positivist and Analytical movement had hoped to rescue it, speculative, imprecise, maundering about with "the great human questions" such as the meaning of the universe, of life, of death. One would have to judge that the Analysts had failed in their larger attempt to straighten out man's muddled thinking and put him at last on the right track. They were able to do this only by so shortening the track that it led nowhere in particular. And their own conclusions pointed to a prominent place for nonscientific, noncognitive modes of thought.

This last trend should be noted. Post-Wittgensteinian Analysis not only showed great respect for the language of everyday life, but became interested in such loose but interesting modes of discourse as history. It no longer tried to impose a scientific vocabulary; rather, it was content to examine and classify the language that people do in fact use in their affairs. Philosophy came back to the richness and diversity of everyday speech. The wheel had come almost full circle. In the beginning Logical Positivists had had a crusading desire to restructure language in order to revolutionize knowledge of the world. In the end they relaxed and floated with the same old irrational human discourse, which, on the whole, now delighted them more than it irritated them.

The Novelist as Philosopher

The abdication of philosophy as a feeder of hungry sheep looking for answers to the Big Questions of life, together with the general decline of religion, had—so it was frequently observed—left the novelist as the leading bearer of values for contemporary man. "In our world today, serious literature has taken the place of religion," James Joyce's brother Stanislaus remarked. Emil Brunner, a distinguished man of religion, agreed: "The novelist in our time has taken the function of the preacher in other times." If fiction is currently the most widely read form of literature, it is also the form on which public attention is likely to focus and where we have had the singular spectacle of really ambitious works reaching the top of the best-seller list: whether by a Boris Pasternak, a John Barth, an Iris Murdoch, a Henry de Montherlant, or a Günter Grass.

The serious novelists most respected in the immediate postwar years had for the most part made their reputations earlier. It had been a great literary generation. The giants of the Modernist revolution, which had begun around the turn of the century or perhaps a bit earlier, blazed on the public's attention just after World War I, with the authors of *Ulysses, Women in Love,* and *The Counterfeiters* leading a host of others, and continued to light the sky through the 1930s. Joyce climaxed with the incredible *Finnegans Wake* in that decade; D. H. Lawrence, dying prematurely in 1930, left a growing reputation behind. Brecht and Hesse belonged to the same era, up-to-the-minute modern though they seemed as late as the 1960s. Germans and Frenchmen, as much as Americans, still admired Ernest Hemingway and William Faulkner. European writers such as Franz Kafka, Thomas Mann, André Malraux, and André Gide were familiar to all literate men on both sides of the Atlantic. This brilliant crew cast so long a shadow that it obscured its successor, dominating the world of letters years after it had passed its zenith. Its classics were already fifteen to forty years old in 1950, but they were still being discovered with delight by young readers and acknowledged as the modern masterpieces.

Those writers had been "existential," whether or not they knew the meaning of the term. A composite portrait of their themes would show paradox, complexity, struggle for identity and values, a sense of the hopelessness of public things but also of the individual's long fight to win for himself some authentic personality. Germaine Brée and Margaret Guiton wrote of André Gide that "he sees man as a being thrown into the world without any divine guidance or revelation, but with innumerable possibilities of 'becoming.'. . . All Gide's novels present a search for integrity. . . . What Gide describes in his novels is the incongruity of any human being's position." [11] A sceptical awareness of human limitations—we can no longer believe in anything absolutely; we know that man lives by myths, science being no less a myth than religion and Marxism no less an act of faith than Christianity—goes along with a passionate romanticism that will not let the ego give up its promethean demands. In this respect the French artist epitomized his remarkable generation.

After the war existential themes appeared in countless novels, poems, and plays. Of course, the existential "philosophers" themselves often preferred to put their ideas into the form of stories, since a primary article of their creed was a distaste for abstract and inhuman thought, as well as for finished, as opposed to malleable and changing, thought. One must seek Camus's beliefs in such works as *The Plague, The Stranger, The Fall, The Rebel,* and "The Myth of Sisyphus" and Sartre's in part in *The Flies* and *No Exit,* as well as *Nausea* and *The Age of Reason.* "For me," declared Colin Wilson in a typical statement from a self-avowed Existentialist, "the instrument of philosophy is not the huge metaphysical tract, but the personal journal, the case-book—or, best of all, the novel. . . . If an idea cannot be expressed in terms of people, it is a sure sign that it is irrelevant to the real problems of life." In D. H. Lawrence's view, the novel was "the one bright book of life," where we can see man whole, grappling with life in its entirety, not just thinking man but thinking and feeling and *living* man.

In some cases it is difficult to distinguish specifically Existentialist themes from generally pessimistic or antisocial ones. Graham Greene's vision of man's inhumanity to man came to him from somewhat older sources. André Malraux was one of those who were apparently Existentialist without knowing it. Angus Wilson, while preoccupied with moral questions and sufficiently aware of Original Sin, did not admire metaphysical novelists equipped with modernistic attitudes. Iris Murdoch, who wrote a book about Sartre, denied that her novels were philosophical. Violence, bestiality, and predacity haunt the serious modern novel, but why should they not, in the age of Bergen-Belsen and Hiroshima and Vietnam, whether or not there is any philosophy behind them? William Golding's celebrated *Lord of the Flies,* a classic of the fifties, seems to be based on Thomas Hobbes. If "an anguished sense of alienation in a hideous and decomposing world" (the description is of Pablo Neruda, a famous Chilean author) is typical of the modern poet or intellectual, it has been so for at least a century and can hardly be claimed exclusively for Existentialism. Those Germans like Heinrich Böll and Günter Grass who had experienced Hitler and the war had no choice but to find symbols for a grotesque hell. In Hugo Charteris' *The Indian Summer of Gabriel Murray* (1968), we meet a misanthrope who rejects the world and consorts only with wolfhounds and ospreys; the gesture is as old as Byron, though the nuances look to Nietzsche and Lawrence.

But when in John Barth's *End of the Road* (1967) we find a man who cannot believe in his own existence, we may feel ourselves justified in thinking that the hand of Sartre was upon this novelist, who has been tagged as an Absurdist. Then there was the Theater of the Absurd, preoccupied with the collapse of ideology, inauthentic existence, and the problem of communicating. We meet people who have no real identity; we are told that the human situation is basically absurd. A serious religious or metaphysical quest goes along with a suspicion of all formal creeds and dogmas. In Archibald MacLeish's play *JB,* the false comforters include a Marxist and a Freudian along with a Christian, and the solution lies in forgiving God and turning to one's own inward resources ("Blow on the coals of the heart"). In Harold Pinter's plays of the 1950s, a nameless menace blankets life—the *Angst,* or ontological anxiety, of Existentialism.

One lived after all apocalypses. They had happened, and life went on. (Stephen Spender made the point in *The Struggle of the Modern,* 1963.) Armageddon had come in 1914; then there was the Lost Generation; the climax to all history had been greeted in the guise of the Russian Revolution. Hitler's Twilight of the Gods thundered to an end in the agony of World War II. By all reckonings the world should have ended, but it went on. Who could believe any longer either in endings or in Second Comings? One was back with the same old human nature. "I hope and believe that the whole civilized world will be wiped out in the next 100 years or so," wrote Henry Miller. Perhaps it will; perhaps most people would agree with Miller's prediction if not his hope. But when the end might come—in ten years or a hundred—no one could say. Georges Bernanos opined that a civilization, unlike a person, might die and still go on standing." [12] Yet if death had already overtaken European civilization and only a hollow shell survived, the stubborn fact remained that individual life went on. One looked nowhere except at the immediate situation—and at that very closely. Or one simply waited, like the two men in Samuel Beckett's famous play.

The turn away from "ideologies," the feeling of an utter exhaustion of beliefs, the numbness that followed the ghastly apocalypse of World War II were as obvious among the postwar fashions in ideas as was the emergence of Existentialism as a desperate counterassertion of pure life-force, irrationally affirming a will to live in the face of all horrors and all failures. But nothing remained constant in the restless neurasthenia of modern life, and no one theme could possibly impose its rule on the teeming contemporary world. There was to be movement and change. In most respects, the first twelve or fifteen years after 1945, roughly the 1950s, had a different spirit than the 1960s. This contrast is one worth developing as a key to understanding the recent past.

NOTES

1. For a note on withdrawal from publication of books critical of the Soviet Union, and of Trotsky's *Life of Stalin,* see *Partisan Review,* 9, no. 2 (March-April, 1942), 173, editorial note, and George Orwell, letter of May 4, 1946, in vol. IV of his *Collected Essays, Journalism and Letters* (1968), pp. 194-195.

2. Paul Oestreicher, in *The Christian-Marxist Dialogue: An International Symposium* (1969). For another exposition of the thesis that despite Stalinist perversion Soviet Communism *must* be basically good, see G. D. H. Cole, *Europe, Russia, and the Future* (1942).

3. In *Marxism and the Existentialists* (1969), which incorporates essays that were part of the controversy with Sartre, Camus, and Merleau-Ponty about Marxism and Communism in the early 1950s.

4. See his *In the 1930s* (1962).

5. Cited by Toynbee in vol. V, p. 9 of his *A Study of History* (1939).

6. But one should not overlook Jaspers' wide audience, also. In *Karl Jaspers: an Introduction to his Philosophy* (1970), Charles F. Wallraff says that the German editions of Jaspers' works sold nearly one million copies and translations appeared in sixteen languages.

7. *London Times Literary Supplement,* September 29, 1966. Hereafter cited as *TLS.*

8. *L'Etre et le néant* (Paris, 1943), pp. 444-451.

9. Published in the 1920s, Otto's book of this name tried to analyze the non-rational religious feeling that exists in the mind *a priori.*

10. *New Statesman and Nation,* March 10, 1951.

11. *An Age of Fiction; the French Novel from Gide to Camus* (1957), pp. 26-27.

12. In *La Liberté pour quoi faire?* (1953), p. 193.

2

The Conservative Fifties

Political Quietism

The political history of the 1950s reveals clearly enough its conservative bent. Immediately after the war, hopes of total redemption with apocalyptic overtones assisted a leftward trend. The British Labour Party won a victory in 1945, which to its enthusiastic votaries seemed the glorious culmination of a long journey from obscurity to success, to be followed by a happy life forever·afterward under Socialism. But the party was turned out in 1951 amid doubts and perplexities reflected in bitter internal strife, not to regain office until 1964. And when it returned it had silently abandoned most of its socialist program. The debate between the pragmatic Gaitskellites and the fanatical Bevanities produced as an intellectual by-product some interesting excursions into political theory. But internal controversy was about all the Labourites could produce in the 1950s. So unorthodox a writer as Malcolm Lowry remarked of the Labour Party in a 1957 letter that "they don't give a damn what happens to the country. . . . Labour is for the most part unblushingly reactionary." This widely shared disparagement of Labour by intellectuals accompanied a corresponding upgrading of the formerly despised Tories, who now became intellectually most respectable. The one-time indentification of the Conservatives with a bumbling if amiable stupidity and of Labour with intellect ceased to hold. The former party seemed bubbling with ideas; the latter, chained to a rigid and obsolete dogma.

In France, the decade began with the triumph of a rightward-leaning coalition (1952) and ended with Charles de Gaulle's antiparliamentary Fifth Republic. Konrad Adenauer's Christian Democratic Party easily controlled Germany against a Socialist opposition that was becoming increasingly less socialist and had little else to offer. These were the Eisenhower years in the United States. Even in the USSR, Khrushchev presided over a certain relaxation of Stalinist tensions. Retreat from ideological rigidity or fanaticism, whether of the Left or the Right, was characteristic of the 1950s' conservatism.

The young radicals of the 1960s, however, seemed to think that the 1950s were conservative because the American public was browbeaten by Senator Joseph McCarthy and transfixed by an irrational fear of Communism. The enslavement of half of Europe by Stalin, the Red victory in China, and the Communist attack on South Korea were indeed hard to ignore, while shoring up, economically and militarily, a desperately disorganized western Europe seemed sheer necessity. But the initial response to these challenges came from left-of-center governments, from the Democratic Truman administration in the United States enthusiastically backed (or, rather, prodded) by the British Labour government, 1947–1951. Among the conservatives of the fifties, both President de Gaulle and Prime Minister Harold Macmillan tried to unfreeze the Cold War. Midway in the decade, Soviet tanks shot down Hungarian workers in the streets of Budapest, ending forever the credibility of the myth of the Russian Revolution; this disenchantment struck harder at the old Left than it did the Right. John F. Kennedy, a hero of the Left at the time, in the next decade, as President, picked up a gauntlet in southeast Asia that Eisenhower had almost ignored. While obviously having no sympathy with ideological Communism, and firmly committed to realistic policies of armed strength, the conservative politicos of the fifties are not fairly blamed for a hysterical anti-Communism. It was scarcely their style.

European conservatism possessed elements of a high and distinguished intellectual tradition, with a well-formulated set of ideas. Of these ideas, doubtless the one most characteristic feature was a view of man as imperfect and the world as flawed, in sharp opposition to the optimistic perfectionism of the other side. The world, Samuel Coleridge had said, is not a goddess in petticoats; it is the devil in a straitjacket. Like Martin Luther, Machiavelli, Voltaire, Schopenhauer, and Max Weber—a varied group of believers and sceptics and atheists, priests and cynics and scientists, alike only in the keenness of their vision—the typical man of the 1950s believed that the world is the devil in a straitjacket. Arthur Koestler called for "an active fraternity of pessimists" in the postwar years, while George Orwell pointed out that all utopias are swindles. In large measure the 1950s was prepared to live with a view of man as limited, even tragic. To think of him as ever being perfect is grotesque beyond all imagining; we will be lucky if his dreadful deformations do not destroy us. In politics, as Orwell observed, one can never do more than decide which of two evils is the lesser.

Conflict is inherent in the world and will last as long as life exists. Things, if they have any vitality, will bump into each other, and of all things man is the most aggressively power-conscious and ego-driven. He will give up war only if cowed by the threat of superior force. Power is a factor that cannot be exorcised, only regulated; the best hope lies in a balance of power, in accepting and therefore being in a position to limit the use of force. The fanatic who wishes to abolish war is the enemy of peace, since he normally ends by waging "total war for total peace"; attributing war to the abnormal malevolence of a few wicked people, he thinks that by expunging the wicked you can attain the millennium. The utopia of what Hans Morgenthau called "the disappearance of politics altogether" by means of some mechanical device, or by an effort of the will, could only lead human affairs into ever more hopeless confusion.

So the 1950s, by rough comparison with the 1960s, was a sober and realistic time, wary of utopias, fed up with romantic heroism (what relief to be rid of Hitler and finally Stalin!), disenchanted with schemes for the salvation of the world.[1] But it was hardly a complacent era. "Human society is sick and convulsed as never before. . . . Never have frustrations and disloyalties been so widespread. . . . Never have law and order, canon and discipline, come into such world-wide disregard." This was written not in 1968 but in 1956 (in the *Times Literary Supplement,* December 28) and may be taken as a fairly representative rumination of those years. A young Frenchman, as reported in 1952 in the French magazine *NEF* ("*Mal du Siecle*" number), made the typical remark that "our era is an era of Total Anguish. At a time when all the future holds in store is atomic and other catastrophes, a deep gloom pervades our thinking, and the Existentialist doctrines are no mere accident." The 1950s experienced the Korean War, Algeria, the Suez crisis, Senator

McCarthy, Elvis Presley, the first real impact of television, and many other horrors, including the final years of Stalin's rule, the suppression of the Hungarian revolt, the beginning of the war in Vietnam, and above all the making of the hydrogen bomb and of intercontinental missiles to carry it. The decade began with the full, sickening realization that World War II's visions of a postwar paradise, marked by perpetual peace and friendly collaboration between the great powers, would never come to pass. One of the decade's most sensational developments was the revelation of Stalin's enormous crimes, denounced even in the Soviet Union within three years of the death of their perpetrator in 1953. The full and awful extent of Hitler's mass murders also became known. Near the end of the fifties the most widely read book was perhaps Nevil Shute's *On the Beach,* in which everybody perishes horribly from a nuclear war.

Intellectuals lived under the sign of Sartre, scarcely a benign one. While there is a strong tendency to call the English "Movement" poets, with their quiet introspection, typical of the fifties, no one is likely to forget that through it on his way to self-destruction stormed Dylan Thomas, grappling with the darkness within and trying to say the unsayable. Black humor, "beat" writers, and the theater of the absurd enlivened the decade. It will scarcely pass into history as a pleasant one.

It is only by comparison with what followed that the 1950s have come to seem a relatively placid era, dominated by men in gray flannel suits rather than by hairy hippies and as yet largely unacquainted with riots, assassinations, and eternal obscenity. Even its protests were gentle ones: the March to Aldermaston by the Campaign for Nuclear Disarmament, like the slightly later grand trek of American liberals to Alabama, was funereal in comparison with the rock-throwing, police-baiting, fire-bombing style of the mature sixties. The decade of the 1950s tended to believe that it had solved the race problem, started the non-Western world on the road to happiness and prosperity, reorganized Europe as a cooperative community, successfully introduced mass higher education, understood Arnold Toynbee and Father Teilhard de Chardin—those optimistic systematizers—and in various other ways contributed to the welfare of mankind. Despite its tribulations, it was not nearly so drab, miserable, and demoralized, culturally and intellectually speaking, as the 1960s.

Yet the very horror of life made easy answers, such as social reformers offer, seem grotesque. Sartre's analysis showed that the awfulness of the human situation transcends social orders: the endless exploitation of man by man could not possibly be cured by any manipulation of institutions. And, though Sartre chose the extreme Left, something was said in the previous chapter of a conservative, apolitical element in Existentialism, with its characteristic mistrust of ideologies and mass movements. In addition to Albert Camus, Maurice Merleau-Ponty moved away from Communism after an initial flirtation with it. (In France, Communism started with a much larger store of credit in 1945 than in England. It had succeeded in identifying itself not merely with the struggle against Nazi rule but with the traditions and destiny of French culture in quite a unique way. Louis Aragon's *L'Homme Communiste* [vol. I, 1946; vol. II, 1953] could scarcely have been conceived anywhere else.) Appalled by Stalinism, Merleau-Ponty came to believe, as did many others, that the monstrous tyranny ruling the USSR was no mere accidental aberration but inherent in the nature of things.

A profound disenchantment with the results of the Russian Revolution, which had ended in a classical tyranny, drove André Malraux into the arms of General de Gaulle. He was willing to agree that Russia had perverted Communism into Stalinism—but also that Communism had in it certain inclinations toward internal repression and external imperialism.[2] Malraux saw the Russian path as a steadily downward course from 1917 to 1950, as the Soviet Union became increasingly less free and less creative at the same time that it became more heavily policed and more given to the techniques of torture and degradation. To be sure, it became increasingly more affluent as well. "If I ask you, what have you done with our hope?"—the hope that Malraux the Marxist had expressed so memorably in the 1930s, when he fought in Spain by the side of the Russians, rallying the intellectuals to anti-Fascism— Malraux asked an imaginary Stalin in 1949, you can answer easily, by opening the window and pointing to the great industrialized land, buzzing with the noise of factories, now a World Power. An American leader could do no more. Malraux declared a plague on both their houses, in a gesture popular in the immediate postwar years when Europe cringed between the two barbarian superpowers, at the mercy of one or the other, or both. (Martin Heidegger found

America and Russia the same: "the same dreary technological frenzy, the same unrestricted organization of the average man.")

The result of such reflection can be an apolitical reaction, based on disenchantment. One or another power elite inevitably will put the devil in a straitjacket; the wordly realm is an evil realm and the Spirit dwells elsewhere. Historically a radical dualism was always close to Existentialism; thus Nicholas Berdyaev, who saw this world as wholly corrupt, completely divorced from the Kingdom of God. This Manichean or Gnostic radical dualism often issues on the Left in a violent revolutionism. (Herbert Marcuse, the guru of the New Left extremists of later years, preached a Berdyaev-like existential anarchism: hatred of every ruling group, permanent revolt against all authority, and an eschatological vision of a world built upon complete freedom and creativity to arise upon the ruins of the present one.) But if one decides that society is hopelessly incorrigible, political quietism may be the result; with a gesture either of irony or renunciation, one abandons to Caesar what is Caesar's and cultivates exclusively the inner realm of the spirit. Among those who spoke for this view was the greatest poet of the century, William Butler Yeats, who wrote in "A Prayer for My Daughter":

> Considering that, all hatred driven hence,
> The soul recovers radical innocence
> And learns at least that it is self-delighting,
> Self-appeasing, self-affrighting,
> And that its own sweet will is Heaven's will. . . .

Uncommitted Art

The intellectual taste of the 1950s greatly admired those "reactionaries," Yeats, T. S. Eliot, and Evelyn Waugh in England, and François Mauriac and Georges Bernanos in France. The D. H. Lawrence cult flourished mightily. (Violent hater of modern industrial society as Lawrence was, his remedy was no socialist welfare state but more nearly a return to the better traditions of European aristocracy, to the old *noblesse*.) The new writers of the 1950s, standing in the shadows of these giants, had no wish to repudiate them. The British writer John Wain, in his statement for the symposium called *Declaration* (1959), expressed the mood when he explained why "a deliberate, conscious, limited, cautious poetry of experiences, carefully chosen and rationally explored, is inevitable today." British poetry of the fifties, not only Wain's but Donald Davie's and Philip Larkin's, among others, exhibited "intellectualism and sanity." Its tone was quiet, its subjects the simple events of everyday life—births, deaths, love affairs. Larkin's "Church Going," for example, describes visiting old churches:

> And what remains when disbelief has gone?
> Grass, weedy pavement, brambles, buttress, sky,
> A shape less recognisable each week,
> A purpose more obscure.

This "Movement" poetry (a rather nondescript name given to the kind of verse written by Larkin, Davie, Thomas Gunn, and others) was diffident and subjective and highly self-conscious. As Davie has noted, it did not look at the outer world, either joyously or angrily; it examined the poet's own highly complicated state of mind. At its best, it produced superbly subtle verse, memorably articulating private truths, the things that pass between lovers, ideas that flit through our minds—very much a poetry of ideas, a poetry for intellectuals that partly deserved another name given it by puzzled pigeonholers: the school of University Wits. It owed much to the great academician William Empson, as well as something to the very nonacademic Thomas Hardy. It was a sophisticated, very mature kind of expression, technically most competent, its voice assured and yet more than a little faint from the tedium of life. A sadness falls over it: disillusioned love, blocked-up roads, featureless existence, "desire of oblivion" (see Larkin's "Wants"). It lay under the sign of Empson's mordant insight: "The waste remains, the waste remains and kills."

This fiftyish literary attitude, so a younger generation of writers would soon allege, wholly ignored one existential precept: to be committed, or *engagé*. Doris Lessing wrote in the symposium called *Declaration* that "to say, in 1957, that one believes artists should be committed, is to arouse hostility and distrust." Wain and Kingsley Amis were later to be attacked for their above-the-battle languor, their essentially aristocratic withdrawal from the struggle. The fact is that Existentialism looked two ways. It was against inauthenticity, bad faith, phoniness, false attitudes, against the inhuman and abstract. Who was more guilty of all these things than the socialist doctrinaire spouting slogans, talking in -isms, and promoting propagandistic art? If to be committed means joining a chanting mob the true Existentialist wants no part of it. (Raymond Aron recalled that a member of the board of editors of *Les Temps Modernes* wanted all the editors to refrain from joining any political party, which he thought odd coming from the journal of Commitment. Yet it is easy to see the point of this request.) He believes, with Kierkegaard, that the true knight of spirituality is not outwardly different from other men. He is sincere, personal, and low-key. On the other hand, the Sartrean demand for commitment is hardly to be dissociated from Existentialism; the imperative to affirm and act on values, to find oneself by the wager of faith, is a common element in all brands of it.

The debate about commitment was soon to break out in many places. But for the first dozen years or so after the war, the horror of ideology tended to outweigh any felt need to storm the citadels or fly banners. Revolutions, like everything else, belonged to a stodgy past. Editorializing in 1956 on Jack Lindsay's literary Marxism, the *Times Literary Supplement* found the really damning criticism to be "its jaded and frowsty atmosphere, like that of a room that has not been aired for twenty years." In this decade, nothing was more old hat than proselytizing, which took one back to the 1930s. "Since 1946 nobody above the Jehovah's Witnesses has taken this attitude," John Wain wrote in 1954.

The estrangement from politics stands sharply revealed when one looks for any evidence of commitment in the best novels and plays of the 1950s. "There is, and there has been, no Marxist theater in France," Joseph Chiari noted in a 1958 survey of the contemporary French stage bearing the subtitle "Flight from Naturalism." Sartre was unique among French dramatists in his revolutionist affinities, and the one play of his which looked in this direction was not much admired. The German Bertolt Brecht was an international favorite, but his rather unorthodox Marxism was not the reason for his popularity; the medium and not the message attracted people.[3] Personal themes predominated almost entirely. The most successful French playwright, Jean Anouilh, combined dazzling technique with a sometimes black pessimism in which wit and the search for pleasure mask deep human corruption. The later Giraudoux deserted political themes, too. The most discussed theatrical piece of the decade was probably Samuel Beckett's *Waiting for Godot,* the classic Existentialist statement of human forlornness. In Chiari's view, the greatest French drama was written by Henry de Montherlant, who certainly concerned himself with human emotions and personal encounter. The leading movements in painting and sculpture were quiet and personal, nonideological, detached from any social message, and delicately introspective. This describes the Abstract Expressionism associated with Willem de Kooning and Jackson Pollock.

Popular culture simply became more "escapist" in the 1950s. In Germany, for example, home of a great cinematic tradition, the few years just after 1945 produced some interesting movies that sought in the debris of the shattered country to come to grips with the Nazi years; but in the 1950s, the years of the *Wirtschaftswunder,* people wanted to forget about the concentration camps, and films turned bland. So it remained for the 1960s to rediscover the Hitler theme. Italian social neorealism had a certain vogue, especially in the cinema; but it was an anachronism in the sense that Italian cultural and intellectual development had been delayed by the distortions of the Fascist years, and the phase did not last long. Sophia Loren and Gina Lollobrigida achieved far more renown than did Anna Magnani.

In an inquiry into British women's magazines written in the fifties, Geoffrey Gorer found an "incredibly chaste" fiction, featuring romantic stereotypes of an almost Victorian kind: how the heroine caught her Dream Man and lived happily ever after—enough to send the next decade's Liberationists into a fury. The Dream Man had a short haircut, superior height, a becoming diffidence, and a good job. Sheiks, wolves, and exotics were out; the very "straight" heroine was looking for a very "straight" young man with whom she could settle cozily down to children and domesticity. Not only was the issue of "women's liberation" almost totally absent from the fifties, but whenever comment was passed on the matter, its burden usually was that that battle at least was over. "Gone are the days of vigorous feminism and anti-feminism," the eminent British anthropologist E. E. Evans-Pritchard remarked in a 1955 lecture. "Surely these are . . . 'issues which are dead and gone.'" Women had won their rights, it was thought, in the generation of Virginia Woolf and the Pankhursts, and little remained to be done.

If one seeks anything in the nature of a significant political novelist in England, one comes up against C. P. Snow, a striking figure, who alone wrote realistically and from the vantage point of an insider about political processes in the very Corridors of Power. But the exception almost proves the rule, for Snow was said by critics and most other novelists to be either no novelist at all or a very bad one. F. R. Leavis attacked him violently as a philistine and a materialist, while Snow charged virtually the entire modern literary establishment with being "intellectual Luddites" for neglecting science. (See chapter 7.)

The shadow of what Doris Lessing—herself a writer trying to be more social and "committed" than was fashionable in the fifties—called "the dreadful lifeless products of socialist realism" lay across this generation of writers, who had grown up between the wars, had read too much propaganda, had watched both Joseph Goebbels and A. A. Zhdanov, Nazis and Communists, destroy art by yoking it to political expediency. The next generation protested against this esthetic quietism. But these young writers of the 1960s themselves were at first most hesitant about opting for anything so crude as political propaganda.

That American literary phenomenon of the fifties, the "Beat Generation," largely conformed to the nonpolitical and essentially quietist pattern. The Beats howled against their society, which they looked upon as "crazy" (absurd), but they were neither violent nor doctrinaire. They organized no protests, stoned no policemen, burnt no college buildings; they fled, childlike, to sex and drugs and what they fondly conceived to be the wilderness. They studied "Plotinus Poe St. John of the Cross telepathy and bop kabbala . . . ," in which respect they prefigured the flower children and hippies of slightly later vintage. The spirit of Zen hovered over them as they pursued inner tranquility and peace of mind less with pills than with philosophy. They had given up working, presumably because in affluent America one could always somehow scrounge enough money to live, but like Alan Sillitoe's young British proletarians they sought escape from a life-destroying culture in rambling, booze, and girls. In a strangely naive way they discovered America for the first time, almost three-quarters of a century after the real frontier had disappeared, visiting such places as Iowa and Arizona as if they were Shangri-la—surely a triumph of the imagination. At the time, European writers were usually shocked by the crudities of Beat, whose writers, like Jack Kerouac and Allen Ginsberg, began the degenerate drift toward porn and pot. Two decades later, Beatniks looked like the gentlest of mystics, not always very good poets but authentic human beings, waiting for God in the manner of Beckett, rejoicing in the small and real things of life (in their very different way) quite as much as Larkin.

To take but one more example, the widely read, semiautobiographical novels of the American Mary McCarthy reflected a savage disenchantment with the naive, muddle-headed left-wing liberals, vintage 1930s, among whom she had spent her youth and against whom she now turned bitterly. While crusading for various simplistic public causes, they had shamelessly neglected the real arts of living, and their private lives were a disgrace. A greater interest in private living was assuredly one cause of the turn away from politics, along with the souring of various political dreams. If, as reported in 1952 (*NEF* issue), "Outside the Communists, French youth is almost totally disinterested in politics today," the reason was not entirely, as was later argued, simple numbness and "complacency." It was a shifting of stress from the public to the personal, from the external to the internal. To know how to love was conceivably not less important than to "change the world," and a good deal more feasible.

The elimination of ideas—the virtual elimination of thought or intellect—was the goal of one of the most striking postwar "movements," *chosisme,* associated especially with novelist Alain Robbe-Grillet as well as with a number of other brilliant *nouveau roman* writers, Germans as well as French. Things are to be treated at face value, not seen as symbols of anything or as part of any scheme or system. "The *chosiste* accepts the surface, the apparent, the superficial as the real—without any compulsion to explain it," as Wylie Sypher observed. The object is hermetic in its own right: "let the earth be the earth." "We no longer believe in depth," proclaimed Robbe-Grillet. Allegedly a sister of Phenomenology, *chosisme* also resembled Bertrand Russell's logical atomism, or William James' radical empiricism. In literature it was a rejection of Symbolism, which tried to find a reality behind the object, a deeper stream of life to which the intuitive use of language guides us. There is nothing deeper. We come down to pure sensation, all "interpretation" being mistrusted for having failed. Artists have always responded to the concrete object, and writers have rejoiced in describing pure sensation; but these modernists made a point of saying that the surficial is everything. Gertrude Stein had already said it: a rose is a rose is a rose. A rose is no longer a symbol of beauty and love, or a part of the chain of being, or God's creation, or anything else except just a rose. *Chosisme* may have been a confused philosophy that was not consistently practiced by its self-advertised devotees, but it was significant of a contemporary mood in its determination to do away with the conceptual and the intellectual and to find no meaning at all in things beyond the fact of their own brute existence. In a sense existential, it was totally nonpolitical, expressing the utmost hatred of ideologies and public themes.

Quite a different sort of literature came from the writers whose apotheosis in Britain dates, it is agreed, from John Osborne's play *Look Back in Anger* (1956). In their mood of protest, with its overtones of violence and nihilism, the young "angries" were a herald of the stormy 1960s; but in the case of Osborne and most of his cohorts, that protest was principally rhetorical. To regard their railing at the world as anything other than infantile temper fits might be difficult, and yet it had a strange power and fascination. Some of them were rather authentically working class. While there had been much talk about "proletarian realism" in the 1930s, hardly any novels of the genre had been written by genuine proletarians, and even fewer could claim much affinity with art. Now, such writers as Alan Sillitoe took one persuasively inside a real world of nonwinners. And these characters were proletarians without illusions. Hating the factory, hating the bosses, they wished only to flee after hours to drink and women. They were delinquents, toughs, whose chief delight was in escaping military service, avoiding taxes, outwitting the cops. The Borstal-boy hero of *The Loneliness of the Long Distance Runner* loses the race on purpose just to spite the authorities. At the end of *Saturday Night and Sunday Morning,* the central figure seems to be on the verge of becoming less a drop-out and more of a citizen; but his only coherent ideal is a vague kind of "pastoral anarchism," which sends him out to the country in search of a village communitarianism. For all we know this vigorous young worker, having sown his wild oats, will now himself "make it" and move up to the world of bosses—"the big wide world hasn't heard from you yet, not by a long way, though it won't be long now." Perhaps he will join John Braine's aggressive poor-boy-on-the-make to find some Room at the Top. Certainly this authentically proletarian writer shows us a tough-minded world, where no ideals or revolutionary dreams exist; a sad, sick world, with no joy in work and little dignity in life, against which the vital exuberance of youth sounds an angry but aimless protest. The Sillitoe approach implied the theme of disenchantment with socialist and Communist ideals, insofar as the real working class had ever much responded to those ideals (at all times, arguably, they appealed primarily to distraught bourgeois intellectuals whom the "proletarians" instinctively mistrusted). Later, though he grew more quietly reflective in some of his work, Sillitoe found a real social cause in the Algerian war.

Trends in Political Thought

A revival of conservatism took place during these years in political, as well as in esthetic and philosophical, thought. The conservatism of Burke and Bonald, pragmatic and tough-minded, suspicious of cure-alls and aware of the devil's straitjacket, was, above all, contemptuous of what Michael J. Oakeshott called Rationalism in Politics:[4] theoretical structures, dreams and schemes, visionary nostrums.

Oakeshott's conservative political philosophy was in certain ways highly congenial to the mood of the hour. If Existentialism means letting each person do his own thing so far as possible without interference from others, Oakeshott supported it enthusiastically. The purpose of government is not to impose beliefs on citizens, "not to tutor or educate them, not to make them better or happier in another way, not to direct them, to galvanize them into action. . . ." Its office is to take people as they are and adjust the collisions between them to a minimum by the fine art of politics. This is a politics of repair, which draws on knowledge much more practical than technical. It does not try to ascertain by speculative thought what the good society is and steer toward that goal. Politics is an art unsuitable to the wild and impatient young. Oakeshott did not at all wish to deny the right of young folk to be wild and impatient and energetic and creative; he hoped they would be. But he saw government as rightly an impartial umpire enforcing the rules on everybody, a sanhedrin of the wise seeing to it that as little damage as possible is done to the body social by the diversity of wills and energies within it. In this respect his was an authentic historic conservatism, drawing on the thought of the master, Edmund Burke, who had said that the end of government is "to follow, not to force, the public indication; to give a direction, a form, a technical dress, and a specific sanction to the general sense of the community"—whatever that general sense might be. This particular utopia appeared to rely on the premise that all these energies will be discharged outside of politics; that is, that people, while being creative and energetic, will be content to leave to the umpires a monopoly of political power. The citizenry will act, and the government will adjust—the assumption being that the two are separate and different.

Intellectuals, novelists, and philosophers of the 1950s tended, then, to conservatism. Distaste for ideology and fanaticism combined with a number of distinct doctrines—the Analytical return to plain language, the Existentialist concern for purely personal experience—to produce this effect. The emotional numbness of the times also contributed to the mood; men who had nothing to hope for and not much more to fear waited stoically for the nuclear bang that might at any moment end it all. Even if one wanted to believe in a cause, what was there left to believe in? Or to oppose? Under such conditions men are likely to return to the common modes of existence shared by all men in their everyday lives. Oakeshott stood in the great shadow of Edmund Burke—whom almost everyone now praised—when he deferred to that which has grown and established itself on our soil over a period of time, valuing it above that which is invented and consciously planned.

The intellectual conservatism of the 1950s was highly sophisticated and literate. George Santayana grew very popular at this time:[5] his free-thinking scepticism ranged over the whole human experience and chose to embrace the orthodoxies rather than the heresies. Situated as far as possible from that naive acceptance of things as they are and from that antiintellectual hatred of all questioning which so often pass for conservatism, the so-called new conservatism knew all thinkers and chose as the wisest not passionate and ignorant rebels but the godly mild and worldly wise, the disenchanted, or those angry beyond the reach of utopian gimmicks, those who had plumbed the depths of human corruption. To the oft-repeated claim of the radicals that the greater minds have always been on the Left, the new conservatism answered, "Not so." Just as Plato had been greater than the Sophists, and Swift greater than the Deists, so Burke far outweighed Tom Paine, and Marx was as nothing compared to Nietzsche. The modern giants, from John Ruskin to William Butler Yeats, were all reactionaries. The Left was peopled with clumsy propagandists and social engineers; its mentality was externalized and shallow.

The waxing influence of conservatism in the fifties was reflected in a qualified return to classical economic principles. The "new economics" of Maynard Keynes—product of Bloomsbury alienation—may have ruled the forties and enjoyed a vogue into the postwar years. But rearguard resistance to it was both valiant and effective. In 1947 a distinguished fraternity of economists including Austria's embattled Friedrich A. Hayek, Britain's Lionel Robbins, France's Bertrand Jouvenel, and America's Milton Friedman gathered at Pilgrim Mountain in Switzerland to reaffirm their faith in free markets. At a time when the jargon of the welfare state and "planned production" was on nearly everyone's lips and Adam Smith was a dirty word, this international elite dared to argue that the private entrepreneur in a competitive society is the best bet to increase wealth and distribute it equitably. The market regulates the economy—charging nothing for the service—better than any bureaucrat can do, imposing its discipline, penalizing inefficiency, directing capital into those channels which are profitable because most in demand. Such were the beliefs of many of the world's best economic brains in the 1950s. Germany's unbelievably rapid recovery from what was once regarded as irretrievable ruin (in 1945 the opinion was widespread that it would take at least a century to rebuild that war-shattered country) was achieved by free enterprise capitalism, as, indeed, was the impressive success of the whole European Community area and Spain. The policies of Ludwig Erhard in Germany, Luigi Einaudi in Italy, Jacques Rueff in France, and Wilhelm Röpke in Switzerland reflected the influence of these ideas. (The free market saved the dictatorship of Franco in

Spain. The Caudillo was in severe difficulties in the 1950s, not so much because the Spanish people yearned for liberty as because the economy was nearly wrecked by an excess of statism. International experts recommended liberalization, the Generalissimo gave in reluctantly, and the economy immediately took off on Spain's version of an "economic miracle.")

The whole pressure of Western social life might be toward that "mighty invasion of economic life by government" which had begun about 1880 and which was accelerated by the two world wars and by the great depression of the 1930s: Documents such as the *Beveridge Report* (1942) in Britain made that invasion a solemn goal of public policy right after the war. Assuredly the welfare state fattened from year to year. Many observers defended it and asked for more. But wherever free enterprise was drastically curbed or abolished, economic disaster resulted; wherever it was given a reasonably free rein, the economy boomed. The British Labour Party and the European socialists temporarily abandoned their doctrine of government ownership. In the 1950s even the Russians seemed to be moving toward a decentralized and competitive economy; certainly the erstwhile Communists in Yugoslavia were. In Czechoslovakia, Ota Sik—a man who had long been a fanatical Communist—was enticing his fellow Party members toward a market economy when the Russians cracked down in 1968. (See his book *Plan and Market under Socialism.*)

This kind of conservatism was in fact classical liberalism, a persuasion that had emerged in the early nineteenth century to sweep everything before it in the heyday of the Political Economists. It then became the favorite whipping boy of every twentieth-century liberal from the early years of the century when the doctrines of the new liberalism of the welfare state and the planned economy began to thrive all over the Western world, down to the present. It was ridiculed, flayed, and left for dead by the generation of economic reformers who experienced and tinkered with the great depression of the 1930s. Yet the free enterprise economy still survived, in theory as in fact. The truisms of Adam Smith remained true, at least in the eyes of the economists of the new conservatism: the market mechanism with its flywheel of self-interest seemed still the best means of attaining wealth. Modify it we may, but to attempt to replace it as the basic economic system leads every time to failure and to tyranny. Though a sophisticated brand of socialism flourished in advanced technological societies such as the Scandinavian countries, it proved unsatisfactory as a strategy for economically underdeveloped ones. Certainly the record of countries which, one after another, adopted some form of socialism and plunged dismally into corruption, dictatorship, stagnation, and general economic messiness was a marvelous feature of the postwar world. Such a list would include not only the countries of eastern Europe but many in Africa, Asia, and South America as well. It would embrace countries blessed with wealth and untroubled by civil strife, whose only apparent reason for failure was an unerring instinct for this wrong choice of economic policies—countries like Burma, Ghana, Cuba, Indonesia. And gradually the wiser of the "developing" peoples came to realize the awful truth, to understand they had been gulled by socialist slogans, and to adopt free-market, capitalistic policies. Its funeral pronounced time and again by socialist orators, capitalism lived to bury its would-be pallbearers. Such at least was the not-implausible reading of world economic history by conservatives.

Whether of a free enterprise or judiciously "mixed" nature, the economic policies of the 1950s for the most part yielded prosperity in the West and hence fostered a sense of optimism. At least in the economic sphere, it seemed real progress could be claimed: the economic stagnation of the prewar years had been overcome without the imposition of excessive statism of the Stalinist variety. In Britain the socialists were stunned to see Tories presiding over economic recovery. The leading economic topic of the decade was "growth," along with the "mixed economy" and the "industrial society," whose rules were, after all, not very relevant to the old socialist-free enterprise debate.

The concern about economic growth, which gave rise to so many books in the 1950s, including W. W. Rostow's famous *Non-Communist Manifesto,* vanished almost entirely as a popular public interest in the 1960s. No one wanted to grow any more; one even wanted to contract. In few other areas is the contrast between the first two postwar decades so striking as in their relative attitudes toward economic development. In the relatively optimistic fifties, European countries were recovering from the long drought of the thirties and the years of wartime austerity and postwar trauma, and affluence had not yet palled. The "economic miracle" of the decade in Germany, in France, in Britain, in Italy, even eventually in Spain, appeared as one of man's greatest achievements of all time. The abruptness of the change from celebration of *Wirtschaftswunder* in the fifties to bitter complaint about the overdeveloped society in the next decade was indeed remarkable.

In the 1950s even those who considered themselves "liberals" recognized the regnancy of conservatism. Lionel Trilling, in *The Liberal Imagination,* paused to note that modern European literature is dominated by "men who are indifferent to, or even hostile to, the traditions of democratic liberalism as we know it," by "reactionaries," such as Yeats, Eliot, Proust, Joyce, Lawrence, and Gide. He could have added Ezra Pound, Wyndham Lewis, François Mauriac, Graham Greene, Evelyn Waugh, and any number of others. André Malraux ended his long revolutionary odyssey as an adherent of General Charles de Gaulle, who was backed by a considerable majority of other major French intellectuals.

The Gaullist mystique was, however, conservatism of a very complex sort. It embraced a sophisticated disdain for simplistic solutions, an awareness of the realities of political power, and a willingness to accept authority, as relief from anomie, that was tempered with a fear of absolute power. It was beyond both democracy and totalitarianism. With the gravity and dignity of his remarkable personality, de Gaulle dared to challenge many of the liberal bromides of his opposition. Amid a general disapproval of nationalism (the received liberal gospel was the City of Man, the United Nations, One World), he pointed out that historical tradition, conveyed through the national culture, gives us such civilization as we have. And in regard to the developing countries, he was a better prophet than the progressives; nationalism did, after all, appeal to the peoples of the Third World. Nationalism is antiimperialist: the assertion of one's own national dignity implies the right of other peoples to the same dignity. Willing to preside over the liquidation of the French Empire, de Gaulle skillfully carried out the enormously difficult job of withdrawing from Algeria, a task that involved the interests and passions of more than a million Frenchmen living there. If in the ensuing decade he lost all patience with Anglo-Saxons, it was because he saw them blundering, out of an inability to understand the realities of power, into unnecessary wars.

"Life is a combat," General de Gaulle believed. "To make

yourself powerless is to invite attack," George Orwell noted. "If you throw away your weapons, some less scrupulous person will pick them up." A Gnostic rejection of the realm of power in favor of some ideal perfectionism was repugnant to the conservatives of the 1950s. We shall not, in this world, avoid entanglement in the painful process of living. "On balance life is suffering, and only the very young or the very foolish imagine otherwise," Orwell added in his essay "Lear, Tolstoy, and the Fool." Reinhold Niebuhr made the same point against the Christian pacifists of the 1930s, of whom few were left in the 1950s (though they would spring up again like mushrooms a decade later): become a saint if you will, but do not imagine you are thereby solving the world's problems, for a responsible attitude towards them requires accepting the necessity of conflict and even violence. The person who refuses to face this fact gets mankind into worse mischief than he who accepts it. Applying the pacifist remedy, he destroys the equilibrium of power on which peace depends and forces himself and the world into terrible wars that he moralizes as "wars to end wars," which only makes them yet more terrible. Hence, a prudent, realistic acceptance of the necessities of power minimizes the troubles of man.

The Return to Religion

The conservative case, then, seemed to many intellectuals of the 1950s to be invincible. Is it plausible, R. G. Collingwood asked, that sixty generations of thinkers have wasted their time, and that ours is the first to find wisdom? Is it rational to suppose that those human dilemmas and tragedies—war, revolution, inequality—for which these sixty generations have vainly sought remedies are now suddenly to be solved and assuaged? Why? Because of our science and technology? This does not touch on the matter at all, the matter being human nature. We cannot apply the techniques of our admittedly successful scientific technology to this domain. The social sciences remain in the same simple-minded state as when Montesquieu first dreamed of Newtonizing human affairs. But Newton himself was now, in the age of Albert Einstein and Max Planck, scientifically obsolete, a fact of which the social scientists seem completely unaware.[6] Positivistic science, with all its "behavioralist" confidence, appeared childish to those thinkers who were most advanced in the 1950s.

Eric Voegelin put the modern liberal intellectual under the glass and found him to be a Gnostic. Translated, this seemed to mean that he was shallow, materialistic, infantile in his knowledge of human nature.[7] In such books as *The Irony of American History,* Reinhold Niebuhr similarly poured scorn on those who were naively optimistic about human prospects, who believed that reason and science could bring man to utopia, who failed to understand that "the whole drama of history is enacted in a frame of meaning too large for human comprehension or management." Historian J. L. Talmon scrutinized the fallacies of "political messianism." Here one could draw on the great Max Weber, humane social scientist, widely regarded as one of the century's leading thinkers (Aron, as well as Jaspers, was a direct disciple): if you cannot endure the dreadful disenchantment of the world, and must have a faith, turn not to some upstart academic prophecy but to the arms of the old religion, still there and waiting to take you back.

The mood of the postwar years did look back to something like traditional religion. The Christian Existentialists were rather more numerous than the Sartrean atheist ones and included not merely Kierkegaard's disciples but Roman Catholics like Gabriel Marcel and the Jewish sage Martin Buber, now an oracle. The Barthian Dialectical Theologians still ruled in European Protestant circles and indeed came into their own in the United States, where no prophets stood higher right after the war than Reinhold Niebuhr and Paul Tillich; Rudolf Bultmann became internationally famous. The courage of some Christians, like the martyred Dietrich Bonhoeffer, in resisting Nazism, and of others in holding out against the Red dictatorships of eastern Europe, gained respect for their creed. Christian political parties burgeoned in Italy, France, and Germany. The writings of Jacques Maritain were highly respected throughout the world. Arnold Toynbee's books of history and Father Teilhard de Chardin's testimony to man's spiritual nature were among other works that seemed to restore old-fashioned religion to intellectual repute. The sceptical Aldous Huxley remarked that Christianity, whether or not it is true in the (trivial) literal sense, happens to be true to the facts of human nature.

In England, the spirit of T. S. Eliot, master of his generation in poetry and criticism, still counted for something. *The Cocktail Party* (1950) fired a parting shot at the triviality of merely mundane existence. Eliot's turn from the acme of Modernism to classicism, royalism, and Anglo-Catholicism was much better understood in the 1950s than it had been in the 1920s, when he made that conversion. A more active propagandist for traditional Anglican Christianity was C. S. Lewis, surrounded by admiring disciples at Oxford and author of those scintillating exercises in modern apologetics, *The Screwtape Letters* (1944) and *Mere Christianity* (1952). Any list of the most persuasive and influential writings of the epoch would have to include his books, along with Reinhold Niebuhr's *Nature and Destiny of Man,* Georges Bernanos' *Diary of a Country Priest,* Albert Schweitzer's testimony of faith, and Henri Daniel-Rops' *History of the Church of Christ.* They exposed the imbecilities, as they saw them, of a generation of liberal-materialist vipers, rejected the fantastic dream of secular progress, and called men back to the salvation of their own souls. All false gods were dead; perhaps, after all, the One True God (as Toynbee called him or it) still lived. The work of the Swiss playwright Friedrich Dürrenmatt, who was considered the greatest German-language dramatist of his era, radiated this concern for love of God as an act of faith in a decaying world—the ethic of Lutheran neoorthodoxy. Philip Larkin's "Church Going" was widely anthologized, perhaps, because of this theme: having lost our belief, and forgotten these old churches, we (modern intellectuals) now go back to them, and, if we cannot really recover the old beliefs, we recognize that something memorable happened here.

> A serious house on serious earth it is,
> In whose blent air all our compulsions meet,
> Are recognized and robed as destinies.
> And that much never can be obsolete. . . .

Or, as Eliot had put it less sceptically in "Little Gidding" (1942, one of the *Four Quartets*):

> We shall not cease from exploration
> And the end of all our exploring
> Will be to arrive where we started
> And know the place for the first time.

Varieties of Conservatism

There were a host of lesser conservatisms. To take one example, in the English novel of the 1950s, the experimental-modernist path of James Joyce and Virginia Woolf was largely abandoned for a more traditional way. Once despised Victorians came back into favor. The fiction of Angus Wilson, L. P. Hartley, William Plomer, Joyce Cary, and other favorites of the serious novel-reading public sometimes exhibited extremely modern ideas, but in rather conventional dress.[8] Hardly less imposing in its influence upon men of letters than the war, Joyce's *Finnegans Wake* stood as an ultimate on the Modernist road, beyond which no one could possibly go. If one were to go on writing novels, all that could be done was to try a different road, which led back toward the feelings and the speech of ordinary men. This literary return to normalcy was a counterpart of tne interest of Linguistic philosophers in explicating the language of everyday life.

As René Remond pointed out in a perceptive study of the French right wing from 1815 to the present, there is more than one kind of "conservatism." Remond found three manifestations of the Right in France. One, typified by Bonapartism and Boulangism—the almost Fascist demagoguery of the Right—is doubtfully classified as conservatism, and was certainly not "in" in the fifties. (De Gaulle's semiauthoritarian Fifth Republic was by no means of this stripe, despite what some of its critics said.) The other two are in many ways the complete opposites of one another. One is an embattled doctrinaire reactionism, the romantic foe of everything modern, clinging to its lost causes and impossible loyalties though the world crumble. In French political terms the adherents of this reactionism were the Ultraroyalists of 1815 (or the ultra-ultras), the Legitimists who retired from the arena rather than touch a politics sullied by compromise. (In a more recent, American, context we have the Goldwater, as opposed to the Rockefeller, Republicans.) The other kind of conservatism is realistic, readily accommodating itself to change; suspicious of all doctrinaire positions, including those of the extreme Right as well as extreme Left; and, in general, as far as possible removed from romantic impossibilism. It cultivates politics as the art of adjustment and appeals to the mature, the nonneurotic, the unimaginative (or at least to those who see politics as the domain *par excellence* which poets and intellectuals should *not* invade). These moderates practice the politics of expediency.

Clearly the disenchanted, beyond-ideologies conservatism of the 1950s bore a closer resemblance to the latter conservative type. Niebuhr, Oakeshott, Orwell, and Aron, and even the poets and novelists looking for concrete, individual realities, made it their reproach against the ideologists of the 1930s that the latter saw the world falsely through a haze of abstract ideas. This criticism of course cut equally well against reactionary doctrinaires. Yet the more purple sort of conservatism was not altogether absent. A total rejection of modern life could be discerned among certain literary men. If Eliot, having fallen under the influence of Charles Maurras' French neoclassicism, wanted to return to the seventeenth century, his reaction was mild as compared with that of D. H. Lawrence, who would return to the American Indians, to the Etruscans, or to those slim naked men from Knossos. "They wrote modern poetry to reject modern life," Stephen Spender said in his study of the Modernists. This is surely the most allowable of all generalizations about them.

We can leave the conservatives of the 1950s knowing that their mood did not last. Like all other fashions in the contemporary world it was condemned to transience. A new generation quickly arose which found this spirit first annoying, then intolerable, and finally incomprehensible. The conservatism of the fifties was followed by the radicalism of the sixties, which may in turn prove quite as ephemeral. John Osborne, the young "angry" of 1956, along with Kingsley Amis and John Braine, finally gravitated to conservatism, never able to appreciate the student revolutionism that followed in the wake of his gesture of protest. It may be that there was much of enduring value in this conservatism. It may be that the intellectual world will return to it. But it was destined for bad times in the ensuing years, when it was excoriated for its lethargy, its elitism, its refusal to choose sides and fight. (The latter option, we may again recall, was thoroughly in tune with the Existentialist ethic.) Fashions changed. The quest for novelty is a dominant theme in the modern world, worthy of being discussed separately. It condemns any set of attitudes to a short life, a fact of which the writers of the 1950s were themselves aware. In a well-known poem, "Remembering the 'Thirties,'" Donald Davie noted how the scene of just a few years ago can seem like "worlds more remote than Ithaca or Rome." "Are we right," John Wain wondered in 1954 (*Spectator,* March 19), "or will the Sixties think us as silly as we think the Thirties?" He must have known that they would.

NOTES

1. Malcolm Muggeridge on Stalin worship: "The spectacle of all my heroes abasing themselves before a great tyrant, and purporting to justify all his doings and all his works, cured me of hero worship forever." *Jesus Reconsidered* (1969), p. 89. Sidney Hook once pointed out that in fact Stalin's crimes *were* known in the 1930s, but no one believed them; it was the climate of opinion that changed rather than the facts. The allegations were then made by disgruntled foes of the Soviet regime, especially emigré Mensheviks or former Bolsheviks such as Boris Souvarine. In recent years the mantle of professional scholarship has endowed these same facts with authority.

2. See Janine Mossuz, *André Malraux et le Gaullisme* (1970), pp. 107–120.

3. Brecht's esthetic was drawn from the prerevolutionary era; he was a child of early twentieth-century Modernism. His friends and spiritual intimates were people like the poet Vladimir Mayakovsky, who committed suicide when he found that the revolutionary state of Lenin and Stalin was no place for a poet. Brecht was singular in that after long consideration he buried his repugnance for the USSR and determined to serve it at whatever cost. For some light on this subject see John Fuegi, "The Soviet Union and Brecht: The Exile's Choice," in *Brecht Heute* (1972).

4. See the collection of his essays bearing this title (1962).

5. A front-page review of Santayana's *Letters* (edited by Daniel Cory) in *TLS,* May 18, 1956, spoke of those who "feel they can never have too much of Santayana's writing. . . . A precious additional witness to the comprehensiveness of his sympathy and his intellectual and moral integrity."

6. See Floyd W. Matson, *The Broken Image: Man, Science, and Society* (1964).

7. See, for example, Eric Voegelin, *The New Science of Politics* (1952), an attack on positivism.

8. This theme is developed in Rubin Rabinovitz, *The Reaction against Experiment in the English Novel 1950–1960* (1967).

3

The Radical Sixties

Toward a New Politics

The quiet privatism of the 1950s was followed by the social and political militancy of the 1960s. For this startling change, some well-worn explanations seem plainly inadequate. Certainly it had nothing much to do with the Vietnam War, which the militants later adopted as a handy vehicle for their programs, for the turn toward radicalism preceded the Tonkin Gulf episode and was taken by people who neither knew nor cared much about Vietnam. Why did the Korean War of the early 1950s, so like the Vietnam crusade of the next decade, lead to comparatively little international protest? Oracles who denounced the latter war as a crime had hailed the former one as a triumph for collective security. In the last years of the 1950s bitter charges were exchanged between the government and a pacifist Left as the Algerian conflict threatened to radicalize France; but the successful mediation of that war contributed no little to the prestige of the grand conservative, Charles de Gaulle. If one seeks the answer in political factors, a more plausible case can be made for success than for failure: the long years of economic "growth" and prosperity had given rise to general boredom, leading restless professors to complain that students were apathetic and to try to stir them up. Astonishing though it may seem to some, the angry young men of the late fifties were demonstrably made angry by affluence and the complacence that issued from it.

The simplest explanation for the leftward swing in the sixties is that it was the result of pure reaction, a generational revolt. By a law of chance endemic in the modern situation, what gives one era its *frissons* is sure to nauseate the next; this cycle progresses in ever shorter time intervals as the pace of life constantly accelerates. Thus, the phenomenon can be placed in a long history of similar oscillations.

For the past two centuries intellectuals have swung wildly between the fervent desire to reject politics and the violent desire to revolutionize it. The two impulses are not as contradictory as they seem, since the denominator common to both of them is a sense of alienation from the existing world as reflected by political practice. Unable to accept that world, the intellectuals in their independent realm have alternated between peaceful secession from, and war against, the enemy. At times they withdraw into the ivory tower— give me the highest one possible, cried Flaubert—of scholarship or art or religion, and from there they cast disdainful glances at the disgraceful scenes below and store up treasures against a better day. But after a time boredom ensues, the pervasive ennui of modern life returns, and the mob below increasingly threatens their peace of mind. The temptation to conduct raids into enemy territory grows. And those who have busied themselves in the tower with visions of an ideal society think they see a chance to perform the grandest tour de force of all, by conquering the enemy and imposing on him terms of total victory.

Such tides of political taste can be traced quite clearly through the history of the past two centuries. At the end of the eighteenth century, Chateaubriand's generation, disillusioned with the French Revolution, invented esthetic romanticism as a mode of escape; Victor Hugo's generation returned to the revolutionary mystique, only to suffer extreme disenchantment in the trauma of 1848 and to withdraw, with Flaubert, into the tower. Then Zola and the Naturalists came back to some degree of involvement in society, writing about the lower orders, throwing themselves into the Dreyfus affair. The 1920s were again cynical and disengaged; the 1930s, Communist and committed. The temptation to return in some violent and spectacular way to the political arena has been intermittently as strong as the instinct to shake free from a hopelessly corrupted world.

The men who dominated the literature and thought of the 1950s had for the most part experienced the 1930s and the war in their maturity; they had seen too much of political fanaticism and violence, and could believe in fairies no longer. But by the end of the

1950s a new generation had arisen which knew not Josef. It had not fought in the war or known the experiences which shaped the mind of the previous generation. It was angry with passivity and resignation, with quiet despair, with purely interiorized angst, with cynicism and detachment.

If the revolt was in some respects a phase of this cycle from detachment to activism, it was also deeply affected by all sorts of special circumstances. Those in England who led the revolt of the fifties' "angries," which moved on into violent "militants" of the later sixties, were products not of the old high Oxonian culture but of the new cinder-block or plate-glass universities. Mass education had begun filling the once sequestered seats of learning with hordes of students and of young "teachers" who represented a new kind of intellectual proletariat. In all the countries of western Europe, and indeed all over the world, the educational explosion produced immense numbers of university students (Japan, for example, had 700,000). They were likely to be more interested in sociology than the classics, in Marx than in Plato; the Mills they knew was more likely to be C. Wright than James and John Stuart. Their frequently brand-new institutions were prone to rather drastic experiments in the restructuring of knowledge and were inclined to a defiant consciousness of their radicalism. These universities were often overcrowded, leaving students with a sense of alienation from the huge educational bureaucracy, victims of modern anomie in the very home of the spirit. For all sorts of reasons the suddenly swollen centers of higher or not so high education became hotbeds of ecstatic or sullen revolutionism.

Pretty clearly, too, political extremism fattened on the demise of significant and exciting political issues and personalities in the established arena of public life. The great personalities left politics; the Churchills and Adenauers bowed out, and the last grand figure resigned in France in 1968 after seemingly outliving his time. Stalin and Hitler had been charismatic, if evil; there were now not even any personable villains. In the Soviet Union the path from Stalin through Khrushchev to Brezhnev led from grandeur to mediocrity. Faceless men took over in the Western democracies, and political parties ceased to represent any detectable differences in ideology. The political romanticism of the extreme Left, inventing revolutionary heroes and seeing apocalyptic significance in every local issue, waxed in exact proportion as public life on the national scale waned. Around 1962 a neoromantic cult of youth grew up around John F. Kennedy in the United States and Harold Wilson in England. Even the aging de Gaulle basked in its reflected light as he slew a degenerate parliamentarianism and solved major problems by vigorous leadership. When these idols faded, there followed the cults of Fidel Castro, of Ché Guevara, of Mao Tse-tung.

The New Left dates approximately from the discrediting of the Soviet Union and its official brand of Communism that followed from the Russian suppression of Hungarian freedom in 1956. The Twentieth Party Congress of 1956, at which Khrushchev revealed in considerable detail the monstrous crimes of Stalin, had sent a shock through the Communist world; it was followed within the Soviet Union by a brief interlude of domestic relaxation and at least anticipated freedoms, while abroad prominent Communist voices, including those of George Lukács and Palmiro Togliatti, issued calls to "break energetically with the [Stalinist] past." But after threats of Communist collapse in Poland and Hungary, the Soviets reverted to Stalinism. The Russian intervention in Hungary led to pandemonium among Communists everywhere. There were mass resignations from the Party, defection of veteran leaders, and anguish in the hearts of simple souls who had never before doubted the shining righteousness of the Workers' State. (See Arnold Wesker's *Chicken Soup with Barley.*) The purity of the Russian revolutionary myth had vanished forever; not even the most radical innocence could ever believe in it implicitly again. The Czechoslovakian intervention of 1968 only confirmed the horror of 1956. Not even the best-intentioned Bolshevik could break with the strategy of terror, and the terror was no longer associated with any goal that could possibly justify it.

But the release of the Left from the rigidity of the old patterns was a stimulus, allowing it to seek all kinds of new expression. This coincided not only with the emergence of Chinese and Cuban brands of Communism, but with Existentialist trends as presented by neo-Marxists who, like Sartre or the Germans Ernst Bloch and Theodor W. Adorno, offered freer, more voluntarist, less dogmatic revolutionary attitudes. The Vatican lifted its ban on socialism (1961), and varieties of "Christian Communism" made their tentative appearances. The dialogue between Communism and Christianity began. All was again glorious ferment on the Left; no Stalinist monolith monopolized everything with its tedious scholasticism and its tyrannical discipline. From even the Slavic Communist world came new voices—Yugoslav and Polish revisionists—and, as a bonus, a new Marx emerged from the unpublished writings of the old.

And so in the New Left—or, within a few years, the Newer Left—there was little unity. The movement was composed of numerous and even contradictory elements. It had no one ideology, though it shared generously in the dislike of abstract systems characteristic of Existentialist attitudes. Much of it rebelled against orthodox Communism and traditional Marxism, both of which it hated almost as much as it hated capitalism. It was an amalgam of alienated attitudes ranging from those of hipsters and addicts and pornographers to those of neo-Communists and anarchists and millenarian utopists. In the early 1970s this mixture was represented by the *gauchistes* of France, who stood well to the left of the now quite staid Communist Party with which they quarrelled violently and were bound together only by their position on the extreme left. They themselves were divided into numerous factions calling themselves neo-Trotskyites, Maoists, Anarchists, and International Idiots.

Some of the earlier quakes were much milder. Hans Magnus Enzensberger and his generation of new German writers provide a parallel so close to the English as to suggest plagiarism; but the evidence strongly suggests an independent development in both countries, stemming from similar causes. Enzensberger emerged rather spectacularly as a poet in 1957. He was specifically influenced by Brecht rather than Sartre, and he reacted against Benn rather than Eliot. The symptoms of his malaise were much the same as Osborne's: generalized anger, a desire to be abrasive (to be sand in the world's machinery, not oil, as one of the Germans said), a yearning for political commitment combined with an uncertainty as to just what party to embrace—indeed, a revulsion against parties and screeds, mingled with an even greater revulsion against the simpering world of exquisite private monologues.

The word *Establishment* suggests the vagueness of the enemy. Kenneth Tynan, the influential drama critic who cried for "engagement" and for political themes in art, called also for satire. In a notable debate, he broke a lance with Eugene Ionesco on this score; the celebrated Absurdist rejected the call to political ideology as artistically pernicious. In 1960 four irreverent and talented young men from Cambridge opened a satirical theatrical review called *Beyond the Fringe,* which received much acclaim in London and later moved on to a successful American tour. A spin-off of that review was the nightclub called The Establishment, which became an early 1960s mecca for fashionable bohemia. It was eventually to degenerate into just another tourist attraction in what for a time was "swinging London," swank and sexy. The magazine *Private Eye,* which specialized in insulting politicians, was another part of the Fringe complex; the Profumo scandal became grist for its mill, and for a time during this gamey affair of cabinet ministers and callgirls its circulation shot up. (The Profumo affair was to help bring down the Macmillan Cabinet in 1964, end thirteen years of Conservative government, and usher in six years of Labour ascendancy.)

The type of satire offered by this group was always slipshod and on the verge of being meretricious, though at times it was amusing and brilliant. Like precocious infants, its practitioners stuck out malicious tongues at everything: religion, the royal family, Parliament, the government, sexual inhibitions, the Establishment—a word now expressive of all the vague resentments against nearly everybody except oneself. For the most part savage rather than subtle (though its wrappings were slick), often wildly inaccurate, unfair, and even philistine (it did not spare writers, thinkers, artists, if they had become successful and therefore by definition a part of the Establishment), *Beyond the Fringe* played to the gallery and was inevitably transmuted into a television program. At least "That Was the Week That Was" owed much to the inspiration of The Establishment-*Beyond The Fringe-Private Eye* complex. For two or three years this weekly program and its successor offered the intriguing spectacle of the Establishment BBC promoting a successful anti-Establishment routine. The entire nation seemed to have adopted an adolescent irreverence, accompanied by much off-color humor, toward anything and everything. It was a satire fad, and like all fads, it soon faded, though a certain type of sick humor survived.[1] Still, it belongs somewhere in the saga of the New Left revolution. It tore down the last of the great English monuments and reticences and respects—a change indeed from the heroic resolve and national discipline, not only of the wartime "finest hour," but also of the immediate postwar years. This sort of *incivisme* was certainly new to the English, if not the French.

As befitted the more serious traditions of the radicals, the *New Left Review* (1959–   ) was much more sober than *Private Eye.* (*Studies on the Left* appeared in the U.S. at this same time.) But it abandoned dogmatic Marxism and was disenchanted with the welfare state; it was less interested in wages than in culture; it flirted with Existentialism, even with sex. It seemed more appalled by affluence than by poverty—an entirely new attitude on the left. It faintly foreshadowed the impending conversion of revolutionary into hippie, little though its leaders—writers like Raymond Williams— resembled hippies. It foreshadowed the decay of the old non-Communist, though often fellow-travelling Left—socialist, serious, "square"—that was represented in Britain by the *New Statesman* and in the United States by *The New Republic,* organs which have now become hollow shells of their once great selves.

Trends in specific political attitudes changed sharply from the late forties and fifties to the sixties. It was fashionable in the former period to regard American resistance to Soviet power and to Communism as salutary and progressive. The Marshall Plan and the Truman Doctrine won enthusiastic liberal approval. When the mood changed, these Cold War maneuvers were viewed as reactionary. Political thought had revolved in a perfect circle. Before 1914, and again, even more vociferously, before 1940, earnest students led by professors and clergymen had vowed " *Nie wieder krieg*" as they cursed the flag and presented pacifist plays. They were less violent in their nonviolence than the later harvest of young righteousness, but no less active and earnest. The peak of the between-the-wars antiwar movement came about 1933–1936, when pacifist sentiment could be found on every college campus. After 1936 doubts began to grow about the wisdom of nonresistance in the face of the Fascist evil, and between 1939 and 1941 virtually everyone thought that the lesson that fear of war leads to blackmail by the wicked, ending in slavery, had been forever learned. Eloquent tracts poured from every press bearing the message that war is *not* the greatest evil and that only idiots think it is. (A popular leftist book recounting the fallacies of the American isolationists bore the title *The Illustrious Dunderheads.*) In the 1950s men sternly pointed to the realities of power. Books about power, books called *The New Leviathan* and *The Machiavellians,* books noting the pitfalls of political utopianism, the inevitable flaws of the United Nations, and the multitudes of half-baked sentimentalisms in world affairs flowed from the presses. Hobbes and Machiavelli were in; Woodrow Wilson and Wendell Willkie were out. The people who supported this realist position had seen pacifism lead the world to the brink of disaster in the 1930s by exposing it to the blackmail of Hitler; then they had watched a set of similar illusions about Stalin almost throw away the fruits of the bloody struggle against Nazism. They came to rest on a grimly or soberly realistic belief in balance of power: "containment," tough-minded resistance to the rival.

But in the next decade *Cold War* became a dirty word, power was pornographic, and back came the Oxford Oath mentality of the early 1930s, when youth vowed never to fight again. The lesson of appeasement had been learned so thoroughly that it took nearly a decade and a half to be forgotten. The peace movement returned; the flag was once more desecrated as draft cards were burned and pacifist plays presented. Bertrand Russell began by advocating preventive war and ended a supporter of nuclear disarmament.[2]

Ideologists of the New Left

The thought of the new revolutionaries often seemed something less than profound. The movement mingled with the new barbarism of the hippies. The student rebels threw themselves into the cause with all the exuberance and the unsubtlety of youth. "We revel in being young and despite the great British, Italian, French and German publics, we are going to have a riot," one of them (Harriet Crawley) wrote. Such was the spirit. The term "day nursery of revolution" was used by David Martin, a sociologist at the London School of Economics, who as such possessed a rich store of experience with student rebels. Many others were impressed by the apparent childishness of rebels who, as these observers saw it, lived in a fantasy world, invented their reality, demanded immediate utopia, and threw temper tantrums when it was not forthcoming.[3] Often the radicals were children of the affluent society who were supported by their parents as they lived in mock poverty and rode to revolutionary meetings in the family Citroën. They liked to use four-letter words and to play games. They rejected all discipline and in countless other ways displayed what their critics diagnosed to be symptoms of infantile regression. When Lenin wrote about "left-wing infantilism," he could have had no idea of the potentialities of the term as developed sixty years later by middle-class revolutionaries from the suburbs.

The reviewer of one of the books written by a prominent student revolutionary could only remark, "That Daniel Cohn-Bendit should have won renown as a serious revolutionary is a symptom of the sickness of our time."[4] To him this was the most primitive kind of thought, drawing upon only a few words, incapable of much more than slogans, violently abusive, and chiliastically religious. Depth of feeling, however, was there: all authority is oppressive; all institutions seek to exploit and destroy the individual. Few of the young rebels were really interested in ideology. They dismissed all rational thought as "bourgeois intellectualism" and emoted in a way that resembled the cruder forms of evangelical Christianity. Chanting from the works of Mao Tse-tung or Ché Guevara in wild delirium, disrobing on the stage, and smoking marijuana were happenings quite comparable to those of the ecstatic religious cults of the Reformation (cf. the Ranters of seventeenth-century England, the nudity of early Quakers and Doukhobors). Police baiting, obscenity, and the issuing of manifestos had the calculated intent of somehow shocking a social authority that in fact seemed not to exist. Total freedom, abolition of money, abolition of the "vicious pig power structure," pornography for everybody, the streets for The People (an ideological reversion to early Romantic personifications of an abstract and mythical entity)—the manifestations of the new culture became familiar to everyone in the 1960s, reaching a kind of apocalyptic climax in Paris and Chicago in 1968.

Yet the strange spirit behind the movement had its logic and even its logicians. It is, of course, subject to analysis under the rubrics presented in other chapters of this book. It was an "After Everything" development, erected on the ruins of previous revolutionary ideologies: Communism and socialism in their classical epiphanies were as dead as anything else, and New Leftism absorbed heavy doses of Existential, Phenomenological, and *chosiste* distaste for anything except the immediate situation. It was also related to the necessity for inventing ever new gestures, when all possible gestures seem exhausted. (See chapter 4.) It included a determined attempt to expunge all historical and traditional knowledge (all that being complex and confusing) and return to the naiveté of the child or the savage. (See chapter 5.) Bearded and unbathed, the student revolutionaries presented to the world the very image of anticivilization, heaving their rocks at school windows more often than at anything "capitalistic," burning buildings like the barbarians of old. Heavily infiltrated by McLuhanism, they seldom read Marx's formidable treatises but preferred the simple slogans in the Little Red Book of Chairman Mao. To describe their position as "anarchist" is not accurate, for there have been anarchist thinkers of much coherence and subtlety. The slogan scrawled on the wall of the London School of Economics in 1968 just about summed up student revolutionary thought: "We want the world and we want it now." ("Let's be realistic and demand the impossible" was the Sorbonne version.)

Yet underlying the powerful tide of emotion on which the student movement was borne were a number of serious and important thinkers. Best known perhaps was Herbert Marcuse, whose story was an interesting one. As a young man he had studied under Husserl and Heidegger, whose Existentialist-Phenomenological influence never entirely disappeared from his thought. But in the 1930s he was attracted to the group of neo-Marxian intellectuals who formed the Institute for Social Research in Frankfurt. These German intellectuals already knew about the "other Marx" and were, moreover, disillusioned with *both* the old Social Democracy and the new Soviet Communism. They regarded Karl Kautsky and Lenin alike as barbarians, vulgarizers of the true Marx, whose thought had been profoundly dialectical and who would never have remained prisoner of a system—had he not said he could never be a Marxist? The motto of the Frankfurt school was Nietzsche's remark that "a great truth wants to be criticized, not idolized"; these young Jewish scholars called themselves Critical Theorists. Members of the group included Theodor Adorno and Erich Fromm, whose interests were notably cultural and esthetic. They also showed an interest in bridging the gap that separated Marx from the then excitingly new ideas of Sigmund Freud, and they were much aware of the Hungarian George Lukács, who had distanced himself somewhat from Moscow while probing new frontiers of Marx-oriented theory in *History and Class Consciousness* (1923). The Marcuse who wrote critically of Russian Communism while still trying to position himself on the far Left was thus an authentic product of the Frankfurt school.

But it remained for his old age to bring him fame. With all their talent for theorizing subsidized by wealthy benefactors, these meta-sociologists long remained a coterie without much influence. When Hitler came to power, the Institute left Germany, ultimately to settle at Columbia University in New York City, where its members, largely isolated from their new environment, continued to write in German. Marcuse was the author of rather technical treatises on Hegel, read by few but savants. During World War II and for some years after, he worked for the American Department of State, for which his rivals in extremist politics would later reproach him. In 1958 his *Soviet Marxism* blasted the Soviet Union as a bureaucratic, statist, and dehumanizing industrial society. His emergence as prophet of the student revolutionaries in the next decade, when he was a sexagenarian, was as startling as anything in the annals of intellectual history. Yet the ingredients of his transformation into a New Left pundit had long been present in his thought: Existential-ism, revisionist Marxism, Freudianism, cultural criticism, and a penchant for rather cloudy theorizing about man and society marked Marcuse even more than other members of his circle.

If one doubts that hippie attitudes could emanate from so lofty a philosophical pinnacle, one need only read *An Essay on Liberation* (1969), which extolls drug-taking, four-letterism, and "bodies un-soiled by plastic cleanliness." Yet Marcuse arrived at this position by a process of thought. Like Sartre, though with some differences, he combined Existentialism with a revisionist Marxism. His critique of modern society was unlike anything known to the Marxian revolutionaries of previous epochs. They had accepted without question the belief that industrialism would usher in utopia by enriching everyone and thus permitting spiritual advancement. To attack industrialism itself had been the creed of such high Tories as Bonald and Ruskin. But Marcuse spoke of "overdeveloped coun-tries" and protested against modern industrial society as such as a dehumanizing, corrupting, enslaving society, crushing mind and soul. What Marcuse hated was not "capitalism" as Marx conceived it, but the whole technological-industrial-bureaucratic society. To Marcuse, Soviet society was as bad as Western societies. He shared the widespread disillusionment with Russia expressed in the view that the Soviet Union had become just another bureaucratic, elitist, and exploitative system, with a bourgeois culture and an oppressive government.

Sometimes the root of the evil was identified as group organization in any form, as any "rationalizing" element; one returned in fantasy to the archetypal Golden Age of primitive innocence. In *Negations* (1968), Marcuse attacked all social institutions and urged a perpetual state of revolutionary ecstasy, very much like the Ché Guevara mystique. He held that we can live in revolution and at the same time in pure freedom. But Marcuse also characteristically spoke of a future ideal society which, though he did not think it could be described at all precisely, he could anticipate—a utopian element in Marcuse's thought that was doubtless responsible for its appeal to the always optimistic young and that distinguished it from Sartre's. (For the latter, the contradictions of the human condition cannot possibly be resolved in any conceivable society. People will continue to exploit each other; by his very nature man will continue to be a "useless passion." The cruel enemy of man is man himself.)

Marcuse's future "free society" would be without government and without "exploitation," thus bearing some resemblance to the socialist and anarchist vision. It would somehow overcome the contradictions between the interior being of man and external reality, and it would do away also with guilt feelings about sex. In brief, it was a Freudian and Sartrean as well as a Marxian utopia— all of them rolled into one big happy ball. (Freud no more than Sartre believed in such a utopia, but Marcuse remedied this defect.) "We are temperamentally incapable of embracing the politics of sin, cynicism and despair," confessed another member of this school, Norman O. Brown, who elsewhere declared that its goal was nothing less than "to put an end to politics"—which would be replaced by Love.

Here the modern discovery of Marx's previously unpublished and largely unknown early manuscripts had its effect. Ironically, the Soviet-based Marx-Lenin Institute had discovered and published the manuscripts. The stress in these writings was not on the allegedly scientific analysis of history or of the economic system, not on materialism and economic determinism or even class struggle, but rather on how man has been deprived of his authentic humanity and his wholeness, how he has become alienated from his work and from his fellows and from his own nature, how his culture and his personality have been fragmented and destroyed by specialization, and how after the Revolution human nature will again be whole, its various fragments reunited into integral selves capable of true art and thought. This decidedly "soft" variety of Marxism was never entirely absent from the main body of the master's thought, so it is not quite correct to assign it to a wholly new Marx disinterred from the early writings.

In any case, the "newly discovered writings" were dredged up in Leningrad in the early 1930s. That they were largely ignored until just a few years ago strongly suggests that they were dependent on a change in the *Zeitgeist* for their influence. Still, their impact, taken together with the Existentialist vogue and with the desire after 1945 of eastern European victims of Russian Soviet imperialism to mitigate their lot, created new versions of Marxism. That is why Sartre, with a more or less clear existential conscience, could declare himself a Marxist.

Among the stimulating neo-Marxists of the postwar era, none was more stimulating than the Italian Antonio Gramsci. A founding father of the Italian Communist Party, he was imprisoned before the curse of Stalinism set in and, dying in 1937, gained the prestige of a martyr to Fascism. His enforced retirement from public life did not prevent him from engaging in intellectual activity (Il Duce did not treat his enemies quite as badly as did Stalin and Hitler). Gramsci's *Letters from Prison* and *Selections from the Prison Notebooks of Antonio Gramsci,* published after 1945, reveal an acute and perceptive mind, productive of a subtle and sophisticated Marxism. As a victim of Fascism, Gramsci enjoyed much posthumous fame in post-Mussolini Italy, not diminished by the fact that he criticized the old idol, Benedetto Croce. His writings were translated into many other languages. Here was a Marxist who had written (as early as 1918, under the influence of hyper-Leninism) that *Das Kapital* was a bourgeois book! Dynamic will, freedom, creativity, as opposed to the passivity of mechanical Marxism, nowhere received shrewder expression than in the epigrams of this poor Sardinian hunchback, who was indeed one of the insulted and injured of the earth, yet a remarkably clear, even serene thinker.

Unfortunately Gramsci offered little to the spoiled children of the bourgeoisie. In his hard-boiled Leninist thought there was not much of that consolation to the sensitive ego which Marcuse presented. Writing from prison about his own daughter's mental difficulties, Gramsci coldly advised her to stop whining and come to terms with industrial society, even holding up Henry Ford as a model. "We're absurdly romantic, and in our efforts not to be bourgeois, we fall into Bohemianism, which is in fact the most typical form of bourgeois behavior." It hit too close to home to permit Gramsci more than a peripheral role in the ideology of the youth rebellion of the 1960s. There was more consoling fare elsewhere.

A prominent post-Freudian source of the youth creed was another German, Wilhelm Reich, in whose thought sexual mysticism accompanied the ascription of unhappiness to "society" in a neoromantic assertion of the natural benevolence of man when freed from sexual repression and all forms of discipline. This lax creed promised paradise after sexual liberation and a social revolution. "It was he above all who forged the most characteristic items in the intellectual armory of the *secessio iuventutis*," Ernest Gellner observed in reviewing Charles Rycroft's book about Reich in the Fontana Modern Masters series. Freud of course had regarded sexual repression and the resulting neurosis as inescapable in any society and likely to get worse as "civilization" progressed. The eccentric Reich, who in his later years exhibited a religious belief in the power of orgastic love and invented a device for the storing of this energy (he died in 1957 after being arrested for marketing boxes of sexual potency), fathered a theory that failure to achieve proper sexual discharge is responsible for virtually all the ills to which man is prey and is caused by a repressive society that, working through the authoritarian family, wishes to keep people emotionally crippled and therefore submissive. (See especially *The Function of the Orgasm: Sexual-Economic Problems of Biological Energy*, 1942.) For this bizarre but highly dramatic deviation from Freudianism, he was expelled from that remarkably intolerant organization, the International Psychoanalytical Association, yet his flamboyant and sincere personality earned him much attention. A one-time Communist who also left, or was asked to leave, that community, Reich was another of the central Europeans who moved to the United States in the Nazi era and found in the New World a strangely congenial environment. His views were far less subtle than Marcuse's; but his main point, linking Marxism to Freudianism and hitching both to a radical critique of existing society that stressed the function of sexual repression, provided a family resemblance. Reich and Marcuse agreed that by changing society one might do away with all sexual repression and thus produce perfect bliss.

In 1971 another Reich, Charles A. Reich, writing out of Yale University, told the youth culture that it was destined to redeem the world by revealing the natural benevolence of man when released from sexual inhibitions and social discipline (*The Greening of America*). The switch from Old Left to New was remarkable for this hedonistic element, so lacking in the spartan purity of the old socialists (who wished, for example, to rescue womanhood from the debaucheries of the capitalist). And with this change came a move away from the traditional "proletarian" image.

A distinctive feature of Marcuse's revised Hegelianism-Marxism, this loss of faith in the proletariat was not entirely new in leftist circles. Georges Sorel lost faith in the working class in 1910, from which moment it is possible to date the rise of Fascism. The *embourgeoisment* of the working class had been an anarchist theme ever since Bakunin. In 1897 George Bernard Shaw perceived that "wage earners are far more conventional, prejudiced and 'bourgeois' than the middle class." Marx expected the revolutionary working class to rise against capitalism and destroy it; instead, capitalism engulfed the working class. So Marx was wrong, not in seeking the destruction of a vicious social order, but in the means by which he expected it to take place. Not the proletariat, which has been absorbed into the "system," but the outsiders who have not are in a position to destroy capitalism. In Lukács' thought this idea is turned into an apology for Leninism, stressing the elitist Party which must perform the proletariat's mission for it. Hopelessly degraded, the real proletariat cannot unaided carry out the task of destroying capitalism and ushering in the perfect society. This must be done by the few, the saving remnant, organized as the Communist Party. However, Lukács, like Lenin, saved appearances by arguing that the Party "really" or "objectively" represents the proletariat. Student revolutionary thought often similarly declared that a drugged proletariat might wake up and resume its proper revolutionary role after being exhorted to do so by the young. Some links with the older revolutionary tradition might thus be kept; yet there was a decided shift of emphasis.

In New Left thought, revolt against the existing society remains dialectically necessary. But such revolt must be carried out by those completely outside the society and thus in a position to negate it. The young, the outcast, joined perhaps by the "underdeveloped" and formerly colonialized peoples, must and will totally reject society. From Frantz Fanon came an Algerian blast against the West, whose workers as well as burghers he declared to be exploiters one and all: an echo of Mussolini's old strictures on have and have-not nations. Nothing progressive and socialist outside the Third World!

Third World influences of course were strong. The outer world bore in on the West as never before, partly because the latter had lost faith in itself, but mostly because exciting things were indeed happening where the formerly awed and subdued peoples of Asia and Africa obtained their independence. In Peking, Hanoi, Tunis, Conakry, Havana, and many other places, they accompanied their self-assertion by violent demonstrations of hostility against the whole Western system. Yet at the same time, it should be noted, the "new peoples" were in fact usually tied closely to Western intellectual culture. African leaders wrote English or French more often than Swahili or Fulani, and their ideologies of nationalism, socialism, or technocratism were European-born. China's new mandarins kowtowed to a Germanic ideology disseminated through Russia. It is indeed somewhat disenchanting to learn that Fanon, the putative spokesman for Africa and all the "wretched of the earth," was born into a bourgeois family in the West Indies and was less well known in the Third World than he was among disaffected Americans. Nevertheless, a close connection sprang up between these jaded and rebellious Western intellectuals and leftist movements of the Third World with their exotic scenarios but familiar slogans.

The deproletarianizing of Marx was a significant trend in thought. It was pointed out that Marx's idea of the revolutionary proletariat had been a conceptual and semantic error. No such entity ever existed; it was a blurring of two different types.[5] Revolutionaries had long existed, especially since 1789, but they were almost never proletarians; they were alienated upper-class intellectuals or members of the old artisan class. An industrial working class dated back about as far, but it was the least revolutionary of classes, being composed partly of men on the way up and partly of sodden wretches incapable of any sort of informed action. The nineteenth-century revolutions that Marx hailed as hopeful signs had nothing to do with the proletariat or industrialism; they were caused by defeat in war, as was the Russian Revolution of 1917 and the Parisian in 1871. It is significant that the Communist parties in the West (for example, the French) officially declared in the 1960s that they no longer sought to appeal to one class only and asked the intellectuals and the technocrats to join their movement.

Can the outcast remnant succeed in its task of total destruction? Can it then create a brave new world of freedom and happiness, without power, dominance, or even rules? What would such a world look like? Would it have automobiles, flush toilets, and electric lights? Would it consist of happy young hippies or barbarian warrior bands? The Marcusians, like the Marxists, deferred such questions until the immediate task of revolutionary destruction should be accomplished. They accepted the case against state power and planned to create anarchist local organization. They also shied off from big industry; their ideal was an agrarian, communal hippydom. The flight from megalopolis and from centralized power appealed to contemporary idealism, which criticism of mass society, of anomie, of The Lonely Crowd (David Riesman) deeply affected. A German emigrant with a knowledge not only of Hegelian-Marxian philosophy but of the sociology that, stemming from Ferdinard Tönnies and Max Weber, has continued to focus on the search for a viable social framework for uprooted modern man, Marcuse extracted from this sociology a moralistic element always incipiently present in it. "The teachings of Marcuse are more religion than sociology," Kai Hermann noted in his book *The Student Revolts*. In its elemental form, Marcuse's religious message is a promise of the apocalyptic destruction of Babylon to prepare the way for the Kingdom of Heaven. But in the higher reaches of Marcusianism there lay considerable deposits of modern sociological and philosophical thought. This aging leader of the young was a professor, a savant and even a pedant, but he was also the inspirer of a religion of destruction.

Marcusianized or not, the New Left as compared to the Old was far less disciplined, more radically individualistic, and far more alienated from the basic premises of modern technological-industrial society. It is not surprising that critics perceived in it certain Fascist affinities. Fascism, and especially Nazism, spoke to the same declassed, outcast elements to whom Marcuse appealed: drop-outs, beer-hall intellectuals, "truants from school," as Thomas Mann called them. They too had despised society and had demanded total revolution followed by total renewal. Yet Marcuse and all the Left, it goes without saying, indignantly rejected Fascism. Marcuse himself sought to show that classical liberalism and totalitarian Fascism are much alike (an extraordinary exercise in New Left logic). Dialectically—which is the way Marcusians like to regard everything—it is quite possible, and as plausible as other such examples of the dialectic, to say that the New Left was a synthesis of the Old Left and Fascism. But stronger in its makeup than either, it would seem, was the anarchist element.

In China the young Red Guards rebelled against the Communist Party itself—against the organization and structure unavoidable in a huge industrial society. Some of the young Europeans still voiced Marxist slogans about productive forces now outstripping social relations, implying that in the future society of their dreams there will be more production, more industry. But even when they used this language, it was clear they did not really believe it. The authentic voice of the young was heard in the books of Georges Perec, the French student whose message is that of utter hopelessness (*Les Choses,* 1965; *Un Homme qui dort,* 1967). Perec sits in his room, a book about Industrial Society on his knees, knowing that the industrial society has no place for him, that he is superfluous and useless in such a society. The voice was heard also in Marcel J. Moreau's *La Terre infestée d'hommes* (1966), a conscious cry of rage and disgust, a sustained invective. Osborne's young angry, compared to this one a decade later in a provincial French town, was positively amiable. Anger grows apace.

Though they shouted against "capitalism," everything suggests that it was not in fact capitalism the young radicals hated but technological society—capitalist, socialist, or whatever. Studies revealed that factory workers did not want to socialize the factory; they wanted to escape it. Max Weber's Iron Cage closes in, whether on the assembly line or in the office; even in the professions or the research laboratory, life and labor grow rationalized and specialized to a degree that the human spirit cannot tolerate—a spirit that is, of course, at the same time being freed and expanded in other ways. The romantic ego expands along with the technological society, and between them they squeeze the soul in an ever-tightening vice. Drug-taking, hippyism, and bombings are its screams of pain.

This much, surely, one must grant to the New Left: its motives were relatively pure, disinterested, idealistic. Its innocence might be staggering and its ignorance terrifying, but it could claim to be the first revolutionary movement in modern history without an axe to grind. Marx asked the proletariat to rise up in order to gain power. Lenin and Stalin sought power in order to seize wealth from its possessors. Strikers demanded more wages, farmers higher prices— all the classic movements of modern protest were frankly materialistic. The new rebels asked for spiritual things. They talked about love and community and not being dehumanized. It might be that some were against war because they feared to fight, but one must grant that on the whole this aspect of the New Left too was motivated by an honest idealism. One might complain that they did not know the world, or man, that their ideas were primitive. But one could not really deny that they asked for the Kingdom of Heaven and that most of them wished to enter into it humbly. (Those who asked for it with bricks and bombs were after all a small minority of the groups.) Marcuse's "great refusal" is heroic if futile; abandoned by every political and economic organization, the few who will not be bought off or drawn into the machine reject the whole "system" in the name of ideal humanity.

New Left and Old

The New Left by and large was an enemy of the Old. New Leftists argued that the Soviet Communist state represents nothing revolutionary but a change of masters (the beggars have changed places but the lash goes on) because it has kept the technological-industrial-statist system. No worker is freer because he toils for the state rather than for a private corporation; he is in fact less free and probably materially worse off. What matters is that the effect on his spirit of factory labor and a consumer economy is much the same, whether he lives in the Free World or behind the Iron Curtain. While the New Left had no unity on this point, or any other, the trend was strongly against Russian and even Chinese or Cuban Communism. The anniversary of the Russian Revolution in 1967 produced a spate of evaluations of the Soviet Union, and its critics on the left were about as unfavorable as any. For example, *Fifty Years of Russian Power,* a symposium published by the Marxist

Monthly Review and contributed to chiefly by Western Marxists, depicted Soviet society as a police state with a bourgeois culture that served neither freedom nor human dignity but worshipped power and wealth as they had never been worshipped before. It "makes the memory of Asiatic tyrannies grow pale," one contributor observed. As the reviewer of a New Left book noted in 1969, "Anyone who still has the temerity to suggest that the USSR is leading anyone anywhere except up the garden path is treated with silent contempt in places where people still think." What a change from the 1930s! Bernadette Devlin, heroine of the revolutionary Irish, said that "I think that Russia and Mao's China are capitalist states. The ideal Social state is yet to be founded." In a similar vein, the British playwright David Mercer, who called himself a Marxist, conceded that "I have never joined a Marxist organization because I have not encountered one in my lifetime which I could give my allegiance to without abandoning my critical intelligence."[6]

The Communists declined heavily in terms of the numbers of their really dedicated followers. The circulation of the French Communist newspaper *L'Humanité* fell from 2,800,000 in 1947 to 400,000 in 1965; the Party in France to fewer than 300,000 members. Communist ranks continued to decline in the wake of the brutal crushing of Czechoslovak independence in 1968, which further shattered the international unity of the movement. In any case, the Communist Party today in France and Italy is no longer a seriously revolutionary party. It expects that capitalism will continue to exist for an indefinite period of time, and it works within the system, both economically and politically. Communist parties have become a practically effective political force to the precise degree that they have ceased to be an intellectually appealing doctrinal movement.

Moscow for its part treated the New Left as a decadent bourgeois movement. *Pravda* called Marcuse an agent of the CIA! Cohn-Bendit, who spoke of "obsolete Communism," was condemned for stirring up youth to revolt. That apocalyptic and prophetic explosion of 1968 in Paris was so inexplicable to the old guard of Bolshevism that they honestly supposed it must have been some sort of reactionary conspiracy to discredit the Party.

There were, to be sure, the other, revolutionary Communisms, but to a degree disenchantment with even these regimes also quickly penetrated the ranks of revolutionary youth. The penchant for hero-worship, which manufactured immortality overnight, led to an exalted idealization of Mao, Guevara, and Castro but was countered by an inability to tolerate any of the necessary compromises to which actual governments, no matter how revolutionary their intentions, were forced. A dozen years after Castro's ascendancy, the Stalinist phase of the Cuban revolution was apparently beginning. The once ardent love affair between Castro and the radical intellectuals cooled very rapidly in 1970–1971, as the Cuban leader bitterly denounced some formerly zealous Castroites (for example, René Dumont, Hans Enzensberger, K. S. Karol) for their published uneasiness about the growing Stalinization of Cuba. He also closed down a university and arrested student leaders for criticizing him. The arrest of the Cuban poet Heberto Padilla and his wife, who were released after signing an abject apology manifestly written by the police, marked this mutual disenchantment of Castro's dictatorial regime and those he now contemptuously called "coffee-house literati" and "decadents." Under such circumstances the Cuban mystique seemed destined to fade rapidly, as the mercurial left-wing intellectuals moved on to new heroes.

Some attrition of idealism could not but follow so many broken idols. In the swiftly moving years from 1945 to 1970, a list of revolutionary *führers* at first commanded the breathless adulation of those claiming to pay allegiance to democracy and liberty and then, under the harsh light of political reality, paled into mere politicians—cynical, pragmatic, leading the way not into a brave new world but only into a rather cowardly old one. Such a list might include Tito, whose Yugoslavia was now gay and somewhat affluent but as capitalistic as any Western country, and a succession of African strong men like Kwame Nkrumah, Ahmed Ben Bella, or Sêkou Touré, who had proved to be either incompetent or corrupt or brutally tyrannical. Such was the way of all political flesh.

Condemned to disillusionment by its perfectionism, the extreme Left in the 1960s tended to fall rapidly apart after moments of intense revolutionary ecstasy. The myth of Ché Guevara shattered in 1967 in grandiose attempts to revolutionize and Vietnamize South America. A few years later messianic faith in the Revolution was already on the wane. Kidnappings and assassinations by uncoordinated bands of extremists only reflected the decadence of the movement. Real revolutions are not made of such pranks.

The one golden moment of youthful militance proved ephemeral. Writing in *Le Monde* a year after the collapse of the student revolution that flared so dramatically in the celebrated Paris demonstrations of May, 1968, Maurice Duverger remarked that "a certain prophetism of the Left, preaching the good word and announcing the Promised Land in a frenetic voice, rejoices those who confuse political action with magic incantation, but discouraged a great number of sympathizers."[7] The romantic anarchism of the new militants ensured their failure as a movement. They rejected organization on principle but were incapable of it in any case. Relying on spontaneity alone, they could produce temporarily impressive effects but could not make them last. To recall a phrase of Charles Péguy, they refused to permit their mystique to become *politique,* and so it melted away. They repeated here all the sins of "revolutionary infantilism" of which the Marxists had accused the Anarchists and Blanquists in the nineteenth century. Orthodox Communism was as dismayed by the 1968 students as was any Gaullist burgher. A common dislike of irrationalism brought the offspring of Karl Marx and Adam Smith together at last.

But there was hardly any such thing as "orthodox" Communism after the great schism in the 1960s of the Chinese Communists from the Muscovite papacy, followed by a general disintegration of the discipline once imposed on world Communism in Stalin's time. An astonishing liberation of even the more conventionally Marxist minds took place. A schismatic Venezuelan Communist, Pompeyo Marquez, establishing a *second* Communist Party in his country—something previously unimaginable, much like a second Roman Catholic church in Ireland—declared that "no one party can claim to expound all the richness of Marxism-Leninism" and expressed an openness to outside ideas: "We do not feel that Marxism is the sum of all the truth and knowledge acquired by man." Abhorrent though such ideas obviously were to the gerontocracy that rules the Soviet Union, they could no longer be rigidly controlled by ukases from the Kremlin. Dialogue between Marxism and Christianity got under way in the 1960s. East European Marxists, profiting by the enlarged Marxian canon and the general post-Stalinist relaxation of authority, were able to introduce apparently small but actually critical changes in the gospel. The Reformation had come to the Marxist church, bringing with it much chiliastic excitement but also dissolving Marxism's monolithic unity and threatening to corrode the implicit faith of its true believers.

But for their spirit of revolution, the *gauchistes* of the 1960s drew on many other sources than Marx, and for their essential spirit, perhaps not on Marx at all. At worst they looked to the drug culture, the pot-porn underground. Their heroes included such figures as Timothy Leary, high priest of the acid heads. *Play Power* (1971), a book by Richard Neville, veteran of the British underground scene, was dedicated to the philosophy of having fun, rejoicing in all the "hippies, beats, mystics, madmen, freaks, yippies, crazies, crackpots, communards" who have one thing in common: they avoid work.[8] One thinks of how the old socialists despised idleness above all else, their main reproach against "capitalism" being that it fostered an unproductive class. For his part, Dr. Leary hailed as the true prophets who were bringing about the "great revolution of our age" the dope peddlers, the rock musicians, and the underground artists and writers.

At this level, the young radicals were subject to the criticism that they represented no more than the disastrous results of contemporary affluence, suburbia, and decayed values; they were the first generation to have absolutely nothing to believe in and an abundance of leisure in which to do it. They had a precursor in the poet Francis Thompson, a dropout from medical school, who wrote: "I did not want to grow up, did not want responsibility. . . . So I had my great toy of the imagination, whereby the world became my box of toys." Inventing ideal worlds with the great toy of the imagination is far easier than grappling with the real one.

At this level, too, entirely destructive personalities, politicized juvenile delinquents, waged "revolution for the hell of it." Serious nineteenth-century revolutionaries believed that it was possible to construct by an exercise of the reason a social order infinitely superior to their own and have it installed in toto; or later in the century and under the influence of Marxism and other historicizing creeds, they believed that there is a predetermined path of history that leads us through the higher to the highest phase, in a process we may accelerate by our actions. Even the anarchist desire to destroy the state, in some cases by acts of terror, was not mere blind destructiveness but rested on the philosophical conviction that destruction of the state would lead to the good society. Without some such belief in a better order or a better future, revolution makes no sense. Only in recent times has there appeared the revolutionary who holds that the act is good in itself, because it does something for the individual or because—in a more typical view— the existing society is so horrible that to smash it up is a virtue, even if one has no reason to expect anything better in its place. The "Situationists" of the 1960s held that breaking up a congealed pattern is in itself good, because *something* new can emerge. Many of the most recent crop of revolutionaries would seem to have lost the foundations on which revolutionism rested, while continuing to cling to the revolutionary mystique. Absurdism as the basis for revolution could not long sustain a serious movement. Only the Old Left could really believe in the myth of revolution.

Even the more serious prophets of revolutionism were grotesquely unfitted to lead a "revolution of the people," or any revolution, or indeed anything at all. They were embittered and alienated intellectuals whose spiritual dwelling places were as far as possible from the haunts of ordinary men. Jean-Luc Godard, filmmaker for the New Left, was such a case of extreme alienation posing as revolutionary populism—as wild a schizophrenia as the contemporary world exhibits. His film *Weekend* (1968) was filled with some of the sexual titillation so much a part of the new revolutionism and so different from the austere puritanical spirit that pervaded the old. It was also stuffed with such horrors as the butcher-knife murder of the wife's mother by a married couple who have been plotting to kill each other, and the subsequent eating of the husband by the wife. "It is necessary to surpass the horror of the bourgeoisie by still more horror," said Godard. Here was the old game of baiting the bourgeoisie, with gestures appropriate to the alienated artist who hates the whole of modern society. Yet the film contained a great deal of declamation about revolution which, one feels, Mallarmé would have found extremely vulgar. Subsequently Godard, while continuing to claim that the function of the cinema is to help bring on the Revolution, made films of a sort bewildering to his young admirers looking for some straightforward socialist message. (One of them, though, was an attack on the 1968 Soviet intervention in Czechoslovakia, which claimed that the real purpose of the Russians was to keep the Czechs from throwing off the shackles of Wall Street!) And he has said that "I aim my films at people I know, people with whom I can achieve something politically. They amount to something like two out of every thousand."[9] Yet, astonishingly, he also claimed to be speaking to or for "the masses" and involved with "the proletariat."

The phenomenal Jean-Paul Sartre reemerged in the 1960s as a revolutionary ideologist. Sartre's political thought was less impressive than his philosophical, psychological, or literary ideas. It comes close to saying that in an absurd world we might as well choose the most absurd cause. An uncritical swallowing of the crudest official Party line characterized Sartre until 1956 (he defended the Nazi-Soviet pact in 1939, for example, and accused the Americans of germ warfare in Korea) when the Soviet invasion of Hungary disillusioned him as it did so many others. But he continued to argue that one applies different moral standards to Communist countries, which represent the Future. This was strange doctrine from the proponent of pure freedom and indeterminism. Philip Thody, who attempted to defend Sartre's one-sided criticisms of the West and his silences about Russia, conceded that the high priest of Existentialism had been "ready to accept particular untruths, however glaring they may be, provided that they serve the general good." Such a creed, which seemed to be deliberately argued in *Dirty Hands* (1948), is, one cannot help feeling, hopelessly at variance with Sartre's own ethic; Camus was right.

In the difficult *Critique of Dialectical Reason* (1960), Sartre announced himself a convert to social rather than purely personal issues; groups and forces rather than individual freedom received his attention. Yet the face of anarchy remained clearly visible under this mask of socialism. Only in moments of revolutionary ecstasy, it seems, do the lonely *pour-sois* manage to fuse into a collective consciousness, which is really the individual person writ large. Sartre's typology of social groups resembles Max Weber's in that ossification and disenchantment soon overtake social institutions; the revolutionary moment fades into modes of terror, as Robespierre replaces Desmoulins and Lenin gives way to Stalin. To live authentically in society, it seems, we can only be part of a revolutionary mob. Since this is impossible save for fleeting moments, man once again is seen as a useless passion.

Sartre in his unlikely role of realistic politician was utterly impractical. His causes excited only a handful of intellectuals and, at least until the apotheosis of 1968, gained no victories. And the triumph of 1968, as we know, proved ephemeral from want of the sort of clear guidance that might have produced a unified and directed movement. In 1971–1972 Sartre again stood virtually isolated, associated with a small number of ultraleftists whose spirit was, admittedly, very strong but whose determination to outrage the majority prevented any political success other than those of the pricks and stings of gadflies on the body politic. At bottom Sartre was anything but a proletarian revolutionary; like his friend Godard, he speaks to two in a thousand when he talks politics— to other highly sophisticated intellectuals, not to working people. In 1968 most of the Parisian workers stood apart from the transported students, whom they viewed as quite mad.

Of Sartre, Thody also observed that he "had no conception of family life, no understanding of religion, little interest in members of the working class who are not politically minded, and no awareness that members of the middle class are not inevitably self-satisfied swine or tormented intellectuals." This universal genius of our time was cut off from almost all that is everyday human. Simone de Beauvoir noted that to Sartre even the family is an enemy of authentic being, forcing us to play roles (her "dutiful daughter") rather than be ourselves. To the nineteenth-century socialists of Charles Fourier's time, the family was a bastion of bourgeois individualism and private property. To the Existentialists, it is evidently much too social. Sartre found life and freedom only among complete outsiders, including criminals like his "Saint Genet." If Sartre is right, we can look forward only to the total destruction of existing society; as in Genet's play *The Balcony,* we would do well to turn it over to the denizens of whorehouses. But it is impossible to imagine Sartre being pleased with *any* society. It will hardly do to dismiss as "bourgeois" those sentiments and practices that have, after all, marked the vast majority of the human race in all ages and places. Sartre's utopia is only for a small coterie of the avant-garde, an elite of intellectual mandarins.

The revolutionary movement of the 1960s, impressive as it was as an outburst of the tormented human spirit in the rationalized, bureaucratic, industrial society, was basically Sartrean and thus condemned to futility. It was a desperate strategy that suffered from all the diseases of present intellectual life—"After-Everything" nihilism, faddism, intellectual confusion, neobarbarism, divorce of thought from reality.

Some therefore found reason to believe that the modern myth of revolution, born in 1789 and nourished on 1848 and 1917, was growing senile and could not survive indefinitely. Such analyses as Camus's *The Rebel* (1951), which touched off a major debate between Sartre and Camus, foreshadowed a number of others, particularly Hannah Arendt's *On Revolution* (1963), which told us among other things that revolution is a game that can be played only a limited number of times. One could rebel against the King in the name of the People and feel virtuous. What if then (as certainly will be the case) many feel disillusioned with the new government, the government of "the People"? Well, they can deny that it really *is* the People's government; they can accuse it of fraud and assert that it actually is the disguised rule of an oligarchy. Suppose they make another revolution, one that really is in the name of the People. And the new government turns out to be of much the same sort, or worse. How long can this go on? Sooner or later it becomes evident to all that all governments are much alike and that there is not much point making a revolution—and one runs out of slogans with which to inspire revolution. The Russian Revolution has solidified into just another tyrannical oligarchy: under what flag can there be a revolution against it? Having been led to ruin by the Nazi Revolution, are the Germans likely to try another one?

Another reason often given for the easy obsolescence of revolution is the sheer size and complexity of today's political units. A revolution succeeds only in proportion to the compactness and simplicity of the offending government. If your aim is the total reformation of a great modern country (Lenin had in mind nothing less than *world* revolution), you are in for a great disappointment, for you will lose both your way and all rational control. Total reform of a single institution, such as a large business corporation or, say, the University of Wisconsin, is difficult enough; total reform of the United States, in a single process over a short time span, is physically and humanly impossible.

The dream of ever-fresh revolutions is evidently an obsessive symptom of modern decadence. It is not the cure but a part of the sickness. Against such arguments, however, the convinced Marxist is immune. For Marx provided him with an answer. Any niggling doubts and petty obfuscations are to be explained as products of capitalist decadence; they are the last refuge of bourgeois intellectuals against the coming storm.

In the aftermath of the perishable ecstasy of 1968, there was a tendency on the part of some revolutionaries to retreat into a more orthodox kind of Marxism. Under the rubric of "Trotskyism," it was possible for them to reject, at least in part, the Soviet Union and perhaps other "workers' states," while insisting that Lenin and Marx had been betrayed by false leaders. All one had to do was return to the road not taken and follow the man Stalin had outmaneuvered and murdered. Trotskyists reaffirmed "the international working class" as the hope of the revolution. (See, for example, Tariq Ali, *The Coming British Revolution,* 1972.) The new Trotskyists assailed the older ones for their dogmatism and authoritarianism. They perhaps overlooked the fact that the historical Trotsky was by all accounts an even more ruthless man than Lenin or Stalin (it was he who invented some of the more refined forms of totalitarian terror, such as holding relatives as hostages). The new Trotskyism was decidedly pale, reiterating all the old slogans about capitalism, imperialism, exploitation, and so forth, in a way to make us wonder whether their magic isn't about exhausted. Long dead as science, Marxism is also wearing thin as myth, and such desperate alternatives as neo-Trotskyism take their place along with existentialized Marxism as one of the phenomena of its dissolution.

Yet there remains Sartre's conviction that Marxism—whatever its objective truth, which is an irrelevancy—is *the* ideology for contemporary man, the only all-inclusive philosophy capable of speaking to his condition. And we must concede it a remarkable staying power. As early as 1848 it was being said that socialism had run its course. Benedetto Croce said the same in 1911, as had others in 1871; "the end of the socialist myth," as Raymond Aron termed it in the 1950s, has been pronounced many times in the last century and a quarter, but each time socialism has bounced back. We cannot be sure it will not swallow us all in the end, as Marxists are sure will happen. Yet in 1970 the forces of dissolution looked stronger than ever before, for Marxism as much as for other authoritarian structures. In its despairing nihilism the radicalism of the 1960s swept aside even its own intellectual constructions.

Conservative Counterreaction

In the turbulent 1960s had arisen Castro, Guevara, the Soviet-Chinese rift, the Vietnam War. The violent student protest movement had flourished all over the world, in Zagreb and Tokyo and Mexico City as well as in Berlin, Paris, Rome, London, New York, and Berkeley—indeed practically everywhere two or three students gathered together. The uprising of the Red Guards in China, which threw that country into a prolonged turmoil, was essentially a youth movement. That famous spring of 1968 in Paris, when for a moment it looked as if the embattled students would overturn society, climaxed a ten- or twelve-year trend.

The violence and apparent mindlessness of all this produced a reaction that possibly heralded a swing back to the right. Those who turned away from the New Left in disgust often turned away from the Left altogether. Some of those who had fomented this period of radical rage—the young "angries" of the fifties—deserted, as did John Osborne with his 1971 play *West of Suez.* "Goodbye to the Left," John Braine wrote (*Spectator,* July, 1968), recording his progressive disillusionment from about 1964 on with socialism, the Labour Party, the Left Establishment, internationalism, the Committee for Nuclear Disarmament, not punishing criminals,[10] and so forth. Oddly enough Braine found himself an admirer of the United States, that incarnation of all evil for the Left; he found at least a modicum of freedom there. Braine has adopted no alternative ideology to his past leftism; as a conservative he is content to "judge each issue on its own merits and not in relation to any philosophical system." What a relief to be released from orthodoxy! It is to be feared that the normal course after such a *bouleversement* is a steady drift in all respects to the right. Apt to follow are such strange emotions as love of country, regard for law and order, respect for the political and judicial system, uncomfortable feelings at the mention of "civil liberty," a benign toleration of the average doltish citizen (considered less harmful than the average enraged reformer), a willingness to fight against Communism, and the like.

A similar renegade from the left, Kingsley Amis (see *Lucky Jim's Politics,* 1968), made it clear that repulsion, and not attraction, was the motive force: "There is only one thing more horrible than Conservative philosophy and that is Socialist philosophy"; "half an hour with a convinced Lefty is enough to make even the most progressive person wonder a bit whether Conservatism might not have a little more to offer." Conservatism has long survived as a reaction to the follies of the Left. Returning from Brook Farm some one hundred twenty years ago, Nathaniel Hawthorne declared that "no sagacious man will long retain his sagacity, if he lives exclusively among reformers and progressive people." Dr. Samuel Johnson grew to be a Tory in reaction against the shallow optimism of some of the *philosophes.* Marvin Fisher, author of a comparison between Hawthorne's and Johnson's conservatism, remarked that "like advocates of conservatism today, Johnson and Hawthorne are united not so much by what they advocated as by what they opposed."

So the law of reaction ensured a return to conservatism after an interlude of trend-setting by the Left. A high school paper in Toulouse, quoted by *Le Monde Weekly,* April 28, 1971, declared, "The one way to be truly *anti*-revolutionary is to follow the dreary, senile leftist missionary pricks"; referring to Mao, Ché, Régis Debray, the Little Red Book, it said, "Stuff them all." Such strains became far from unusual even in the underground press. The revolutionaries of yesterday became the bores of today. Graham Hough, writing in *Encounter* early in 1971, declared that the majority of students were now altogether weary of revolutionary drivel and "sick of the dreary hypocrisy of those who want to shelter behind their privileged status and at the same time destroy the life and reputation of the very institution that guarantees it." Suburban subversiveness, at any rate, seemed to have overstayed its time. The 1970 generation of youthful rebels threatened to rebel against the revolutionary gods of the 1960s; here as elsewhere one could pass from swinging avant-garde to old fogey overnight. Reading the Little Red Book or cutting sugar cane for Castro might soon date one as crushingly as a taste for the music of Lawrence Welk. In France, the "gauchistes" who, though boasting of the patronage of

Sartre, Simone de Beauvoir, and Godard, tried to outflank the traditional Communists on the left, were so disunited and incoherent that they could safely be ignored. Among many other straws in the wind, there was the case of Norman Podhoretz, influential American editor, who in 1970–1971 did a complete turnabout and began to attack the New Left in the pages of *Commentary,* a prestigious American intellectual journal that had earlier shown sympathy to that movement.

American campuses grew quieter in the early 1970s; but visitors to Germany were struck with what one of them reported to be a totally hysterical political style, and not everyone would agree with Hough's generalization about the British university scene. In the spring of 1974 a handful of radically fanaticized leftists succeeded in terrorizing Essex University in England. One could plausibly argue that the ideas of yesterday's intelligentsia were trickling down into the popular mind, in accordance with a fairly well established law that what the elite thinks today will sooner or later be what the masses think. According to this theory, the great bulk of the intelligentsia, at most times since 1900, have thought pink; at long last and by sheer perseverance they have imposed this stamp on the majority, which until very recently lived in the early nineteenth century. If this theory is correct, as in part it is, we are in for a long siege of low-level radicalism. Should this be the case, it may well drive the intellectuals into the opposite corner.

Whatever the future may bring, future historians are certain to find something memorable in the revolutionary outburst of the 1960s. What that will be depends on the shape of things to come. If our civilization collapses in nuclear war or total anomie, the turmoil of the sixties will seem like the roll of thunder announcing the end. If we end in Orwellian tyranny, it will appear as the last defiant expression of free individuals. In the unlikely event that we go on to solve most of our more urgent problems and to live a reasonably happy existence in some sort of technological subtopia, the sixties antics will suggest an adolescence happily outgrown. More probably, as we muddle along in much the same indeterminate way we have always done, they will be revealed as simply one more exhausted option. And so a new one will have to be invented.

NOTES

1. A type exemplified by John Lennon's jokes about cripples and ill people and jews (*sic*), in *A Spaniard in the Works* (1965).

2. Russell could even forget completely that he had ever held an earlier position. In 1947 the famous philosopher stated that if the Russians refused to internationalize atomic weapons, as the United States then proposed, they should be forced to do so by the threat of atomic bombing. In 1953 he called "the story that I supported a preventive war against Russia . . . a Communist invention . . . a slanderous report." In 1958, as he subsequently wrote (*Listener*, May 28, 1959, p. 937), certain people "brought to my notice things which I had said in 1947, and I read these with amazement. I have no excuse to offer." If this could happen to one of the strongest minds of the century, how many others were capable of totally expunging memory of yesterday's politics?

3. E.g., Alasdair C. MacIntyre, *Herbert Marcuse: an Exposition and a Polemic* (1970): ". . . idealised students who have produced. . . . what is more like a new version of the children's crusade than a revolutionary movement."

4. *TLS*, November 28, 1968, review of Cohn-Bendit's *Obsolete Communism: The Left-Wing Alternative.*

5. See, for example, Heinz Lubasz, in *Praxis*, 1/2 (1969), 288. Published in Zagreb, this journal was a stimulating source of revisionist, undoctrinaire Marxism. See also Ludwig Reichhold, *Abschied von der proletarischen Illusion* (1972).

6. See Karl Miller, ed., *A Listener Anthology, 1967–1970* (1970), p. 229. Mercer had been chided by D. A. N. Jones ("Mercer UnMarxed") with being utterly un-Marxist in his writing: "His stories are about the difficulties of solitary idealists (usually artists and students) confronted by institutions and organizations that cramp their style." In reply Mercer affirmed his Marxism but defined it as "the view that history is a complex of forces, of property and of production relationships, in a state of ongoing dialectical change," a definition so vague that, one supposes, any capitalist could accept it.

7. In a piece significantly titled "La Maladie infantile du gauchisme." (See weekly edition of *Le Monde*, March 27–April 2, 1969.)

8. This sanction for play is found, of course, in the high theorizing of Marcuse: pleasure is the highest goal, the "performance principle" (work ethic) is dehumanizing, and in the vaguely adumbrated utopia postindustrial people will play, not work.

9. *Le Monde Weekly*, April 29–May 5, 1971, p. 7.

10. A curious and interesting role in the British reaction was played by the so-called Moors murder case, a sadistic torture-killing of children by two people who had read much pornographic literature. Braine comments on his rebellion against the left-liberal dogmas of opposition to capital punishment, crime as the fault of "society" and therefore not to be punished, etc. For somewhat similar reactions, directed also against the corrupting influences of degenerate pornography encouraged by a permissive society, see Pamela Hansford Johnson, *On Iniquity* (1967). But it should be noted that the Moors murderers' political reading ran along Nazi-Fascist lines.

4

The Disease of Modernism

Neophilia

In a book of the early 1970s Christopher Booker coined the word *neophilia,* "love of novelty," to denote the most significant quality of modern culture. At the lowest cultural level, neophilia is reflected in the ephemera of popular music, clothing fashions, slang, and life style, which may change annually if not weekly. But more recently the higher culture has been swept into this neurasthenic frenzy, too; art styles, political attitudes, and fashions in ideas became as subject to it as anything else. Words like *trendiness* and *neophilia* appeared as a criticism of this unseemly instability in what, some instinctively felt, should provide us with more or less unalterable standards of excellence. "We live in a moment of history where change is so speeded up that we begin to see the present only when it is already disappearing," the eminent psychiatrist R. D. Laing observed, adding that "we are living in an age in which the ground is shifting and the foundations are shaking." Perhaps it is significant that these remarks are found in a book in which he argued, to put it bluntly, for the normality of abnormality, the sanity of insanity.[1]

More than a century ago Baudelaire identified the fundamental malaise of the modern era as boredom, ennui. Modernism is the rejection of tradition for novelty, and novelty quickly palls, leading to the quest for ever fresh novelties. Writing in anger and bewilderment toward the beginning of the specifically "Modernist" movement in the arts, Leo Tolstoy (1897) could only suggest that art had been reduced to the level of an amusement: "Every amusement wearies you at every repetition. In order to make an amusement which has wearied you once again attractive, you must somehow

87

import novelty into it: if Boston wearies you, you must invent whist, if whist wearies you you invent preference, if preference wearies you you invent something else new, and so on" (*What Is Art?*). But late-nineteenth-century writers were not, as Tolstoy implied, frivolous; they were terribly serious about art, even if some of them wished to detach it from life because they found the life around them hopelessly vulgar and decadent. They nevertheless felt impelled to invent a new style and mood in order to mark themselves off from the previous generation. Its style had been "Naturalist," that is, quantitative, scientific, deterministic, interested in common people, and they had to reverse all these qualities, not just because they wanted to be different—though that was a part of it—but because they experienced in the deepest parts of their being a genuine revulsion against them. The Symbolists were bored with Naturalism. In the course of time men would grow bored with Symbolism.

"Tides of taste," though in a slower rhythm, can be traced back many centuries. The fashions of the Italian Renaissance gave way to the Baroque and the Mannerist, following which came a reversion to severe (neo-) Classicism, thence to a Rococo softening, and so to Romanticism—even before the latter mood introduced change and subjectivism as a more or less constant feature. And these were only the higher waves, within which nestled smaller ones remembered only by savants. We seek in vain for a stable Golden Age when all was serene good taste and no one was bored. Nevertheless, it is reasonably clear that objective standards of art and taste once existed (Classicism by definition possessed them) and that fluctuations were relatively both slow and narrow. In modern times they have increased in intensity and become ever more rapid. Styles which used to last a century, and then a generation, now may be good for a season. The fever rises. Art, therefore, moves toward its dissolution, victim of its own kind of anomie, or disappearance of standards. "We see that modernism leads not only to the destruction of traditional literary forms, it leads to the destruction of literature as such" (George Lukács).

The Modernist movement, it has been said, was not just another novelty but a new sort of novelty. "I do not see how anyone can doubt," wrote that confirmed anti-Modernist C. S. Lewis, "that modern poetry is not only a greater novelty than any other 'new poetry,' but new in a new way, almost a new dimension." It is true that many of the things modern art did went outside the old channels of change: the abandonment of naturalistic perspectives in painting and the rejection of all prosy exposition and description in poetry are examples. So also is the novel's exploration of dreams and the unconscious. Arthur Rimbaud's "reasoned disordering of the senses," Paul Valéry's demand that poetry begin where prose leaves off and do something utterly different, the Symbolist avoidance of direct statement—these were startling and unprecedented innovations, which have, of course, their equivalents in painting and sculpture and music. Joyce revolutionized the novel.

But was this "new in a new way"? What Lewis had chiefly in mind was the plunge into obscurity. He went on to claim that there has never been nor will there ever be agreement even among experts on what a T. S. Eliot poem means. The apparent obscurity of the Romantics or of Robert Browning was the result of a strangeness that could wear off, not of any inherent incomprehensibility; Browning is in principle understandable, and, indeed, it is today hard for us to see how anyone could have regarded him as obscure. But Mallarmé, Eliot, and Joyce—so this argument runs—are not in principle comprehensible at all. They present worlds so private that no one can enter them, and they use modes of expression so complicated that no one can decipher them. They made a radical break with statement that is direct, logical, and public, and hence subject to a least approximate sharing by others. The older writers communicated within the boundaries of roughly a single language world. With the new literature we enter a wilderness of personal languages and horizons.

The Modernist Neurasthenia

In a book about nineteenth-century art, Werner Hoffman found a tragic split developing at the end of the century between past and present, or between history and life. It began with that sharp rejection of the older "classics" by the first Modernists, of the 1890–1920 generation. It widened to the point of agony as the twentieth century moved on. The life-philosophy, Dionysus, presentism, permissive individualism, post-Freudianism—all these pervasive Modernisms urged us to cut loose from tradition, abolish the past that enchains us, and trust happily to our animal instincts. But art requires form and structure as well as fire and spirit. Dionysian art leads eventually to the abandonment of all attempts to communicate, as with recent composers who relinquish form in favor of "happenings," letting each instrument in the orchestra go its own way. Great art and successful living demand that tradition and innovation work together, toward what Dr. Hoffman calls "the integration of an antiphony." But contemporary art rejects tradition altogether and builds only on innovation. It is a strange situation, and literary scholar Morse Peckham, in his essay on the subject, noted that "in the entire history of art nothing so strange has ever happened as the astonishing developments of the 1960s."[2]

In this respect the Modernist style only reflected the conditions of a fragmenting culture, creating something "appropriate for the bewildering and bewildered society that had emerged" (A. Alvarez). We would seem in fact to have to take into account several different dimensions in any appraisal of Modernism. First, what Alvarez describes as "the continual and continually accelerating change from one style to another" is largely a function of the pace of today's technological society. *Everything* has speeded up, since communications have done so, and group interaction has become more intense. One is tempted to try to reduce this to a law of acceleration, in Henry Adams' manner. Writing about 1900, the French literary critic Émile Faguet, who believed modern European man was suffering from a kind of intellectual indigestion brought on by too many ideas coming in too rapidly, observed hopefully that "we need not assume that because we go ten times as fast from Marseilles to Paris today as in 1840, we will go ten times faster still in 1950." But in fact this just about occurred. Faguet estimated the time of that journey as 150 hours in 1840 and 15 hours in 1900. Ten times faster would be an hour and a half, which seems a conservative estimate for this distance of some 450 miles in the jet age.

The whole pervasive life-world of modern, urbanized, democratic, technologized man germinates the doctrine of incessant mobility, and this is bound to affect the arts. In any field, the popular mind most readily accepts the view that "not keeping up with the times" is the cardinal sin. Publication of any book is guaranteed if its message is "it's not up-to-date," it isn't changing, it's run by old fogeys, it's not with-it—"it" can be politics, the press, education, the church, anything. This is an outlook shared by Left, Right, and Center; it is the consensus. All agree that what is old is bad, that yesterday's ways will not do today, that everything must adapt or perish. If Leftists call for a New Politics (nothing less, after all these centuries), clergymen now demand a New Morality, and the most extreme conservatives are conditioned to think in terms of new technology and new business methods. And if anyone suggests that the principles of politics and morality and even business do not much change, or that good education does not depend on a reformed curriculum, he is thought odd.[3] Small wonder that the arts, too, are expected to introduce annual new fashions, just like television programming.

And, driven by the gnawing hunger for recognition that afflicts the modern ego in a vast impersonal society, each creative person is impelled to do something different. Only a few years after T. S. Eliot, Hart Crane reads him, admires him, is jealous of him, determines to use language in a different way; he cannot stand to walk in the shadow even of a giant. Repeat this story thousands of times, and you have the pattern. (Those who insist that nothing is really new might cite John Donne more than three hundred years ago: "Every man alone thinks he has got /To be a phoenix, and that then can be /None of that kind of which he is, but he.")

A second major and familiar element in Modernism was the distancing of the artist from society in a far more extreme way than ever before. Esthetic and intellectual types, the tender-minded and introverted, became increasingly alienated from a commercial, vulgarized, democratic, "bourgeois," rationalized—call it what you will—culture. Sociologists and others vied in trying to find terms for modern society. To Comte it was "positivist," to Carlyle "mechanical" and "cash-nexus," to Marx "bourgeois," to Walter Bagehot "matter-of-fact," to Max Weber "rationalized" and bureaucratic, to Durkheim anomic, to Barrès deracinated—and so on. (To Charles Fourier it was simply "civilization.") Science, democracy, capitalism, urbanization, and sheer bigness were some of the villans. To withdraw from, rebel against, scandalize, *épater* a "hideous society" was the deepest motive of the artists who began Modernism. Flaubert had dreamed of burning down Paris; Mallarmé thought he had perfected the art of driving the bourgeoisie mad by writing verses they couldn't understand.

Alfred Jarry, creating his King Ubu, who demanded to be made a slave in the age of Equal Rights and who created the Institute of 'Pataphysics, belonged to a generation (c. 1890–1910) that carried gestures of this sort as far as they could really go; everything since has been anticlimax. Its outcast poets (dying in slums and ditches like Ernest Dowson), its cult figures like Alfred Jarry, Oscar Wilde, Marinetti the Futurist, who made their lives as grotesque as possible, carried perverse eccentricity to the utmost limits. In *The Banquet Years, The Arts in France 1885–1918* (1958) Roger Shattuck gave us a portrait of Jarry, archetypal surrealist personality, whose persona defies short description. Vladimir Markov's *Russian Futurism; A History* (1968) describes David Burlyuk, who appeared "wearing a top hat, with an earring in his left ear, a wooden spoon in his buttonhole, and his cheek painted with a bird sitting on a tree." An English cult figure, recently much discussed, who with allegedly brilliant gifts wrote practically nothing but scandalized Europe by his outrageous behavior in the Bright Young Thing era, was Brian Howard. These bizarre shenanigans of the early Modernists reached the masses a couple of generations later, vastly satirized and vulgarized, in television programs like "Laugh-In."

Modernism is also—its third dimension—a function of the intellectual complexity of modern times, the "overburdened mind." Direct statement became discouraging because one has to say so many things at once. The philosophical perspective reflected in F. H. Bradley's *Appearance and Reality* (Bradley, we are reminded, was T. S. Eliot's professor) and in the new physics of Albert Einstein and Max Planck (said to have directly influenced Cubist painting) was that there is no one truth; rather, there are infinite truths, depending on one's position and purpose. So many new ideas flooded in that statements had to be multilevelled, able to suggest several levels of truth. If one wished to cope with all the knowledge available, one had to invent some new mode of communication. "In a world of fragmented values," Stephen Spender wrote in his valuable study of the Modern, "everything has to be reinvented." The chief of the writers who presided over the modern idiom were in fact fabulously learned men trying somehow to embrace the whole of an inheritance both long in time and rich in content. Consider Joyce's *Ulysses* and *Finnegans Wake,* with their compressed, encyclopedic content, almost like shorthand textbooks of Western civilization; T. S. Eliot, the resources of the whole civilized tradition at his poetic command; Pound ransacking the Orient; Yeats pursuing the lore of the West back to Byzantium. No modern statement can be simple unless it is self-consciously so; and even then, this false simplicity has to be given some sort of novel form.

Small wonder, then, that the Modernist styles have been "difficult, disciplined, complex, aware, elliptical, and unprecedented" (Alvarez). So is the modern condition. This condition is now nearly a century old—the specifically modern consciousness germinated in the 1880s and 1890s. The maturing of André Gide as artist, immoralist, and homosexual belongs to this time. A dozen other examples come to mind: Sigmund Freud and Havelock Ellis, Ernest Dowson and Oscar Wilde, Henri Bergson and F. H. Bradley, William James and Edmund Husserl. Modernism in all its aspects flowered at this moment. As early as 1888, John Davidson was lamenting that "the world is old; it has been satiated with originality. . . . A public man must therefore be extravagant in order to distinguish himself."

Nietzche had analyzed "the dissolution of art" (which to him was not much different from the dissolution of man) several years earlier, in *Human, All Too Human*. The arbitrary limitations with which neoclassical principles sought to bind art—the unities of action, time, and place in drama; the rules about sentence structure, choice of words, verse patterns and meters; all the elaborate formalism of the old literary culture—had seemed absurd to the Romanticists, who threw them off to exult in a glorious freedom. But without certain basic limitations we are adrift, as in a game without rules. The strongest art is that which manages to conserve an illusion of freedom while actually knowing how to bind itself, as "one learns to walk gracefully on narrow paths over dizzying precipices." (One might, in a crasser analogy, compare it to the truly great athlete who can get away with seeming to break the basic rules of his sport, because he has mastered them so thoroughly.) But "once the thread of development has been broken" we are condemned to ceaseless experimentations. Nietzsche, talking specifically about dramatists, thought that after Voltaire—"the last of the great humanists" and "one of the last men who could unite in himself the highest freedom of spirit with an utterly unrevolutionary temperament"—we have "the modern spirit with its restlessness, its hatred of standards and limits," conquering in all areas. In this restless experimentation we have tasted joys; "but for how much longer?" Our poets are condemned to "become experimenting counterfeiters, foolhardy copyists," be their strength ever so great. In place of the curbing and organizing of creative power, we have power valued for its own sake, inspiration for inspiration's sake— Dionysus without Apollo. "Yes, one has thrown off the 'irrational' fetters of French-Greek art, but thereby, unnoticed, one finds that all fetters, all limitations have become irrational—and so art moves toward its dissolution. . . ."

After Modernism

The years after 1945 saw the Modernist style move perilously close to its dissolution. Criticism of it had become widespread. It declined into barren coteries, "Lilliputian claques," and into fads, idiosyncracies, hysterias. The avant-garde repeated itself, spawned anachronism, cultivated old styles eclectically, parodied itself, parodied everything—but created nothing more after the one great generation of Modernists. These had tended to do what could never be done again, and they knew it. "After us the Savage God," said Yeats. After Picasso's generation, that corruscatingly brilliant age that produced Klee, Kandinsky, Chagall, Mondrian, and others, "modern art" entered into the desert. "They [the great modern innovators in art and literature] led in the direction of an immensity from which there was bound to be a turning back," wrote Stephen Spender, "because to go further would lead to a new and completer fragmentation, utter obscurity, form (or rather formlessness) without end." There has never been so much poetry and so much painting as in recent years, but none of it succeeds for more than a season or rises to more than local prominence.

The art of modern times has been isolated from life and is therefore absurd, meaningless, rooted in nothing except the stray and puerile insights of rootless individuals. Its schizoid subjectivism reflects the absence of common values in society. There may be form without content since, not sure of what they want to express, writers tinker with technique; typically an almost frightening level of technical competence goes with a feebleness or morbidity of ideas. Artists by and large have continued to spurn the vulgar multitude and have appealed to coterie or small-magazine audiences, if indeed to any at all.

The playing out of the Modernist phase of high art has caused all save certain small and isolated groups to lose interest and has created a vacuum into which have rushed all manner of weird substitutes. The almost month-by-month artistic and even intellectual fashions are suspected of being as vulgar and certainly prove to be as ephemeral as seasonal tastes in the length of ladies' skirts or the cut of men's coats. Increasingly bizarre experiments permit "in" people to adopt airs of knowing superiority and put down the unfortunates who have not kept up. But is any of it art? The average intelligent citizen cannot easily distinguish fraud from genuine if desperate esthetic avant-gardisms and is tempted to give up in disgust. The disease does indeed seem to be, as Mr. Booker named it, neophilia.

It is hard, for example, not to think that serious music has reached the state of total decay, a victim of this ailment. Figures who command much respect and play a large role in music give off an alarming scent of modish decay. John Cage, an Absurdist and extreme eccentric, abandoned music altogether in favor of "environmental sounds and noises," so he declared (*A Year from Monday; New Lectures and Writings,* 1967). Though a recent history of twentieth-century music calls him the most influential composer of his generation, few of the general public know his name. Cage encouraged the divorce between society at large and the small circle of real artists (see also his *Silence*). He wanted to abolish the composer; abolish notation; in the end, abolish music. Here was the phenomenon of artistic antiart, ending in a death wish. In the quest for novelty, with ever diminishing returns, where else to end? Cage's disciples went back to the shenanigans of the Satie and Dadist era, including nonsensical demonstrations. They took up bizarre living. But this too is old hat. It was done long ago. In the end, the most startling novelty is to bring art to an end.

But much was created. Music pushed onward in a restless wave of experimentation, adding to such older novelties as atonality and serialism new devices of electronic music, computer composition, "concrete" music, and so on. It could not be denied that this music showed a fierce dynamism, an urge to express new ideas and invent new techniques. But this very dynamism carried it into a wilderness where there was no significant audience. A sympathetic commentator, Henry Barraud, described the course of twentieth-century music as "a fearsome evolution, in which new systems have violently abused the old tonal techniques, revolutionized all our habits and reactions, and in which apart from a limited group which is very aware, the great majority of the music public, confused and stunned, bridle at a phenomenon which is too much for them, even if it does not offend them." Hence the frequent judgment that serious music, "classical" music in the grand Western tradition, is dead or dying, no longer having any roots in society. (Arthur Honegger, an eminent modern composer, said as much in *Je suis compositeur,* 1951.) The audience for serious music that still existed wanted to hear the familiar sounds of Beethoven and Brahms, not the weird experimentations of a Xenakis or Penderecki. (The anguish of their times clearly affected the composers: Penderecki's "Threnody to the victims of Hiroshima" was naturally without any harmony at all.) Distressed enough in their own lives, people came to the concert hall for relief, not agitation. At the same time many young music lovers turned to the new jazz, whose upper borders were close to those of the serious avant-garde. But theoreticians of the high culture such as Theodor Adorno equated jazz with the dehumanizing mindlessness of a decadent mass society. They seemed to confuse the various levels of pop music, ranging upward from primitive drum-thumping rituals, with the almost classical jazz of a Hubert Laws—a serious confounding of genres, surely, but quite understandable in all the din and confusion.

The true music of the bourgeoisie was surely not Pierre Boulez but something between Lawrence Welk and Johann Strauss. The serious avant-garde received support only on the eccentric fringes of a polymorphous society. To call this music "bourgeois decadence" as Marxists did was only a further confusion. The point was underscored by the sterility of music in the Soviet Union, as the deadening hand of state ideology slowly strangled one of the world's great musical traditions. The cutting edge of modern music was indubitably composers like Penderecki and Boulez—a scintillating blade but one far too sharp for the democratic mass society of today. Isolation and eccentricity reinforced each other in a vicious circle, threatening the death of art from a radical separation of the artist from society.

The dissolution of art was matched by the frequent dissolution of the artist, who continued to be an outsider driven toward self-destruction. One of the leading literary discoveries of the 1960s was Malcolm Lowry, author of *Under the Volcano,* whose compelling prose emerged from the interstices of a chaotic, drunken life. Lowry, predating the drugged generation, was a victim of alcohol. *Under the Volcano,* it has been said, "is a novel about Hell"; Lowry put his life, which was a hell, into it. His restless wanderings, seeking a place quite outside of and beyond "society," are typical of the modern writer of genius, Lawrence being the best example. Lowry, born in England, took to sea in his youth, later drifted to Mexico (the nominal setting of *Under the Volcano*), and finally settled for some years in a cabin on the lonely shores of British Columbia, where he did his best writing.

Sylvia Plath, the brilliant young American poet, committed suicide in 1963 (a famous case, preceded by some poems of a frightening power). So, in 1970, did the man many called the greatest German-language poet of his generation, Louis Celan, who had come to believe that communication was impossible. Celan, whose real name was Paul Antschel, was an international wanderer whose life might well serve as an epitome of the story of modern Europe. He was born in an area which had been a part of the old Austria-Hungary, belonged to Rumania at the time of his birth in 1920, and became Russian in 1940. The Germans took it in 1941 and sent Celan's Jewish parents to death in a concentration camp. He survived and left Russia for Rumania in 1945, moving to Vienna in 1947 and Paris in 1948, where he married and spent the rest of his life. For understandable reasons he did not care to live in Germany, but he wrote in German, the tongue of his youth, and was much honored in the German literary world. It is hardly surprising that his haunting poems are filled with images of death and destruction.

Another suicide was perhaps the greatest American poet of the time, John Berryman, a decidedly nonconformist personality who killed himself in 1972. That same year the English critic and poet A. Alvarez, who had known Sylvia Plath, wrote *The Savage God,* a book on self-destructive tendencies in modern art. Genuine commitment to literature or art is likely to be a destructive force in modern times. Yvor Winters found Hart Crane to be a typical case: this major American poet ended by drowning himself, after having tried alcohol and homosexuality along with poetry. He, too, had begun with a faith in the Word and had lost it. Since Rimbaud, the man of letters— C. P. Snow was right—has been a scandal. If he has taken to drugs, this is hardly new, for Rimbaud and Baudelaire continued a practice familiar to the Romantics of the early nineteenth century, which has only become more widespread today.[4]

Confusion in the arts was compounded by the repetition of old movements which were announced as new ones. Since there have been so many changes over the last century, and since revolutionists usually are too impatient to study history, they fall into that trap which Santayana noted: being ignorant of the past, they are condemned to repeat it.

There were numerous revivals, evidence enough of the insecurity of contemporary style. Everything has come back at some time, arousing fears of a sort of endless regurgitation, the death of culture in an emetic paroxysm. There was the revival of Art Nouveau, signalled by the Aubrey Beardsley exhibition of 1966 in London. Beardsley images appeared on the covers of record albums by the Beatles. (With their staring eyes and mask-like faces, the Beardsley ladies impressed young people as obviously "stoned.") But this was only one of a number of revivals. There was a popular cult of the 1920s; then one of the 1930s; finally even a revival of the 1950s— ready for resurrection from the lethean gulf, already ancient history, by 1972. In its ever sicker hurry, modern life seemed to devour styles as an addict pops pills, needing more and more each time. Unable to assuage its thirst for novelty with styles supplied by the existing avant-garde, it devoured past styles too, reviving and rereviving them and forgetting them betweentimes.

A. Alvarez, writing about poetry, commented on "the odd phenomenon of the latest *avant-garde* being largely a rewrite of that fifty years ago."[5] If avant-gardism itself wears out as a gesture, so does the supply of possible avant-gardes. As Oscar Wilde quipped a long time ago, the danger of being too modern is that you may find yourself suddenly old-fashioned. Examination of the numerous "little magazines" which flourish ephemerally in all Western countries turns up little that is really new. "Concrete" poetry, after all, goes back to Apollinaire's "simultanism" of the 1900s, if not earlier.

The Futurists invented the "happening" in 1913. Mixtures of "sex, sadism, and socialism" were original, if at all, only in the combination, not the ingredients. There were gimmicks like pages printed in the shape of inner soles, so that you can wear your poetry—humor in a well-worn tradition. Some still thought that to write without punctuation or capitalization makes stale ideas daring. For the rest, the offbeat magazines offered either Marxist polemics or standard modern poetry and criticism.

"The artist's brave cry of freedom has turned into the shout of a buffoon," Ken Baynes declared sadly in surveying the field of "little magazines." [6] Of much recent art it is hard to decide, indeed, whether it is just buffoonery or in some obscure way significant. In 1967 (as reported in *Time,* May 26) a fashionable Pop artist exhibited among other things "a 6-ft.-long stuffed-and-sewn canvas loaf of raisin bread, with six detachable slices and 42 removable raisins; a 12-ft.-tall droopy white canvas 'ghost fan' . . .; a collage made out of cigarette butts . . .; a brobdingnagian girl's thigh for hem-hoisting London." Worse lay ahead, for in 1971 a Bulgarian named Christo persuaded enough people to put up money for "a 1,500 foot long, 8,000 pound curtain of tightly woven orange-hued industrial nylon" to be hung across Rifle Gap in Colorado, there to billow temporarily in the wind (Futurism and Dadaism on a gigantic scale). The "conceptualizing" artists did not paint at all; they invented the ideas for paintings and sold them as do-it-yourself kits. Art of this sort is clearly satire, or the contemporary equivalent of it (when we are beyond mere satire, something more brutally aggressive is necessary). Pop art, a leading vogue of the early 1960s, was beyond Modernism; at the same time its apparent return to themes of everyday life was sardonic and often contained the most extreme Modernist hatred of everyday life.

It seemed impossible to sustain a movement longer than a few years. Alain Robbe-Grillet's "new novel" was the hottest avant-gardism about 1960, one with more than usual distinction, backed by its brilliant creator's fascinating novels as well as by his theory about how he thought he had created them. But by 1970 he had become an object of attack, not only because the *nouveau roman* had grown stale but because it had become the Establishment, its prophet an international celebrity, man of property, and member of the literary *status quo.* From revolutionary to reactionary in one decade—perhaps even in one or two years—is the usual story of recent artistic fashions.

In a book surveying the French novel in the decade 1960–1970, R. M. Albérès found no one theme nor even any identifiable group of great names, such as one might readily compile for the previous generation (Malraux, Bernanos, Montherlant, Sartre, Camus, Mauriac); instead he found countless tendencies and a host of writers all good and none recognizably better than the rest. No directions and no main lines; only stimuli. No river flowing in one direction, but a lake. Similarly, an attempted survey of *Movements in Art since 1945* (1970) by Edward Lucie-Smith resembles a catalogue of innumerable movements and artists none of which or whom proved of any enduring significance—at least none stands out from the crowd. The age of Braque, Matisse, Klee, Mondrian, Picasso, Kandinsky gave us the giants of Modernism; the epigoni seem to be interesting dwarfs. An unfavorable review of Lucie-Smith's book complained of its "almost unfailing flatness, praising all and sundry," but one wonders what else he could do, unless he were to dispraise all and sundry. Art has come to be like *haute couture*, its history like the history of fashions, with little to be said except that thus it was at such time: catsup bottles succeeded optical illusions as midi-skirts succeeded mini. And, as was frequently pointed out, it was subject to a cynical commercial manipulation by the moguls of the art market, who treated it like a branch of advertising.

Some Recent Themes

Within these mingling waters various patterns might be discerned, though not very clearly and sometimes in bizarre contradiction. Violent hostility to the social environment was naturally a common thing. "The refusal of the world as it is" always and ever lies at the bottom of modern poetry and art. In a discussion of contemporary novels (1972), Professor W. M. Frohock found a substantial proportion of their themes divided between one or another kind of withdrawal—either by physical flight, by a drop-out way of life, or by escape into a realm of fantasy—and a wild lashing out at the world. The flower child and the militant seem to be reflected in this literary dualism; in the end, the schizophrenic and the manic. In either case, of course, we have a reaction to a hostile and intractable milieu, not felt to be subject to management or even coexistence but only to be violently assailed or fled from. Yet modes of accommodation also appeared. Pop art is an example. Whatever one thinks of soup cans, Roy Lichtenstein and Andy Warhol were as significant as any contemporary artists. Doubtless their gesture toward the nonesoteric was ironic and was meant as an antiart. (The alienated became alienated from their traditional alienation. To be "square" is a daring novelty.) But one cannot quite be sure. Serious jazz supplies an example of a popular genre capable of interesting the intellectuals and thus bringing highbrow and lowbrow within measurable distance of each other.

Remarkable, too, were the poetry readings which attracted large crowds of far from highbrow people. In 1965 a large crowd filled Albert Hall in London to hear a poetry recital. It was an astonishing event and reflected a quite widespread interest extending from Russia to California. The poetry read by Pop and Beat cult figures hardly gained approval from those poets who, usually sheltered from the masses in some university post, carried on the great traditions of high culture; in fact, they indignantly pronounced it sloppy and sentimental. Sometimes it was embarrassingly self-advertising. On the other hand, it could not have pleased the pure philistines accustomed to reading *Playboy* magazine and James Bond novels, if indeed they read anything at all.

At its most vacuous, Pop poetry calls to mind the American Rod McKuen and the Canadian Leonard Cohen. Childish fantasy, simple political rhetoric, Bob Dylan or Beatle songs made up the subject matter of much of it, and it is significant that it has been identified in England with Liverpool. But poets such as (the British) Adrian Mitchell, Christopher Logue, and Brian Patten did at times come close to what the Western civilized tradition regards as good poetry. The verdict of a recent critical survey, that Pop "largely failed" as poetry because of its simplistic ideas and impoverished language (see Michael Schmidt and Grevel Lindop, *British Poetry since 1960,* 1972), does not prevent recognition of its importance. One of the chief developments of the 1960s in poetry was this "underground," anti-Establishment verse, out of which occasionally emerged work of real merit, which contained a fresh if naive vision, and which did at least reach large numbers of people. (Typically it was meant to be recited to an audience, not read in a book, a feature that accounts for its popularity but also for some of its lapses in taste.)

An important book appraising trends in the American novel of recent times—surely a brilliant generation, with Saul Bellow and Ralph Ellison and John Updike towering above a host of interesting lesser talents—and bearing the title *After Alienation* (1965) purported to find the chief trend in a movement toward a sort of reconciliation with ordinary life. Yet this trend was followed mainly by those partially attuned to the spirit of the conservative 1950s who felt challenged by the new wave of extremely alienated writers in the 1960s—writers who were likely to look upon Bellow and Ellison as quite hopelessly Establishment types. The "radical innocence" in which Ihab Hassan found a key to the American novel was only the bruised romantic ego retreating to its ultimate lair, giving up protest only because the world is beyond protest.

Some serious academicians, influenced by the modish radicalism of the era, trained their fire on "elite" culture and claimed to find no grounds for preferring traditional high culture to popular culture, Stravinsky to the Jefferson Airplane, or Shakespeare to the underground film. In the main, academic culture and pop culture remained apart. In his introduction to *The Survival of Poetry* (1970), Martin Dodsworth described the two schools as each in its own way sterile. The one, though often formally excellent and retaining some contact with tradition, lacked emotional content and the taste of reality; the other could move people but was typically formless and mindless. Between these cut-glass flowers and rank weeds, there was very little really sound and authentic poetry.

That the great bulk will not survive is not surprising; great poets are always rare. Yet in the absence of clear standards almost anything has a chance of acceptance, and some recently prominent schools of poetry are in fact very bad. As an example, the American "Black Mountain" school combined a cult of obscurity with much posturing, self-advertising, and quaint erudition. Yet it was regarded in some quarters as the leading movement of recent literature; its leaders were highly prestigious, enormously successful. Despite its undeniable sincerity, their verse is really a pseudopoetry by poseurs playing at being poets. Even at its best, the Black

Mountain school radiated an eccentricity and a preciosity which are in the highest degree unnatural and testify that something is radically wrong somewhere. We might even suspect fraud, as with much of pop art. But its ideas were modishly appealing in rejecting technology and Modernism, calling for a return to the rural past or to the Indians and preaching a neotribalism as a relief from a fragmented society.

In pluralistic America especially, but to a scarcely lesser extent in other countries, numerous local schools of poetry sprang up. A San Francisco school, as well as a New York school, was able to establish a tenuous claim to wider recognition. Most English professors have heard of *it;* but not even English professors know of all the wayward groups, flourishing momentarily in Philadelphia or Bremen or Edinburgh, producing ephemeral little magazines printed on brown paper or worn in the soles of shoes. The profusion of such publications is a tribute to the vitality of the human spirit in our allegedly sterile age, but it also suggests the diffusiveness and aimlessness of contemporary art. Few broad trends can be distinguished.

To some extent the arts did mirror the movement from personalism and quietism in the 1950s to an often startlingly violent political chiliasm in the 1960s. Standing out slightly from the crowd of miscellaneous painting in the earlier postwar years was the Abstract Expressionism associated with De Kooning and Jackson Pollock, a form certainly detached from any social theme or message. In the next decade attempts at "revolutionary" art might be feeble, but Pop and Op were both aggressively social and objective and more ideological than Expressionism. And, in the 1960s, there was an ideological poetry (for example, Lawrence Ferlinghetti's) which was not good poetry by any academic standards but had the power to move deeply young political militants intoxicated by visions of utopia and the myth of heroic revolution. In general, the arts could be counted on to reflect trends in ideas.

The response of the arts to the new radicalism of the 1960s was extremely interesting. The New Left was not the Old; there could be no return to the simple-minded (as it now seemed) "proletarian realism" of the 1930s. Novels in which the bourgeois hero finally casts off his capitalistic heritage and sinks happily into the arms of the Party—which once was the plot of a majority of left-wing novels—had become obsolete, along with those emotional exhortations to join the union and march on the picket line. (Unions were now for the most part hopelessly, and happily, Establishment.) Lives of Lenin, propaganda movies from the USSR, celebrations of the Ten Days That Shook the World had lost their savor, of course; better to memorialize the futile revolt of the Kronstadt sailors *against* Lenin's new tyranny. Utterly hopeless revolts, in the spirit of Camus's existential rebel, proved generally attractive. Guevara's gesture of seeking the most desperate odds possible seized the imagination; so did Nat Turner's slave rebellion and even (with tongue in cheek) the Charge of the Light Brigade.

But in accordance with the eternal esthetic cannibalism of the Modern, new forms and devices had to be found. There was certainly a fecundity of experiments. If we take the London stage of the sixties as our case study, we find something of a bizarre renaissance. Cruelty, terror, drastic attempts to shock were much in evidence. A baby was stoned to death on the stage (*Saved,* Edward Bond, 1965); soldiers were kicked to death and burnt alive (*Dingo,* Charles Wood, 1969); a spastic child's father attempted to kill her (*A Day in the Death of Joe Egg,* Peter Nichols, 1967). There was all manner of (unnatural) sex, stopping just short of the sodomic rape featured on the New York stage (*Ché!*). It was in the main a "drama of despair." The multiplication of horrors included an extension of the Absurd to madhouse situations, considered more sane than a totally insane world. One of the more important British dramatists, Joe Orton, a former convict, was murdered by his homosexual roommate—England's answer to Jean Genet. Such youthful cult figures tended to make the old kings of drama—Robert Bolt, Terence Rattigan, even Harold Pinter—look antiquated and very "square."

In this drama of cruelty, brutality, absurdity, and despair, what political thought there was expressed a radical innocence, a thoroughgoing anarchism that treated all authority with contempt. Spitting on the flag was carried backward in the retrospective harrying of Queen Victoria and Winston Churchill, who were portrayed as clowns and criminals. (With no Vietnam War on which to vent their fury, the British resurrected the Crimean War, the Indian Mutiny, and World War II. For some reason World War I fared better—a Lovely War.) And over all of this the spirit of McLuhan hovered, for the medium was the message. Plot almost vanished, submerged in random experience, inconsequential ideas, all kinds of fantasy and buffoonery. What made plays go was dazzling stage technique. Reduced to a bare summary, almost the whole of the drama of the 1960s sounds utterly childish and boring. If, in fact, it excited considerable interest to the point of being hailed as a revitalization of the theater, this was because it came off better in performance than on paper. Some of its formidable tricks were verbal and stemmed from a keen ear for popular speech, as well as from the newly available shock of obscenity. (Censorship of the stage, long a British tradition, ended finally in 1967, prior to which the Lord Chamberlain had intervened on several occasions.) Others, in stagecraft and direction, suggest that technique prevailed over subject matter. The latter turned an exuberant anger on everything, producing fireworks capable of brilliantly illuminating a theatrical season. One must admit the vitality, the sheer energy, of this kind of theater. But the total effect was intellectual incoherence.

All of this suggests that, in a certain sense, it may now be impossible to write history about contemporary culture. For we do not find movement, development, but only random change. It is as if a river whose course one could follow ended in a swamp or in innumerable rivulets going off in all directions. One can follow out each of these trickles, but the river as a whole has ceased to have a determinate direction. Perhaps it has ended in a sea where all waters mingle confusedly together. There are all kinds of currents, but the sea, containing everything, is not moving anywhere. We can describe a particular area of it, but this is not "history." Paul Valéry, in some remarkable essays written around 1932, had this intuition of a past to which we can no longer look for direction: "It is useless to try, on the basis of a knowledge of the past, to conjecture what will be the sequel to our state of general bewilderment." Our ancestors were sure they could trace the direction of the human stream. Possibly they were deluded, but they did see great general movements in the history of mankind. Now, in the universal melee, there are no beginnings and no ends, only an endless milling about.

This may of course be a delusion, since few large trends or directions are discernible at the time, and since little history written in its own time reveals what posterity can see. Nevertheless, the absence of detectable direction seems a valid short-run judgment. Modernism has come to an end; what will follow it? Can anything, except the death of art?

The Pornographic Revolution

It is possible to discuss the triumph of obscenity and pornography in the context of Modernist neophilia. Any cultural historian looking for major themes in recent times must of course grant this trend an important place. Whether he sees it as the ultimate decadence of a dying culture or a hopeful signpost on the road to human liberation, he can hardly ignore it. He might link it to the new political radicalism; but while the abundant use of four-letter words by the student revolutionaries helped gain them attention, it does not seem to have had any organic connection with their politics. (Of course, the kind of infantile revolutionism which simply wished to create a scandal found an obvious ally in the obscene expression. Notable organs of the California school included *Fuck You* and *Horseshit.*) In 1896 Alfred Jarry could touch off a scene of pandemonium by beginning his play *Ubu Roi* with "Shit!" ("Merdre! Shite!") But the law of diminishing returns affects improper words, too. And improper acts.

To those who would argue that the drift toward permissiveness in language and behavior represents a long-term erosion of social order, there can be no serious objection. "An ordered society is necessarily a censoring society," Samuel Hynes observed in *The Edwardian Turn of Mind,* "because any society that is stable enough to have established values will naturally act to protect them against disturbance." The drift toward promiscuity and individual freedom against the claims of social order is an aspect of anomie, the breakdown of standards upheld by social authority, and has been going on since at least the seventeenth century. Nevertheless, a crucial change in that drift took place in the twentieth century, and a most significant part of this change was the secession from order on the part of respectable or *good* writers.

That pornography has existed about as long as has literacy surely cannot any longer be disputed. One of the achievements of recent scholarship has been to exhume the "other Victorians" along with the buried pornography of the seventeenth and eighteenth centuries, fully revealing material which had long suffered from neglect. There was pornography in ancient Greece, as the word itself indicates. It was revived in the Renaissance and thence handed down to the seventeenth century. In the latter period it seems to have become more endemic, and it played a significant role in the "liberation" of the mind in the eighteenth-century Enlightenment.

But until about 1914 pornography was almost always an underground or clandestine product, most of it disreputable, created by writers who neither were nor deserved to be regarded as having anything to do with the canons of literature. In 1857, at the high tide of Victorian respectability, the Obscene Publications Act was enacted by the British Parliament in response to a mounting volume of "poisonous publications." Thirty years later, the National Vigilance Association and other defenders of propriety arose in response to such booksellers as Henry Vizetelly, who boasted he had sold a million copies of "the worst class of French novels." Many of these were of the French Naturalist school—Zola ranks as perhaps the first great writer since Rabelais to go over to "indecency"—but clearly most of these publications were still of the gutter-press variety.

Edwardian England was the scene of a significant drama involving bolder and bolder attacks on Mrs. Grundy, which, while still arousing the ire of social conservatives, more and more attracted the support of the best writers. Battles about censorship broke out on a broad front. H. G. Wells, the pioneer sexologist Havelock Ellis, the socialist Edward Carpenter, and others not only approached sex with a new frankness but preached a New Morality, breaching the traditional tabus on premarital or extramarital sex relations. The forces of law and order fought back mightily but with little consequence. The dike was broken just about the time the Great War came. Oscar Wilde was crushed in 1895, Freud was hissed from the platform in 1910, and Joyce's *Dubliners* was refused publication for eight years after its completion in 1905. But it was published in 1914, amid the emergence of that brilliant group of new writers which included D. H. Lawrence. Purity continued to fight rearguard actions, but the struggle was really lost with the brilliant success of Joyce's *Ulysses* and Lawrence's *Women in Love* just after the war. (In Germany, during the postwar breakdown of government, there was an outburst of sexually daring films until censorship was reintroduced in 1920; in the 1920s Berlin's night clubs became centers of sin.)

Great writers embraced not only explicit sexual descriptions but also four-letter words. Joyce, in the most powerful of literary passages, dredged up the sexual preoccupations of the secret mind. He and his fellows rendered pornography obsolete by turning the erstwhile feeble efforts of Grub Street hacks into powerful and moving literature. Their books were not obscene but reverent, believing in the dignity of the sexual act, of which Lawrence made virtually a religion. No civilized man could put them in the same category as French postcards or *Captain Billy's Whiz Bang.* As early as 1933 Joyce's *Ulysses* was granted a special exemption from American laws banning the use of four-letter words. (No one else could use them, though blanks gradually gave way to the first letter followed by three astericks; George Orwell reminds us of a breakthrough about 1946, when it became possible to write f**k. Henry Miller's *Tropic of Cancer* could not legally be published in England or the United States.)

So the great moderns obliterated the distinction between good literature that was pure and bad literature that was dirty; good literature could in part be dirty, and increasingly one thought of much pure writing as very bad. Ruskin's "fair and foul" no longer held. But when every scribbler thought he must imitate Joyce and Lawrence, the results were dismaying.

The battle of *Lady Chatterley's Lover* in 1960 is frequently said to have prepared the way for the pornographic inundation of the 1960s, during which decade the student radicals, the underground press, and all manner of novelists—as well as film makers and playwrights—began using more explicit terminology and dealing more explicitly with sexual activities. With the triumph of Penguin Books over Her Majesty's Government in behalf of the unexpurgated edition of what everyone concedes was one of Lawrence's poorer works, the floodgates were opened and in poured those deliciously or hideously naughty works of past and present which hitherto had been confined to sinister quarters and dark corners.

In actuality the story was hardly that simple. The Lady Chatterley case itself was brought on by a new British law (1959) apparently designed both to deal more effectively with an already mounting tide of obscenity and to allow more latitude to serious works of art. During the proceedings, witnesses for the defense time and again made the point that anyone could buy salacious trash at Charing Cross, while Lawrence's book, which really treated sex with great reverence, was banned. During his address the defense attorney was at pains to assure the jury that this particular case would not, must not, constitute a license for "any scribbler writing any kind of novel" to use the same words. Yet in fact, for all his reverence, Lawrence was an advocate of both the four-letter words and the explicit descriptions—far more stirring in the hands of a real literary artist than in those of a pulp magazine hack, however brave his intentions. And if these were permitted to *Lady Chatterley's Lover,* it would be hard to deny them to other novelists. In a democratic age one can hardly insist that a man be a certified genius before gaining certain obviously advantageous literary rights. How, in any case, does one certify genius?

The way was clearly open to all manner of would-be Lawrences to venture as far into the tempting field of sexual frankness as their boldness and ingenuity allowed. Literature that had been considered indecent was no longer confined to the gutter but emerged to join respectable society. No longer outcasts, Justine and Fanny Hill were admitted to polite society, where, with Lady Chatterley or members of Mary McCarthy's Group, they enjoyed the highest prestige. "In the twelve years since the passing of the Act the development of 'literary frankness' and pictorial nudity has been almost incredibly swift," C. H. Rolph remarked in reviewing the process of which he had been a part (*TLS,* January 14, 1972). The tide flowed so inexorably against the forces of decency that the respectables felt like Canute.

The French version of the Lady Chatterley trial was the de Sade affair, which reached the courts in 1956–1957. Pauvert, publisher of the works of the scatological eighteenth-century nobleman, was condemned, but an appeal overturned the conviction in 1958. A new law of 1958 in France, as in Britain, tried to establish some controls over obscene publications. The arrival of President de Gaulle ushered in a period in which the once wicked French became "more Puritan than England or the United States." *Fanny Hill,* which circulated freely in the latter countries, was banned in Paris. The imprisonment of Ralph Ginzburg in the United States for publishing obscene material was not really typical of an erratic but unmistakable trend toward permissiveness, which by the end of the sixties led to dirty movies on every downtown street corner and only slightly less dirty ones in suburban movie houses. Slickly packaged photographic sex made vast fortunes for such magazines as *Playboy* and *Lui*. More important, in the name of high philosophy Sartre praised the Divine Marquis along with Genet; writers as talented as Günter Grass, Alain Robbe-Grillet, William Burroughs, and John Updike produced heavily pornographic works. Dirt was divinity; the obscene was the exalted.

What had really happened was the vast vulgarization of something intended initially, and in fact successfully used, as a means to the revitalization of literature and of human emotions. The coinage had been debased. Joyce used scatological terms for a purpose, with calculated effect, to make legitimate points. He put obscenity to artistic use. Dirty words and eroticism were not their own end, in a *Playboy* or James Bond way; they were used (sparingly) where they belonged and because they belonged. Joyce's obscenity had such great effect because it was not overused. It shocks us where shock is appropriate, and not elsewhere. Of Joyce and Lawrence, Anthony Burgess remarked that "every dirty word had to tell, being transmuted into an exact technicality or else into a symbol of mindlessness." Their actually quite economical use of the forbidden words was esthetically effective *because* they were forbidden. Gongs are effective only if you do not keep striking them. Make the four-letter words as commonplace as any others, and you destroy the possibility of using them at all for literary effect.

You also eventually destroy the ability of literary sensationalists to exploit them for profit. Writers like Norman Mailer who debased their talents by succumbing to the allure of gaining fame and fortune and flooding their books with an incessant stream of scatology and obscenity could not go on long in that vein. Those who got books of no real quality published because they used the language of the streets could not repeat this feat indefinitely. The flood of pornography cheapened the literary market not just because it was pornography but because, by leaning on this crutch, writing became poorer. Many noted the antipathy between pornography and art. The restrictions placed on earlier writers had forced them to convey meaning imaginatively rather than simply through four-letter words. Pornography typically has no structure except that round of constant "fucking" which is the subject matter of all eleven volumes of the notorious *My Secret Life*. It is artistically and psychologically simple-minded: a clumsy fist, Storm Jameson noted, mashing what is complex and paradoxical—the human feelings involved in love and lust—into a flat anatomical mass.

The effect of this fashionable novelty must soon wear off. There were signs of this at the end of the decade which may go down in history as the Salacious Sixties. The inclusion of between three and six clinical descriptions of sexual acts in every novel had become a convention, a ritual, as rigorous as the old Aristotelian rules about the unities. And most of them were as tedious as the incessant repetition of the act itself is likely to be. All perversions had been explored, but there is, after all, a distinctly finite number of these. In seeking to expand this number the imaginations of desperate authors went too far, and the limits of all credibility were exceeded. Drawings and photographs of every possible position in the end had the same disenchanting effect. Pornography was clearly in danger of becoming the last and greatest bore of all. Even Herbert Marcuse, who was often blamed for having begun it all, seemed to draw back when faced with vulgarized permissiveness (see *One-Dimensional Man*). This was not what he had meant! In much the same spirit, veteran civil liberties advocate Morris Ernst wailed that he had wanted to defend *Ulysses*, not sodomy on the New York stage. Similarly Wilhelm Reich, so widely known as the prophet of unlimited sexual liberation, came to reject "random fucking" as not what he had intended to sanction. As for the boredom, it was much commented on. The highly liberal *New York Times* reflected that "the insensate pursuit of the urge to shock, carried from one excess to a more abysmal one, is bound to achieve its own antidote in total boredom. When there is no lower depth to descend to, ennui will erase the problem" (April 1, 1969).

A revival of purity threatened: "Come back Snow White, all is forgiven," one reviewer of films implored after seeing an underground movie. He had also seen, and found incredibly boring, a movie called *Assault*, as well as *Beyond the Valley of the Dolls*, *Myra Breckenridge* (reversal of the sexes), and one about a penis transplant. In 1971 this was a normal week's crop. While no one could imagine a return to the arms of Mrs. Grundy, it did begin to look as if the scatological shock effect would wear off, leaving the seeker of novelty very much where he was before—but with one less option, and disillusioned about the last mystery. In a 1971 John Mortimer novel, a man says that sexual love "has been greatly overrated by the poets" and suggests that "it is pretty uphill work if you ask me."

Certainly all this looked very odd from a distance. At the International Writers' Conference held in August, 1962, at Edinburgh, with all the contemporary crew of writers displaying their considerable egos, a visitor from India interjected the simple comment that his country had too many bigger problems to have much time for such neurosis and self-pity. If Western literature can plumb exciting depths of personal feeling, it also exhibits loss of social purpose; its self-indulgence and its hippie attitudes mark it a victim of the affluent society. The preoccupation with drugs and pornography is profoundly decadent, not because sexual and psychological experimentation is bad, but because a healthy society has interests that preclude preoccupation with such matters. In this sense pornography and eroticism are "escapist." (Norman Mailer turned to his "hipster" cult of sex and scatology after becoming disenchanted with utopian politics.) In no healthy society are these elements allowed full play in their physical, not to mention intellectual, manifestations. They are overridden by social needs that require energies to be directed elsewhere than to erotic fantasy. Only an idle, leisured class—including successful novelists—can afford to indulge itself thus. Rejection of pornography is found in working-class, not upper-class, circles. When in 1968 a British jury, in a temporary reversal of the permissive trend, convicted the publisher of an American scatological novel called *Last Exit to Brooklyn,* the publisher complained that he had drawn a working-class jury rather than an "S.W.3" (affluent-professional) one.

The women's movement was also a source of protest against pornography, which feminists saw as the product of male fantasy based on the humiliation and subjugation of women. "The whole pattern of pornography is one long woeful saga of female degradation," Jill Tweedie wrote. "Almost all pornography is written by men for men," Steven Marcus noted in *The Other Victorians.* The most literarily successful pornography, for example, Alain Robbe-

Grillet's (see *Project for a Revolution in New York*), would seem to bear this out. Kate Millett's attack on male sexual fantasy as intolerably arrogant—she singled out Norman Mailer's and Henry Miller's—was printed in her widely read *Sexual Politics* (1969). An element of sadism almost always enters in, the woman being treated as an object, a slave, the victim of brutal masculine lust. Thus while one of the most striking of sado-pornographic works, *The Story of O*, was evidently of feminine authorship, and the merest glance at contemporary literature reveals women's interest in the frank treatment of sex, including "perversions," it is nevertheless true that some of the backlash against what Robert Brustein called "the perverse imagination" stemmed from another avant-garde movement, the aggressive Women's Liberationists.

Often, too, the backlash accompanied a reaction against the lifestyle of the dropout and drug culture, or the "demonic students" of the later sixties. Kingsley Amis's 1972 novel, *Girl, 20*, is an amusing lecture on how sordid the young barbarians are, how silly it is for anyone of culture to try to get on with them; it was an aspect of that wry and witty writer's swing far to the right. Not a few other quite sophisticated people joined him in casting a hesitant vote for decency along with soap, for not always taking off one's clothes at an instant's notice, and for questioning the virtues of heroin.

Yet is must be recorded that among those who called for the freedom of the four-letter word were the intellectual leaders of the time. A 1970 assembly of British writers voted overwhelmingly in favor of it. True, David Holbrook, a well-known and hardly reactionary British author, burst forth in the January 15, 1972, issue of *Spectator* with a complaint that "pornography has now become a horrible epidemic in England that threatens our country's psychic health," and a similar statement ("The Politics of Subversion and Rage") by Masud R. Khan in *TLS*, February 4, 1972, related pornography to an impoverished esthetic and a dehumanized society. But the reactions to their statements as reflected in the correspondence sections of these journals suggested no agreement with them. It is futile, as well as illiberal, to forbid pornography, to censor any kind of literary or artistic expression, a consensus of the intellectual community held. Nasty as much of it is, it must be tolerated as the price of freedom; if the alternative to putting up with salacious trash is Mrs. Grundy, we have no choice at all. "The end of obscenity" (no forbidden words or scenes) would supposedly mean sounder psyches, fewer hang-ups, serener sex lives. The warning that it might lead to a devaluation of love and thus a cheapening of life itself did not get much attention.

Extreme confusion among those smitten by a deep sense of alarm at the revolution of pornography and permissiveness was quite apparent—for example, in the *Longford Report,* printed in England in 1972. Much in evidence in that document was highly amateurish sociological and historical talk about modern degeneration, traced to such varying causes as the demise of Christianity and the failure to be scientific enough (or perhaps to be sufficiently unscientific) about sex. In 520 meandering, poorly written pages, opinions gathered from a host of literary and public figures sought to estimate to what extent we are "damaged" by salacious literature, to what extent censorship might pose a greater danger to "freedom of speech," but provided no consensus.[7] The appeal to the mores of society runs aground on the simple fact that there is no single set of positive moral values shared by all or even most of society's members. If there is a consensus, it is the liberal assumption of a pluralist society open to all opinions that are not demonstrably a clear and present danger. That the publication of matter regarded as nasty by many people is such a danger is hard to prove.

Such considerations evade what Freud considered the real issue: complete sexual liberation destroys love: "In times during which no obstacles to sexual satisfaction existed . . . love became worthless, life became empty" (Sigmund Freud, *Contributions to the Psychology of Love,* 1912). Freud added that "the ascetic tendency of Christianity" had "raised the psychical value of love" in a way that paganism could never do. The contemporary soul prizes romantic love as the highest value, yet in its indulgent insistence that it be made easy for all (in a democratic age) destroys that value. Only that which is hard to attain can have value. If Freud and all the others who have made this point were right, contemporary man is frustrating himself in the realm of sexual love and will end either by a reversion to the barnyard or the renaissance of a new puritanism. (Something like this had, in fact, happened at the end of the eighteenth century to bring "Victorianism" into being: an orgy of libertinism in high society brought an extreme reaction toward virtue and chastity.)

Some Consequences of Neophilia

Pornography, then, is a phase of Modernism: the quest for ever more startling novelty, the need of each generation of artists and writers to revise and stupefy its predecessor by some new twist of style or structure or content. If originality has become the obsession of twentieth-century authors, as Paul Valéry once remarked, the quest for originality has made the bizarre and the forbidden the most striking features of modern artistic expression.

This pressure toward nonconformity, this *drang nach neuheit,* inevitably leads the artist ever farther away from the normal or average modes of feeling and expression. "The picture of American society that one might glean from a study of their novels would be a very strange one indeed," Auberon Waugh commented in the course of reviewing some American novels. "It is a world peopled almost entirely by dropouts, dope fiends, nymphomaniacs, roadside philosophers and suchlike parasites on the body politic." The writers not so much reject as ignore the world in which the vast majority of Americans (who presumably provide the reading public for these novels) live. The latter world no longer pays attention to any sort of serious cultural statement (as the memorable Anthony Burgess / Stanley Kubrick film *A Clockwork Orange* seemed to say).

It would be interesting to see the results of a Gallup Poll concerning how many Americans had even heard of the greatest American poets of recent time: Sylvia Plath, John Berryman, Robert Lowell. (If some have now heard of Plath it is because of the sensational features of her death.) It is even less likely that more than an infinitesimal percentage of the public could identify an outstanding living artist or serious musician, showing knowledge of his work and its significance. There *was* an interesting poll taken a few years ago by one of the little literary magazines, which revealed that most people who bought "significant" novels did not actually read them. Of the eighty-one buyers of John Barth's *Giles Goatboy* whom it questioned, the magazine claimed, only seven read the book through and fifty-three did not read any of it. *The Confessions of Nat Turner* did no better, and John Updike's *Couples* did even worse. And indeed these novels, like many others, are quite unread- able, though undeniably "significant." They celebrate the bitter absurdity of modern life.

The wave of neosuperstition—occultism, witchcraft, shaman- ism—which broke over the avant-garde and counterculture world in the 1960s was an "After-Everything" phenomenon relating particularly to the decline of art. It was a refuge against the rationalized technological society, as art had once been. Edward Coley Burne-Jones painted his angels in defiance of materialistic science. What does one do when there is no painting? The poets and artists of the nineteenth century, from Rimbaud to Jarry, from Dante Gabriel Rossetti to Ernest Dowson, expressed their protest against society with the grand gesture of Art for Art's Sake. The exhaustion of this gesture, with the exhaustion of art, left a vacuum that has had to be filled. It may still be filled by popular poetry or art of an increasingly weird sort, but these are no longer what they were. The substitute gesture is sought for and found in various ways. Occultism clearly is a defiance of the "square" world with its rules and roles, its science and bureaucracy, its "rationalization" princi- ple. When one cannot any longer be a poet, one becomes a witch.

The much-discussed "generation gap" was, of course, largely the result of neophilia, the restless neuroticism of modern life. Fashions in everything change so often that only people of very nearly the same age can share those intimacies of culture, such as songs, jokes, books, vocabulary, that are the instruments of personal understand- ing. Youth and age, inevitably different in their views of life, could once at least share the same classics of literature and art and music, the same dances and stories and blandishments. The frenzied replacement of all styles every few years imposes a further obstacle to social intercourse and augments the isolation of modern souls.

Beginning humanists were often dismayed to discover that even the realm of scholarship was prone to a neophilia that rendered truth apparently less significant than topicality. The old classics of history, for example, which had seemed timeless and had given pleasure as well as a sense of reality to generations of readers were dismissed as "obsolete"—Burckhardt on the Renaissance, to take one case—because their familiarity had palled, and sophisticated contemporary historians thought of new questions and new techniques. Burckhardt had not understood the use of computers, had not analyzed the economy of Italy with the aid of regression analysis or counterfactuality, had said nothing about the index of social mobility. In social studies, fads such as these swept across the academic landscape from year to year. Black Studies were in one season and out the next, a fate that also overtook courses on Latin America, Africa, and other exotic regions; swarms of young historians rushed to study them when they appeared prominently in the news, only to find later that interest had waned and there were not enough academic posts for all the Ph.D.s. (Auberon Waugh wryly observed in 1972 that there were more people interested in writing about Africa than in reading about it.) Guessing the trends became a game necessary to graduate students, as they plotted strategies for getting a job by hitting the market just right, having a dissertation on feminism or occultism ready while these topics were still fashionable. Trendiness thus infected some of the most august realms of research, where it seemed likely to exert a profoundly demoralizing influence.

Incessant novelty, a result of the disease of Modernism, had one further consequence, worth discussing as an additional theme in the next chapter: it filled the world with an immense quantity of intellectual matter. Such material had been accumulating for centuries in the Western tradition, piling up a body of literature and thought too vast for anyone's comprehension; but this accumulation accelerated in ever increasing proportions with the death of tradition and the enthronement of novelty. "Has the line of Western tradition become too long?" Professor Giovanni Sartori asked. A tradition can endure for millennia, as many examples prove, if men have not learned to question it. But a part of the Western tradition was the expectation of change and of improvement. Viewed from this perspective, the inherited body of thought becomes an awkward encumbrance.

NOTES

1. *The Politics of Experience* (1967).
2. *The Triumph of Romanticism* (1970), p. 231.
3. The only sign of conservatism in the popular mind in recent years was resistance

to the introduction of a new and lower skirt length in 1970, a trend that conflicted disturbingly with the New Morality. It is possible for novelties to clash with each other in this way.

4. Experiments with drugs for literary purposes were undertaken in the 1950s by such eminent and respectable figures of the older generation as Aldous Huxley and, in France, Henri Michaux.

5. See his book *Beyond All This Fiddle: Essays 1955–1967* (1968).

6. See "The Changing Guard," *TLS,* August 6 and September 3, 1964.

7. The collection of essays edited by David Holbrook, *The Case against Pornography* (1972), was also decidedly uneven though deeply impassioned—a rather inarticulate cry of pain and outrage.

5

The Overburdened Mind

Intellectual Fragmentation

"The difficulties of education had gone on doubling with the coal output, until the prospect of waiting another ten years, in order to face a seventh doubling of complexities, allured one's imagination but slightly," Henry Adams wrote in his wry way at the beginning of this century. Calculating the acceleration, he thought it likely that civilization would reach an end by 1921, destroyed by the sheer diffusion of energies. Perhaps it did. That was very nearly the year in which Yeats wrote "The Second Coming":

> Things fall apart; the centre cannot hold;
> Mere anarchy is loosed upon the world,

and the Dadaists said that it no longer makes any difference what words are used; in which Paul Valéry recorded the disintegration of European civilization, and Ezra Pound declared that there is no organized or coordinated civilization left, only scattered individual survivors (1922). Eliot's Waste Land or Unreal City was a heap of broken images. Knowledge went on, but it became a dry stone, a dead tree. Wyndham Lewis's "Cosmic Man" was man with technology but without culture.

Much of modern thought relates to the theme of the destruction of cultural unity, and the main dramas of thought in action in the period between the two world wars centered on this theme. The bloody agony of Fascism and Nazism was the gigantic contortion of a civilization reaching with all its energies for a community, a *Gemeinschaft* (Hitler's Völkisch state), that now lay beyond the power of all energies. The equally incredible embracing of Com-

119

munism by intellectuals and artists in the 1930s reflected their yearning for integration into an ordered hierarchy of intellectual discipline. These last desperate flights from cultural and intellectual anarchy proved to follow false trails, leading to horrors that made anarchy, by comparison, look like paradise.

Even if one gives up the quest for integration and, giving it the pleasing name of pluralism, finds anarchy acceptable, one cannot escape the awesome facts of intellectual fragmentation. At least any historian who writes about the recent epoch and thus, presumably, endows it with some sort of unity, must face them. He may, paradoxically, find here his chief unifying theme, an outstanding characteristic of modern times, one that goes far to account for a large number of cultural phenomena: the malaise of students, for example; the violence of revolutionaries, the hysterias of popular culture, the resort to drugs, even the inability to think clearly—amid a welter of "information"—about foreign and domestic policies of all sorts. This is the age of specialization, of intellectual fragmentation.

The fact has scarcely escaped notice, yet one may wonder if it has been noticed enough or its consequences observed. "Literature today is fragmented. . . . Scholarship is fragmented too; so is life. We are all confined to our own antheap, which is generally dusty, small and low." So, in 1968, remarked historian H. R. Trevor-Roper, who himself always tried commendably to combine the necessary expertise with breadth of interests and of outlook. If literature and scholarship are fragmented, as manifestly they are, life must be fragmented too. The death of culture, or at least of *a* culture, must certainly have momentous implications for all of life, must indeed be the greatest single event yet in the history of humanity.

To be sure, the unified, organic culture, wherein all men were whole, is a Golden Age myth. Henry Adams thought that in the thirteenth century there had been an integral culture, after which a steady disintegration increased in geometrical proportions until final dissolution occurred in modern times. Nearly a century earlier the pioneer socialist Henri Saint-Simon similarly believed that "the political malady" of his age, which was "egotism" and social disorganization, could be traced back to "the dissolution of the European spiritual power, a consequence of the insurrection of

Luther," since which time "the human spirit has detached itself from the most general views and has given itself over to *specialization*." But in fact medieval culture was not simple; indeed, the revolt against its intellectual authority in the seventeenth century, led by Francis Bacon and René Descartes, can quite easily be seen as a revolt against complexity, an attempt to simplify by declaring the whole cultural heritage to be nonsense and beginning all over again with a few axioms. And the early nineteenth-century Romantics, who were to be accused of fomenting cultural anarchy by invoking the autonomy of the subjective ego against all rules, actually thought of themselves as rescuing the unity of knowledge from Enlightenment scepticism. ("Knowledge is one," declared Jules Michelet.) Each great thinker or movement of ideas tended to see itself as restoring wholeness, but was viewed by its successors as only adding to the confusion. Complaints about the "overburdened mind," familiar in our time, have in fact been heard in all ages. No man has ever been able to grasp the *totum scibile,* but every thinking man wants to.[1] As José Ortega y Gasset said, man is the only being that misses what he never had.

This being conceded, it is still hard to deny that the present age has fallen victim to acute intellectual indigestion as no other ever did. The sheer fact of numbers confronts us. We may look back to a time when, for example, Sir Walter Ralegh said that he bought *every* book that was published. In western Europe and the United States today, there appear to be at least 100,000 new books published every year. (Recent figures of 23,000 for Great Britain and 22,000 for the United States give a rough idea.[2]) As many books were published between 1945 and 1970 as in the entire five hundred years from the birth of printing to 1945. There were 4,750 periodicals listed for Britain, 39,000 for the United States in 1970. Willing's *European Press Guide* listed over 50,000 Continental newspapers and periodicals. Who could read them all? Ten thousand men doing nothing else could not read 1 percent of them. There is a flourishing industry in abstracts, bibliographies, bibliographies of bibliographies, indexes, "retrieval" systems. If it is said that most of this huge output is without serious intellectual content, the reply must be that we cannot be so sure. For the intellectual historian, little at least is without *interest*. In any case, there was a generous profusion not only in low-level literature but in quite advanced or at least pretentious fields. Hardly less remarkable than the abundance of learned journals, in all zones of knowledge, was the proliferation of "little magazines" of poetry, art, criticism, philosophy. Specialists are needed just to keep up with the art movements, which are spawned by the dozens almost every week. One striking recent development, it would be generally conceded, is the impulse, exemplified by Pop art, to abolish distinctions between highbrow and lowbrow culture, to fill in that familiar abyss between artists and masses. If 99 percent of what is published is trash, as always was true, it is at any rate necessary to sort it out, and this is now harder than ever before to do. The task of the intellectual historian of the present age is a formidable one.

Equally striking figures exist, of course, for the growth in university population. In Mark Pattison's day, only a century ago, it was taken for granted that the treasures of the *totum scibile* could be made available to no more than a few thousand students. No one in all history had ever imagined that more than a small minority was capable of entering the sacred temple of knowledge, until just a few years ago. In 1870 there were 14,000 university students in Germany, the most advanced nation in the world in respect to its proportion of university members. (This was the age of Marx and Darwin and Mill, of Ruskin and Dostoyevsky and Nietzsche, as well as of Hertz and Clerk-Maxwell and Pasteur—in other words, the age of the men whose conceptions and discoveries still largely shape our minds.) By 1920 the number of university students had grown to no more than 80,000 out of a population of some 50 million. France had 42,000 in 1914, and only 80,000 in 1939. The educated world before 1914 consisted of somewhere around one person in every thousand, while minds capable of securing acceptance as intellectually creative were of the order of one in fifty thousand. In England on the eve of World War I, it would not be far wrong to say that about a thousand persons represented Knowledge and Culture—a little world consisting of Oxbridge and London dons plus some nonacademic men of letters who had won acceptance by their works.

Today, the number of university entrants exceeds one-third of the populace in the United States and is rising rapidly everywhere. It was over half a million in Britain in 1970 and is expected to reach a million in another decade. France in 1969 had 600,000. More than doubling itself in the 1960s, Italy's student population reached

600,000 in 1971; West Germany's stood at over 400,000, and was still growing. In the United States in 1971, over 800,000 *graduated* from colleges. There are tens of thousands of scholars and teachers in every one of dozens of fields of study. There are some 15,000 American historians, many more college teachers of literature, only slightly lesser numbers of sociologists, psychologists, political scientists, and economists. This is only at the "higher education" level; in addition, tens of thousands of high school teachers are reasonably well educated. The total "intellectual community" of western Europe and the United States must now greatly exceed a million people, by any sort of reckoning. "Quantifiers" could busy themselves with attempts at statistical accuracy in such matters—which could never succeed because of the necessity of arbitrary definitions—but humanly speaking the results are obvious. A "knowledge explosion" of immense proportions has provided the contemporary world with a shock equivalent to that of the discovery of the immensity of the cosmos upon Galileo's generation and to that of the immensity of time upon Lyell's.

And so, as Trevor-Roper remarked, we are all confined to our antheap. No one can "keep up" with more than a small area of specialization. In the 1960s, for example, more books were published each year on recent American foreign policy than were published fifty years ago on all of American life and culture. From such a degree of compartmentalization, many revolutionary consequences were bound to flow. It is no use arguing that we can store all this information up in computers and thus avoid being overwhelmed by masses of knowledge. The information is already stored in the books themselves, if what concerns us is merely its storage in inert receptacles. The point is that the living, creative mind of man, which has a personality and belongs to a culture, cannot keep up with the knowledge, cannot integrate it in any way. And this must have decisive consequences for human history, whatever is done by computers.[3]

Attempts at Synthesis

Professionalism began to take over the various realms of learning (converting them into industries, as Arnold Toynbee observed) about 1880—from which year the founding of professional societies and the proliferation of learned journals, the decline of those old amateur "men of letters," and the coming of the professional scholar can be approximately dated. As a child, Toynbee watched the process in a scholar's library, seeing the works of Edward Gibbon, Thomas Babington Macaulay, and Henry Hallam give way to rows of professional journals and inscriptions edited by German professors. Viewed from this perspective, specialization has grown faster than we may think. Not so terribly long ago the University of Edinburgh (we are reminded in a history of that august institution by D. B. Horn) possessed a Chair of Technology and one of Universal History. Undeterred by ugly facts, not enough of which had perhaps yet been discovered by hordes of subsidized research-ers, those grand nineteenth-century sociological and historical generalizers spun theories embracing the entire human or even cosmic realm.

The collapse of such generalizing efforts was evidenced in the post-1945 years by the fate of Arnold J. Toynbee's remarkable assault on world history. The first six volumes of this massive work were completed just before World War II and aroused great interest; after the war, Toynbee extended *A Study of History* to ten volumes (1954) and lectured all over the world, publishing volume after volume of more popular expositions of his thought, while *A Study of History* was abridged for even readier popular consumption. For a time in the fifties, he was almost sage of the Western world. Undoubtedly his work has been the most ambitious attempt in the century at a total synthesis of human experience. But as a system of history it was soon seen to be a failure. Striking out at academic industrialism and mourning the passing of the great historical generalizers, Toynbee saw himself as a scientist, like Buckle or Comte, classifying specimens of the genus Human Civilization and finding the pattern of its life. As such, it was evident to those with a knowledge of history that his huge opus was largely myth— immensely erudite, imaginative, fascinating, yet simply not true. Whilst the Existentialists were discovering the irrationality and brokenness of all human history, Toynbee claimed to find orderli-ness and purpose, in which respect he was wildly out of step with the times—a throwback to the nineteenth century. His battle against the specialists in behalf of a total world history was, in his own words, as futile as trying to drink the ocean. His popularity certainly revealed a decided public nostalgia for that older function of history, revealing to us the path behind and before. But in hundreds of essays and books, the learned community recorded its negative verdict on Toynbee and pronounced his grandiose structure a failure, though it also frequently recorded its grudging admiration for his boldness. Most academic scholars did not follow in Toynbee's footsteps; they went on writing detailed studies and ignoring "metahistory."

Erich Heller once remarked of Oswald Spengler, who had earlier tried something similar to Toynbee's assault on the historical process, that he had achieved a "highly topical oblivion": everybody knew he should be forgotten. This became the case with Toynbee. Those twelve massive volumes with their enormous footnotes and "annexes" were consigned to a special oblivion on library shelves, where everyone passing by smiles knowingly or sadly shakes a head. Man's last attempt to understand the past *in toto* and to use this knowledge for his redemption expired in these titanic but fruitless labors.

Others, less ambitious, who tried to play the role of Victorian sage or "man of letters," received equally severe rebukes and, one feels, largely deserved them. They appear as mountebanks, as "phonies"—that most scathing contemporary epithet. For example, John Kenneth Galbraith's dissection, almost with contempt, by economic specialists in the pages of learned journals was only to be expected; but more thoughtful sections of the semipopular press also dismissed him as a fraud.[4] Kenneth Minogue once remarked that Galbraith in full stride resembles nothing so much as a pyromaniac in a field of straw men, a phrase that also seems strikingly applicable to Bertrand Russell's numerous excursions into the fields of politics and morals. Galbraith is a brilliant (if conceited) man, able to stimulate public discussion of significant economic and political issues as few can: the Affluent Society; Countervailing Power; the Administered Economy. But he and others like him arouse suspicion. They claim an omniscience one knows they cannot possess. They mask their superficiality with glibness and cultivate a mock profundity. There are many of them; indeed, in accordance with the laws of neophilia, every season now produces its would-be sage. In one or another subculture, some of them manage to maintain a reputation among the gullible and half-educated. A dozen names come to mind which it would be kinder not to mention. None can come close to passing inspection as a genuine master able to give us a synthesis of the modern mind, able to knit together the numerous compartments of knowledge that are increasingly divorced from one another.

Father Teilhard de Chardin supplies another example of failure. "Most biologists find little scientific value and professional philosophers very little precision or originality" in his thought, Raymond Aron correctly observed of the widely read author of *The Phenomenon of Man,* the nearest twentieth-century approach to a total evolutionary philosophy such as Herbert Spencer once attempted. Perhaps this is as much an indictment of his critics as of Teilhard; yet the problem remains—that of finding any generalization that can escape devastating criticism by modern experts. Like Toynbee, Teilhard gave us insights and added phrases to our vocabulary. (See chapter 9.) Neither giant succeeded in knitting up a fragmented world into a tidy whole; they only added further material to its diverse cultural burden.

Bertrand Russell's vast corpus of nonphilosophical writings might be further cited. The dean of modern philosophers, equipped with awesome technical mastery of mathematics and logic, was never content to rule over this narrowly specialized kingdom of professional academics but, carrying on the aristocratic traditions of his distinguished clan, wanted to be an intellectual leader of his times: a reformer, a utilitarian and socialist, a commentator on every issue of the day, moral, political, economic, social. He wrote a shelf of books marked by a lively, witty style and a considerable superficiality of content. The alter ego of this modern Kant was Voltaire. But like Voltaire he achieved a chaos of clarities, as each lucid exercise contradicted the last one. Politically Russell was never able to stay long in one place. With "a mind like a circular saw," he methodically undercut every position he ever adopted. The passionate sceptic drew apart from a cause as soon as he found one and went his lonely way. At the same time he kept up the desperate pretence that every issue was really very simple, given a Russell to explain it almost condescendingly to the masses. In the end his masterpiece, like H. G. Wells', was his autobiography—the story of an endless quest. One of the wonders of the century, Russell left nothing on which to build a system or a synthesis.

Small wonder that failure of communication has been a leading theme of modern literature. In Ionesco's play *The Lesson,* a professor kills a student because she cannot understand him. C. P. Snow's Two Cultures, scientist and humanist, assumed a great deal more unity within the two camps than actually existed—as well as more desire for solidarity. Sociologists are parted from historians, poets from artists, economists from psychologists; the "humanist" camp is a shambles. Scientists who yearn to know more about the world of "culture" can find little to grab hold of. (Snow conceded at least one basic cleavage among the scientists, that between engineering and "pure" science.)

One sign of the times is the rapid increase in research that attempts to keep up with other research on a subject: proliferation of the type of article in historical journals, for example, titled "Recent Writings about . . ." or "Recent Literature on . . ."; also, the tendency for the subjects of such articles to become ever narrower, so that "Recent Writings about the German Socialists, 1890–1912" or "Recent Literature on the Origins of the Progressive Movement" became typical. A large percentage of historical articles and even books is now of this sort. The trend reflects, in part, a Modernist subjectivism which no longer sees one objective past in the reconstruction of which each scholar submerges his personality, but rather as many subjective pasts as there are scholars to discern them. But mainly it reflects a desperate desire to keep afloat in the flood of writing, to take account of what has been written about a subject— which, obviously, one must do if historical research means anything. There is so much published material that taking account of it quickly turns into a major project in itself. The *reductio ad absurdum* will be articles about the articles about the articles about the literature of a subject.[5] (There are now many bibliographies of bibliographies; perhaps we shall soon need bibliographies of bibliographies of bibliographies.) Another sign is the proliferation of absurdly specialist journals; we have *Blake Studies, Studies in Burke, Dickens Studies,* the *James Joyce Quarterly,* the *Shaw Review, Yeats Studies,* even an *Evelyn Waugh Newsletter,* which the departed spirit of that great comic writer must surely find delightful. And so on indefinitely.

The alternative, not keeping up with the literature of a subject, causes students in different universities to write the same theses or dissertations in complete ignorance of each other's work, as undoubtedly happens frequently, especially in the humanities. This sort of research can be justified only as an exercise, of value mainly to the person who writes it; it can hardly be justified as a "contribution to knowledge." Either way we turn, it seems that the sheer quantitative factor destroys knowledge as it has always heretofore been sought and transmitted and justified. The context of knowledge from ancient times down to very recent times was the small, highly literate elite. Socrates scarcely needed an army of research assistants to stay abreast of Hellenic thought; he could do so by walking around the agora. Twenty-two centuries later, the British public that bought up *The Origin of Species* on its first day of publication in 1859 and eagerly debated it was still a reasonably coherent intellectual community. A century beyond that, there was no such single intellectual community capable of debating anything.

The inflation of knowledge by people who are something less than sublimely creative cannot easily be dismissed, much less stopped. Literary criticism is a field in which this practice is perhaps especially flagrant. Writers are studied to death. Line-by-line exegeses, studies in opinions-of, analyses-of, symbolism-in and uses-of-words-in great writers—to this must be added all kinds of impossibly subjective or arbitrary interpretations (Browning, as a recent example, has now been given a Kierkegaardian interpretation), and in addition some systems of literary classification and analysis which are truly ingenious but largely meaningless: the depths of Structural Linguistics must be sounded to be believed. Yet this type of writing is not, surely, altogether blameworthy. Can we have too much knowledge? Who is to say that it is bad that thousands gather around Joyce and Eliot and Proust and other great writers? If they seem like vultures stripping a carcass, the answer surely is that not all people can be prophets or workers of miracles. Nevertheless, the result is the multiplication of books and articles beyond anyone's ability to assimilate them and the addition of very little to the normal person's understanding and enjoyment of the great authors.

Consequences of Fragmentation

It can hardly be doubted that the remarkable outburst of student protest in the 1960s was related to the phenomenon of fragmentation, though the connection was not often made. More typical was the complaint that students are bureaucratized, smothered with rules, and impersonally treated. Obviously these latter complaints are related to the sheer size of university populations. But faculty overspecialization was a leading target for student criticism. In a British symposium on this subject (*Anarchy and Culture: the Problem of the Contemporary University,* edited by David Martin, 1969), Peter Wiles observed that the average don is specialized, reluctant to risk broad generalizations, "has learned disillusion and self-control, usually at the cost of emotional richness," is not interested in politics, but busily—and usually happily—cultivates his own small plot of assigned intellectual ground. New Left students opted for the extreme opposites; they were fuzzy and ignorant but "involved" and excited by large ideas, emotional, chiliastic, political. Under such circumstances, talk about "understanding between teachers and taught," more student-faculty get-togethers, and other hopeful slogans and nostrums were vain. There was a gulf that the nature of modern knowledge has imposed. It was not the fault of the university or the faculty, nor was it the fault of the students. The organization of present-day knowledge demands specialization, just as the extent of present-day knowledge breaks down all of those vast generalizing structures, which even in the nineteenth century were vulnerable to empirical criticism. Yet youth will not be content with the dry husks of academic scholarship; for emotional reasons, it will have its Marx, whatever the facts may be.

The astonishing distance between academic, professional thought and nonacademic, amateur thought about politics, economics, society, and international relations has been one of the noteworthy features of our times. A small minority of academics has joined forces with the revolutionary students, but the behavior of this group is not typical. (Sometimes the professional in a nonpolitical field became the enthusiastic amateur in politics, a phenomenon of which there are some remarkable recent examples: distinguished professors of linguistics shouting slogans and leading student mobs.) On the academic side, there is a strong body of thought whose conclusions are sophisticated and on the whole conservative and realistic, as far removed as possible from visions of utopia or drastic one-shot solutions to all the ills of man; it offers a huge medicine cabinet of concepts which, after long study, the adept may hope to master. (Or, rather, not one cabinet but several, since we have separate specialists in economics, international relations, political philosophy, political theory, and so forth, who generally have little time for any laboratory but their own.) One entering this domain finds much of interest but little to suggest the imminent discovery of some dramatic cure for war and other social ills. University faculties are not filled with wild-eyed revolutionary fanatics, as some appeared to believe, but with utterly unrevolutionary investigators absorbed in the patient study of a reality so complex it takes years to master. The brighter young undergraduate or even graduate students are impatient with this wilderness, mystified by its sinuosities, convinced that the world needs a speedy nostrum, and disgusted with these sages who do not even attempt to provide anything of the sort. If the students persist in academic studies, however, they gradually lose their innocence and are drawn into the professional maze.

The surfeit of matter contributes to the neophiliac trends discussed in the previous chapter. Trendiness, ever changing fashions, incessant novelty in the arts stem in part from the sheer abundance of would-be "artists" seeking recognition. There are today hundreds of thousands who paint; art shows appear in every suburban school and shopping center. If 99 percent of these artists are totally without claim to distinctive merit, the remaining 1 percent, or even less, supplies far more art work than can be digested by a national or a world public. Ten thousand eager artists, all with *some* talent, clamor at the door of eminence, most of them necessarily in vain; only luck and chance will decide which few get noticed by the national magazines, hung in the important galleries, and bought by investment-minded collectors. So many are clamorous, so many ingenious at devising ways of getting attention, that the competition inevitably encourages endless changes of fashion. And in this bedlam of shrieking would-be geniuses—some no doubt genuinely inspired—no one can find a fixed standard; all is permitted, anything goes, each week produces its flashing meteor. What is true for the painters and sculptors is almost equally true for most kinds of writers.

Sheer quantity, then, contributes to fragmentation, to the destruction of standards, to the neurasthenia of culture. These trends reinforce each other. "Modernization," rending the fabric of traditional society, creates the anomic society of individual egos increasingly released from social discipline, ever freer yet ever more frustrated. The price of one's freedom is that countless others are also free; the cost of everyone's creativity is a debasement of the creative coinage.

Assaults on the Heritage

Faced with an impossibly large and disconnected inheritance, one strategy is simply to ignore it, to pass it by. Saul Bellow's Augie March glanced at the world of learning and retreated: "Considering how much world there was to catch up with—Asurbanipal, Euclid, Alaric, Metternich, Madison, Blackhawk—if you didn't devote your whole life to it, how were you ever going to do it?" So much for education! Augie soon quit college, to embark on other adventures. He might have tried to drink the ocean, like Arnold Toynbee or Thomas Wolfe, but he could well have died of it and preferred not to try. Had he stayed in college, he might have gone on to academic expertise and missed the *totum scibile* anyhow. So he went off to "live," which is different from to "know"—*praxis* is totally divorced from thought.

The "average" man today is no doubt much like Augie March: he cheerfully ignores the intellectual or grand cultural realm to live in some sort of subculture, composed of hobbies (model railroading, bridge, reading on some hobby-subject like sci-fi or the Civil War), of television and movies and the evening paper, of a little paperback or slick-magazine sex. "Each individual must find his own way of dealing with chaos," as Harry Bamford Parkes has said of Americans. The teenagers create their own bizarre countercultures.

If the *homme moyen sensuel* is content to cheerfully ignore the whole realm of serious knowledge and higher culture, all kinds of academicians and specialists live largely in microworlds made up of their own specialties, plus perhaps a modicum of general culture (a reasonably serious journal, an occasional topical drama, a concert now and then). There is a painful grasping after culture of this sort, quite in evidence in any Little Theater group, adult art class, or evening course at the city university.

If neither Toynbee nor Teilhard could unify the immense quantity of modern knowledge, which Existentialists were prepared to take as evidence of the fundamental absurdity of things, others would seem to have tried in various ways to annihilate, evade, or erase some or all of it. A large amount of recent intellectual history might be placed under the heading of strategies of antiintellectualism, little wars on culture. There is a long list of these assaults. The object, avowed or not, evidently is to wipe out the intolerable superabundance of knowledge—to unburden the mind.

An impulse to get out from under the load had been experienced by the writers of the 1950s. They stood in the monstrous shadow of *Finnegans Wake,* and they had to move away. The Movement poets, like Larkin, wished to throw off some of the weight of tradition. They reacted against the heavy burden of history and culture that the giants of Modernism, Eliot and Pound and Joyce, had taken upon themselves. Donald Davie, in a book about Pound, reproached him for doing this. Larkin spoke disdainfully of the "myth-kitty" and of "terribly educated" poets drawing on the ancient world and other arcane knowledge.[6] He seems to have felt— although his own apparently simple art conceals enormous amounts of knowledge—that he was rejecting a complicated, technique-ridden verse for something fresher and simpler. The search for roots and traditions wearied the Movement poets; they relaxed and floated with the experience of the moment, worrying little about the cultural inheritance even as they obviously bore a great deal of it silently within them. So even these conservative and sophisticated writers exhibited the instinct of this "After-Everything" era to wipe out that intolerable burden of history and tradition.

A recurring theme in the content of the serious contemporary novel is neoprimitivism; shaky as any generalization must be, given the flow of novels today, one is tempted to call it the leading one. The flight from civilization, which may be as old as civilization itself, has been a potent force since the era of Nietzsche and Joseph Conrad (pre-1914). In the 1920s Lawrence turned to the Indians and Lorca to the gypsies. "That is what is the matter with us," D. H. Lawrence wrote. "We are bleeding at the roots, because we are cut off from the earth and the sun and the stars. . . ." One might consider the frequency with which contemporary novelists show us a situation like that of Pierre Moinot's *Le Sable vif:* a small number of people cast away in a primitive environment. If primitivism is a favorite of film makers anxious for reels of sweaty passion, it is also a leading theme of serious novelists. The historical novel has declined; the novel of society, despite brave efforts such as Anthony Powell's *Music of Time* series, arouses little interest; and despite the popularity of the TV version of John Galsworthy's *The Forsyte Saga,* the *bildungsroman* is no more fashionable than the old *roman fleuve.* Wholly out of place would be brilliantly intellectual novels of debate and discussion by highly civilized people such as Aldous Huxley gave us in the 1920s, or those long social-political sagas identified with Jules Romains and Roger Martin du Gard (not to speak of Upton Sinclair) in the 1930s. Instead, evident on every hand is the attempt to strip away all that is social and civilized and traditional, leaving men and women in elemental situations. Henri Thomas' *Le Promontoire*—to choose another example from recent French fiction—throws us into a rural Corsican atmosphere of myths, superstitions, and primeval customs which quickly takes over the mind of the weak and uneasy European intellectual. The plays of the important British dramatist Harold Pinter are about human isolation and loneliness—about the existential predicament of consciousnesses battling to escape self-imprisonment. These are but examples, of course. A type of primitivism or radical innocence appeared in the British drama of the 1960s, suggested by the names of Tom Stoppard and Peter Terson. This was the television generation. One of the greatest American novels, John Updike's *Rabbit, Run,* like Nelson Algren's *Man with the Golden Arm,* studied contemporary primitivism.

The serious interest in the primitive displayed by anthropologists and students of religion is noteworthy. Claude Lévi-Strauss and, in a slightly different dimension, the Rumanian-born Mircea Eliade have attained stature as among the most remarkable of all contemporary scholars. The phenomenal world of the savage deeply engages their attention, and they believe that it has much potential meaning for us. One striking thing about Eliade's anthology of world religions was its inclusion of generous attention to the so-called lower religions as well as the higher. Though his book is a long way from Rousseau's writings—his method is sophisticated and knowledgeable in the extreme—we see in it a profound movement back to the primitive, a movement in some respects begun by Nietzsche, and carried on by Lawrence and his cult of healthy animality.

Another persistent idea was that a literary and humanistic culture had not staved off degeneration. It had not prevented Hitler. "Not only did the general dissemination of literary, cultural values prove no barrier to totalitarianism," wrote the eminent critic George Steiner (*TLS,* July 26, 1963), "but in notable instances the high places of humanistic learning and art actually welcomed and aided the new terror." If the antiintellectualism of the Right harped on the defection of the "intellectuals" to Communism, an antiintellectualism of the Left dwelt on the numerous instances where men of culture had welcomed Fascism or Nazism. (Many distinguished Italian philosophers and artists like Croce, Giovanni Gentile, Pareto, Arturo Toscanini, and Giacomo Puccini had initially done so, and so had many distinguished Germans, including Martin Heidegger the philosopher, Gottfried Benn the poet, Leni Riefenstahl the movie maker.) In almost every case, to be sure, profound disenchantment subsequently set in. It is true that men of science were also collaborationists; but one had expected more from the humanists. Thought had been discredited by touching the dirty skirts of political monstrosity.

One might ask why it is the special duty of artists to see that politics are clean, or one might point to the many cases of heroic resistance to Hitlerism and Stalinism, wherein men of humane culture went into exile, were imprisoned or killed because of their ideals. Or one might ask how it is possible to be so sure that the brutality of these political tyrannies would not have been lessened by a wider dissemination of culture. Was not real culture all too scarce? How does one know that more and better education would not have changed matters? The masses who followed Hitler were, like the Führer himself, demonstrably half-educated; it was, after all, by deluding the masses, not by attracting the intellectuals, that Hitler gained power. Nevertheless, this line of argument, specious or not, was frequently voiced. It was repeated during the Algerian civil war of the early 1960s—if civilized Frenchmen could murder and torture, what was civilization worth?—and again during the Vietnam War.

Immortalized in Kingley Amis' novel *Lucky Jim* was the discovery that the knowledge industry, like everything else, is a racket. As the number of university people multiplied, the coinage of scholarship was inevitably debased, and it became easier to believe what had perhaps always been a popular conviction, that solemn treatises by Ph.D.s consist in the main of pretentious or ludicrous verbiage dressed up with footnotes and that academic gradgrinds transport heaps of meaningless data from one place to another in order to pad their bibliographies for promotion. Hardly anyone denied that there was *some* truth to this. F. R. Leavis and the *London Times* officially complained, in the name of humanism, of the publication of badly written and unilluminating scholarly make-work. That there was now (not only in the United States) an "academic marketplace" where professors sold their services at an auction conducted largely on the basis of the length of their bibliographies might be a sign of educational progress, but to many it somehow degraded the arts and sciences.

The impulse to wipe the slate clean of knowledge and thus unburden the overburdened mind also appeared in the frenetic writings of the curious savant-pundit, Marshall McLuhan. The vogue for his works, which made "McLuhanism" a stock phrase and swept McLuhan himself to magazine-feature notoriety in the 1960s, can scarcely be explained on other grounds than their appeal to this sort of antiintellectualism of the intellectuals, though he did embrace some other fashions, such as one-worldism and the desire to understand technological revolutions. The heart of his message was his assertion that the electronic mass media presage an end to the Age of Books and thus the downfall of the divisive tyrant, Intellect. What Aldous Huxley and others had experienced as nightmarish, McLuhan, if we are to take him seriously, found consoling. (That McLuhanism was all a gigantic leg-pull, conceived in irony—the greatest joke of all being that the irony was not appreciated by a technologically drugged populace—remains a possibility.) Words put down visually and linearly on the printed page have heretofore ruled the world and have made a mess of it, creating exactly that fragmented chaos we accept as "culture." The electronic media herald the reign of pure sensation, which will enable mankind to achieve a primitive unity and wholeness. Dwight MacDonald described McLuhan's utopia as consisting of noble savages equipped with computers; in McLuhan's own words, "a Pentecostal condition of universal understanding and unity," a "state of collective awareness" induced, it would seem, by all the world sitting around and watching the same television programs.

The spectacle of so many billions of people not reading or thinking seemed to please McLuhan, who oddly enough expressed all this in books. These were admittedly written in a rather disorderly way and contain wildly inaccurate information, as critics have not failed to point out.[7] They also contain some brilliant insights and aphorisms. Some saw a comparison between McLuhanism and drugs, pornography, and mysticism, those other fashionable solutions to the befuddling problems of our cultural chaos. McLuhan's unthinking electronic collective offered a haven of blissful release for a certain type of contemporary intellect: with one magnificent gesture we can dismiss the whole Gutenberg Galaxy. A successful, much-acclaimed young movie producer interviewed in the *New Yorker* (November 21, 1970) described himself as "a child of McLuhan" in that he had never read any books. He expressed a desire to make a movie out of *The Three Musketeers* but had obtained his knowledge of the Dumas classic from a comic book version.

McLuhan's animosity toward the written word was associated with his yearning for a lost community and his keen sense of fragmentation. The empire of Sound made possible primitive man's intense group spirit, his lack of individual egoism, for which "tribal trance" McLuhan betrayed a considerable nostalgia. That other factors than that sinister invention, the alphabet, caused the breakdown of a perhaps mythical solidarity seems obvious to the historian (were not some literate societies quite community-minded because they were small and culturally homogeneous?); but McLuhan was concerned to call attention in the most forceful way possible to the fact of this breakdown. In the last analysis, McLuhan's was a cry from the heart against the chaos and confusion of modern life, and a cry that had to be louder than Matthew Arnold's a century before, or T. S. Eliot's a half century before. The extremity of the situation induces ever more extreme responses.

Knowledge of the early McLuhan reinforces this interpretation of him; he had exhibited a conservative agrarianism akin to that of Ezra Pound and Wyndham Lewis, a "cultural nostalgia" (Jonathan Miller) or "high patrician anguish." He was born and brought up in the western provinces of Canada. Miller sees him as an extreme humanist reactionary of the T. S. Eliot sort, who rather than sinking into testy irrelevance adopted a strategy which enabled him to seem ultramodern while attacking Modernism; more specifically, to undermine scientific positivism and its dreary child, technological efficiency, under the pretence of celebrating their triumph. If he could have pulled it off, what a coup! But he was too clever by half.

McLuhan's appeal was enhanced by a switched-on style reflecting some of the qualities of the electronic media whose virtues he appeared to extoll. (McLuhan argued, however, that he only pointed to the existence and impact of those qualities; he did not sponsor them.) Yet he himself was not a TV personality but a scholar who had, until relatively late in life, written learned articles on literary topics. In 1951, in *The Mechanical Bride,* he tried to seize on the automobile as a symbol of modern man, an attempt which met with less success than his subsequent foray into the communications field. The combination of sensitivity to advanced ideas with an apparent preference for television shows made the Canadian a marvel to intellectuals. Another appealing contemporary idea of his was an interest in form rather than content. In *The Medium Is the Message*, he suggested that the most important thing is the kind of medium TV is, rather than the specific content of its programs. Whether we watch a "soap opera" or a play by Ionesco does not much matter; what matters is that we watch it on *television.*

But McLuhanism was most significant for its assault on the printed page and thus on the whole literary inheritance. We may again observe that McLuhan paradoxically wrote this in books, communicating it to other intellectuals. It provided in turn an occasion for many other books, discussing, criticizing, evaluating McLuhan. At least one of these books, interestingly enough, consisted in part of the transcripts of radio and television interviews with Professor McLuhan. The printed page would seem to have one powerful advantage—it remains in existence for others to ponder and reply to. Without it, an intellectual tradition is impossible. Only if one wishes to annihilate intellectual tradition does one prefer the spoken word.

The failure of verbal communication in general—the demise of the Word—was a theme far from peculiar to McLuhan. The observation of Herbert Read in 1950 that "reading—leisured, absorbed, and curious—is rapidly ceasing to exist as a characteristic activity of modern man" was, after all, hardly more than a banality, even before the television plague. In 1963 George Steiner predicted that Samuel Beckett would end by writing a play in which nothing was said: "Monsieur Beckett is moving, with unflinching Irish logic, toward a form of drama in which a character, his feet trapped in concrete and his mouth gagged, will stare at the audience and say nothing."[8] In fact, Beckett went a step further and dispensed with characters: "Samuel Beckett's latest play premiered Sunday night at Oxford University with no actors, no dialog and no action, just a pile of trash on stage and the sounds of a baby's amplified cry and breathing. It lasted 30 seconds" (News story, March 9, 1970). Beckett's movie, called *Film* (1964–1965), contained no dialogue and had only one sound, "Sssh!" Beckett is one of the most unflinchingly honest of contemporary writers. The failure of communication and the breakdown of expression are contemporary ideas, met with frequently.

An illustration of this idea is that mode of nondiscourse known as "concrete" poetry, quite fashionable in the 1960s. "Concrete" poetry is a nonoral poetry, converting words into designs. Any meaning it may possess is deliberately made staggeringly simple. (For example, a Swedish volume of concrete poetry consisted of designs made from the numbers of prisoners at Auschwitz together with the names of products, such as motor oil and soap, into which their bodies were made.) But the nonverbal arts displayed a similar desire to annihilate tradition. In painting, both Pop and Op had this desire in common. Serious music disowned its past, or at any rate its continuous tradition; there were attempts to go all the way back to medieval music, the idea being to wipe out as much as possible of the great Western musical heritage from Bach to Brahms. Otherwise, there were John Cage's "environmental sounds and noises" and there were musical computers. This desire to produce antiart— art that will, while creating something, express disgust against all acts of creation and against the very idea that there should be artistic *genres*—made its appearance in films as well as in painting, sculpture, and music. In literature, some of the *nouveau roman* writers—following in André Gide's footsteps (*The Counterfeiters*) but going even further—displayed hostility to the novel as something written or finished; they would like to show the record of themselves engaged in writing a novel but constantly changing it as they change. M. Francis Ponge carried this practice even to the area of academic monographs; he produced a book about Malherbe, fruit of some years of research, which consists of his notes arranged in no very coherent order, as if to reproach the false fluency of professors who write in old-fashioned, logical-continuity ways—an antimonograph.

The urge to scramble the traditional artistic *genres* goes back to the dawn of Modernism, when Baudelaire and Wagner and Mallarmé yearned for synesthesia, for colored poetry and music that paints. Today it is often accompanied by a revolt against the very concept of artistic modes. Revolt can hardly go further.[9]

But the strategy of ignoring the inheritance really cannot work any better than the strategy of trying to overcome it. Tradition is, after all, there; if one agrees to pretend it isn't, one knows nevertheless that this is a pretense. Somebody is sure to tell and to scorn the pretender. To be a pretend-savage is scarcely possible. There is no innocence after such knowledge. Millions of people, to be sure, honestly have never heard of the great inheritance or, if they have heard of it, know so little of it as to make no difference. We do have barbarians, honest ones; they are the great multitudes of newspaper readers and television watchers. But the minority whose mission it is to bear culture cannot revert to barbarism. They are a part of the inheritance even in making this gesture, which is the outcome of it all. They are responding to their awareness of the cultural inheritance when they seek to escape it. Only a mighty cataclysm which physically destroyed all record of it—all books, paintings, buildings, sculpture, music—and all the people in whose minds it is imprinted could get rid of this weight of the civilized past. Of such a cataclysm—Giambattista Vico's roll of thunder, announcing the return to barbarism and the renewal of the cycle—men have in fact been dreaming all through this century. It was Nietzsche's vision, and George Sorel's, and Stefan George's. It was very much a part of the spirit of 1914. Perhaps it will yet come, in the form of nuclear war or the poisoning of the air. Meanwhile, life goes on.

If we speak of attempts to annihilate the inheritance, the diversity of contemporary intellectual life forces us to note the opposite phenomenon too: there were desperate efforts to preserve and use it. Never was the past so ransacked, so anxiously studied. Packs of industrious scholars descended on Burke, Mill, and de Tocqueville, on Nietzsche; on Joyce, Yeats, and Lawrence; on every major figure and quite a few minor ones. The works of these writers were handsomely reprinted, and they were edited down to the last laundry list. Essays by the thousands were written about them. A Byzantine scholarship lingers over every line of their works. Although this may be in good part a result of the exigencies of contemporary university life, there have nevertheless been enterprises of extraordinary value. Such landmarks of scholarship as Leon Edel's work on Henry James, or Gordon Haight's on George Eliot, or George Painter's on Proust—to select only a few outstanding examples—cannot be dismissed as professional busywork. They are monuments of learning testifying to their creators' boundless zest for their subjects. The massive, sometimes multivolume biography—exhaustive in its research, scrupulous in its scholarship, even elegant in its expression; labored over for years, "definitive," fixing (one supposes) the canon forever on great men of the past—is a feature of our times that does credit to academe. To the examples from literary history cited above, one could add such political biographies as Robert Blake's *Disraeli*, J. H. Plumb's *Walpole*, Max Braubach's *Prince Eugene*—and innumerable others. Among great editors of collected works, Theodore Besterman gave us close to a hundred volumes of Voltaire letters, while scholarly industries have been built around the issuing of the complete writings of Edmund Burke, Jeremy Bentham, John Stuart Mill, Thomas Jefferson, John Adams, Woodrow Wilson, and others. It need not be said that hordes of historians are industrious. In *Doing History* (1971), J. H. Hexter remarked that two things are true of historical writing today: never so much bad, and never so much good. The level of technical competence in the best professional work is amazingly high. No age has so studied its past. If all this only adds to the monstrous profusion of books, it suggests a heroic resolve to try to cope with the burden of the past. The latest generation of scholars has provided the tools for such an undertaking in an unparalleled manner.

But it largely gave up synthesis. Awareness of the ungraspable complexity of empirical reality and the frailty and tentativeness of all attempts to cope intellectually with that reality has been the dominant theme of modern thought, expressed in its basic philosophies (Linguistic, Phenomenological) and reflected in its literature. "Thought is crude, matter unimaginably subtle," Aldous Huxley remarked. Historians have grown accustomed to see the past as subject to an infinite number of "interpretations," depending on the historian's position and purpose, no one any "righter" than the others. Inexhaustible in content, the record of human events is something from which one creates almost at will any sort of pattern—"a sort of Rorschach blot into which the writer can project almost any shape he wants." Literary scholars, suspicious of all efforts to talk of "the spirit of the age" or even of schools or trends, simply dissect individual writers or individual literary works.

There have been more brutal dismissals of the cultural tradition. Those who followed intrepid militants such as LeRoi Jones and Eldridge Cleaver threw out all the "white man's culture": if we only have jazz and soul, we do not need Beethoven and all that. One could ask whether, in the West, black culture is not an integral part of white culture (really great Negro writers such as Ralph Ellison knew that it was) and whether jazz, which *does* owe something to Beethoven, can endure if subsequent generations dismiss all cultural tradition in a similar manner. But for the moment no matter; we have cleared our minds of much. Similarly, the subintellectual student cult of "relevance" was often no more than a device for getting rid of anything that one would rather not at the moment take time for. The crude versions of Marx and Freud were still available with their now venerable strategies of "reduction," by which ideas and art forms may be dismissed as "really" just instruments of exploitation and domination or the projections of subconscious guilt feelings.

The profoundly antiintellectual aspects of popular Marxism are less frequently noted than they should be. If, as John Morley once wrote, labels are used by talkative people to save themselves the trouble of thinking, Marxism is a supreme case of labelism. An assiduous second- or third-rate mind can memorize the Marxian categories and then employ them to sweep aside whole realms of experience. Modern art and literature become "nothing but" the morbid excrescences of a dying culture. Politics, the play of personalities, parties, issues, is a puppet show that may be ignored, and all sorts of ideas and philosophies are "objectively" the devious conspiracies of capitalists to divert, stupefy, or confuse the mind so as to prevent people from thinking about exploitation and revolution. International relations may be interpreted as a clash of economic interests, the diplomacy being only a disguise. Marxists are constantly at work reducing the rich diversity of life to an elemental simplicity.[10]

Other reasons for ignoring whole segments of knowledge came from the student radicals of the 1960s, who yearned to pitch the whole academic curriculum in the drink and often did not bother to justify their desire; an obscenity would do. In a 1969 symposium, Perry Anderson, editor of the *New Left Review*, argued that British intellectual life had been the victim of a huge international conspiracy, an invasion of "white" refugee intellectuals. Wittgenstein, Bronislaw Malinowski, Lewis Namier, Karl Popper, Isaiah Berlin, and other foreigners, reactionaries all, because *emigrés* (the New Leftist did not seem disturbed by the fact that most of them fled from Hitler rather than Stalin), had moved in and taken over. Therefore British youth should disregard all academic teaching. The wild implausibility of this thesis—influential as the immigrants have been, they were no more than a small element in British intellectual life, whose native sources are obviously rich and diverse—was hardly more striking than its illiberal implications ("foreigners" are not to be trusted; those who fled from either Fascist or Communist police states are unreliable reactionaries.) But no matter; this served the purpose of cutting down the dreary academic rigamarole. Having dismissed all formal knowledge as a reactionary conspiracy, one could go out and disrupt meetings with a clear conscience.

The hippies and yippies of the 1960s were barbarians in the sense of their almost complete lack of any received culture. The disavowal of that culture was their religion, the source of their courage, the source of their (for some) charm; they were utter innocents, who looked at things as if they were the first ever to think or to feel. Their heroes were Indians and other primitives. Their dramas were savage rituals. They wrote their poetry oblivious of all previous poetry. They achieved staggering simplifications about war and society because they were ignorant of all those problems that have perplexed men through the centuries. They talked about love and peace as if no one before them had ever heard of these things and as if all you have to do to get them is to want them. The badges of barbarism in their dress and appearance reflected the long-haired state of their minds; the Goths, compared to them, were sophisticates. They may be the "barbarians from within" who, in the absence of outside barbarians, are the potential destroyers of a weakening civilization. Like the early Christians, they gather in the catacombs to dismiss as foolishness all the knowledge of the Greeks and to become as little children. Two thousand years of book learning flow above their heads and they do not know it. They may attempt to build a "counter culture," but on no traditional European foundation.

"Good writing is counter-revolutionary," one of them wrote in 1969 (*New American Review,* no. 7, p. 217). Literature and intellectualism are for bourgeois finks, "mandarin" types, and other disgusting agents of the Establishment. Only action, that is, fighting in the streets, is worthwhile. To put pen to paper, or paint to canvas, is to betray the struggle. There is nothing to talk about; all has been decided (by some secret consensus of the young and alienated); it only remains to do it. Those who think thereby doubt. If this creed of the new revolutionaries did not prevent them from publishing books bearing such titles as *Steal This Book,* it at least turned those books into tools of sabotage, antibooks. Some slight reason might remain for writing as propaganda, since "ideas are weapons," but none whatsoever for writing in the disinterested "pursuit of truth"— words apt to provoke paroxysms of laughter in these "radical" circles. And McLuhan, rather a hero of the New Left, was cited in behalf of the view that the electronic media were now much more significant than the printed word. Putting on a spectacle for the TV news cameras provided far better propaganda than the old-fashioned tract. The path from Marx to Lenin to Rubin was in intellectual terms a steeply descending one.

NOTES

1. For a note on the ideal of this "sum of the knowable" as a nineteenth-century scholar felt it, see John Sparrow, *Mark Pattison and the Idea of a University* (1967).

2. To be exact, there were, according to the *Bookseller,* 23,207 new books and 9,106 reprints and new editions published in Britain in 1969, representing a small increase over 1968. The figures for 1970 were about the same. In the decade of the 1960s there was a steady year-by-year increase. On the book explosion, see Robert Escarpit, *La Révolution du livre* (1969).

3. Nevertheless, it was not unusual for people of a scientific-technological bent to argue that there was nothing to worry about since "in the very near future computers operating from different nations will be able to communicate clearly with one another. . . . These computing systems will form an international network of information retrieval and processing systems well able to master the information

explosion and the demands of the educational set-up." *TLS,* January 1, 1970, p. 1. Such people think of knowledge as "information" which we "retrieve" when we need it for some practical purpose, a view deeply shocking to "humanists."

4. See for example Arthur Shenfield, "On the State of Bad Economics," *Spectator,* March 22, 1968, and "Dominie's Economy," *TLS,* November 23, 1967.

5. In 1973 the Rockefeller Foundation reported awarding a grant for a study on the findings and effects of other grant-supported studies on a certain subject (Appalachia).

6. Earlier in this century, the Imagist poets and at about the same time the Georgians tried to do much the same thing—to "release poetry from the burden" of tradition. The Imagists sought the naked, unthought-about image. The Georgians retreated to bucolic simplicity.

7. The author of a dissertation on McLuhan, Frank W. Oglesbee (1969), found him citing sources that apparently do not exist—evidence, perhaps, that it is all a send-up, unless we are to accuse McLuhan of out-and-out fraud. But it is only fair to add the remark of Jonathan Miller, in his book on McLuhan, that he "created the possibility of truth by shocking us all with a gigantic system of lies."

8. *TLS,* July 26, 1963. See also Steiner's essay "The Retreat from the Word," in *The Listener,* July 14, 1960.

9. The vogue of Eastern thought fits well into this scheme for annihilating tradition. For it is well known that knowledge of the deeper reality, the *atman* or world-soul, "is not to be obtained by instruction, nor by intellect, nor by much learning." Yogis were at one with primitives in recommending noncerebral modes of perception. Somewhat similarly, Africa's distinguished statesman-philosopher Leopold Senghor has declared that "writing impoverishes reality," that the art of the spoken word is the highest art. The non-European cultures, bearing in so strongly on the faltering consciousness of high Western civilization, brought a message that seemed on the whole to agree with the antiintellectual, antiliterary stance of much of Western culture.

10. Each of the great modern reductionist ideologies undercuts the other; though there have been many interesting tentatives of accommodation, the true Marxist sees Freudianism as bourgeois decadence, and the true Freudian construes Marxism as a type of fantasy produced by the unadjusted personality.

6

The Other Culture:
Science and Scientism

Humanist Versus Scientist

"The intellectual class," Jacques Barzun wrote, "which ought always to remain independent, has been captivated by art, overawed by science, and seduced by philanthropy." Of its captivation by art and its seduction by philanthropy (social crusading) we have largely spoken thus far. It would certainly be wrong to leave out that which has always overawed some intellectuals and which continued to do so in the contemporary era.

The scientific mind works differently from that of the humanist. Though the preceding chapters have presented on the whole a picture of cultural fragmentation, of too many ideas flooding in upon modern man, it must be admitted that this has been far from a universal opinion. So great a thinker as the philosopher Alfred North Whitehead said, not long before his death in 1947, that his greatest fear was "lest a rigid system be imposed upon mankind and that fragile quality, his capacity for novel ideas, for novel aspects of old ideas, be frozen . . . until he and his society reach the static level of insects." Paradoxically, an age subject to frantic and incessant change feared stagnation; an age that suffered from cultural anarchy lived in dread of totalitarian regimentation.

It would be difficult to persuade a congress of world intellectuals to vote against innovation in the realm of ideas, and they might well agree that Whitehead's fear was well founded. It has been a commonplace opinion that mankind needs "new ideas"; one could get money from governments and foundations if only one could think of a new name for a course or a program. Writing at the end of World War II and his own long life, H. G. Wells, speaking as always for the scientific mind (*Mind at the End of Its Tether,* 1945), declared the basic trouble to be that physical conditions change more rapidly than men's ideas, which run a losing race and fall ever farther behind. (To which, in behalf of the "humanists," Georges Bernanos replied that "civilization isn't something one runs after.")

By Wells' analysis, we need more, not fewer, new ideas; the mind is not overburdened but understaffed. There was no concern here about integration of thought, but an atomism that sees a myriad of problems posed by the environment implying a need for a myriad of ideas with which to meet these problems. (Though he later abandoned it, the scientific-rationalist mind of Bertrand Russell once proposed such a "logical atomism" as his basic philosophical position.) Scientists, John Beer complained (in *The Cambridge Review,* November 7, 1959), "live in a makeshift world. They throw up a structure in the full knowledge that tomorrow it may be knocked down to make way for a better."

We have been mostly looking at matters from the viewpoint of the humanists—poets, novelists, a certain kind of philosopher. The opposing viewpoint was by and large that of the scientists. We can hardly ignore one of C. P. Snow's Two Cultures. In 1959 the well-known novelist, administrator, and scientist gave a lecture on this theme, which promptly drew a series of replies, elicited much discussion, and led Sir Charles himself to take a Second Look several years later. A full bibliography of the Snow controversy would be enormous. For that reason alone, the historian of contemporary thought is likely to seize on it as a landmark.

Though ending with a conventional plea to heal the breach and pull together, Snow's tract amounted to a counterattack from the side of science. As such it bore some of the marks of its hour. The lecture included expressions of admiration for the Union of Soviet Socialist Republics for having disciplined its maverick intellectuals and made them serve the technological society. In 1959 the capitalist countries were going through a time of shame mixed with panic at having been outdone by the Russians in the space race. They were afraid they would be beaten to the moon, and the assumption of Soviet superiority in scientific and technical education led to laments about the backwardness of a European educational establishment too heavily committed to the humanities. The same panic in the United States resulted in lavish new subsidies to science programs. In England *Two Cultures* was part of a debate on education waged within the framework of an Oxbridge elite on the defensive, of proliferating new universities and much interest in alternate curricular patterns. Yet it inevitably raised much wider issues and recalled older "battles of the books." Scientist versus humanist signified an ancient schism in the Western soul.

Nietzsche, baffled by the schism, had once dreamed of a man with a double brain, one for science and one for nonscience, able to bring the two together without blurring. In the classical tradition, logic and rhetoric were paired as opposites—the cool, analytical, reasonable method versus an art frankly aimed at arousing human feelings. (Highly formalized, with precise rules, classical rhetoric sought to channel and control this irrational element, being itself a sort of science of persuasion.) But in the high Middle Ages, logic won out and crushed its rival. In revenge, Renaissance humanists ridiculed the logic-choppers and exalted the arts, which mold the personality by evoking moods and feelings and ideals. Though the modern scientific movement of the seventeenth and eighteenth centuries assailed Scholastic logic as much as Humanist rhetoric, this earlier clash somewhat resembled the more recent tension between scientists and their humanist or esthetic foes. Fundamental types of mind are involved.

Perhaps the greatest seventeenth-century mind, Blaise Pascal, was torn agonizingly between science and religion. Samuel Butler's "Hudibras," the Restoration satire, directed its barbs not only at Puritans (at that time the "progressive" camp) but at the scientists' Royal Society. Molière was as hard on doctors as on religious hypocrites, and Jonathan Swift, with his fellow Scriblerians, mercilessly ridiculed the scientists, that haughty newfangled crop of barbarians who imagined that their dotty antics were going to replace the classics of literature. And, also in the early eighteenth century, Giambattista Vico tried to lead a humanistic counterattack on Descartes' powerful scientism. If the high Enlightenment secured an armistice through Newton's good offices (neither Voltaire nor Dr. Johnson, opposites in so many other ways, attacked science), the nineteenth century strenuously renewed the conflict. Matthew Arnold's Archimedes Silverpump, Ph.D., is as much a figure of fun as the druggist in *Madame Bovary* who disinfects everything. "The more materialistic science becomes," said Edward Burne-Jones, "the more angels I shall paint."

Attacks on Science

This antiscientific wing of the modern intellectuals, familiar at least since Swift and very familiar since Burne-Jones, hardly needs an introduction. To a certain type of intellectual temperament, "science" has long stood for (a) the barbarism of technical know-ledge crowding out the liberal arts which civilize men; (b) the tyranny of a rationalized and mechanized society pushing out all that is not immediately and obviously "useful" (money-making or comfort-breeding); (c) the pretentiousness of people who are really half-educated and have vulgar minds but who claim to know everything. And perhaps it has stood for other things as well, including diabolical qualities. C. S. Lewis' "cosmic trilogy" (1944–1945), a kind of contemporary *Gulliver's Travels,* was so anti-scientific that the biologist J. B. S. Haldane complained about it (*Modern Quarterly,* August, 1946): the scientists in the trilogy are almost all sinister figures, cast quite literally in the role of devils, obsessed with greed and lust for power. Lewis was admittedly an extreme case, yet the "mad scientist" abounds in pulp literature, grade B movies, and television. But the scientists generally saw themselves as unselfish, dedicated wholly to truth—the "real he-roes" of modern times, Snow declared.

Aldous Huxley commented that D. H. Lawrence's "dislike of science was passionate and expressed itself in the most fantastically unreasonable terms. 'All scientists are liars,' he would say, when I brought up some experimentally established facts, which he happened to dislike." (We may be reminded of Samuel Butler, nineteenth-century writer—"The men of religion tell a lot of little lies for one big truth. The men of science tell a lot of little truths for one big lie.") Although the scion of the distinguished biologist Thomas Huxley was himself a reasonably acerbic critic of scientists—Lord Tantamount cannot lift his eyes from the microscope to see anything really important[1]—Lawrence's violence mildly disturbed him. Yet Lawrence's was a typical Lorenzian "gut reaction," a highly intuitive, emotionally charged hatred of all that "smelled of death." Instinctively Lawrence knew the enemy of the artist, of life and freedom and joy.

George Orwell was hardly a delicately refined esthete, but he did not think much of science. It was all right in its place, but any person exclusively educated in the scientific manner would be narrow and ignorant: "his political reactions would probably be somewhat less intelligent than those of an illiterate peasant who retained a few historical memories and a fairly sound aesthetic sense." He met a young chemist who informed him that he "could not see what was the use of poetry." It is to be feared that this appalling young man, whether typical of the natural scientists or not, fitted the humanist's image of them. Orwell's *1984,* like Huxley's *Brave New World* and most of the "dystopias," as Chad Walsh called them in *From Utopia to Nightmare,* displayed the horrors of a world that is run by scientists and has totally succumbed to scientism—meaning roughly to the extinction of personality and spirit and art, to the total dehumanization of man. The most representative plays and novels could be relied upon to work this theme. To take but one example, Jean Giraudoux's *The Madwoman of Chaillot,* as popular a serious play as the postwar generation watched, is a witty sermon on the cluttered madness of modern life with its mechanical confusions and distracting complexities. Dress up this idea and one was assured of an audience.

Up until about 1914 distinguished writers produced visions of the fair society that might materialize in the future, when scientific reason prevailed. Since then, and most especially since 1930, distinguished writers have produced visions of the hideous society that all too possibly will evolve if the same reason (science, technology, rationalization) continues to prevail. Of the reverse utopias written in the post-1945 era, Orwell's *1984* and Constantin Gheorghiu's *Twenty-Fifth Hour* were only the most celebrated; there have been many. They are nightmares made from the stuff of nineteenth-century dreams. They show us equality, literacy, democracy, science, material comforts, the triumph over nature, the achievement of happiness—all those goals of progress turned sour and nasty. Equality means standardization and facelessness (everyone wears the same plastic mask in L. P. Hartley's 1960 dystopia). Literacy means the half-educated who can be the more readily manipulated; science means people dehumanized by drugs or kept in herd-like subjection by amusements like television or "the feelies." It also means sinister organizations enslaving people in order to mold humanity to a laboratory blueprint. Bland happiness—the happiness of the drugged or lobotomized—is the horrible fate awaiting equalitarian, technological mankind. The dystopias were not all of one mind on details but the above is a fairly accurate presentation of their main drift.

To the humanist, the scientific mind seems philistine, deficient in the esthetic sense. Virginia Woolf's scorn for Arnold Bennett, who described only the outside of things, is a paradigm of every artist's horror of the H. G. Wells mentality, the A. J. Ayer syndrome. The poets know at the bottom of their hearts that scientific rationalists scorn poetry and religion and metaphysics, and cannot understand a man who wants to paint angels. The warfare has not changed much since the beginning of the nineteenth century, when Jeremy Bentham's "steam intellect improvement" appalled Coleridge and Carlyle and Blake; Bentham, the great Utilitarian who made fun of religion and saw no use for poetry, was spokesman for the modern era as he triumphantly paraded his alleged destruction of metaphysics. Charles Darwin, who lived during the nineteenth-century period of transition into the Age of Facts, remarked in his *Autobiography* on the atrophy of his esthetic tastes, which he regretted losing. In his youth he loved poetry and music, but in his later years he could not bear to read a line of poetry and was wearied by music. Whatever the irenicists may say, it does look as if science and art are natural enemies.[2]

In recent years an existentialized intelligentsia has been prepared to view science as well as technology with the gravest suspicion. Its members believe that the serious problems facing mankind, the only really interesting ones, are those with which the creative writer deals. These are not scientific questions; the rational intellect has but little to contribute to their solution. Such people usually agreed with F. R. Leavis that "science is obviously of great importance to mankind." But it is not of the highest importance, because it does not and cannot grapple with the deepest issues. These issues concern human experience as a whole, the human personality and its search for a viable emotional life through experience. When the scientist cheerfully allows literature and art a place as "entertainment," the contemporary civilized person is likely to laugh or to cry in dismay. We will not find our destinies in the laboratory. Science and technology can provide some of the instruments to use in our quest for the good life, but cannot tell us what that good life is.

Science lost prestige first of all because it was associated with a destructive element. "Science means Bikini," André Malraux declared early in our period, referring to the first nuclear bomb tests. And if science meant the shadow of universal destruction and unthinkable terror, it also meant dehumanization and manipulation. "Computerized" was a nasty word to all kinds of unhappy consciousnesses; most of the militants of the New Left were utterly "romantic" in this respect, wherein they differed from practically all past revolutionaries. If it be objected that computerization is technology and not science, the answer is that the two have become more and more closely associated. Science has sold itself as that which propels us to the moon and builds ever bigger intercontinental missiles. It has also tied itself to commercial research, churning out ideas for ever more consumer goods. For science as the lonely pursuit of truth, for the science of Descartes and Pasteur and Einstein, one could no doubt discover much reverence, but the modern Pasteur runs a huge government-financed research project, perhaps on bacterial warfare, and the present-day Descartes works for General Electric or the Rand Corporation.

There was growing and widespread doubt about the worth of what technology produces. If, as Jacques Barzun claimed in 1964, "during the past 30 years the articulate have unceasingly cavilled against the tyranny of scientific thought, the oppression of machines, the hegemony of things, the dehumanization brought about by the sway of number and quantity," during the 1950s and 1960s the chorus swelled. Two examples, randomly chosen but typical of diverse ranges of thought, may be given. In *The Myth of the Machine* (1966; 2nd vol., 1970) that earnest and industrious champion of trends on the moderate left, Lewis Mumford, who in the past had generally been all for technics and machinery, declared his purpose "to question both the assumptions and the predictions upon which our commitment to the present forms of technical and scientific progress, treated as if ends in themselves, have been based." And a convert to the right, Montgomery Belgion, in *The Worship of Quantity* (1969), lamented that "the world has entered the era of the computer and the bureaucrat." On the left, Mumford confirmed the switch reflected in the book of another weather vane, John Kenneth Galbraith— *The Affluent Society,* which turned from the demand for more goods and more utilization of machinery to a concern about the "quality of life." Mumford had, to be sure, written in 1959 *(The Conduct of Life)* that "we can no longer naively believe that human improvement will follow directly from man's conquest of nature." But compare *Technics and Civilization,* in 1934: "To understand the machine is not merely a first step toward reorienting our civilization, it is also a means towards understanding society and towards knowing ourselves." He then praised "the calmness, cleanness and order" of the "neotechnic" (humanized machine) age just dawning! The path of Mumford's progressive disenchantment with machines from 1934 to 1966 is an index of the progress of the liberal mind on this subject. On the right, Belgion carried on a long tradition of antimodernism and antimaterialism, but with a rather new concern about science and technology *per se.*

Even the scientists sometimes doubted science. A considerable scandal was created in 1969–1970 by the defection to "political activism" of an outstanding young Harvard molecular biologist, in what was hardly a unique case. "Science and its technologies are today on the defensive," the director of the Oak Ridge National Laboratory wrote in *Science* magazine in January, 1970. He identified several rather different antiscientisms, including not only Lorenzian abolitionists but more moderate questioners of proper national priorities. Clearly in the 1970s science was getting less money from governments and commanding less prestige than in the previous two decades. In the 1950s those who held the public purse strings loosened them as far as possible at the very mention of the word *science.* Twenty years later, despite all the attempts to arouse more lay interest in science (a sort of Snow job, one might say), there appeared to be less and less of such interest. In October 1970 announcement was made of the impending merger of the only two British magazines dedicated to popular science, because there were not enough readers to support both; and the journal marked for disappearance was the more thoughtful and scientific of the two

(Science Journal). Physics and Engineering Ph.D.s joined the ranks of the unemployed.

From the political left came attacks directed at scientific tie-ups with government and with military activities. New Left thought featured rejection of the ethos of a scientized and hence "dehumanized" society. In England the visionary hippie John Michell received messages from beyond the earth portending the end of one great age and the beginning of another marked by a new "expansion of consciousness." The youth culture offered the shaman in place of the scientist. Books with a theme of "beyond affluence, let's learn how to live maturely" (some of them very bad) appeared in considerable numbers and in some cases became best-sellers. The kind of science that sought wealth and power, many would say, had had its day. As a writer recently declared, "The crucial issue for the contemporary writer as well as for Western culture as a whole is not one of people fighting to make a living, but of people fighting to make a life, to learn how to *be,* in a time of physical affluence and psychic impoverishment." Little though it wanted to let go of it altogether, the Western world seemed sick of its Faustian ego and eager to find another self. The reaching out to Asia and Buddhism, the primitivist yearnings, and all the different antiscientific cults like astrology and belief in visitors from outer space (taken half-seriously by some semiintellectuals)—in fact, the whole hippie complex—were signs of this desire on the popular level.

The potentially frightening power that the new, sensational scientific discoveries about the mechanism of heredity might place in the hands of a few was much discussed. The discovery, in the 1950s, of the exact ways in which a nucleic acid carries the "genetic code" that determines hereditary characteristics was one of the most exciting scientific achievements of all times; it raised the possibility of artificially determining the inherited characteristics of any living organism, including human beings. And, of course, the mighty clamor raised about pollution of air and water—of "the environment" generally—which arose in the late 1960s blended with the mood of disenchantment with the technological society. Practically everybody used to laugh at those bumpkins who tried to keep the railroads out of their pastures in the 1840s—funniest reactionaries in history! Now politicians who opposed the further development of aircraft became progressive heroes.

That science itself, unlike art, is genuinely progressive was the foundation of the whole ideology of progress that arose in the aftermath of the seventeenth-century Scientific Revolution, became the emblem of modern Western man in the nineteenth century, and is still popularly entrenched. Achievement is cumulative: "each generation begins at the point where its predecessor left off," and goes on from there. Critics might urge that when we put all our energies into science, there is an inevitable loss elsewhere; that when we agree to consider only the measurable as real, we destroy something valuable in nature; that scientific habits of mind cause us to degrade personality and cheapen life (man becomes "nothing but" a collection of atoms or glandular functions, or the determinate product of environment and heredity, and may be regarded as a thing). They might urge many things, but they could hardly deny that scientific knowledge is progressive. How do we know? Its solid fruits are apparent—we become richer and richer, build bigger and better machines, make gains in measurable efficiency. We cannot prove that a humanistic education butters any bread, though we may suspect that it does. We can prove that science does.

But is the assumption of scientific progressivism any longer really valid? The production of machines, it can be argued, has clearly reached the point of diminishing returns. We do have knowledge that is helpful and that we would not wish to abolish. But is there anything obviously progressive about building larger airplanes and wider television screens? Has the time come to call a halt? The vision of more and more has become a nightmare rather than a dream.[3] Such a book as Jacques Ellul's *The Technological Society* (1965) presented a point of view destined to burgeon in the next few years. Technology has conquered both Communist and capitalist societies of the West and is about to fasten its lethal grip on the "underdeveloped" countries, destroying the last locations of genuine culture and human dignity. It should be resisted, not encouraged. That they are underdeveloped is much less certain than that we are overdeveloped. To Ellul, the trouble with the technological society is not just that it chokes us with material things. We are the slaves not merely of machines but of the ethos of efficiency, of the habits of quantifying, which cripple the spirit of man.

A flow of books from reputable presses struck the fashionable note of antimaterialism, antirationalization, easily sliding over into antilogic, antiscience, antireason. They might historicize: modern man is doomed unless he ceases his worship of the false gods and comes to terms with his "deep subjectivity." Or they might moralize and psychologize along similar lines. No publisher's list was without a few such books in the early 1970s, though one suspected some of them were left over from the later 1960s. At the same time, the literature on occultism, previously referred to, swelled to a flood (see the number of titles under this subject in the 1973 *Books in Print*), and this subject became academically respectable, with popular courses being offered on it.

The Attraction to Science

Yet science also attracted the intellectuals. It has done so persistently at least since the Enlightenment. Partly in reaction against Romanticism and Idealism, the great mid-nineteenth-century Positivist generation hailed science as queen and applied it everywhere: Ernest Renan, the Parnassians, George Eliot, Feuerbach, and Marx tried to make literature, morality, religion, politics conform to its model. Émile Zola and the Naturalists carried on this trend. Then, early in the twentieth century, the brilliant sociologists of the Weber-Durkheim era, who identified themselves with the scientific spirit, won the admiration of all. Socialists, whether Marxist or Fabian, thought they were using scientific methods or following a scientific analysis of society. (One thinks of the notorious blindness of Beatrice and Sidney Webb to all imaginative literature.) Freud attempted to subdue the disorderly psyche itself with the weapons of science.

These intellectuals typically looked on science as rational, sensible, orderly thought replacing myth and superstition and unverified random beliefs. It meant an increase of wealth, but it also meant intelligent organization of human society with the goal of enriching life in other than material ways. Released from the drudgery of excessive labor, men would have leisure to pursue the good life, to attain freedom, peace, community. The myth of science as purveyed by the politico-scientific wing of the intellectuals suggested a superman hero leading poor humanity out of its age-old miseries into a fair haven of enlightenment. Its subscribers believed, as had Shelley, in "the power of science to raise humanity and combat evil."

This had been the basic belief of the eighteenth-century Enlightenment; there was never an absence of outstanding thinkers to carry it on in the nineteenth and twentieth centuries, in a lineage suggested by the names of John Stuart Mill, H. G. Wells, Julian Huxley, John Dewey, A. J. Ayer. It seemed to include in this basically proscientific tradition the American Pragmatists, the political economists, the sociologists and psychologists (who in the overwhelming majority read Carl Jung out of the profession for the sin of mysticizing, and who even viewed Freud with deep misgivings despite his loyalty to what he regarded as scientific methodology), the Logical Positivists, and—until quite recently—virtually every shade of socialist. Permeated as it was by the idea of progress, which at bottom rested on the progressiveness of science as a mode of knowledge (unlike all others—the arts do not progress, they only change), the leading nineteenth-century ideology clung persistently to science until the last decade or two. If Matthew Arnold expressed elegant disdain for that "great rope" with a philistine on each end, Victor Hugo was more typical in writing a hymn of praise to the Atlantic cable, "The Hymen of Nations," a technological miracle that would knit mankind together, enrich human existence, open up new potentialities for the spirit. We heard the same thing about atomic energy, television, and space exploration that the Victorians heard about electricity, telephones, and automobiles, with poets and thinkers leading the parade of platitudes. They were joined by the political ideologues, who held with Léon Gambetta that the locomotive was republican; democracy, liberalism, social progress went hand in hand with the advance of industrial technology. Only very recently has this attitude changed.

Throughout his long life—or at any rate until his dotage—Bertrand Russell held to the view that to act on any knowledge not derived from scientific investigation—that is, verifiable by experimental inquiry and controlled by logical, mathematical concepts—is to travel toward fanaticism and invite destruction. This view was confirmed by the rise of Nazism, which Russell saw as a result of the abdication of rational thought in favor of a wild mysticism. He was prepared to accuse D. H. Lawrence, as others accused Henri Bergson, of being the effectual accomplice of Hitler because he undermined logic and science with his support for instinct and intuition.

Unquestionably some even among the humanists were oblivious

to most of the themes we have presented heretofore: an Existential-ist angst, a sense of decadence and an exhaustion of creativity, an apprehension of cultural disintegration, as well as a revolutionary anger at the most absurd of societies. Judith Shklar, in her enter-taining and wide-ranging book of a few years ago—*After Utopia: The Decline of Political Faith* (1957), one of the most ambitious attempts at recent intellectual history—could only look uncompre-hendingly at those she described as victims of the "unhappy consciousness." She called them "Romantics," and swept into the pile so labelled George Orwell, José Ortega y Gasset, Jean-Paul Sartre, Aldous Huxley, and quite a few others who are Romantics only in her sense of finding something not quite right about the modern world. (Those who think it sick can just as well be, and often are, quite classical in temperament, from Arnold and Flaubert to Leavis and Lewis.) She grasped with her intellect what bothered these people, but she did not empathize or sympathize with them. She did not see why anyone should be bothered by the fragmenta-tion of culture unless he were quite a morbid sort of hypersensitive, and she scolded her unhappy intellectuals for snobbishness, political apathy, lack of practicality. Her veiled indictment was quite similar to that offered by Snow in his *Two Cultures*. Though a humanist by trade, she is evidently a scientist by temperament, as many histori-ans and social scientists are.

The most striking schism in the ranks of historians at the beginning of the 1970s was not between ideological radicals and conservatives or between those who would adhere to an austere Weberian standard of objectivity and those who would frankly use historical writing to promote some valued program; though these divisions existed, the sharpest was between those who embraced a cult of "quantifying" techniques, which aspired to be clinical, exact, "scientific," and those who regarded such research as essentially barbarous. The latter, traditionalist camp was by no means assured of victory. Of the spectacular career of sociology in the postwar world, more will be said later.

The importance of Marxism in the postwar years, and especially in the 1960s, has been noted, and is indeed too obvious a pheno-menon to require emphasis. Much of the most interesting work on Marx in recent years has been a reinterpretation that plays down the "scientific" Marx, equating this with a vulgar dogmatism that is the offspring of Engels and Lenin, and presents a metaphysical and humanist Marx found chiefly, though not exclusively, in the early manuscripts. Sometimes under Existentialist influence these new interpretations have tried to rescue the great Communist from the demerit of being a sterile Positivist or a dogmatic system-builder, as these "scientific" qualities go out of style. But this has aroused indignant opposition. The primary factor in the refusal of many orthodox Communists to accept Sartre's offer of Existentialism as a better basis for revolution than old-fashioned Marxism is their reluctance to give up the claim to be scientific. The elements of materialism, determinism, and rationalism in the Marxist ideology constitute a core of values to which its followers insistently cling. They reject types of thought such as Existentialism and other Modernisms, calling them decadent bourgeois mystifications, because at bottom they fear and mistrust any departure from what they think of as "scientific" thought. In vain one might seek to show that theirs is a pseudoscience resting at bottom on blindly affirmed values; the faith in science that sustains them is too strong to be shaken by any kind of argument.[4]

The above are samples of the continuing proclivity for science found among all kinds of intellectuals. Scientism may be found even in the ranks of the esthetes. If a derisive hostility toward all that science stands for, in the Lorenzian manner, has been common among the artists (epitomized perhaps in that institute of anti-science, "'Pataphysics," lovingly perpetuated by the disciples of Alfred Jarry), another strain is represented by the Futurists, with their enthusiastic acceptance of the power of steel and the fever of speed; by the urban-industrial esthetic of Le Corbusier, who wanted to build machines to live in, but machines with beauty and grace; by Paul Valéry, who saw the classical beauty of pure science as most akin to his dream of a modern esthetic. This strain represents a distinguished branch of Modernism, which has had a pronounced impact on contemporary life. Le Corbusier was a giant, Valéry a more intelligent and thoughtful Modernist than most.

These artists tried to establish a modern order to replace the murky chaos of romantic fantasies. They were close to classicism (what admiration Valéry had for Descartes and Voltaire!) and therefore to logic and mathematics; at this point they touched science and technology.

Is science itself not just one mode of art? Clearly there is an esthetic element in science, as there is a scientific element in some esthetics. Euclid alone saw beauty bare. The word *elegant* regularly crops up in scientific discourse, to describe a theory or a technique. As Ernst Cassirer would explain, science is only one of various "symbolic forms" men shape.

The young underground acidheads and dropouts, needless to say, regretted in typically extreme form the whole of modern industry and technology, but at the same time they took for granted all its products. In this they but caricatured the contemporary viewpoint. "I think New York should be levelled and turned into a buffalo pasture" was a typical remark by one such person, whose heroes, he said, were Chief Joseph and the Dalai Lama. This young man was, at the time, in receipt of a research grant from one of the foundations—endowed of course by funds derived from industrial capitalism—and was in the habit of tape-recording his material.[5] It seems safe to say that he could not have survived half an hour in a buffalo pasture nor communicated with Chief Joseph; his natural habitat was Greenwich Village, much as he affected to despise it. Many hippies lived on family income derived from the technological society and would have been lost without their Hondas. True, some of them took to the wilderness, but it was likely to be a wilderness served by electricity and within easy range of movie houses. Their ambivalence in this respect was typical of present intellectuals, who alternately curse and worship the terrible gods of technology and science. (To orthodox, old-fashioned Marxists, this "neo-Luddism" is a deplorable error.[6]) Thomas Molnar, in his *Sartre: Ideologue of Our Time* (1968), is among those who noticed that Sartre and Mme. de Beauvoir lived scandalously comfortable lives for people so contemptuous of "bourgeois" practices and showed no reluctance at all to share in the material fruits of a civilization they condemned for its materialism. The same, of course, could be said for any number of lesser talents, including artists, movie directors, on down to pop music "stars" who exploit fashionable antitechnological themes for profits on which they live jet-set lives.[7]

Few humanists were so extreme as to suggest that we ought to abolish science, which after all staves off disease, increases comfort, protects society, and also uncovers knowledge that is far more than utilitarian. A reviewer of J. F. D. Shrewsbury's *A History of*

Bubonic Plague in the British Isles (*TLS*, April 30, 1970) was driven to exclaim, after observing that "pestilence was woven into the texture of our forefathers' lives," that this book "should be prescribed reading for anyone who believes that there could be, as an attainable alternative to a scientific and technological civilization, some form of society in which, clothed in white samite, we can move about gracefully, uttering beautiful thoughts, breathing unpolluted air, eating simple unpolluted food, and occasionally peeling off our spotless garments to swim, joyously naked, in some unpolluted stream." The prescientific age was far more "polluted" with death-dealing germs than ours. When in an excess of zeal, ecology-minded reformers demanded a moratorium on technology, there was an outcry from the "undeveloped" Third World countries which showed that these peoples quite definitely do not want to stay undeveloped, despite the views of American and European intellectuals alienated from their own technological societies. The undeveloped peoples virtually accused the ecologists of joining the imperialist plot to keep them in poverty. They live in no preindustrial paradise but in squalor, ignorance, and disease from which they wish to escape via technological progress. They will take their chances on the price of affluence.

And indeed it is widely recognized that any serious attempt to turn back the clock and adopt a belated Luddism could only result in disaster for highly developed societies. There is no way to cut off technology from modern society. The richer peoples look to technology to solve all kinds of problems that grow out of their advanced technology. There is here a natural momentum that cannot be checked by anything short of the total collapse of existing society.

The Clash of Cultures

Whatever the occasional reactions against science, it has been built deeply into the structure of modern consciousnesses. Science fiction, which J. R. Tolkien described as the "most escapist of all literature," has been the contemporary form of fantasy. Malcolm Muggeridge complained that "toward any kind of scientific mumbo-jumbo we display a credulity that must be the envy of African witch doctors." In a reply to Snow, Michael Polanyi (*Encounter,* August 1959) saw even the "traditional culture" of the humanists relying too much on science— "the supreme intellectual authority of the post-Christian age."

The encroachments of science on personal lives, emblemized in the sexologists, was one of the most startling developments of the post-1945 era. Sex became scientific in the early fifties with the fabulously best-selling Kinsey report and its many sequels.[8] As Lionel Trilling noted, people now feel that only science is capable of dealing with intimate problems, which were formerly handled by religion and folk knowledge. Though presented as a neutral survey of what in fact people do, the Kinsey report was looked to for guidance, mantled as it was with the mana of science. To the annoyance of humanists, sexology incorporated an implicit naturalistic value system. There was a tendency toward quantitative considerations, appropriate for the scientist. A little inclined to encourage the average American male to step up his weekly production of 3.2 orgasms, the report radiated a conviction that any concern about the qualitative aspects of the sexual act, or any aspects other than the physical, might lead in the direction of guilt complexes; the goal is to remove all such moral concerns and in effect to mechanize the sexual relationship. Well-scrubbed and appropriately cosmeticized couples consult the chart, perform the act, and arise wholesomely free of hang-ups. Trilling (in *The Liberal Imagination: Essays on Literature and Society,* 1950) feared they would also emerge free of humanity and observed with some irritation that love was formerly the preserve of poets and other imaginative writers. "Surely it is sad to have the issue all confused again by the naivete of the men of science," he remarked in connection with a problem "solved four centuries ago by Rabelais."

Though *Fanny Hill* was popular, it was to manuals such as Kinsey's rather than to Rabelais that people normally now turned for guidance in sexual matters. Even the young protesters, who despised most aspects of the technological society, followed the lead of the sexologists. In this respect Orwell's *1984,* which saw the totalitarian society repressing the dangerous power of sex, and Huxley's *Brave New World,* in which sexual pleasure was dispensed as a means of social control, proved equally wrong. What developed was an attempt by science to render sex harmless, all its power and all its magic rationalized away. Sex was now taught in the public schools (or in churches!) like hygiene. While earlier sexual preparation had a sacred character, Suzanne Lilar wrote in *Aspects of Love in Western Society* (1965) that "modern sexual education is primarily a form of demythologization . . . profane, rudimentary and disparaging." She thought it basically a denial of Eros, a dehumanization. There were many who agreed.

Such were the positions adopted in a bitter debate between sexologists and outraged humanistic traditionalists—a debate closely related to that about pornography and permissiveness. The sex researchers, who pressed on far beyond Kinsey's questionnaires, were by no means inarticulate. At the Washington University Medical School in St. Louis, Dr. William Masters produced not only mechanical phalluses for his Reproductive Biological Research Foundation but also diatribes against "cultural fiction" about sex purveyed by "literary traditionalists." He saw himself sweeping away the clouds of ignorance damaging to countless lives. He was answered by those who thought laboratory sex the ultimate in grossness and folly—copulating couples wired and cathoded and photographed, something grotesque beyond the imaginings of Swiftian irony. Dr. Masters and his astonished critics were barely within shouting distance of each other.

The conditions of contemporary life sharpened the clash between humanist and scientist. Driven to the fringes of society and shocked to the depths of his being by it, the poet saw the scientist as a comfortable member of the power Establishment, wealth and prestige on his side, happily catering to the needs of suburbia for more affluence. But scientists, tired of being vilified by dilettante artists, went on the offensive in the postwar years as they basked in the glow of public admiration and the security of plentiful public funds.

Both, of course, had become narrower as an inevitable result of specialization. The older scientists were seldom products of specialization but men of a broad liberal education who could at least debate philosophical and cultural issues. The older humanists were more public and more responsible than their contemporary counterparts. Victorian scientists and humanists shared many more values and experiences than present-day equivalents—could one imagine fruitful dialogue between, say, Edward Teller and Sylvia Plath?

Contemporary values are much more polarized. C. P. Snow's book was called forth, indeed, by what he felt to be an increasing estrangement—no longer the frozen smile, more often the snarl of rage.

The terms of the debate had also changed somewhat since Victorian times. In the Snow-Leavis encounter, the lines of argument were superficially similar to the joust between Matthew Arnold and Thomas Huxley just eighty years earlier, but there was a difference. Speaking for the scientists (behind a rather thin disguise of neutral peacemaker), Sir Charles suggested strongly that the men of letters and arts are enemies of society. They are "politically silly and politically wicked." Their irresponsible refusal to go with the evident course of events—and Snow's ultimate argument for science was the historicist one that the scientists "have the future in their bones"—makes the humanists reactionary foes of "liberal democracy" and even accessories to Auschwitz. (We are reminded of Russell's accusation against Lawrence.) Though a little dull, the scientists are decent folk, responsible citizens, and optimistic believers in progress. The literati, on the other hand, are filled with a black pessimism, a hatred of life, a mad disregard for reason and progress and freedom and all the respectable modern gods. Snow virtually posited a dichotomy between the liberal scientific Establishment and the reactionary literary outsiders.

This opposition is not what Arnold and Huxley represented, a fact which goes far (as Lionel Trilling perceived) to explain Leavis's fury. Arnold spoke, on the whole, for the intellectual Establishment against an upstart rebellion of scientism. He certainly did not doubt that literature was a force for morality, decency, and progress. He thought that science was likely to prove subversive. It was the scientists, Thomas Huxley and Herbert Spencer, who were bulls in the Victorian china shop, assailing the orthodoxies at every turn. But in the more recent debate the men of letters assumed the role of rebels and outsiders.

To the charge of dropping out of politics and neglecting the common life, the writers and artists were surely vulnerable. The gesture of Virginia Woolf and Bloomsbury exemplifies their position. Mrs. Woolf's Mrs. Dalloway, wife of a leading politician, did not really believe in him and his life and half wished she had married someone else. She was weary of the "public-spirited, British Empire,

tariff-reform, governing-class spirit," which was for so many generations the pride of England and of its major writers, including
Shakespeare, Milton, Burke, Macaulay, almost all the great men of
letters down to the end of the nineteenth century. Her dislike was
partly of security and order and being part of an Establishment,
partly of the formalities and hypocrisies of official society, but
mostly of its neglect of private sensibilities and the esthetic life.
Prime ministers could once be men of letters—as late as William
Ewart Gladstone, even if he inspired some secret amusement among
the real scholars and writers. "What was important to Matthew
Arnold was important to Mr. Gladstone. Nothing that is important
to me is important to Mr. Harold Macmillan," Stephen Spender
wrote in 1963. (The same could perhaps not have been said of de
Gaulle by Malraux. But Harold Macmillan was a cultured man by
comparison with other politicians one might name. His own memoirs were an outstanding literary achievement.)

Burke and Dr. Johnson might have had their differences, but they
met as equals. John Stuart Mill could move easily in both the
political and intellectual worlds. But beginning with the esthetes and
dropouts of the 1890s, the same forces that alienated the artist from
society alienated him from politics, except sporadically as extreme
critic or revolutionary—which role is really based on rejection of
politics, on a failure to understand and be a part of it. Mrs.
Dalloway, by and large, spoke for the modern temper of the literate.
Of that there can be little doubt. Politicians belong with business-
men and bureaucrats in the circle of the damned. Snow was right in
charging the most significant portion of the modern intelligentsia
with deserting politics as well as technology (which politics cannot
hope to avoid, since it must deal with the existing forces of society).

He was outrageously wrong, however, in charging the Victorian
writers with neglect of social questions. Carlyle, Dickens, Ruskin,
Morris, and even Arnold were keen and intelligent critics of society.
To dismiss the whole of this highly significant heritage of social
thought as no more than "a scream of horror" betrayed ignorance
most unbecoming in a defender of scientific methods.

F. R. Leavis, who took up the cudgels against Snow, was no rabid
Modernist. He had earlier, with considerable solemnity, taken upon
himself the not inconsiderable burden of saving modern man by

rescuing literary standards, to which end he had created the famous journal *Scrutiny* to winnow the crop of authors past and present, delivering Arnold-like judgments on the best and the worst that have been written. Against the *Scrutiny* clique had been raised the objection that it was a self-appointed elite passing judgment from a rather arbitrary and even narrow standpoint. Leavis had been reluctant to approve modern and experimental writers. He was a great advocate of Lawrence but not of Joyce. The fierceness of his strictures against Snow, whom he treated as a barbarian and a boor, seemed partly due to his own jealous proprietorship of the realm of high culture, as if the voice of civilization could only be the voice of Leavis.[9] Leavis belonged among the literary traditionalists for whom, it was alleged, the logical desideratum would be a hierarchical, aristocratic society within which an official Academy censors the arts and keeps them pure.

Yet Snow, too, was at heart a mandarin. He clearly fell within the H. G. Wells school in wishing at heart for a world run by the scientists—a utopia in which politics would be abolished, wild and inconvenient people eliminated, and all would go smoothly because perfectly rational solutions would be provided by the scientist rulers, computers at their elbows. It is an equally tidy, classical, aristocratic system. Were Leavis and Snow not so violently prejudiced against each other's point of view, they might have agreed on a ruling elite consisting of both. As in Louis XIV's time, an Academy of the Sciences and an Academy of Arts and Letters would sit at the King's either hand.

The sciences and the humanities are, after all, necessary components of any ordered and civilized society. Their radical separation is one of those "schisms in the soul" that Arnold Toynbee found to be characteristic of dying cultures. This divorce is also a function of modern complexity, since the sciences have advanced to the point where a man has no time to study anything else except his specialty in one small area of research. It is, in fact, wrong to suppose only Two Cultures: Snow himself conceded a basic difference between theoretical and engineering types within the scientific camp. (He later discovered a Third Culture, too.) The so-called humanists were even less united, being badly split on both political and esthetic issues.

Attempts at Mediation

Mediation between the two camps has never quite succeeded, but there have been many attempts. Early in the history of modern philosophy, Immanuel Kant sought to make it clear that the two realms are separate and the gap almost unbridgeable, an analysis that has left its mark down to the present. In William Golding's novel of the 1950s, *Free Fall,* Sammy Mountjoy perceives the Kantian dualism. The world of science is real, but has nothing to do with the moral world, the world of human choices and actions. We cannot impose rule and reason on our inmost selves. Attempts to make science of human affairs lead to the erection of ideal types such as "economic man," which is an abstraction from one sort of human behavior but cannot be used to guide or understand a real person in his existent situation. Or it forces us to see man, as John Locke and Adam Smith saw him, as determined and unfree.

Kant's postulation of an incurable schizophrenia in our knowledge left each part flawed. Science secures clear and certain knowledge at the cost of confining it to externals, to that alone which can be perceived by the senses; while knowledge of the noumenal thing-in-itself, the spiritual reality behind the phenomena, can never achieve more than a cloudy imperfection. The two are not in conflict, unless noumenal knowledge claims exactitude or phenomenal knowledge claims to know ultimate essences. Of course, each in its arrogance has done so, all through the nineteenth century and right up to the present; but Kant had at least suggested a solution for the puzzle. Each of our necessary modes is inadequate, and we cannot have complete knowledge. The best we can do is be clear about the status and limitations of what Kant called the pure and the practical reason.

Some recent formulations stressed that scientific knowledge in the physical-science sense, which became the classic model for such knowledge—that is, generalizing, law-finding science—achieves its result at the cost of losing concrete reality, which may be what we are really after. In human affairs particularly, abstraction withdraws the most useful as well as the most interesting kind of understanding. The physicist sees the fall of an apple, the motion of a planet around the sun, and the clinging of the atmosphere to the earth all as examples of the law of gravity, ignoring the differences between apples, planets, and gases. And this is both splendid and useful. The historian or political scientist might similarly see Alexander the Great, Henry VIII, and Hitler as examples of tyranny, but to do so involves taking them out of context and ignoring those differences between them that are vital to a correct and useful understanding of any one of them. In this case the particular, and not the general, may be what we most want and need.

Each type of knowledge is (if you like) a "science" in its own way. The generalizing or law-finding sciences are not the only valid mode of knowledge. Yet it must be confessed that many dedicated Positivists, such as Carl G. Hempel, stubbornly insisted that there is only one science and that its name is General Law. On this issue a fierce debate in the philosophy of history has gone on all through our period, beginning with a Hempel paper in 1942. But probably a majority of historians have followed the brilliant lead of R. G. Collingwood (*The Idea of History,* 1946): history's methods, which are scientific in being critical and orderly, aim at an understanding radically different from the law-finding of Positivist science, whose model has indeed done much damage to historical studies. The aim of history is not classifying objects but recreating a unique past in order to illuminate the unique present.

Albert W. Levi, in *The Humanities Today* (1970), repeated the Kantian insight in arguing that scientific and humanistic thought represents "fundamentally discordant approaches to life." Art, metaphysics, and literature the Positivist feels to be a menace, while the Idealist or Existentialist instinctively rejects the methods and results of science "because they are all too often irrelevant to the emotional requirements of man and to the facts of his human condition." Both are necessary. A healthy culture tolerates and even rejoices in a creative tension between them. Dying cultures may suffer from *radical* schism in the soul, but vital ones are not monolithic.

The important philosophical school of Phenomenology also seemed to suggest a mediation. In one way, Phenomenology undercut science. It subverted traditional deterministic and materialistic science, not by denying the possible uses of its method, but by rejecting its claims to be the basic truth, the bottom reality. Science itself is a free creation of the autonomous consciousness. Life precedes science, and science therefore cannot explain life.[10] Modes of human desire, such as love, justice, and artistic creativity, are anterior to and beyond the reach of the kind of limited understanding that science is capable of—science being directed towards things, toward the phenomenal and not the noumenal realm. Kant, Nietzsche, and Henri Bergson had all said something similar earlier, but Husserl's fashionable school made the point with greater precision. This science of the unassembled mind, as it were, put science itself under analysis and showed how it is made up of a set of values and attitudes—a set of ideas—which grow in the garden of human consciousness. Rationalism itself is a convention, a strategy.

Yet some Phenomenologists did not draw irrationalist conclusions from this but proposed instead to study as carefully as possible the operations of the human mind. Phenomenology offered itself as the ultimate science, "transcendental subjectivism" replacing "physicalist objectivism" as the deepest perspective. Husserl attacked Existentialism, with which his Phenomenology was often confused and to which, because of its irrationalism, it undeniably stood close. Not only did Husserl insist that Phenomenology is a "rigorous science of philosophy," but he argued that science had once had broader aims than those of the positivistic variety that arose largely in the nineteenth century. Positivism was a pitiful residue of the once rich body of Western inquiry, which had bartered its substance for the illusion of precision. It is necessary to return to the prespecialized age. Plato, Aquinas, and Descartes were scientists, but they were also philosophers who used their reason to the larger ends of human understanding. Husserl hoped for "a reconciliation of science and life." Possibly from the intellectual ferment of our age such a reconciliation may emerge as the most notable achievement of all.

During the astonishing twentieth-century revolutions associated with Einstein, Planck, and Heisenberg, physical science became more like art or even religion. Gone was its once confident monism and materialism; it conceded the multistructured nature of reality and found reality itself dissolving in a cloud of ideas. Up-to-date minds found it less and less possible to draw disparaging contrasts between the certainty and purity of physical science and the tentative, probablistic conclusions of human studies. That there is abundant room for a religious, a metaphysical, an esthetic view of things became a truism, reinforced by the expert judgment that methodologically the scientist seizes his fructifying hypotheses from outside the realm of empirical fact. Such a book as Pratima Bowes' *Is Metaphysics Possible?* expresses this widely shared position: the religious, the metaphysical, the esthetic, and even the common sense are realms with an equal claim to validity. The claims of science to answer all questions and supersede all other modes of knowing are well behind us and cannot be sustained, though this vulgar nineteenth-century view lingers on in popular thought.

Scientists indeed have become mystics. In 1973 the great German physicist Weizsaecker was reported (*Time,* April 23) to be communing with an Indian Yogi and declaring that "mysticism is one of the great discoveries of mankind." The mysterious universe that surfaced between 1881 and 1927 amid the Einsteinian ruins of the old billiard-ball universe has grown ever more mysterious. The atomic bomb used the rubble of whole cities to prove its absurd paradoxes to be more than just speculation. The postwar years revealed the expanding universe, blown up from something about the size of a baseball to something many billions of light-years thick and destined to continue growing until, after more billions of years, it would begin shrinking again—a vision uncannily like the world cycle conceived centuries ago by Indian mystics. The subatomic jungle of strangely behaving particles also has grown even more strange, apparently a device for the production of the craziest possible happenings. (In *The Roots of Coincidence* Arthur Koestler calls attention to the neutrino "which has no mass, no electrical charge, and can hurtle with ease through the entire earth.") One can hardly any longer reproach believers in ghosts, astrology, visitors from outer space, and other occult phenomena for deserting scientific reason; the goings-on in the laboratories of any great scientific institute can make these tired old superstitions look like models of common sense. The last certitude, science, has become the last refuge of the illogical.

The Behavioral Sciences

A large chapter in the history of recent attitudes toward science relates to the aggressive emergence of behavioral science and a vogue for sociology that threatens the traditional humanistic studies with consignment to the academic slums, as well as to a strong reaction against this trend that includes the charge that this alleged social science is a fraud. Social and psychological science found itself under sharp attack even as it appeared to be consolidating extensive gains. Basking in the warmth of public admiration and stimulated by the free flow of public funds, their institutes and centers thriving, the social scientists looked down at swarms of critics eating away at the foundation of their imposing edifice.

Enemies claim that the term *behavioral science* was invented as a device to get government money out of antiintellectual but gullible legislators at a time when anything labelled "science" would cause the coffers to fly open. Grants would be forthcoming for any project that managed to twist itself into a semblance of science, the main attributes being technical (use of methods and instruments resembling those employed by physical and natural scientists, such as mathematics, computers, graphs, and charts) and conceptual (use of metaphors taken from physical and natural science, such as input/output, equilibria, systems of forces).

Critics were never lacking to attack all this as spurious. Yet one could hardly dismiss it as only a cynical game played by academic empire-builders. Its practitioners believed in it fervently. In such a book as Harold D. Lasswell's *The Future of Political Science* (1963), the vision of a world ruled over by political science seminars, gathering facts on a vast scale and transmuting them into scientifically derived policy decisions, reached heights of sheer delirium. Lasswell, one of the *doyens* of the American academic world, had become a science-intoxicated man. In his utopia, graduate students scurry about with questionnaires, while newspapers and other media spill their contents into the center where Lasswell and his fellow professors sit surrounded by computers, engaged in "intellectually integrating" all this data and sending forth a stream of certified political decisions. Such visions of glory emanated primarily from the United States, a fact from which some Europeans might draw the darkest of inferences concerning technologized and dehumanized man. They would not be entirely right, for the eminent academicians who spawned such schemes believed themselves to be fighting on the side of the angels. In American university departments of sociology and political science, an immense amount of work was being done by eager converts whose projects combined abstruse and involved flights of metaphysics with the furious use of computers.

It was not only in the United States that social and political science, often vaguely unified under the banner "behavioral," experienced a boom. In Great Britain sociology, formerly almost a neglected discipline, was the academic darling of the 1960s, while in France and Germany it also flourished vigorously. The basis of this strength was somewhat ambiguous. Sociology was associated with the new universities, though it also managed to secure a foothold in the older ones from which formerly it had been contemptuously excluded. Thus it wore an air of progressiveness, of being with-it and swinging and not Oxbridge-stodgy, of being politically "activist" and "relevant," too, sharing some of the mana of these fashionable terms—a curious role, perhaps, for a discipline identified with the objective and rational treatment of social problems. Some British sociologists, like David Martin, grew immoderately disgusted with student revolution. But others were among its intellectual leaders. Low-grade sociology often was a thin disguise for polemics—an academic refuge for frustrated revolutionaries who, under the pretext of studying them objectively, could expose, ridicule, condemn the ruling class, the Protestant Establishment, the military mentality, or perhaps, furtively, glorify various social movements.[11]

In the eyes of some intellectual mandarins in Britain, sociology smacked of intellectual vulgarity and ranked as a study suited to the lesser talents of provincial teachers and limited students: recent democratic intruders into the citadel of higher learning, who populated those upstart plate-glass or cinder-block universities. ("More is worse," Kingsley Amis said of the higher educational explosion.) Hugh Lloyd-Jones suggested, in the course of reviewing a quite long and evidently dull book on the sociology of British academic life (*Spectator,* June 5, 1971), that sociology has functioned as "a convenient soft option" for the marginal student unable to do mathematics or languages and put off by the rather severe discipline of historical research, which normally demands wearisome hours in the archives. An indulgent study, "it often takes the form of instruction in the very beliefs which the student's emotions have already led him to embrace." Lloyd-Jones even saw it as the new theology—uncritical, devout, and tedious. The prolix solemnity of much sociology supports this view, but obviously not all of it fitted into this dismal category. Sociology's popularity extended to the younger generation of historians, who wanted to be scientific and use computers and end indecisive and dillentantish muddling around, as well as to "get involved" with contemporary issues—a curious blending of early nineteenth-century Positivism, long considered discredited in historiography, and fashionable existential commitment and presentism.

At any rate, there could be no doubt about the vogue for sociology; the discipline "has become almost frighteningly fashionable in Britain," Peter Wilmott observed in 1968. It gave rise to an enormous literature. There was the sociology of nearly everything: the neighborhood, the city, the country; the family, the church, the school; labor, management, industry; politics, government; homosexuality; and so on and on. *Behavior* was almost as popular a word as *sociology*. Likewise, *structure:* social structure, political structure, economic structure; the social structure of modern Britain, the social structure of a town, a suburb, a school, even a pub. Books on sociological methods became common. One, *The Strategy of Social Inquiry,* came equipped with a Data Pack containing "magnetic tapes, computer data and programme tape, and 80 column punched cards." Faced with the evident popularity of such do-it-yourself field survey kits, articles in the press actually showed concern for ethical questions raised by the frequency and intensity of interviewing; the problem arose of citizens beset by hordes of sociological inquirers demanding information on their private affairs.

The flexible boundaries of an ill-defined discipline appeared in a claim by a publisher that a history of the blacks in South Africa is "sociology." (Anything about race has to be sociology, the reasoning must have been.) A book called *The Sociology of Progress* turned out to be a potted history of the idea of progress—skimmed from J. T. Bury's old masterpiece—capped by a few moral generalizations. A good deal else called sociology is, obviously, similar to what in past epochs would have come under the heading of journalism, travel, literature, description, or even sermonizing. One of the more popular works of recent British sociology, Peter Willmott and Michael Young's *Family and Class in a London Suburb* (1960) might almost as well have been written as a novel, as a memoir, or as several articles for the Sunday supplement. Nell

Dunn's *Up the Junction* was classed as a novel but came close to sociology of the Wilmott-Young sort. An account of how lorry drivers work, what they feel about their work, and how others feel about them was presented as sociology.

The constant temptation of this discipline, which produced many estimable and interesting, if minor, studies of this sort, was to try to justify its claim to be a science by interpolating pretentious terminology and pseudoprofound generalizations. Sociologists are in general agreement that they differ from historians in seeking, and presumably finding, general rather than particular social patterns or relationships (the assumption being that "human activity is patterned or ordered in a way that is similar to the patterning of natural phenomena") and that they differ from novelists, journalists, and other unsystematic describers of human social behavior in being rigorous, ordered, and logical in their methods. It can hardly be enough to write an enjoyable and reasonably perceptive account of life in the suburbs. Willmott and Young's book joined such widely read works as William H. Whyte's *The Organization Man* in being refreshingly free of jargon and alleged laws; but it raised an uncomfortable doubt: is it sociology?

When they departed from ordinary language and description to produce generalizing theories cast in novel terms, the sociologists drew upon themselves a withering fire. In an age of sophisticated analysis of language and scientific methodology, sociologists were not allowed to get away with it. "Ponderously obscure description of platitudes"; "abstruse ways of explaining the thumpingly obvious"—such were the deflating comments on the brave attempts of some social investigators to clothe their humble researches in the mantle of high theory. A suspicion of fraud enters when men must say obscurely what can be said simply. Translation of sociological jargon became a favorite indoor sport among the intellectually sophisticated. ("A high degree of interfamilial interaction" means that relatives get together a lot.)

The man considered the most formidable sociological theorist was also the favorite target for attack: Talcott Parsons. His detractors found him to be both incomprehensible and mock-profound, his turgid statements to amount really to no more than the tritest of truisms. One critic suggested that the elaborate structure of Parsonian goal-directedness, cognitive and cathetic responses to stimuli, and the like can be reduced to such statements as "Whenever you do anything, you are trying to get something done," and "You cannot do anything without thinking and having feelings at the same time." [12] Confronted with the need to vindicate their law-finding function, sociologists were all too likely to come up with one of those thumping platitudes, if not with outright redundancies. A prominent textbook on rural sociology informed us (in a "law") that three processes determine the number and distribution of population: births, deaths, and migration. There is presumably a similar law stating that the candidate who secures the fewest votes always loses the election.

Sociology claims to replace common discourse and conventional wisdom about human affairs; yet what it usually does is tell us in new language what men have always known. It transcribes traditional knowledge into scientific-sounding vocabulary for an age that can only think in this way. If, having lost Rabelais, we must learn about sex from Kinsey, the same applies elsewhere: having lost Dickens and Tom Jones' friend the poacher's daughter, we must learn about life from "social inquiry." In a stratified society we do not meet any real truck drivers, so we must read a book about them; and as the time when we might read about them in a poem by John Gay is over, we must read about them in a sociological treatise.

Thus the popularity of sociology was balanced by a ferocious criticism usually on a rather advanced philosophical plane. Such a book as A. R. Louch's *Explanation and Human Action* (1966) used all the tools of advanced linguistic analysis to argue that "the idea of a science of man or society is untenable"; that this radical and pernicious error of scientism inheres in "the univocal theory of explanation that all explanation consists in bringing a case under a law," which "as applied to human performance is totally irrelevant." Louch's barrage against the behavioralist fortress was aimed from the trenches of philosophy, where formidable forces under the strategic command of Wittgenstein, Ryle, J. L. Austin, and the Linguistic school think it is their business to clarify the confused concepts of other investigators. If this means clarifying them right out of existence, so much the worse—or better. Possibly a handful of investigators as astute as Louch could level every intellectual discipline and thus save the taxpayers endless amounts of money. These austere analysts are out to spoil everyone's fun, and some people have detected an emotional aridity in their methods. But the Louchian assault on the social sciences was undeniably effective and hence helped to lead us in a direction exactly opposite from that of their practitioners. It was an appeal to the richness of experience expressed in the piecemeal, tentative, and moralistic ways of everyday language, to conventional wisdom against the narrowing formulae of the social scientists. This, as we have seen, is the tendency of much recent Analytical philosophy.

The judgment of Louch that "a sterile scholasticism has possessed the behavioral sciences. . . ." was repeated by H. P. Rickman (*Understanding and the Human Studies,* 1967): "To model the human studies entirely on the sciences is, I believe, intellectually misguided, scientifically sterile and morally dangerous." Such critics thought that the behavioralists left out the essential element—mind. The behavioristic sociologist or political scientist tries to treat human actions as mere behavior, taking into account only external results while getting around that inconvenient interior dimension. But the understanding of this interior dimension is what really matters. The rich and wonderful world of human "intentionality" that the Phenomenologists are interested in exploring—so strange and unpredictable, capable of that "gratuitous act" that Gide saw as the most valuable of all things because it is an expression of the self, quite spontaneous and quite useless, wholly unrationalized and hence truthful and satisfying—this is what we must understand more and more if we are to advance in self-knowledge and thus avert self-destruction, and it is exactly what behavioral science ignores.

In *The Sociological Imagination* (1959) C. Wright Mills criticized both pretentious theoreticians like Parsons and mere empirical data gathering of the psephological sort and called for a creative combination of theory and investigation. Mills' own books, such as *White Collar,* came close to meeting these exacting requirements. Few others did.

Psychology

Herbert Blumer, in *Symbolic Interactionism: Perspective and Method* (1969), represents a groping from within the profession towards a less positivistic sociology; it would be wrong to suggest that behavioralism is without opposition among sociologists. But it seems the dominant mode, and this is also true recently within academically respectable psychology. In 1972 the veteran American psychologist B. F. Skinner, known for his work on rats and pigeons, published a popular book called *Beyond Freedom and Dignity,* attacking nebulous entities not subject to the iron laws of conditioned reflexes and assailing what Skinner called "autonomous man," who, unlike a pigeon, cannot be made to peck to order. Although such enthusiasts for "human engineering" seem incredibly foolish and naive to their humanist foes, they continue to pin their hopes for human improvement on science, and the success of Skinner's book suggests that their cause is by no means lacking in popular appeal. At the opposite pole stand Phenomenologists and Existentialists, who declare that, even if we could know all the external stimuli playing on a human being, we could not predict his response, because of that radical, totally unpredictable freedom which is the very nature of the human consciousness and which is not to be found in any other kind of being. The distance between Skinner and Merleau-Ponty, both prominent sages of our era, can only be measured in intellectual light-years. It would be hard to imagine greater polarization of viewpoints.[13]

The academic trend in psychology has been away from the "depth" school of Freud, Jung, and McDougall, which was considered to be too speculative, bordering on metaphysics or mysticism. Faced with these awesome depths, into which the intrepid pioneers of Freud's age had thrown a tentative flare, the average academic psychologist drew back. This revulsion becomes more understandable when we contemplate the extremes of sheer mysticism reached on the wilder post-Freudian shores, where dwell such far-out figures as Norman O. Brown (*Life Against Death: The Psychoanalytical Meaning of History,* 1959, and *Love's Body,* 1966) or the Reich-Marcuse school, which adapted Freud to the uses of the social revolution. Psychologists preferred behavioristic experiments on rats. These experiments, on the anlaysis of Louch and Rickman, prove utterly sterile when applied to human beings. Yet behavioral psychology flourished; whole libraries, journals, and institutes were devoted to it. Its extremes are suggested in the description of a recent learned book titled *The Psychiatric Programming of People*

(1972): "The book is based on the author's premise that man is, for psychological purposes, a computer. . . ." Armed with shock treatments and "ethological" concepts, these practitioners of behavior therapy promised to do away with personality aberrations, possibly by making possession of them a more unpleasant liability than at any time since the Middle Ages.

But psychology, the focus of much interest—for what is more fascinating to modern man than this subjective element?—belongs to no one school. It is a scene of wild disorder. Existentialist or Phenomenological psychology, brilliantly expressed in such works as R. D. Laing's *The Divided Self,* is far out on the opposite wing from the behaviorists and physicalists. Taking its point of departure from the philosopher Martin Heidegger, Existentialist psychotherapy was first developed by Ludwig Binswanger and by Medard Boss of Zurich, once a student of Freud and Jung. It has stressed ontological security, "identity," the need to make oneself an authentic person by awareness of one's freedom to choose. It rejects the mechanical aspects of Freudianism, seeing this approach as a kind of technology of the soul using pseudoscientific dogmas. The Existentialists view the problem of the human personality as a moral and cultural problem, not as a medical one. "Disease" as applied to the psyche they consider to be a barbarous misnomer; Laing came to feel that the "insane," by failing to adjust to a grotesque society, may actually be exhibiting true sanity. In any case, one should not "treat" them as if they are abnormal; rather, one should regard them as spiritual pilgrims of an unusual sort. At the opposite extreme are psychiatrists to whom schizophrenia is only a matter of vitamin deficiencies. There are also Gestaltists and Structuralists.

By and large Freud—the genius of the first third of this century, founder of the huge industry of psychoanalysis, author of an assumed science of the mysterious forces within the psyche—did not hold up. His genius was recognized, but his scientific claims were sharply questioned. In a situation somewhat comparable to that of Toynbee and Teilhard, Freud came under attack from the clinical behaviorists on one side and from Existentialists on the other. Contemporary man, it was argued, suffers from quite different ailments of the spirit than those hysterias Freud had found. No need now to worry about sexual repression and guilt; the dirt once kept confined in the bottom of the mind is now all over the street. The great Viennese turns out to have been a thinker only for his own time. Psychoanalysis, two writers on the subject declared in 1965, "is the biggest hoax ever played on humanity."[14] An extreme opinion, it is by no means a rare one in recent literature. Freud as male chauvinist was a discovery of Women's Lib: his libido is masculine; he believed that women envy the male his more substantial organ of sex.

The same fate that overtook the Marxists befell the Freudians as well. The impact of Freud had been so enormous that his mark would always remain on the modern mind, his words indelibly planted in language. Towards him even those who came, often with regret, to realize his imperfections might feel with W. H. Auden:

> If often he was wrong and at times absurd,
> To us he is no more a person
> Now but a whole climate of opinion.

But the new psychology had to be post-Freudian, in other words, had to go beyond Freud; caught in the toils of Modernism, it could not remain frozen in a dogma. Dogmatism had always been a problem for the Freudians. The Master had been among the most dogmatic of men, largely unable to confess any error—a "right man" in the terminology of A. E. van Vogt. The International Psychoanalytical Association took on qualities of an ecclesiastical court, expelling members for heresy. Like institutionalized Marxism, institutionalized Freudianism congealed into a sterile and intolerant theology. So dry a shell was bound to fracture.

In the *Crisis of Psychoanalysis* (1970) Erich Fromm pointed to the utter fragmentation of the movement. There is an extreme right wing of affluent consultants serving respectable burghers willing to pay to have their tensions relieved or their family arguments settled. (Needless to say, books are not lacking to prove that, like nearly everything else, psychiatry is a part of the Establishment, plotting hand in hand with the Pentagon and Wall Street to "uphold the status quo.") There is an extreme left wing of far-out prophets of complete liberation through unlimited sex, who are favorites of the counterculture. In between, dozens of aberrant psychoanalysts preach their own pet modifications of the Master's dogmas.

It need hardly be repeated that the influence of Freud remains powerful. "He has in large part created the intellectual climate of our time," the *TLS* remarked in 1956. Psychoanalysis is an established industry, increasingly resorted to by troubled souls or harried marital partners. Most psychiatrists would probably still acknowledge their primary debt to the great Viennese. Yet the reaction against Freud seems equally unmistakable, as much from the restless young who find his "mechanization of the soul" repellent as from the laboratory Positivists who find his hypotheses unverifiable. The more thoughtful and creative psychologists have pushed well beyond dogmatic Freudianism, which threatens soon to become as dead as dogmatic Marxism. And to dissolve the dogma meant dissolving the Freudian school as a specific entity, though fragments of Freudian insight continue to float amid the intellectual debris of the modern age.

The existential psychiatrists, such as Laing and Boss, reject Freudian scientific "reductionism" and mechanism. We must take experience at its face value. The "unconscious" is a superfluous concept, the product of Freud's attempt to make the psyche a machine. We do not explain what dreams "really" mean; we take them as they are. The therapist (not an "analyst") does not maintain a clinical objectivity, as Freud's alleged doctor of the mind is required to do; he relates himself to the experiences of the other person in a fully human way. This revolt against an inhuman regimen of behavioral science as applied to the individual mind is, again, close to being a return to conventional wisdom.[15]

Similarly, Carl Jung, of far more interest than Freud to young people who participated in the mystique of counterculture and "expansion of consciousness," has lost much credit with the "scientists." There seems no way of proving the existence of an archetype of the collective unconscious. And Jung in his later years spoke openly as if archetypes contained hints of something "beyond the frontiers of knowledge." His late works, including the posthumous, autobiographical *Memories, Dreams, Reflections* (1963), aroused dismay among skeptics by their frank mysticism.

The more intelligent and creative psychologists of the recent generation—for example, the American Abraham Maslow—wandered restlessly between behavioralism and the various varieties of Freudianism. Such men shared the distaste for systems found so widely in the post-1945 world; they chose to drift close to a nearly Phenomenological interest in intentionality, to reject all reductionist and mechanistic styles, to refuse to believe that any one psychological rule could account for the rich exuberance of human experience.

In the end, the attempts of Freud and Jung to bring the soul under the rule of science only added a few metaphors to our vocabulary. "For Jung, the unconscious was a populous mythological pantheon," Aldous Huxley wrote. "Freud saw it rather as an underground urinal, scribbled over ... with 4-letter graffiti." No one is likely to deny either the myth-loving or the scurrilous aspects of the psyche, but all its other aspects cannot be reduced to these. Along with many other qualities of the mind, they exist; that is all one can say.

The Age of Computers

Computers did not invade only the "social sciences." Driven by a law of professional specialization which decrees that one's work be made as arcane and as formidable looking as possible, in order to earn academic prestige and justify promotion, even professors of literature turned eagerly to computers. They can be used in literature chiefly, it seems, to analyze sentence structures and create concordances. What was formerly reserved for the Holy Bible and Shakespeare, and carried out laboriously by the devout over many years, can now be performed in a short time for every writer, so that we will perhaps eventually have concordances for Ian Fleming and Edgar Wallace. We may also have elaborate data on the average length of the sentences in these authors' works and their preferred words and forms of speech. International conferences were held at Cambridge (1970) and Edinburgh (1971) at which numerous papers were delivered on just such subjects.[16] The work done appeared to be suggested, not by any rational human need, but simply by what computers can do. Small wonder there was violent protest against this sort of thing, which nevertheless rapidly became more frequent.

Already in the field of literary criticism and scholarship—beginning in the prewar period but sweeping on to academic triumph after the war—was the so-called New Criticism, an intellectual development rather comparable to the behavioralist advance in the social sciences or the Analytical trend in academic philosophy. In its broader meaning, the New Criticism was a victory of technique over content. Objective and astringent, its disciples despised mere "literary appreciation" as embarrassingly old-fashioned, just as the political scientists now felt that reading the classics of political theory, Plato and all that, was too amateurish. They sought a method of criticism more suitable to an age of specialists, one that explicated, counted, analyzed.

The New Critics seemed to distrust literature—a strange spirit to dwell among teachers of literature, one might think, but teaching, as is well known, had now become the least of a rising young professor's concerns. The turn toward computers was only an extension of research habits well entrenched in English departments before the quantifying vogue. To murmur "how beautiful" over a passage of Milton offered far less opportunity for advancement than a counting of the exact number of times Milton inverted his sentences or used bucolic images. It became necessary to point out that the study of literature can never become an exact science.[17]

The debate went on. Behavioralism in political science was obsolete, according to some who talked about the revival of political theory, or political philosophy.[18] The aridity of behavioralism had "turned off" youth and forced it to slake its human thirst for values and larger patterns of meaning at the dubious fountains of antiquated metaphysics. To confine oneself to observable external behavior is to eliminate that which is most human and most interesting. Like Logical Positivism in philosophy, its demand for clarity and certainty had forced behavioralism to eliminate too much. We must speak about many things even if we cannot speak about them in ways that satisfy the tests of the laboratory. Moreover, behavioralism's refusal of all normative and speculative functions incapacitated it for criticism of society, since it implicitly accepted the existing framework within which action takes place.

At the bottom of the heap of "behavioral oriented" studies, so modern in appearance, lies the old Saint-Simonian impulse to set up a ruling class of scientific mandarins. Can government be left to chance, to the vagaries of democracy, to politics? Let the citizen deliver himself into the hands of "an unbiased source dedicated solely to reporting scientifically on the probable costs and consequences of alternate proposed policies or solutions" (statement of Behavioral Research Council, Great Barrington, Mass.). C. P. Snow himself revealed an unmistakable desire to abolish politics and set up a scientific elite to govern. If we really believe in the science of politics, we must insist that public policy yield to it and stop floundering about in a pre-Galilean stage of superstition.

Such attitudes as this, of course, may lead to a desire to abolish culture itself, with which political ideologies and attitudes are closely bound up. Reactionaries who are aristocrats and *literati* and traditionalists; revolutionaries who share a *mystique;* liberals captivated by a vision of free minds in an open society— all these people's political irrationalisms are linked to culture. Scientists want a rational, cosmopolitan man who is deculturalized: a "cosmic man," in Wyndham Lewis' term, who only knows how to do science. His education will be carefully supervised—by the scientific elite (who may, of course, try illegitimately to shift the burden to computers).[19] *Quis custodet custodes?* Our scientist-rulers will hardly command universal assent; people cannot be depoliticalized and deculturalized, unless they are coerced or manipulated. If it should gain power, this well-meaning scientific elite, like other self-appointed saviors of mankind, would perhaps soon become a despotism, exterminating enemies (the humanists would be the first to go!) and then quarrelling with each other until some Lenin of the behaviorists arose to still every dissenting voice. Such is the humanist suspicion.

Skinner's beehive was not conceived in happiness but in gloom; it is hardly right to describe it as a utopia. Some scientists turned bitterly pessimistic. Once the harbingers of progress, they had sternly stressed determinism and, quite often, the amoral struggle described by Darwin. The biologist Jacques Monod's *Chance and Necessity* (1971), a neo-Darwinian revelation of the reign of chance and necessity, lashed out bitterly against the "lies" of religion, progress, humanitarianism. It was a kind of reply to the fantasies of the youth culture about Eden served on a platter. It agreed with Sartrean Existentialism insofar as it saw the world as absurd and man a stranger in it: "He wakes at last to the realization that, like a gypsy, he lives on the margin of an alien world." This science, like Max Weber's, is no cheery offering of the rewards of conquest of nature.[20] It is a grim picture that we will confront only if we are strong enough to stand the truth. Monod thinks we are better advised to forget our dreams.

One wonders how long science can remain on the pedestal of popular esteem if it is going this route. At any rate, we are a long way from Snow's contrast between bitter, antisocial artists and responsible, constructive scientists. The scientists, to judge by this and other recent cases, are as bitter as the artists, and even less hopeful.

The Case for Scientific Reason

In the 1960s men got to the moon—and found there was no thrill in the accomplishment. Within a few years, complaints about spending excessive funds on such sci-fi adventurism multiplied. Nothing better illustrated the ambivalence toward science and technology.

Many other technological marvels, including color television and supersonic airplanes, raised the "standard of life," but opinion turned against material goods. Medical science itself was not immune from the disparaging comment that it has prolonged suffering as much as it has life, perpetuated genetic defects, and inflicted burdensome expenses on society. In the chorus of Cassandras on the topical subject of pollution, the more extreme rejected technological progress altogether and condemned economic as well as population growth; they predicted almost certain doom by the end of the century, or soon thereafter, from contamination, the exhaustion of resources, or the unbalancing of nature. The choice, in their view, was only one between deaths. If by some chance we escape nuclear war, we shall perish from famine, or asphyxiation, poisoning, lack of water, depletion of metals, shortage of power, or some other technological horror. So reckless were some of these claims, backed by unverifiable conjecture rather than solid evidence, that one might suspect them to be more an emanation of ideology or religion than of science. Indeed, responsible scientists seldom joined the Cassandras. The widespread conviction that technological and population growth has become a menace to human happiness is a moral judgment, a questioning of the values by which Western civilization has long lived.

Science was in trouble; but some wondered whether rational thinking was not thereby discouraged, to man's great detriment. Can we so easily reject the rule of reason? Released from some of the errors and false trails, scientific approaches to social and political questions in the wider sense surely offer hope. They cannot solve all "problems," but they can palliate many. They are better than the depressing struggle of ideologies that has embittered our era and strangled communication between peoples.

Ideology raises the hackles and inflames the mind. Shrill voices hurl charges and countercharges that are the more envenomed because they do not submit to rational proof; they are beyond evidence and beyond logic. Are "the workers" "exploited" by "capitalism"? Does "Communism" threaten "liberty and democracy"? Does "liberalism" lead to "Communism," or is a "reactionary" a "Fascist"? Ninety percent of such argumentation must rest on sheer emotive expression, on an inner twist of the mind which is not interested in evidence, which in effect says with Jean-Jacques, "Let us begin by setting the facts aside, for they have nothing to do with the case." A good example is that of a distinguished writer and scholar who said, in expressing his opposition to United States involvement in Vietnam, that he did not intend to argue logically about the question of the Vietnam War at all.[21] Our defecting linguist did not bother to become a social scientist; he became a "political activist," presumably about to descend into the streets to toss a few rocks. The Two Cultures debate perhaps died in those days of 1968 when scientists and humanists clasped hands over the bleeding body of the university. (Federico Mancini in an article on the Italian student revolts said that "physics and humanities students led the revolt.")

Strategically, sociology is a mediating discipline, whereby the critic of society, withdrawing to a distance, judiciously reflects and weighs. His rhetoric is at least cool, his approach rational. Much recent political writing is marked by an extreme irrationality. Not only are there the conspiracy theories, but in other ways there is a retreat into deep fantasy. War, for example, is said to spring from pornographic impulses, or from psychosexual urges; politics, to such as Norman O. Brown, is a form of rape. (Brown spoke for a whole youth culture in avowing an intent "to put an end to politics" altogether, replacing it by poetry or Love.) Faced with such obfuscations, we may yearn to have back Thomas Hobbes, whose clear mind knew perfectly well what war and politics are about: men want things. Sociology at its best, in the tradition of Hobbes and Montesquieu and de Tocqueville and Max Weber, contains keen-minded dissection of myths, high-powered tools of analysis. Some of contemporary sociology belongs in this tradition. German sociology was the scene of a bitter debate between (roughly) an element represented by Herbert Marcuse and Theodor Adorno, prophets of the neo-Marxian, and a more objective group led by Ralf Dahrendorf.[22] In France, similarly, the disabused clarity of Raymond Aron, who called himself a sociologist, has done battle with the school of Sartre.

In the Soviet Union, too, a kind of sociology has emerged to exert a moderating influence, presenting more realistic and informed views to combat the fanaticism of religious certitude; it is a device for tempering dogmatic Marxism without seeming to be a reactionary opposing ideology. (See Alex Simirenko, ed., *Soviet Sociology,* 1968.) One cannot come right out and say that all the official claims are nonsense, but one can present sober factual evidence in the name of social science. The Kremlin tyrants send their poets to mental asylums or labor camps, but they evidently listen occasionally to their sociologists. Likewise, in the West, studies such as the Frenchman Serge Mollett's *The New Working Class* (1963), which examined social class with clarity and respect for fact, contributed to the newer social movements by discrediting the simpler-minded stereotypes of old-fashioned Marxism. Many hope that in the wider sense a scientific—that is, rational—attitude toward political questions will make headway. The pernicious model of the physical science, "behavioralism," may have to go. Whole empires of pseudoscientific jargon will be demolished utterly. The cruel light of philosophical analysis will play on many an ugly sociological construction, as well as on the primitive vocabulary of the ideologists. The work of destruction will be a formidable task, but men of good will hope that it goes forward. Some of the worst enemies of false science are ranged on the scientific side of the Two Cultures war, while others are on the humanist side. Reason is a frail and often indiscernible wisp of hope flitting somewhere above this unseemly brawl between computerized barbarians and maddened humanists.

NOTES

1. In *Point Counterpoint* Huxley, as Quarles, appears to agree with Lawrence (Rampion) that "the machine means death." And in *Brave New World* Huxley practically invented the antiutopia in which all humanity has been drowned in a sea of scientific hedonism.

2. In his Romanes lecture "Science and Literature" (in *The Hope of Progress,* 1972), Sir Peter Medawar, citing Lowes Dickinson's remark that "when science arrives, it expels literature," argued the reverse, that "when literature arrives, it expels science." A considerable body of modern criticism has explored the alleged "dissociation of sensibility" (T. S. Eliot's phrase) created by modern science beginning in the seventeenth century. See especially Basil Willey's *The Seventeenth Century Background* (1934). There is a discussion in Charles Davy, *Towards a Third Culture* (1961).

3. "If I project the dream into the future there seems no outcome," Malcolm Muggeridge wrote, "only an infinitely extended projection that at last disappears into gray nothingness—our economy expanding year by year to double, treble, quadruple . . . color television, three-dimensional, on a large screen, on a still larger screen; more and more motorcars; wider and wider roads; faster and faster airplanes, supersonic, super-supersonic, with louder and louder bangs; anti-missiles, anti-anti-missiles, anti-anti-anti-missiles, and so on *ad infinitum.*" *Jesus Rediscovered* (1969), p. 91.

4. Those who accuse the Marxists of being unscientific mean that they ignore or distort patent empirical realities. But Marxists do this because of their fierce wish to have a social or historical system that is rational, orderly, predictable, law-like. They will have it whether it is there in reality or not.

5. See Don McNeill, *Moving through Here* (1970), p. 80.

6. The utopia of a proponent of the Feminist Revolution (Shulamith Firestone), wnerein after the women of the world have arisen and lost their chains mankind joins womankind in living in "sexuate" perfection, included test-tube babies and machinery to do all the housework. It is difficult to get science and technology out of either the utopias or the dystopias.

7. For one example, the successful, eccentric, uninhibited British theatrical director Joan Littlewood, according to Kenneth Tynan, called herself a Red, but owned a "sumptuously decorated house," often went yachting, and was a notable gourmet. Similarly, Alastair Horne has commented on the remarkable adjustment to bourgeois comfort achieved by Chilean Communist Pablo Neruda and the Chilean socialist president Salvador Allende.

8. The sharpness of the change is suggested by the fact that, in the 1930s, a psychology professor lost his post at the University of Wisconsin for using questionnaires on sexual experience. A. H. Maslow's insightful surveys were buried in the *Journal of Social Psychology.*

9. The intrepid Leavis engaged in a subsequent quite violent exchange with Noel Annan (see *TLS,* May 29, 1969, April 23, 1970, and April 30, 1970), an educational administrator advocating more science in the British universities. Annan found Leavis's humanism intolerant in that "in the name of creativity [it] would impose . . . a straitjacket upon the play of free minds."

10. The wit of G. K. Chesterton had perhaps anticipated the somewhat ponderous conclusions of German philosophy: "It is idle to talk of the alternative of reason and faith. Reason is itself a matter of faith."

11. The student revolutionaries, however, typically asserted that academic sociology, like other studies, was used to prop up the existing social order and that, come the Revolution, it would presumably vanish, along with almost everything else except some speeches by the Leader.

12. See G. Mortimore and R. Enfield, "Their Language and Ours," in "What Is Sociology?" supplement, *TLS,* April 4, 1968.

13. For an interesting clash of views see T. W. Wann, ed., *Behaviorism and Phenomenology: Contrasting Bases for Modern Psychology* (1964).

14. Edward R. and Cathey Pinckney, *The Fallacy of Freud and Psychoanalysis.*

15. "The student of human nature is apt nowadays to forget that most of what we know about the mind of man is to be learnt from the writings not of scientists but of men of letters--the poets and philosophers, the novelists and the literary critics." Sir Cyril Burt, cited by Arthur Koestler in *The Act of Creation* (1964), p. 18.

16. See *TLS,* April 21, 1972.

17. See William Righter, *Logic and Criticism* (1963); also some remarks on attempts to scientize literature in Kathleen Nott, *A Soul in the Quad: The Use of Language in Philosophy and Literature* (1969).

18. Dante Germino, *Beyond Ideology: The Revival of Political Theory* (1967) tended to see the revival not so much following behavioralism as accompanying it. Within political science, behavioralism was always criticized, and it never entirely won the day, though about 1960 it was almost ready to claim decisive victory.

19. The expectation that somehow computers will resolve the impossible task of teaching all modern knowledge is found in George B. Leonard's *Education and Ecstasy* (1968), which introduces us to a 2001 school where children go to computers and "electronic identification devices" to get "the full bank of the basic, commonly agreed-upon cultural knowledge arranged in dialogue form." One wonders who it is that reaches agreement upon this essential "cultural knowledge." One also feels sorry for these children, forced to listen to debates between machines.

20. For an example of such an outlook, with its "breezy materialism," see L. V. Berkner, *The Scientific Age* (1965); but see also the disgusted review in *TLS,* February 25, 1965.

21. Noam Chomsky, *American Power and the New Mandarins* (1970). The exact words were that he did not "accept the presumption of legitimacy of debate."

22. The German debate between neo-Marxians and Weberians was discussed in a *TLS* lead article, March 12, 1970.

7

Dissolutions

The Communist Schism

In the eye of the future, the most recent period may be looked upon as decisive in the dissolving of structures of authority. We have referred to the dissolution of art, partly through the springing of the trap set by Romanticism and baited by Modernism: a trap of subjectivism leading to incessant novelty hunting. Prevalent for centuries under the rubric of Classicism, discipline in the arts weakened steadily over the past two centuries but reached its complete dissolution in the past two decades. We have referred to a similar crisis in scientific thought. Authority in the matters of the mind lasted longer in other areas of perception and behavior. In the 1960s two huge systems of thought that had directly and immediately affected the lives of hundreds of millions were in trouble. One was relatively new and the other very old in the West; both were religions, that is, dogmas accepted by faith, beyond rational proof, offering consoling visions of the world as orderly, purposeful, and meaningful for man.

Despite the total scepticism of an intellectual elite, the Christian religion has remained meaningful for millions of people. The leading secular religion which supplanted it in 1917 in Russia, and subsequently among a fervent minority in many Western countries is by no means unrelated to Christianity. Marxism might claim to be a science or a tool of historical analysis, but plainly, as Arnold Toynbee wrote in his deliberate way,

> the elements which have made Marx's version of Hegelianism an even more explosive mixture than Chang Ling's version of Taoism are not

189

derived either from Hegel or from any other modern Western philosopher; they most of them bear on their face their certificate of origin from the ancestral religious faith of Western Christendom. . . . And such of the dynamic elements in Marxism as cannot be traced to Christianity can be traced to Judaism. . . .

(*A Study of History*, vol. V)

Deny it though Marxists did—and do—this view of their creed as basically similar in its structure to the messianic-eschatological type of religion became widespread and seems almost too obvious to debate. Books such as Jacob Taubes' *Abendlandische Eschatologie* (1947) or Norman Cohn's popular *The Pursuit of the Millennium* (1957) elaborated in a scholarly way on the connection between Judaic-Christian ideas and modern secular versions of the same archetypal vision. The latter placed the Promised Land on earth rather than in heaven, but so did some deviant Christian eschatologies all through history. (Joachim of Fiore, the medieval Christian revolutionary, has become particularly well known.)

It is significant that thoroughly analytical minds like Bertrand Russell could never regard Marxism as other than, in Russell's words, an "irrational dogma" that belonged to the realm of religion or "superstition," not rational thought. From the socialist side, realization that Marxism is a "myth," a work of the imagination, struck a significant number of unusual people who began as Marxists in the orthodox sense, that is, by accepting the creed as truth revealed by rational scientific inquiry: Georges Sorel, Henry de Man, Nikolas Berdyaev. In the 1930s converts to Communism frequently put the case on the grounds of its capacity to inspire zeal rather than its cognitive value. This great movement was one of faith, not reason, as one after another of the converts fervently confessed. The recent tendency for Christianity and Communism to draw closer together in a "dialogue" offers further evidence of their basic similarity.

Most historians came to view Marx's system as one of those primitive kinds of conjectural or purely theoretical formulations of the past, as it might have been or should have been, which can be affirmed only by blinding oneself to a multitude of inconvenient facts and forcing the others into a preconceived mold. As such, it was of little scientific use except as it might suggest some striking hypothesis to be tested against empirical reality. But as a heuristic device of this sort, it also had severe limitations, for it was a crude tool that had to be twisted out of all recognition before it could be applied. It is not true that all history is a record of class struggle, for it is precisely the most striking fact about the eons of premodern history that little class struggle occurred. Or, again, to say that one can extract from man or society a "material" side that is the "basic cause" of historical change—if indeed this is what Marx said—is to fall into linguistic confusion. And the abstract formulations of Marx about "feudalism," "capitalism," and "socialism" ignore the elements of particular national or regional contexts that shape history as it happens.[1] Yet there remained some historians who found Marx's approach interesting and useful, if only as an initial approximation of the truth.

Sometimes there was a schizophrenic discrepancy between the alleged theoretical foundations and the actual historical work. Many Soviet scholars obviously learned to play the game of avowing their dedication to Marxian precepts in the first and last chapters of their works while writing quite undogmatic history in between. Less sophisticated young Western historians sometimes combined an announced dedication to Marxism with "empirical" research, the two elements coexisting in the same book without really coming together. Apparently they believed they were using Marxism to interpret history, but clearly they were not. (Marx himself, when he wrote about actual situations, tended to forget his theoretical formulations. See, for example, his *Civil War in France*.) A review of a book about contemporary Africa (1971) by an ardent New Leftist noted that the book could be read on two almost entirely separate levels: the first two hundred pages tell something only about the ideology of the New Left; the second two hundred pages are a fairly accurate and reasonably objective account of African politics, which scarcely relates to the ideology at all.

Economists, too, with the exception of a tiny minority, looked upon Marx's fantastic system as, in Keynes' phrase, "an obsolete economic textbook." And so in other zones of thought. But Marxism had been transformed from a curiosity of the infancy of the social sciences into a vital, dynamic faith for twentieth-century man because it had captured the mind of a political genius, Lenin, and had gained power when the Russian government collapsed under the intolerable weight of the First World War. It thus became an armed prophecy, a religion backed by the power of a mighty state governed by a dedicated theocratic priesthood whose zeal to succeed and to expand its power was equalled only by its drive to achieve and enforce doctrinal purity. For Marxism inherited the universalism as well as the eschatological hope of Christianity.

All this is a familiar part of the general history of out time. In 1945, after Russia's victory at a terrible price over Germany and an easy inheritance of half of Europe as its reward, the morale of Soviet Communism stood high, its prestige throughout the world great. In 1949 the Communist victory in China seemed to presage the world victory of the cause. But in the 1950s and 1960s, the dream began to disintegrate.

Communism alternately attracted and repelled Western intellectuals in ways we have already discussed. The radical ambivalence of Sartre's stance—utter philosophical rejection yoked to complete practical acceptance—is a paradigm of their position. Many embraced Communism in 1932, cast it off in 1939, came back to it in 1941, rejected it in 1948 or perhaps 1956, and in the 1960s found it appealing again. But throughout these vacillations a steady erosion of credibility undeniably occurred. The law of the disenchantment of the world—Max Weber's law—caught up with Communism. Its charisma wore thin. Its mystique became *politique*. Its heroes turned into tyrants. Indeed, they were found never to have been heroes at all. Finally, Communism suffered from the disintegration of its ideological monolith. Schism and heresy overtook the Communist church in the 1960s.

The Russian Communist Party fought a stern battle against the forces of change. Its continued repression of artistic novelty—indeed of Modernism generally, in which it saw a threat to its stability as great as from any political movement—was a notable feature of the postwar world. The hideous features of the Stalin-Zhdanov era, when the crudest of Party bureaucrats were made overseers of the arts, ended in 1953 with the death of Stalin, which was thought to portend a thaw in the deep freeze of Russia's cultural, if not political, life. Despite brief interludes of relative freedom and a few sparks of esthetic revolt that deeply interested those outside the Communist world, such a development failed to occur. Yet, little by little, the Stalinist terror was eroded.

It was with intense excitement that the outer world watched the apparent beginnings of the liquidation of cultural Stalinism, as the great spirit of Russia stirred once again. *Not by Bread Alone!* The very titles of the new Russian works were an inspiration. Boris Pasternak seemed another Tolstoy, summoning the whole world to a spiritual revival from the brooding depths of the Slavic soul. Anyone in the least aware of contemporary culture knew the names of Solzhenitsyn and Yevtushenko. The possibility of fruitful dialogue between Russia and the West arose as the dismal atmosphere of the Cold War dissipated.

Subsequently, the courage of Russian writers and artists warmed the heart, but they were crushed beneath the state machine. Andrei Sinyavsky and Yuli Daniel were arrested and tried for Grave Crimes against the State: they had published without permission. In December 1965 there was a demonstration in their behalf in Pushkin Square. Offspring of the older Soviet Establishment, including a Litvinov, joined the protest. The meeting was broken up by the police and the writers were sent to prison. At the trial Daniel called the long roll of Russian writers and artists who had perished in prison camps. A handful of scholars and intellectuals testified for him and paid the penalty of loss of livelihood, although Nobel prize-winning Soviet novelist Mikhail Sholokhov *(And Quiet Flows the Don)* demanded their execution in the name of the Revolution. Vladimir Bukovsky, who organized another Pushkin Square demonstration in 1967, was committed to a mental institution before being sentenced to three years in a labor camp. He had written for an underground literary magazine! News of all this got out of Russia into the West, where the books of Solzhenitsyn, Pavel Litvinov, and others were being published. Solzhenitsyn's *Cancer Ward* became a best-seller. A book highly critical of the USSR by the Soviet scientist Andrei Sakharov was published in English in 1969. Pavel Litvinov's *The Demonstration in Pushkin Square* was published in England in 1969, and the record of the Daniel-Sinyavsky trial appeared in English in 1967. In 1972 Peter Reddaway's collection *Uncensored Russia* and Roy Medvedev's *Let History Judge* added to the flow of dissident literature out of the Soviet Union; the poems of the courageous Natalia Gorbanevskaya were also printed. Since these writers had something to protest against and ran real risks, they aroused great sympathy. But their martyrdom seemed in vain.

Despite occasional imperfections of form, the Soviet literature of dissent breathed a realism not possible in the West. When Solzhenit-syn boasted that he used his writing to "warn in time against threatening moral and social dangers," he was dealing with real dangers and taking real risks. What Western writer, hurling his obscenities at a ghostly "Establishment" in full awareness of his complete liberty to do so, could make this claim? When Andrei Amalrik refused to rewrite his history thesis to conform with the party line, he was expelled from Moscow University; a British or American graduate student who *conformed* to the official line in the 1960s would probably have been laughed out of the profession. Among the charges on which Amalrik was tried and condemned in 1970 was that of possessing a copy of George Orwell's *1984*, at a time when most European intellectuals were condemning Orwell as a reactionary because he mistrusted Communism. Amalrik's real crime was posing the rhetorical question, *Will the Soviet Union survive until 1984?* On his involuntary journey to Siberia, Amalrik might have taken comfort from the protest against his arrest lodged by sixty-four French historians, but many thousands of other historians, in Germany, Britain, America, said nothing, perhaps because they could not understand how any dissenter could attack Communism rather than capitalism, the backer of North Vietnam rather than the backer of South Vietnam.

In 1962, at the height of the "thaw," the powerful Russian Expressionist sculptor Ernst Neizvestny put his work on exhibit for a few hours; outraged Soviet officials led by Premier Khrushchev himself promptly closed the display, and Khrushchev and Neiz-vestny reportedly had a shouting confrontation. It was a crucial moment in the history of Soviet culture. Neizvestny was not sent to the uranium mines as some demanded, but he was muzzled, deprived of materials, and reduced to doing etchings, a few of which found their way out of Russia. (They were shown at the Musée d'Art Moderne de la Ville de Paris in January and February, 1970.) Still, Soviet policy grew less brutal than in Stalin's era: artists were less often shipped off to prison camps but, more typically, were sub-jected to a combination of subtler harassment and efforts to draw them over at least in part to the side of the Establishment. (It is ironic that some European intellectuals who had remained loyal to the Kremlin all through Stalin's era because Stalin had con-cealed his worst crimes protested and broke away from the Party when they were able to read about the sentencing of a Daniel. Under Stalin, there would have been no trial at all.) Such blandishments evidently worked on the poet Yevtushenko, who, once a symbol of rebellion, became a kind of tame liberal, exhibited by the Establishment and used to rebuke more extreme recalcitrants. Other intellectuals were less tractable, as the trials and condemnations of such people as Daniel, Sinyavsky, and Bukovsky showed. Jews seeking the right to emigrate to Israel were also harassed and persecuted.

More than any other figure of the Soviet opposition, Alexander Solzhenitsyn made himself the symbol of protest against the uneasy heirs of Stalin. The sheer mass of his literary achievement earned him a world reputation, and he was compared to Tolstoy—whom he admired and sought to imitate. (The novel *August 1914* is the first part of a larger work that aspires to be another *War and Peace*.) In 1974 Solzhenitsyn added crushing weight to his indictment of the Communist system with his *Gulag Archipelago,* a massively documented report on the treatment of political prisoners. In the wake of this international best-seller, smuggled to the outside press in defiance of orders to hold his peace, the Soviet author was first imprisoned and then expelled from the country by an embarrassed Kremlin officialdom.

The Soviet ruling class took art seriously.[2] (So did the Nazis, who organized an exhibition of "degenerate art" in 1937.) It can hardly disturb the sleep of the average American politician that the latest avant-garde art is on exhibit; he probably does not even know what it is. Writers may mouth their obscenities at will for all he cares. But the Soviet leaders, trying to preserve their closed culture against the forces that threaten it from all sides, sensed danger in every modernism and fought a constant battle against contamination from without. Despite their concentration camps, they are probably destined to lose in the long run. Theirs is not the final answer to decadence and disintegration, as they imagine, but a brief and precarious hiding place from it. Their quaint nineteenth-century ideology assures them that history is on the side of a new, integral, socialist, working-class culture rising as an "organic" order on the ruins of the crumbling old, bourgeois-capitalist culture. But history seems much more on the side of ever mounting cultural fragmentation through complexity, subjectivism, and specialization, which convulsive counterefforts such as Nazism and Communism can only momentarily stem. "Lenin's heirs have been . . . protected," Ronald Hingley observed in *A Concise History of Russia* (1972), "from such nuisances as industrial strikes, demonstrations against official policy, assassinations of leading statesmen and the pronouncements of permissive-minded clergymen, as well as from hippies, yippies, junkies, sex supermarkets and protesting students." But for how much longer?

Such success as the Russian Communists had in holding back the tide was due much less to Communism than to Russia herself—a less sophisticated society than those of the West, still closer to a traditional peasant folk culture, in some ways not yet fully caught up in "Modernism." Yet caught up it will be, for, ironically, the Communists themselves are the agents of modernization. They imagine that they can industrialize and urbanize without becoming culturally modernized, and in this they are surely wrong. They have only the comparatively frail dike of their Marxian ideology to pit against all the powerful forces of cultural change endemic in the sweep of modern civilization. The fact that Modernists dare to protest today, and can smuggle their works out of Russia, represents in itself a change from the Stalin era when neither protest nor publicity was possible. Experts on the USSR point out that by no means all the offending rebels are silenced; while much is made of the few big fish caught and punished, like Daniel and Sinyavsky, many smaller ones slip through the clumsy nets of bureaucratic officialdom. The underground magazines and newspapers have increased in numbers. And in the "people's democracies," cultural controls are more rapidly disappearing.

Some Soviet intellectuals—for example, the physicist A. D. Sakharov—believe that Soviet industrialism itself cannot proceed much further without greater political freedom. The dictatorship is responsible for an ever growing Communist lag behind the Western technologies, especially in their most advanced segments. Economic problems motivated the détente with the United States in 1972, a course likely to open Russian society to more outside cultural influences in spite of all precautions taken against this effect.

From *Pravda* itself one can learn such interesting things as that Soviet publishing houses misguidedly reprint huge quantities of that bourgeois author Agatha Christie; and that self-employed construction workers go around the country doing a land-office business in private-enterprise contracting. Obviously neither ideological nor economic purity exists. Other well-informed observers of the USSR claim that the volume of *samizdat,* or illicitly printed books and magazines, is huge, reaching into countless homes. Only a return to Stalin's dreadful methods can hope to stamp out this underground literature of subversion, and the Kremlin bureaucrats are extremely reluctant to undertake anything like that. Making examples of a few in order to discourage the others, they only create silent sympathy for the martyrs.

Meanwhile, a large category of literature and thought in the satellite states experimented in strategies of softening or "humanizing" official Communism, attempting as much "revision" of party-line Marxism as it seemed possible to get away with. According to the Polish revisionist Leszek Kolakowski, ideology can never be eliminated, but it can be softened, "its predatory and 'imperialistic' grip upon intellectual life can be lessened and perhaps eventually broken." Such quasi-Marxists of the Communist world, who had felt the awful grip of organized and institutionalized ideology, tried to break that grip so far as possible. For example, the Polish writer Adam Schaff conceded that "alienation" can continue to operate under socialism; that is, the moral question transcends social structures, surely a sweeping concession to the Christian position. (Schaff's article "Alienation and Social Action" appeared in *Diogenes,* the Paris-based international journal of ideas, in 1967.) The Yugoslav heretic Milovan Djilas passed, like Eduard Bernstein among the German Social Democrats at the beginning of the twentieth century, beyond the pale of all orthodoxy and, like Bernstein, stimulated lively debate. The Polish philosopher Kolakowski dealt less directly than Djilas in political terms but undermined the Marxian ethic with admixtures of Kantianism. The naturalistic ethics of Marxism forces one into the unpleasant position of approving whatever serves the cause of advancing the historical process, that is, moving it forward toward the Revolution and the ultimate utopia. In the hands of Lenin, and especially of Stalin, such a creed prepared the way for monstrous and bloody crimes, against the innocent as well as the guilty. Kolakowski urged the necessity of adding to Marxism at least one ethical absolute from outside the historical and social order—one that affirms the dignity and value of the human personality.

The Hungarian George Lukács and the East German Ernst Bloch, among others more or less tolerated in the East, were Marxists with a difference, being engaged in that occupation so fashionable in the West: existentializing Marx. Bloch opted for the "warm stream" in Marx as opposed to the "cold stream" of pseudoscientific determinism. These currents, flowing out of a slowly thawing Communist intellectual world, mixed with similar currents in the West to form that combination of Marxism with Existentialism and Phenomenology which has become so important.

The distinguished Marxian scholar Auguste Cornu was allowed to publish in East Germany the several volumes of his long biography of Karl Marx, a work that, though far from unfriendly to Marx, is at least careful and objective, while the scholars working at the Marx-Engels Institute in Leningrad painstakingly edited and published every last scrap of Marx's writings, contradictions and all. The full truth about their founding father, at least, must not be suppressed,[3] and he turns out, like the founder of Christianity, to have been a far from simple man.

Where ideology was directly concerned, resistance was of course greater. The Leninist, Stalinist, and post-Stalinist Russian state steadfastly insisted upon maintaining, by force, the purity of a doctrine alleged to be the final and complete truth that can be neither added to nor altered. After Stalin's death in 1953, there was no erosion of the belief in a single orthodoxy, though there was a gradual weakening of the will to enforce it. "Revisionism"—that is, any change in the received, official version of Marxism-Leninism —continued to mean much the same thing to the Communist as bourgeois-capitalist-imperialist-reactionary-class enemy. The wicked of the world, conspiring to do in the workers' society, strive above all to undermine its intellectual foundations by weakening the fabric of its delivered truth, and it is necessary to stand guard against such subversion.[4] Faced with such fanaticism, backed by the power of a huge totalitarian state, those who must live under that state could only with difficulty proclaim themselves critics of its creed.

Yet this allegedly immutable truth changed almost monthly, according to the dictates of the official priesthood. This was true not only in political but also in scientific and philosophical matters. The myth of scientific Marxism suffered a severe blow in the celebrated case of Trofim D. Lysenko, who had persuaded Stalin and the Kremlin power structure that his non-Mendelian, Lamarckian genetics was the key to magical transformations of Russian agriculture. This proved to be an illusion that resulted in immense damage to food production, and Lysenko was eventually exposed as a charlatan; but he had managed to hoodwink the Communist leaders for many years by exploiting their ideological conviction that somehow, somewhere, there was a Marxian, Communist science that was much better than bourgeois, capitalist science.[5] Truths about chemistry, genetics, logic, linguistics, and the evaluation of great writers were all abruptly changed by official decree, as well as were what Russians were supposed to think about Tito, Stalin, the Arabs, or the family. After all, Leninism itself was originally a daring revision of Marxism. And there developed several different priesthoods within the Communist family of nations, often vociferously discordant. Marx himself had wavered between different views on important matters: no Marxist he. It was possible to appeal from Stalin to Lenin, from Lenin to Marx, and from one Marx to another. Faced with such multiplying heresy, keepers of the citadel of orthodoxy became like Browning's bishop, fearing that to deny one iota of the creed leads to atheism. When the pope has spoken, let there be no further debate. But there were now several popes, and the Protestant virus spread fast among the true believers.

Meanwhile the *praxis* to which in principle Marxists appeal— they claim their theory fits and explains empirical reality—was at work betraying them. The happenings of the postwar years made a total shambles of Marxian theory in so many ways that it would be an almost endless task to describe them. One need only mention the area of international relations. Theory declared that quarrels between Communist countries could not occur. Theory declared that the capitalist countries would be fatally hurt by the loss of their colonies. ("European capitalism has survived the loss of its African colonies very comfortably; in fact, far from being choked by an excess of frozen funds, the main difficulty for the capitalists in the 1960s was to find enough capital," historian Trevor Lloyd wrote concerning the venerable, now discredited Leninist theory of "imperialism."[6])

In regard to the former colonies of the Third World themselves, theory declared either that they would have to go through a capitalist phase before arriving at socialism or that they might follow the example of Russia, skipping the bourgeois-capitalist stage and achieving socialism under the guidance of an elite Communist Party. But what actually happened in the new countries of Africa and Asia was so chaotic, and often so stunningly disastrous to Moscow, that it could be fitted into no possible pattern of coherent Marxism, however frantically the logicians of Communism might juggle their categories.

In the end, the wide world eluded these intellectual nets. Non-European leaders might borrow the rhetoric of Western radicalism, knowing no other; theirs was nevertheless a different world. The theories of Americans and Europeans who wished to chart a neat course for all the *jeunes états,* so that they would arrive at the blessed pinnacle occupied by the Western capitalist democracies, were as irrelevant as the Marxian categories; but the democracies had not claimed infallibility for their theories. Marxism would never again be the same. Its particular way of ordering a disorderly world had failed like all the others. That its metaphysics is obsolete perhaps signifies less than that its sociology is Euro-centered.

So Communism was as obsolete as Christianity or Judaism. That was the meaning of the wild outburst of radicalism in the 1960s. Uncomprehending burghers shouted that the Communists were breaking loose, but these were post-Communists; that is exactly why there was such a wild outbreak. An element in the Student Left of what is better called nihilism than anarchism was obvious and frequently noted. Although they sometimes made hasty and slip-shod efforts to adjust their thinking to intellectual categories, these young leftists felt most keenly the urge to destroy all "authority," to tear down the whole "system." Total rejection, total negation was their avowed goal: the tags of Marxism were no more than an afterthought. "Burn, baby, burn" was closer to their hearts than "Workers of the world unite." Explicitly scorning the now tame Communist Party as a part of the Establishment (in such countries as France and Italy), and scornful too of the extinct volcano of Soviet Russia, the young revolutionaries admired Castro and Mao only insofar as these less tarnished figures symbolized revolutionary guerrillaism. The latter is not so much akin to Marxism even in its Marcusian reincarnation as it is to those Christian recipients of the Spirit who felt themselves released from all laws to act as they wished.

The Beguines and the Beghards unleashed their desperate antino-
mianism in the last days of the great medieval intellectual tradition. Their actions find an echo today.

The Christian-Communist Dialogue

A world not unaccustomed to surprises was at least mildly astonished in the mid-1960s to learn that Communism and Christianity
had entered into earnest discussions—the phrase was "dialogue."
Although France's leading intellectual Communist, Roger Garaudy,
was expelled from the P.C.F. for an excess of enthusiasm for that
dialogue, this did not halt what soon became an international
vogue. Beginning in France and Italy, it spread to all quarters and
received eager encouragement from elements in both camps. The
literature grew vast. The dialogue was especially welcomed by
slightly deviant, liberated Marxists—a description which now fitted
nearly all the intellectually live ones. Their journals featured discussions of the question (see, for example, *Marxism Today,*
1966–1968). From the other side, representatives of a fragmenting
Christianity were just as eager to try their hands at something new,
something "relevant," something that might possibly revive a
sinking church. Within Catholicism, these forces received encouragement from the extraordinary 1963 encyclical of Pope John
XXIII on liberal thought and social action in the church, and indeed
from the whole tenor of his brief but electrifying pontificate. Both
sides were in the throes of a crisis that had the effect of weakening
dogma and liberating experimental currents, even if it threatened
ultimate dissolution. A symposium, *The Christian-Marxist Dialogue* (1969), stated quite frankly that adversity was a factor
drawing the two old foes together: neither one was doing particularly well, each needed an ally. But the deeper cause of the
association was a basic intellectual affinity, the shared principle of
"eschatological hope," as a Christian recently put it. The Jewish-
Christian doctrine of the apocalypse is the root source of modern
revolutionary ideas: the message of "last things" with the expectation of an enchanted rendezvous at the end of the historical road.
   That the two faiths had once been mortal enemies only supplies
evidence of their similarity, for it is a familiar feature of human

nature that, as Coleridge put it, "party men always hate a slightly differing friend more than a downright enemy." In the 1960s the erstwhile foes each moved closer to their common center. As Marxism grew more spiritual and individualistic, Christianity became more social and worldly. Writing on the Christian-Marxist dialogue in a German publication (*Neues Forum,* 1967), Jan M. Lochman noted that the old animosity fostered by the concept of "idealism" versus "materialism," which had made each of these creeds a scandal to the other—the Marxist talking scornfully of other-worldly pie in the sky, the Christian shocked by a crude hostility to mind and soul—had largely evaporated. The new dialogue rested on a mutual interest in immanence and transcendence. Christians sought to give their faith a content in this world; Marxists wanted to leaven their worldly creed with a bit of ethical transcendence. Together, they flatter themselves, Marxists and Christians can provide a total philosophy, a neat amalgamation of both worlds, the mundane and the spiritual.

The tide of Modernism pulled the church in a direction suggested by such slogans as "adjust to the modern world," "meet contemporary needs," "become relevant." To "get with it," to reach the young and speak their language, even to the extent of replacing the organ with the guitar and the hymn with the folksong, became the ob-object of dedicated clergymen in many sects. Many other churchmen went well beyond this. Bishops recommending pornography and clerics leading mobs of protestors finally ceased to be any more surprising than the New Testament written in "hip" or ghetto language. In the name of "situation ethics" the churches drew close to Hugh Hefner. The chaste neoorthodox theology of Karl Barth and Reinhold Niebuhr was suddenly out; rather than reject contemporary social trends, it was assumed, one should go along with them.

"Honest to God" theology talked of religionless or atheist Christianity. Dr. Paul van Buren and the Bishop of Woolwich led this vogue for "secularist" theology, the burden of which was that if Christianity can't beat the modern world it had better join it. The foes of this trend claimed that it represents, to quote the Reverend Eric Mascall, a capitulation to the spirit of the age, when Christianity "ought to be radically examining, assessing, and correcting it." The early Christian church drew apart from the Roman Empire in an absolute refusal of the secular world, which eventually gained it power when that world crumbled. The modern church is an integral part of the world and will crumble if it does. But the accommodators asserted that the church cannot speak to modern man at all unless it adopts his lingo; they felt that at least a *little* of Christ's message can get across this way, whereas if traditional modes are adhered to *none* of it will. The choice is between dying quietly and putting up a fight.

A sense of both crisis and opportunity pervaded the Christian churches. On the one hand, they felt "out of it," losing influence and relevance, unable to communicate; afflicted with an idiom of the past, they were a victim of the neophilia which demands ever new gestures and modes of discourse. At the dawn of the Modernist era, now nearly a century old, Nietzsche had said "God is dead"; Péguy's horror at "a world without Jesus" dated from only a few years later. Since then, a moribund religion had sunk deeper and deeper into bourgeois quicksands, except when, during World War II, the challenge of Nazism had forced a valiant few to choose martyrdom.

If the churches seemed unable to respond to the needs of the present, an opportunity to do so was presented by the manifest spiritual yearnings of the 1960s. Curious quasireligious communes and cults proliferated on the fringes of the youth culture. All kinds of occultisms flourished. The naked, bearded, rock-festival-attending, stoned adolescent talked in exalted tones of a sort of religious conversion, and looked for signs and wonders. "We need a society in which people love each other" was a message that could "blow the minds" of naive young people, who, if they did not march forth in a mob to attack something, might retire to the equivalent of monastic poverty. All the features of a great religious awakening were present, as in the age of the Reformation or at the beginning of the nineteenth century. "And what rough beast, its hour come round at last," Yeats had asked, "slouches towards Bethlehem to be born?" The opportunity was too tempting to pass up. The church was challenged to reap this harvest of eager souls even if it had to alter its very language. As sanction for doing so, it might turn to Kierkegaard, to Bultmann, to Bonhoeffer, and to other existential sages who preached that the husk of doctrine is nothing, the life-meaning kernel everything.

Thus a familiar personality of the 1960s was the swinging young priest who set out to modernize the church. It did not much matter what church he represented—Anglican, Roman, Methodist were alike in the style of their Modernism, as sectarian barriers began to melt in an "ecumenical" sun. Though somewhat older, the ecumenical movement reached a peak in the early 1960s. Old structures were becoming irrelevant. In the later years of the decade, familiar, too, was the revolutionary priest who went wholly over to a position not easily distinguishable from radical or Communist political militancy. The message of Christ, he assumed, was not basically different from that of Marx. Arm in arm, the erstwhile foes who had long abused each other with "godless materialism" and "opium of the people" marched off to fight the revolution for social justice. Such religious militancy, found all over the Western world, became particularly prominent in South America. Argentina's frankly revolutionary *Movimiento de los Sacerdotes para el Tercer Mundo* was estimated in the early 1970s to number as many as a fourth of the clergy among its supporters. (Rejecting Marxist socialism, the movement advocated an "authentically national" Argentinian socialism; in other words, it was composed of *Peronistas,* followers of Juan Peron. The revolutionary church, it appears, is prepared to render up quite a bit to Caesar.) Brazil had a similarly large and active segment of revolutionary priests preaching hatred of the native rich and of American imperialists—and not only plain priests, but an archbishop.

The ease with which Christianity as a social ethic or a political position can be absorbed by other causes suggests a basic weakness in its doctrine. Except in the vaguest terms, it lacks a social ethic. Devout Christians have themselves noticed this; the New Testament, Lord Acton remarked, says much about private but remarkably little about public life. There is no specifically Christian statecraft. As generations of critics have noticed, Christians have not been noticeably wiser than anyone else in these worldly arts. In recent times they have moved with the crowd: they enthusiastically supported both world wars, and just as enthusiastically repented afterwards, vowing eternal pacifism. Biblical passages can be quoted on both sides of most political questions. The only tangible content of the Christian social message is a passionate hopefulness that encourages expectations of utopia without supplying the means to attain it—and in this way it is very akin to the mood of youthful revolutionism.

The most primitive kind of radical economics came from priests converted to Marxism. Possessing a rhetoric built around vague generalities such as justice, brotherhood, and humanity, the social Christian finds nothing in his creed to indicate a specific content for these abstractions, and so he easily adopts the program of whichever secular movement he consorts with, coloring it with his emotional fervency. Embattled clerics, who often were the most militant of the militant and in whom the spirit of the Crusades burned once again, flavored the new Children's Crusade with their fanaticism and intolerance and courage. An aspect perhaps of the church in dissolution, their revolutionary impulse was nonetheless authentically Christian in that it drew upon an old and deeply laid tradition, that of chiliastic, millenarian, messianic religion. "They shall hunger no more, neither thirst any more . . . and God shall wipe away all tears from their eyes."

Secular Christianity

By no means all contemporary theology falls into the category of secular Christianity. Most clergymen were as uncomfortable in its presence as historians were when they found a textbook entitled *Hang-ups from Way Back*. Most clergymen, needless to say, continued to distinguish sharply between Karl and Jesus. "Honest-to-God" thought was severely criticized, on the grounds that by leaviny any objectified God out of the picture, it left human nature very much as it was without Christianity and became another form of paganism. Such conservative reactions were by no means rare. One of the most important recent schools, associated with Professor W. Pannenberg of Mainz, rejected Rudolf Bultmann's demythologizing (in which biblical stories became merely examples of basic human situations, the specifics being of no great consequence) in favor of a return to the defense of the historicity of the Christian Gospels, a kind of neofundamentalism under highly learned auspices.

Sometimes, rather than surrendering to socialism, the church gave in to modern capitalism. In the story of the Roman Catholic church's adaptation, or surrender, to the modern world, the organization known as *Opus Dei* may in future accounts of this process be found to have played a significant role. This new Catholic order, reminiscent of the Dominicans and Jesuits of earlier times, and like them originating in Spain, was founded in 1928 by a young priest, José Maria Escriva de Balaguer. It was originally a secret organization and attained prominence only in the 1960s when Escriva's pamphlet *The Way* (*Camino*) almost rivalled the *Thoughts of Chairman Mao* in some places as a primer for the young. The *Opus* was in some respects a pious response to the challenge of a beleaguered church surrounded by the forces of socialism, liberalism, and atheism; yet it frankly practiced policies of accepting, and penetrating, the functioning apparatus of a secularized society. In recent years it has helped preside over the economic modernization of Spain. Although the *Opus* drew on itself the indignant wrath of liberal and socialist groups for its insidious tactics, in the last analysis it would seem to be doing much of their work for them. It has in any case become rich and powerful, its disciples filling important offices of business and government, and seems in danger of losing any specifically Christian message.

Despite some "good works," the *Opus* for the most part elected to join the forces of capitalism and technocracy. Other branches of Christianity, as has been earlier described, have chosen to go the road of Karl Marx rather than John D. Rockefeller, hailing the prophet of atheistic Communism as a boon companion of Christ in the work of saving the poor. In either case, the implications for the church and the Christian religion as such seem clear: both are being dissolved into one form or another of Modernism. The *aggiornamento* of the church, as the Italians call it, may lead to its extinction. (*Aggiornamento* means "modernization"; but it also means "adjournment.") The trouble with earthly causes, as Muggeridge observed, is that sooner or later, alas, they triumph. All specifically Christian doctrine seems to be dissolving. As someone says in a recent novel by P. H. Newby, "The modern Protestant theologian believes so little nowadays that there's very little doctrinal reason why everybody shouldn't be a Christian." The same might have been said of modern Catholic theologians, who from about 1965 on engaged in a veritable outburst of criticism of the church itself. In May, 1972, the Vatican weekly *L'Osservatore della Domenica* wrote of a wave of criticism "often graver and more offensive than even Protestant authors would dare to make"—mentioning the Swiss Hans Kung, among others—and, with reference to the United States, declared that "a tremendous earthquake is shaking the Church to its roots."

Theology has been very active in recent times. The graduate schools of divinity produced an abundance of eager young men nourished on the exciting works of Barth, Heidegger, Bultmann, Tillich, Buber, and many another master; and as some of them undertook to revise these now antiquated thinkers, new schools arose. One found here the same kind of profusion of academicism as in other areas. Professional theology became as specialized as any other branch of learning and, hence, increasingly divorced from the average man, a fact of which theologians were uneasily aware. Literature proliferated; a host of paperback books endeavored to keep up with the "New Theology," but it remained incomprehensible to the man in the street. In this regard theologians were caught up in the trends of the times, unable to escape either the toils of specialization or the tendency toward faddiness, revisionisms, something new each season.

All these developments suggest a severe crisis, from which it does not appear that traditional religion will recover. Perhaps religion will survive; perhaps it will even be strengthened. But few think it will bear many similarities to traditional religion. Perhaps in the modern catacombs a new world religion is rising among hippies who reject the world. "Jesus freaks" were not uncommon among them; "Jesus Christ Superstar" was a pop hit. Toynbee led many in supposing that out of the present mingling of cultures and ideas, and (on his analysis) out of the breakdown of Western civilization, a global faith would come into being comprising portions of all the major world religions—an amalgamation of Christianity, Islam, Buddhism, and perhaps others. Obviously a great deal of mixing was going on. While American youngsters aspired to be Buddhists, there were Asiatic bishops of the Roman church, American black converts to Islam, and attempts at syncretism such as Baha'i from Islam and Ramakrishna Vedanta from India. But that this portended a global synthesis seemed most unlikely. Students of world religion pointed out that there was more diversity and less unity than ever before.[7] On a projection of existing trends, what seems more likely to happen is an ever-increasing dissolution of formal structures, as in the arts, in favor of individualized religions or ideological styles. Likewise a similar trendiness, a fashionable prophet for each season (witness the cult of the fifteen-year-old guru in 1973), each more bizarre than the last. It is also possible, some speculated, that technological and cosmic man, living off mass-cult

TV and cinema fare cunningly manufactured to soporize the impulses which give rise to transcendent aspirations, will not have any religion, nor any art.

At any rate, predictions of the dissolution of the church were often voiced. "I personally shall be very surprised if a decade or so from now anything remains of institutional Christianity," Malcolm Muggeridge wrote in 1969, adding that quite a number of church leaders actually hoped for such a condition. The attempted alliance with radical social causes seemed a desperate strategy for survival that might wane with the loss of interest in the extreme Left. That traditional Christian morality must dissolve in the age of sexual freedom was a fact conceded even by the churches themselves, or at least by all but a few of the more conservative of them. It need hardly be added that the traditional humanists and scientific positivists continued to insist on the irrationality of religion. Alan Isaacs' *The Survival of God in the Scientific Age* (1966) suggests that science has happily released us from such antiquated notions though we might be able to find some use for the concept of God as a hypothesis in ethics![8] Such old-fashioned "rationalism" might itself be a quaint survival of the eighteenth and nineteenth centuries, but it continued to exist.

Other Dissolutions

Other structures, too, have been attacked. A challenge to existing sovereign states came from various ethnic movements, which were in some ways only an expression of old nationalist impulses, but which were revived with a new stress. This was a significant trend in the 1960s, embracing French-Canadian separatism, the renewal of Scottish and Welsh nationalism, the Provençard or "Occitan" movement in France, and in America, of course, black nationalism and the similar programs of Chicano and American Indian groups. The color of radical politics was seen in complaints that a particular region and its people were "exploited" (the French Canadians treated as "white niggers," the Occitans cheated by hard-fisted northerners, the Scots bled by Westminster). Underground publications and urban guerrilla tactics imparted a New Left flavor to causes that were an obvious frontier for restless revolutionary youth in search of grievances. In the 1950s American black intellectuals fought for an equal place in an integrated society; in the 1960s some turned to separatism and black nationalism. The reason was in part that national independence makes an excellent revolutionary cause, as long experience has proved, and was thus suited to the revolutionary spirit of the sixties. To rally all the black brothers together in a struggle against "whitey" was easier and much more dramatic than to carry on the hard, often frustrating work of racial accommodation. And obviously, there was the further appeal of living local cultures against bigness and the faceless society.[9] Even in quite nonrevolutionary circles, there was a new feeling for regionalism, for decentralization, for local autonomy, as witness trends in France, Italy, Yugoslavia, and indeed almost everywhere. The trend of thought and feeling was often to resist tendencies towards ever more centralized statism.

Needless to add, educational structures were also breaking down. The 1950s created brave new universities which were to lead the way into an era of better and more widespread education. The next crop of students tore them down. It would seem that it was precisely those institutions which were considered out in front that suffered the brunt of the student revolutionary attacks. Such were, for example, the Free University of Berlin, into which the intellectual resources of the new Germany were poured under the supervision of the foes of Hitler, who returned from exile in 1945; the new British universities, often boldly innovative in their organization of the realm of knowledge; and the lavishly endowed and very prestigious California university system in the United States. It is true that eventually nearly everyone got into the melee, but in the history of the student revolt, Berlin and Berkeley will probably be accorded special honor—or dishonor—as the birthplaces of the student movement. Both, in different ways, were symbols and centers of all that was supposed to be best in the postwar intellectual world. They raised up young people who scorned all organized universities and were ready to burn them to the ground and whose reply to the knowledge factory was a four-letter word.

In fairness, one must point out that in many places the student revolts took place in a setting of dreadful overcrowding and the almost complete death of institutional life. Federico Mancini observed that the Italian university was "a feudal structure paid for by a huge mass of people living in a condition of utter frustration and *anomie,* and run by a short-sighted and power-crazy oligarchy."[10] Throughout Europe the rapid expansion of university populations had created similarly deplorable conditions, marked by the reluctance of a structure created for a small elite to adapt to mass democracy. In some places the old university was moribund before the students knocked it over.

Cultural chaos was reflected in the widespread tendency of the universities to abolish all "requirements" and to allow students to take whatever courses they chose without pattern or sequence. All structure in education seemed to be breaking down. While students sometimes set up "free" universities on the fringes of the regular ones, and an "open university" was put on television in Great Britain, at a lower level of education harassed teachers rationalized their total loss of control over pupils by inventing the "open classroom," dedicated to doing whatever the children wanted to do. (See, for example, Herbert R. Kohl, *The Open Classroom,* 1970—a voice from the American ghetto, but not without echoes in Europe. The scenes of wildest confusion, with students refusing to listen to the traditional lectures, took place in the venerable old German universities.[11]) Examinations and grades were en route to total abolition. With the decline in the average ability of both students and professors that accompanied the lowering of entrance standards, many courses degenerated in quality so that, by picking his path warily, a student might earn a degree in a quite reputable university without ever having done any serious intellectual work. In the aftermath of the riots of 1968, student control in some French schools terrorized and drove out those teachers and students who dissented from an intolerant leftist dictatorship. Such trends toward student control (usually meaning the influence of a small number of dedicated revolutionaries), total educational permissiveness, and the like are familiar enough to need no discussion. They threaten, if they do not absolutely assure, the dissolution of the traditional structures of education as well as those of the traditional churches.

Amid these dissolving tendencies, some claim to see a basic threat to reason itself. In times of such cultural chaos and intellectual confusion, Lamennais had written during that "ferment of ideas" at the beginning of the nineteenth century, "reason will decay before men's eyes. The simplest truth will appear strange and remarkable,

and will scarcely be endured." The rise of absurdism, of irrationalism, and of antiintellectualism was associated with a serious decline
in the level of political discussion, reflected in all sorts of wild
beliefs. Conspiracy theories and devil theories flourished. The
classical scholar John Sparrow devoted a book to analyzing the
outrageously irrational views about the assassination of President
Kennedy (*After the Assassination,* 1968). The emergence of many
such myths could be connected to the bigness and complexity of life
and the breakdown of any coherent total view amid a wilderness of
specialized compartments. Many a commentator identified the root
cause of political irrationalism as the impossibility of citizens having
anything like the knowledge necessary to comprehend public problems and policy. With half a hundred new countries to know about,
in a world whose perplexities multiplied almost every day, not even
the new media of "news" coverage could help them; indeed,
television may have worsened their situation. Forced to record
fleeting visual images of a tiny fraction of the world's events,
television could manage only a weirdly distorted picture of objective
reality, suitable to a Kafka nightmare.

Yet the supposedly informed intellectual community surmounted
the problem scarcely more effectively than did "the man in the
street." Louis Halle, in *The Ideological Imagination* (1972), noted
that rational discussion about Indochina was *least* possible in the
academic community, among "intellectuals"—as anyone who has
lived in academia in recent years is in a position to testify. As an
example, Godard believed that Soviet bureaucrats secretly connive
with American capitalists to suppress Czechs who really want to be
super-Communists.

Existentialists had declared that we manufacture our own reality.
"New Left" historians often seemed to boast that they invent the
past for purposes of present propaganda in an ideological cause. A
reputable American historian announced that "it is past time . . . for
the admission that for American historians history begins and ends
with ideology." No less than in the Soviet Union, except on the
other side (against and not for the Establishment), scholarship was
to be guided by political purposes. Historians of this persuasion
grew fond of saying that Clio is inevitably a whore and might as well
be made an honest one. To historians who happened not to share
their political biases, these partisans seemed to gravely distort the

past. One such quite respectably published work, a history of Britain in the 1930s, was described by Charles Wilson, its outraged reviewer, as "a continuous barrage of condemnation of everybody who does not share the authors' views or conform to their prejudices." Another such book was described by Elmer N. Lear as "political pamphleteering peppered with illicit conversions of partial truth into alleged whole truth."

Aware that no historian speaks with the authority of History itself but must reflect his time and place and temperament and thus present not *the* truth but only one tiny aspect of the truth, one perspective among an almost infinite number, scholars could scarcely doubt that everyone flavors fact with opinion or rhetoric in some measure. Yet faced, for example, with a barrage of books that presented the Cold War as a plot on the part of American capitalists to enslave the world—books with a veritable ideological obsession clearly lurking just beneath the surface—one was tempted to fall back on a myth of objectivity. Far from having ended, ideology came back in the 1960s on the double and in an even more ferocious form, warping minds by almost deliberately closing them against any truth except the one they were resolved *a priori* to receive. The existence of a naive popular mythology, such as Hitler and other demagogues exploited, had long been taken for granted and attributed to ignorance and lack of education; but what was one to say about the demonology of students and professors who led political uprisings from their positions in advanced mathematics or medicine? Or historians who on principle structured events in accordance with their highly inflamed prejudices, leaving out all that which did not conform to their ideological images and tendentiously editing the rest? Under such circumstances, it was quite easy to pray for a renaissance of scientific thought—austerely objective, ruthlessly realistic, disciplined, analytical, contemptuous of what we personally *want* to believe and respectful only of beliefs that can endure the sternest of rational tests. But whether science was not also in dissolution became, as we have seen, a vital question for the last quarter of the twentieth century.

As has been previously noted, Freud's structure was in as much trouble as Marx's. Indeed, the catalogue of ideals that failed in the postwar world would be a long one. The vision of One World with the United Nations presiding over the City of Man, which sustained the dreadful slaughter and immense sacrifices of World War II, was an early casualty of Cold War realities; the UN receded to a position of slight importance as critics pointed out its inevitable impotence and the muddiness of the thinking on which its hopes had been raised. The embattled peaceniks of the 1960s cared nothing for this vanished symbol, opting instead for more drastic programs and far more utopian answers. For a moment in 1945, the ideal and the real had come together around the United Nations symbol; thereafter they gravitated steadily toward opposite poles, and by about 1970 were engaged in combat against each other. Between Melvin Laird and Henry Kissinger on the one hand and Jerry Rubin and Noam Chomsky on the other, there was a gulf that made almost any other schism in our deeply divided world seem small by comparison, but this is too much a matter of public record to need elaboration. And the same could be said about numerous other political issues.

The tarnishing of the idea of democracy itself in the postwar years revealed the corrosion of a formerly vast edifice of faith and authority. A democratic revival accompanied the profound reaction against Fascism and Nazism in World War II and lasted through the early postwar period, when it was reinforced by the disenchantment with Soviet Communism. Though earlier criticized by captious intellectuals, democracy turned out during the war against totalitarian dictatorships to be a Cinderella whose homely virtues showed forth after her gaudy sisters, Fascism and Communism, turned out to be whores, and inefficient whores at that. The intellectuals beat a path back to her scullery.

A large literature in defense of democracy is exemplified by Reinhold Niebuhr's *Children of Light and Children of Darkness* (1944), "a vindication of democracy and a critique of its traditional defense." This low-key defense of pluralistic democracy as, in Winston Churchill's phrase, the worst form of government except all the others—two cheers for democracy, not three (E. M. Forster)—was widespread in the 1950s and fitted the antiideological mood of that era. Some intellectuals, of course, remained for a time under the Communist persuasion; their attitude toward democracy was that expressed by Harold Laski in *Faith, Reason, and Civilization* (1944): since it is remaking man and rooting out the vices of capitalism, the USSR must for the nonce reject Western-style democracy, for which read selfishness and greed. Yet even Laski swerved back toward democracy before his death in 1951.

But disenchantment set in afresh. The radicalized youth of the

1960s treated parliamentary assemblies with scorn as mere fraudulent tools of the economic-military power elite and called for
revolutionary violence rather than the tedious ways of democracy.
They invoked "the People" and talked of "participatory democracy," but the extremely cloudy ideas masked by this revolutionary
rhetoric related to little of the traditional notion of democracy as
free elections, the open society, pluralism and compromise. It had a
closer affinity to utopian visions. And as one East European with all
too much experience of utopia noted, "No utopia can be realized
without terror, and in a little while only the terror remains."[12]

Apart from this, there were many reasons for feeling less and less
confidence in democratic government. Few of them were new, but
most were stronger than ever. The "myth of democracy," evidence
suggested, had scarcely any appeal in Germany and Italy, not much
in France, and surprisingly little in England.[13] The ever growing
complexity of the world meant a steady decline in whatever remained of the well-informed citizen. Faith in democracy as an
ecumenical destiny of man, like the Soviet Marxist belief in a similar
expectation for socialism, was a casualty of the widened horizons of
these years, for the numerous *jeunes états,* almost without exception, passed under various sorts of dictatorships. One might reflect
that democracy is a luxury that only our kind of civilization can
afford, or one might more ambitiously theorize that democracy
turns out on a closer inspection, in the light of knowledge and
historical perspective, to be a phase in the transition from a
traditional to a "modern" society and not even necessarily the only
possible such phase. There were evident trends away from it,
suggesting that the fully technological society can ill afford such
casual inefficiency as government by numerous popular elections
provides. Parliament lost power to the Cabinet and the Cabinet to
the Prime Minister; Congress lost power to the President; and all of
them lost power to the permanent bureaucracy. There were paradoxes discovered, such as Harry Eckstein's finding, stated in *Theory
of Stable Democracy* (1961), that a degree of voter apathy is a
requirement for "democratic" success.

In another wing, of course, waited the political scientists who, by
their authoritarian methods, insisted that sooner or later government would have to replace the sloppy guesswork of the old order.
Even reformers, liberals, and progressives were likely to move away

from the sovereign people. In America such widely approved humanitarian reforms—approved, that is, by the liberal intelligentsia—as equal rights for blacks, abolition of capital punishment, legalized abortion, tolerance of pornography, and legislative redistricting were imposed by the fiat of the nonelected courts and would have been voted down in any popular referendum.

A subtle and wide-ranging discussion on the issue of democracy, as on other issues, was notable more for its negations than for its affirmations. It had the effect of tearing away most of those illusions that once had surrounded democracy as rule of the people, hope of the future, fulcrum of faith in man. There was little disposition in more responsible circles to propose nondemocratic alternatives. The pluralistic, technological society would have to struggle on without a total ideology, without a simple system, without even any very credible myths. In certain ways it might even become more democratic (as through the wider implementation of consensus finding). But the old Democratic Faith, such as Lord James Bryce had found in the United States at the end of the nineteenth century, such as even Lord Bryce's own Britain in the era of Gladstone had glimpsed, was almost certainly dead beyond recall. It was only one more of the dissolutions of the twentieth century.

NOTES

1. Marxist reductionism is obscurantist insofar as it diverts attention from the specific, unique world of politics, which must be understood in its own right and not dismissed as a mere reflection of economic forces.

2. Andrei Zhdanov: "The Soviet people expect from Soviet writers genuine ideological armament, spiritual nourishment that will aid in fulfilling the plans for great socialist construction, for the restoration and further development of our country's national economy." Harold Swayze, *Political Control of Literature in the USSR, 1946–1959* (1962), p. 37.

3. This does not, however, seem to extend as far as the story about Marx's illegitimate child by Helene Demuth; a biography of Marx published in East Berlin in 1968 suppresses this altogether.

4. Charles Tillon, a French Communist "purged" in 1952 from his position of party leadership, described the remarkable proceedings in a book written in 1970, *"Un Proces de Moscou" à Paris*. Excommunication followed by subsequent ostracism and attempts to turn family and friends against him did not cause this veteran Communist militant, a colleague of Andre Marty, who was also deposed, to leave the party or to publish this account until after 1968, following the repression of Czechoslovakia.

5. See Z. Medvedev, *The Rise and Fall of T. D. Lysenko* (1969), by a participant, and especially David Joravsky, *The Lysenko Affair* (1971).

6. In *Past and Present,* May, 1972. The long historians' debate taking off from the old Hobson and Lenin theses about imperialism as an economic necessity of declining capitalism, to which Lloyd's article was a contribution, ended in the almost total defeat of the Marxian theories. For a round-up, see Kenneth E. Boulding and Tapan Mukerjee, eds., *Economic Imperialism: A Book of Readings* (1972).

7. See, for example, Ninian Smart, *The Religious Experience of Mankind* (1968), pp. 526, 537. Mircea Eliade, in his sourcebook *From the Primitive to Zen* (1967), included primitive religions, protesting against the assumption that only the "higher" religions have anything important to say; this is a typical contemporary view. In *Schism and Renewal in Africa, An Analysis of Six Thousand Contemporary Religious Movements* (1968), David B. Barrett exhibited the thousands of new sects in Africa.

8. Cf. the arguments presented in 1952 by the veteran popular philosophizer C. E. M. Joad for retaining belief in a God in a scientific-rational age—*The Recovery of Belief; A Restatement of Christian Philosophy.*

9. The Occitan culture in France, like the Catalan and the Basque in Spain, had roots in an ancient distinction of language; the language of the south (*langue d' oc*) was the language of the troubadours and was revived in the nineteenth century by a distinguished group of poets. Something is still made of this cultural and literary autonomy by the present asserters of southern independence, but they are more inclined to talk of capitalistic exploitation and of being "colonized" by the industrial north.

10. *Bulletin.* of the American Association of University Programs, Winter 1968, p. 429. Another excellent report on some European universities is Hans Daalder, "The Dutch Universities," *Minerva,* April 1974.

11. Another voice raised in favor of "abolishing educational structures" was that of the Vienna-born priest Ivan Illich, who in 1972 added the doctrine of *Deschooling Society* to his previous mastery of dechurching Christianity.

12. E. Kohak, "Requiem to Utopia," *Dissent,* 16 (1969).

13. See, for example, G. A. Almond and S. Verga, *The Civic Culture: Political Attitudes and Democracy in Five Nations* (1963).

8

Reconstructions

A Rage to Order

"Perhaps at no other time has wholeness been so difficult," George W. Morgan wrote in *The Human Predicament: Dissolution and Wholeness* (1968). "Our lives, our selves, our ways of being, are subject to dissolution." Though some of his examples may have been a little naive, Arnold Toynbee chose perceptively when he placed "schism in the soul" high on the list of his symptoms of disintegration. Previous chapters in this book have suggested themes of fragmentation, dissolution, and cultural chaos. No one could miss them in the realm of intellectual phenomena, which reflect not only the richness of our cultural inheritance but also the fantastic complexity of our society. In *A Primer of Ignorance* (1967), R. P. Blackmur wrote of "the new illiteracy" produced by "fragmentation and specialized knowledge."

It may be that dreams of a lost *Gemeinschaft* or perfect wholeness are just that: archetypes of a Golden Age that in fact never existed. Be that as it may, the historian must record the preoccupation with this question in modern times. It was experienced by the great nineteenth-century prophets Ruskin, Emerson, Nietzsche, as well as by Marx. They feared the radical dehumanization of man through loss of his "whole self" to specialized functionalism.[1] This fear has been felt even more keenly in more recent times and is a key to much of contemporary thought. It is of course deeply significant that Marx in his latest reincarnation emphasizes the healing of "alienation," the restoration of man's whole being, to a much greater extent than his earlier exegetists had supposed.

217

Since early in this century (cf. Paul Valéry, 1907), perceptive people have predicted an age of scientific barbarism, marked by the destruction of civilized whole men. In the context of socioeconomic problems, Bertrand de Jouvenel remarked that "we are faced . . . with the dismemberment, the disintegration of man, and . . . we must increasingly concern ourselves with his integration." The most serious minds of this century have been concerned with this issue. After exploring the Waste Land, T. S. Eliot spent much of the rest of his life preaching the need for traditions, a sense of the past, and the rootedness of art and culture in an ongoing social organism in which the past informs the present. "No poet, no artist of any art, has his complete meaning alone." To D. H. Lawrence, the novel was "the bright book of life" because only through its fullness could "emerge the only thing that is worth anything, the wholeness of a man, the wholeness of a woman. . . ." And the continuing popularity of the novel above all other literary forms is a tribute to this search for wholeness.

Ambitious, despairing, or grotesque attempts to recover the unity of things mark many of the more imposing monuments of recent intellectual history. Toynbee's monumental quest for the totality of man in the historical process, which ended in failure but produced a notable document of contemporary thought, has already been mentioned. An equally celebrated and equally formidable synthesis came from the Jesuit priest Pierre Teilhard de Chardin. Like Toynbee and others we have discussed, Teilhard belonged to the generation affected in its youth by World War I, and the genesis of his thought lies well before 1945, by which time his work was almost done (he died in 1955 at seventy-four, in the same year and at almost the same age as his friend José Ortega y Gasset).[2] His best-known book, *The Phenomenon of Man,* came out in 1940. But like Toynbee, he arrived at fame in the postwar years, when he was widely regarded as oracle or saint, no less attractive because he was rebuked by the then timid church. He presented in his work an ultimately optimistic evolutionary vision, wherein he resembled Toynbee, as well as a deep religious feeling accompanied by the claim that his work was no more than a scientific study of phenomena. Teilhard saw the entire cosmos involved in a process of emerging higher states, none reducible to the lower one: from matter to life, from life to man, from man to God. A day of triumph lies ahead, bringing the unity of mankind, a great expansion of consciousness, the absorption of man into God, the overcoming of all schisms and imperfection.

Bergson, as well as Hegel, influenced him, but Teilhard's spirit as embodied in his remarkable style was ecstatically religious; his writing was a kind of mystic poetry, a pantheistic hymn to the marvels of nature, man, and God, all parts of one stupendous whole. No one was ever more intoxicated than this French priest by the oneness and the plenitude of the universe. His life, however, was an active one, marked by much practical work in anthropology, paleontology, prehistory. He was by profession a geologist, but his real interest was evolution. Near the end of his life, he was dashing off eagerly to see what Louis Leakey was up to in Africa or to someone else's archaeological site. Joy in detailed research, a conviction that faith and science, metaphysics and everyday life ought to merge marked this genial Jesuit. He was a versatile man.

Again like Arnold Toynbee, Teilhard earned the cold contempt of the hardheaded practical men of science (see, for example, Peter Medawar), who could not understand all this metaphysical talk and religious rhapsody and assumed that its source must be a mountebank. In truth Teilhard seems to have been something of an amateur, however zealous, in his chosen fields of research. His biological speculations were far removed from the professional laboratory. He was accused of utopianism, of excessive optimism, or of a kind of intellectual totalitarianism—"prophet of a totalitarian age" (see Bernard Charbonneau's book, 1963).

In theology the Teilhardians opposed the Barthians, so gloomily resigned to evil and imperfection in this world, and encouraged us to struggle upwards towards the more perfect humanity bound to emerge out of the chrysalis of the present age. They earned the approval of some broader minded Marxists like Roger Garaudy and played some part in the church's turn toward "relevance" and social action. They were eager, following in Nietzsche's path (which Father Teilhard approved), to complete unfinished man, to move on toward the superman. In social policy they questioned Niebuhr's sober realism based on an awareness of power realities and often sounded a bit like the vaguer kind of liberal who thinks happiness is just around the next legislative corner—another similarity to Toynbee, who greatly admired Teilhard.

Teilhard's *Phenomenon of Man* gave to millions a fresh if debatable vision of the whole cosmic process; he strewed challenging ideas in his wake, some of which struck in our vocabulary along with Toynbee's striking metaphors (the noösphere, for example, a word for our total environment of ideas; point Omega, a new term for the Blessed Kingdom). As science, the vision failed to convince. Though a splendid tribute to one man's genius and faith, it was not the universal synthesis, the comprehensive overview for modern man. As a person Teilhard was as amazing as Wittgenstein or Sartre or Lévi-Strauss or other titans of our age, which has not lacked towering achievement. His genius was called forth by the urge to knit together a sundered noösphere, but it scarcely succeeded.

Neoclassicism

A small but significant group of modern thinkers would "take their stand" against the whole modern world, diagnosing its turn toward individualism as the root cause of its evils. They have been abhorred and castigated by liberals and socialists—and, indeed, by most orthodox "conservatives"—ever since they began to reject as grotesque heresy everything that has happened since the French Revolution. They are the reactionaries. Among other things, they tend to believe such odd things as that the universe has an objective order, which is ultimately rooted in God; that we get our standards in art and morality—absolute, unchanging—from this order; that in human society the only tenable, God-appointed order is a hierarchical society in which each man has his place, is content with it, and keeps it. Take away "degree, priority, and place"; untune that string; and you begin unravelling the whole social fabric, with the ultimate result chaos.

C. S. Lewis, in *The Abolition of Man* (1943), argued that the abandonment of absolute standards means the abolition of man, through the surrender to arbitrary will. Lewis was among a group of embattled reactionaries more radical than the leftists, who after all accept most of the modern world and merely want to reorganize it in certain ways; they were enemies of Modernism root and branch. One should distinguish this group from those who merely let fly an occasional blast at the modern world, or who, indeed, consistently criticized much of the modern world but nevertheless participated in

Modernism and never dreamed of turning back the calendar to some remote and stable epoch. The latter group was much larger than the former. Yeats could refer to "this filthy modern tide," but Yeats rejected Christianity ("so get you gone, Von Hügel, though with blessings on your head") and classicism ("we are the last romantics"); he was a shaper of the modern idiom who often wondered, indeed, what kind of poetry could follow his ("After us the Savage God") but who never doubted that the stream of life flows on and that man must flow with it. He expressed this belief in his poem "Meru":

> And he, despite his terror, cannot cease
> Ravening through century after century.

It is a bold man indeed who thinks that the dynamism of Western civilization can be halted. Such people have been isolated figures, subject to ridicule. Yet some of the strongest thinkers have occupied just such a position. Faced with the dissolution of art, thought, ethics, and personality itself, they have declared the necessity of calling off the whole modern epoch.

John Ruskin was probably their leading ancestor in the modern English-speaking world, though behind Ruskin stood Thomas Carlyle. Chesterton and Belloc tied crusading democratic reform to Catholic traditions. T. S. Eliot took his stand on royalism, Anglicanism, and classicism. Lewis, during and after World War II, drew a circle of oddly mixed converts around him at Oxford, including Dorothy Sayers (who combined medieval scholarship with the writing of detective stories and brilliant satire directed at the modern liberal-progressive mind), Roy Campbell (semi-Fascist poet of rare literary gifts), and J. R. R. Tolkien (very appealing to children). The remarkably versatile Lewis also wrote some fantasy novels (the "cosmic trilogy") of high quality, imbued with a frankly didactic element: glimpses of prelapsarian perfection of nature, in a society that is, of course, simple, pastoral, pretechnological.

The hold of traditionalism was even stronger in France, with its powerful national ties to classicism and to Catholicism. Around the turn of the century, French literature fell profoundly under the influence of a group of neotraditionalist writers including Maurice Barrès, Charles Péguy, Paul Claudel, Charles Maurras—a group obviously far from being of one mind on all matters but agreeing in their call for a retreat from Modernism. They appealed to nationalism as well as to Christianity and classicism; but this was because they identified the authentic French tradition with these elements, declaring that Romanticism and individualism were foreign imports. Maurras, indeed, was forced to view Christianity as merely a useful national institution without really believing in it, since he stood in the line of an equally strong French tradition of scientific rationalism reaching back through Comte to Descartes. This illustrates the difficulties of anti-Modernism. What *is* tradition? What *is* orthodoxy? Western civilization has accumulated a store of venerable heresies.

The experience of Fascism deeply discredited this group. Maurras demonstrably influenced Mussolini; the anti-Semitism of his *Action Française* left some mark even on T. S. Eliot, and Ezra Pound became a Fascist propagandist. No one ever expressed a neoclassical rage for order more fervently than did Adolf Hitler. Protest as one might against the crudity of equating Maurras with Mussolini or Nietzsche with Nazism, the affinities between them remained disquieting. Like everything else, traditionalism had to assume different guises as time wore on and options were exhausted. It has been driven in some odd directions in recent years. (Consider, as an example, Marshall McLuhan, previously discussed.)

Needless to say, the traditionalist battle has been a losing one. John Wain reported leaving Oxford under the spell of Lewis, but it did not survive his entry into the world. That Oxford should be the home of lost causes and impossible loyalties is itself a splendid English tradition, one that evokes memories of John Henry Newman and the Tractarians. But that kind of receptivity is little more than an academic attitude. Those strong enough to stand consistently against the modern tide inspired admiration but seldom won converts, and ended by looking a little absurd. The American critic Yvor Winters is a good example of such a person. An admirer, Fred Inglis, conceded that often "he is dismissed as a crank, living in isolation outside San Francisco, hanging on to weird neo-classic principles, and writing nineteenth-century sonnets to Melville." Winters disapproved of Eliot and Pound—which reminds us of the curious fact that these great poets were, artistically, the leading Modernists, though their political and social views were wholly antimodern. (They have been called revolutionary traditionalists.) The camp of traditionalism is indeed sundered: F. R. Leavis, who by and large belonged with the literary traditionalists, championed D. H. Lawrence.

Much in evidence was a strategy of drastic simplification. Lewis would have us return to "mere Christianity"—a straightforward matter of God and the Devil, right and wrong, Christ against the seven deadly sins. Winters would have us abide by the rule of reason in the arts—a poem should be clear, logical, and exact. Both men— and they were scarcely unique—possessed a kind of grandeur that stemmed from the linking of their vast learning and imposing intellects to the most archaic of causes. An Oxford don of sophisticated intelligence and far-ranging knowledge who believed in the Devil was a marvel. Lewis could call the Higher Critics barbarians and get away with it. Winters dared to handle virtually all the modern poetic "greats," mainly because his knowledge and his intellectual powers obviously earned him this right.

All classicists and traditionalists made the simple point that we must have clear standards of belief. If we really believe, with the Romantics, that the only measure of poetic value is its subjective intensity, we cannot logically say that Melville or Ben Jonson are any better than Rod McKuen or Little Orphan Annie, and we deserve the cultural chaos into which we have fallen. If we really believe that all morals are "relative" and may be justified by the circumstances of the day, we cannot logically condemn Hitler or napalm bombing. Anyone who declares firmly that gassing Jews or maiming babes is wrong, or who thinks that the music of Verdi surpasses that of Lawrence Welk, is committing himself to values that he derives from some higher realm, or that he affirms as an act of faith. If he describes himself as a "humanist" who acquires his standards just from the observation of man, by wholly naturalistic means, he is obviously not telling the truth. Why should he affirm a faith in art, life, or decency if he merely watches what most men do? Humanists always say that human nature must be improved, enriched, moved forward; to this end they choose some of its features for strengthening and others for elimination. How do they choose the good features and reject the bad, if human nature itself is their only touchstone? How do they know what is "good" or what is "bad"? Obviously they have smuggled in some ethical criterion from outside the realm of empirical fact. Where did they get it? They live by what they have forgotten, Jews and Christians say; they hold to a religious ethic, though they imagine it is something their unaided reason has invented. But in the long run the ethic cannot survive when the religion itself is rejected.

Neoclassicism, of course, purports to be the rule of reason in the arts, and Winters' collected works bear the noble title *In Defense of Reason.* Used in this sense, though, reason is a faith. (Charles Frankel's *The Faith of Reason,* 1948, is the best title ever devised for a study of that grandest of epochs, the Enlightenment, in reality so different from its image.) Neoclassicism, the foe of relativism, possesses an intolerant, aristocratic spirit and specializes in cutting through the defenses of muddled Modernists to reveal the bankruptcy of their permissive, individualist premises. Like Dr. Johnson, the critic it admired most, the Winters school belligerently planted its standard of authority above all fashions and scorned the fools who go tripping after the idols of novelty.

What is its "reason"? Basically, it is what a literate and intelligent elite says it is. This is no doubt a glorious elite, for it stretches back to Aristotle and the Greeks through a long succession of great artists and critics. But today the neoclassicist canon is hardly more than the *ipse dixit* of one faction. We can appeal against it to other lineages—the drunks, as opposed to the sobers, in one analysis of the Romantic-Classicist quarrel—and what can it say, except that we are wrong and it is right? At bottom it is not reason so much as arbitrary faith in certain values that neoclassicism asserts. To the classicist, reason has always been a cumulative product, a consensus of all the wise through the ages, and he is hostile to the presumptousness of any individual who claims a right to overthrow this alleged consensus. "Reasoning pride" is to be condemned. Today, however, the classicist is in the intolerable position of finding that in fact no consensus of past wisdom exists; he is forced arbitrarily to ignore or reject a good deal of "tradition," a situation that scarcely existed prior to the eighteenth century.

The authoritarian streak in neoclassicism was visible in one of its chief modern creators, Charles Maurras, who did not hesitate to expand his intellectual traditionalism to the political arena. One can hardly have sound art in a decadent society, and so Maurras created that forerunner of Fascism—one of its three faces, in Ernst Nolte's book—the *Action Française,* which undertook to purge the impurities from French politics and society just as Maurras the critic wished to purge the impurities from French literature. Democratic pluralistic society and modern art were inseparable in Maurras's view. The logical extension of his neoclassicism led toward an authoritarian political regime, akin to some species of Fascism: a disciplined, inequalitarian, hierarchical order. (The widely held opinion that Hitler was some kind of a wild romanticist is quite wrong. He was devotedly classical in his artistic as well as his political taste.) The *Action* was anti-Semitic, anticapitalist, antiforeign, antiparliamentary. One feels that Maurras was pushing matters to their logical conclusion. If we are to have back the old intellectual order, we must also have back the old social and political order.

Today intellectual order cannot be restored except in some such twisted form as Fascism. The day of kings and nobilities and churches is gone; if we aim at them we get dictators and storm troopers and concentration camps.[3] Ironically, the would-be classicists and rationalists who still exhibit a "rage for order" are, and must be, extremists and outsiders themselves—a point noticed by one of them, the distinguished American academic Richard Weaver (*Visions of Order: The Cultural Crisis of Our Time,* 1964). Pluralism is the orthodoxy of today; it takes an outsider, an estranged and alienated soul, to notice its radical defects and to seek to "expose and restrain the illusions of our century." Order has become a concept known only to the disorderly spirit; the classicists are the last romantics.

But, though in an impossible position, the Weavers and Winterses and Lewises were interesting minds. Richard Weaver and C. S. Lewis are dead; Yvor Winters is an old man. The breed appears to be dying off, not to be replaced. The struggle for order is too much for human strength. "You keep both Rule and Energy in view," Thom Gunn wrote in his poem to Yvor Winters. No one can any longer do it. Energy disdains rule; those who follow rules are impotent. The neoclassicist belief in hierarchy, the most reprehensible feature of its creed in an age that worships equality, strikes home to the very roots of recent economic life. The economic crisis marked by mounting wage and welfare claims, giving rise to inflation and spiralling taxation; the decline in workmanship and economic responsibility, resulting in ever poorer products at higher costs; the severe financial and social difficulties afflicting cities from which the affluent have fled while the demoralized remain—all these blights of recent years stem basically from a loss of the civic sense. Men will work even in menial positions for low wages if they have a secure place in a human community; they will do their work conscientiously and with pride when they know it is appreciated. Destroy this community, remove all the social checks on greed and corruption and irresponsibility, and you release men to better themselves at a cost that will perhaps eventually destroy society.

There is some point of contact here between the extreme Right and the extreme Left, for both are opposed to the faceless society, the "society of strangers" based on contract and the marketplace. Young outcasts and revolutionaries take to the hills to form communes (though few of them last) in order to regain the lost community. The reactionaries, however, insist that community necessitates inequality and obviates democracy and liberalism along with the other less pleasant features of the Great Society. The organic society is authoritarian and aristocratic; it is hierarchical. (Some of the hippie communes themselves illustrated this point, producing patriarchal dictators, worshipped virtually as gods by the adoring communards.) These venerable items of the conservative creed were not popular anywhere else. Here the Yippies and the Junior Chamber of Commerce were shoulder to shoulder, both claiming to stand for democracy and liberty, though the way they construed these difficult terms varied. Only a few, likely to be scorned as "Fascists," held that the good society is inconsistent with democracy and at least with that type of liberty defended by the Civil Liberties Union. Such despised anti-Modernists, however, form a rather distinguished little fraternity in the contemporary world.

Structuralism

The neoclassicists are an endangered species, but the urge to reestablish order appeared in another form more recently, under the name of Structuralism. Again mainly of French origin, it had an international impact. Structuralism is in some ways extremely modern, especially in its subjectivity and Wittgensteinian view of language. Indeed, its most notable beginnings were among students of language, positing as a basic premise the assertion that languages have an inherent order which imposes itself on ideas, so that, in effect, what we say determines what we think rather than, as generally supposed, the reverse. Dr. Johnson had thought that "language is the dress of thought." But it is more nearly true, the Structuralists insist, that thought is the dress of language. Or in the words of one of the founders of modern linguistics, languages "are invisible garments that drape themselves about our spirit and give a predetermined form to all its symbolic expression" (Edward Sapir, *Language, an Introduction to the Study of Speech,* 1921). From this, one might be led to explore the ways in which languages *differ.* To think in classical Greek or Latin is different from thinking in English or German, and to think in Chinese or Urdu is different from either, because of fundamental syntactical as well as semantic elements; thus we may understand, for example, why much of poetry, indeed even prose, is untranslatable.

From here, however, it is a short step to the reflection that there are after all *some* common denominators in language; we *can* in part translate, we *can* understand each other, however imperfectly, across language barriers. Comparative linguistics affords insight into the ways in which the special conventions of language shape our ideas, while at the same time suggesting certain universal elements, too. The endless, undifferentiated flux of things can be carved up in many different ways; we can, for example, be led by our terminology to believe that there are five, ten, a hundred colors, or even just one. Yet all is not chaos. Structural linguistics has proposed the theory that we can devise a set of symbols that will describe any language. Exactly what this signifies is not clear. But it has provided one of the more exciting intellectual frontiers of our time.

The intellectual ancestry of structural linguistics (or Linguistic Structuralism as it is sometimes called) is another unusual story with international ramifications. Like other recent vogues in thought, Structuralism's pedigree may be traced back into the nineteenth century. Its generally accredited father was the Swiss linguist Ferdinand de Saussure, who died in 1913. Saussure asked that language be studied as a system of relations, and we owe to him the term *semiology,* meaning a general science of communication signs. But the sensational rise to prominence of structural linguistics resulted more from the discoveries of two scholars working in the United States. The older of the two, Roman Jakobson, migrated from Moscow via Prague to the United States, bringing with him the insights of the Russian "formalists." (From this school came the remarkable *Morphology of the Folktale* by V. Y. Propp, originally published in 1928 and translated into English in 1958.) The younger, Noam Chomsky, burst on the world as a prodigy in 1957 with his book *Syntactic Structures,* which quickly wrought a veritable revolution in the staid and ancient subject of grammar and became one of the most discussed scholarly books of our times. Reduced to plain language, Chomsky's discovery was that there is a "deep structure" underlying the surface structure of sentences, which can be expressed in mathematical symbols. In this fact Chomsky, who called his theory "transformational grammar," found evidence of some kind of built-in human capacity to understand basic grammatical structures and convert these into the language which we use. He also suggested the possibility of universally valid structural principles that apply to all languages. (Compare the suggestion offered by, among others, James McCawley that there may be a "universal semantics.")

Often popularly presented in bristling McLuhan-like manner, Structuralism was sometimes a modishly paradoxical avant-garde position from which to deflate intellectual systems. The great anthropologist Claude Lévi-Strauss took it from linguistics and applied it to primitive kinship systems, which he claimed have a necessary logical and universal order implicit in their structural nature. Others then took it up and applied it to poetry, to science, to psychology, so that it became a sort of unifying factor, a point of view cutting across disciplines. In psychology, Structuralism comes close to *Gestalt,* the idea that mental operations involve grasping whole patterns—a weapon against associationalist or behaviorist, mechanistic psychologies, and hence a valuable stress on the human need to find unity. In literary criticism, Structuralism insists on attention to the literary work as a coherent whole, at the expense of its social-historical context or its "ideas" or, again, its purely esthetic features (imagery, use of words, and so forth). Obviously all such features ought to be taken into account, yet the narrower sort of Structuralist tries to rule out the others.

One reason for Structuralism's popularity relates to chapter 5: it is a strategy for the annihilation of intellectual traditions. By concentrating only on the formal aspects of things—the medium and not the message—the content can be jettisoned. It used to be supposed that the soul of an author appeared in what he had to say (much though his success in conveying it depended on how he communicated it), but to literary Structuralists of the more extreme sort, it is only the method of communication, the container and not the contents, that matters. They throw out the baby but keep the bathwater, which they neatly bottle and label. Structuralist analyses of works of art pointedly omit all consideration of period, of ideas, of the work's origins or social effects—of anything, in fact, except its architecture, its immanence as structure. Lévi-Strauss distrusts verbal knowledge, seeks to hew through it to a few simple mythic archetypes which can be reduced to symbols. There is obviously an immense pain behind so unnatural a procedure. When one cannot bear to hear the music, one counts the notes, classifies the measures, and plays mathematical games with the results. The urge to annihilate content is as strong a component of Structuralism as is its hope that by so doing we can restore a kind of inhuman order in thought.

As so often happens, the vogue for Structuralism arose at the time when structures once taken for granted were dissolving. In the great ages of art, Bernard Berenson once remarked, no one bothered to theorize about esthetics; theories about wholeness are a substitute for vanished wholeness. In area after area, structures of a unifying quality had broken down: macroeconomics (the nineteenth-century assumption of a single economic system of which all phenomena were subordinate parts) became microeconomics, for example.[4] Structuralism was taken for granted, it would seem, in earlier times, and so everyone was a Structuralist without knowing it, just as everyone was an Existentialist. Now that we have lost our grasp on the whole, we find that there is an -ism to describe it and, invoking the name, try in vain to recover it. In a notable essay the distinguished historian Lucien Fevre once pointed out that the word *civilization* did not appear in our vocabulary until the later eighteenth century—a curious fact he thought possibly significant.

The achievement of Lévi-Strauss and, to a lesser extent, such mathematical prodigies as Noam Chomsky, nevertheless demands attention as one of the marvels of our time. The sheer virtuosity of the French master's achievement requires that he be classed as one of the few giants of the age. The four massive volumes called collectively *Mythologiques* (1964–1971) constitute an investigation of more than eight hundred North and South American Indian myths, with the ultimate revelation that all of them may be seen, by demonstrable logical development, as variants on a single myth. Whatever their historical plan of development, human cultural creations also have a logical one, and so one may look at the world in an ahistorical way that releases us from the demon of endless evolution. Teilhard and Toynbee were on the wrong road altogether. Time is no refreshing river but a polluting stream. The right method is to begin where the Existentialists began, with Hegel's *Phenomenology of Spirit*—with the external world as given to human consciousness, as a "primal asymmetry" of binary differentiation. The world as given to consciousness is differentiated into nature and persons, high and low, right and left, near and far, adult and child, and so forth. Each binary opposition begets others and thus begins a dialectic which is—as computerists understand—mathematically exact.

Human consciousness is the primary data: Structuralism, as we noted, agrees with other Modernisms in an intense and sceptical subjectivity. Languages, myths do not tell us primarily about the external world but about the human mind. But the human mind has a logic printed into it—why and how we cannot know. Its categories are not those of formal logic, as Kant had thought, but of numbers. Pythagoras turns out to have been right. Russell and Whitehead showed that logic may be expressed as mathematical symbols. To Lévi-Strauss, as to the ancient Greek, the purest order is found in music. *Mythologiques* resembles Joyce's *Ulysses* and *Finnegans Wake* in being itself a perfectly orchestrated harmony.

Lévi-Strauss is very much a child of the present in other ways. The undercurrent of his thought is deeply pessimistic. Civilized man is dismissed as a ghastly error. The spirit can be at home only among precivilized folk. We need not look forward to ten thousand pages from Lévi-Strauss showing us the logic of human civilizations; they are not worth it. The end of the last volume, significantly titled *L' Homme nu*, sounds a bit like a routine prophecy of doom.

Lévi-Strauss is the master of advanced mathematical skills with which few if any of his readers can cope; but this awesome technical skill, combined with massive anthropological scholarship, leads us to rather banal conclusions. In 1949 his *Elementary Structures of Kinship* threw a cat among the pigeons of anthropology by postulating that kinship systems, like myths, have a logical order that can be demonstrated mathematically. There are not just so many strange systems of family connection, a tribute to the caprice of the human spirit; when we look at them all, we see an order that can be tabulated, classified like fingerprints. His *Tristes tropiques* (1955) and *La Pensée sauvage* (1962) were more popular tributes to the spell of the primitive and evidence of an uncanny literary skill. His prose echoes with memories of the language and the culture in a way that seems quite unstructural, very traditional. His vast logic of myths appears likely to join Toynbee's huge opus on a shelf reserved for classics that everyone has heard of but few have read.

What will it teach us? The Structuralist achievement is oddly barren. It functions at so austere a level of difficulty, as well as abstraction, that it does not bear on life. It was with such systems in mind, including Roland Barthès' "semiology," a key to all cultural codes, that Graham Hough remarked, "However esoteric literary studies may become, they must fail of their object unless their results ultimately filter through to the intelligent common reader, and unless they are expressible in something like the language of common life."[5] A young person who simply wants to learn to write well may, if he picks up a recent book on "style," find himself in the presence of no humane tradition, but lost in a strange jargon that he can hardly understand without a great deal of preliminary training, including mathematics. He will probably throw it down and go back to television or rock music. The Structuralist revolution in English studies, at least, threatened to produce only another branch of highly specialized in-group work that is sheer mystification to the public.

Noam Chomsky attempted to give some wider significance to Structuralism. The American-born expert made his reputation by his discovery of significant mathematical structures in syntax. From this he concluded that there are inborn structures of reason in the human mind, hailing the spirit of Descartes while casting aspersions on Anglo-American empirical philosophy. He went on to deduce a new Enlightenment from his Cartesian rationalism, arguing that each individual has within him all the seeds of knowledge and may, if liberated from an authoritarian education and society, live happily in an anarchist utopia. This last leap reminds us of what some of the zanier spirits of the later eighteenth century, like William Godwin, got from Jean-Jacques Rousseau. Chomsky had recapitulated the path from Descartes to Rousseau, and his subsequent adventures as hero of the New Left appeared to land us back in the French Revolution. His pronouncements on the subject of war, poverty, and exploitation were on the level of undergraduate radicalism; whatever we may think of their validity, they could just as well have come from the least literate of leftists as from a distinguished mathematician. Lecturing at Cambridge in 1971 (the first of the annual Bertrand Russell lectures), Chomsky startled his audience by discoursing abstrusely on language and philosophy in the first address and simplistically on utopian politics in the second, passing from the higher mathematics to the lower polemics in a shifting of mental gears almost unprecedented in the history of thought.

Thus with some of these Structuralists we are far from the conservative mandarinism of the older neoclassicists. Mandarins they might be in their field of academic specialization, but they compensated for this by trying to be swinging, with-it leaders of youth as their political avocation. Structuralism's tendency to produce cult figures for the counterculture is illustrated by the French psychologist Jacques Lacan, who believed that the unconscious had a linguistic structure. This does not of course detract from his intellectual importance. Yet clearly a rage to order in one dimension may accompany a rage to disorder in another. Few if any of the Structuralists had much use for tradition and authority. They were children of alienation, whose principle of universal order testified to a yearning for wholeness, but who found it in very far-out places.

And a great deal more of modern thought may be brought under this search for wholeness. Carl Jung said his long quest for the principles of the psyche was a search for the whole self amid the "fragmentation, confusion, and perplexity" of our age. Humanity, he believed, is one, with the same psyche underneath all the epiphenomena of culture. The archetypes of the mind, which dispose all to the same images and symbols, emerge from the collective unconscious of the whole human race. They also, he believed (more notably in his old age), contain hints of something beyond human ken; so do numbers—the great mediator between the human world and the higher world. (See *Flying Saucers,* 1959, p. 142.) Such intuitions have existed all through human history, as Jung's monumental researches into the alchemists and others showed. They have usually been too vague to carry much conviction to the sceptical scientific mind. Now the Structuralists have apparently provided some hard evidence that the mysticism of numbers, which haunted Pythagoras, Plato, Kepler, and Galileo, is really a matter of the way the human brain is built. The unifying principle is within us.[6]

NOTES

1. "Collingwood has suggested that the underlying principle from which all Ruskin's practical thinking springs is the unity and indivisibility of the human spirit, and that this involves a comprehensive belief about the mind, 'the belief, namely, that each form of human activity springs not from a special faculty—an organ of the mind, so to speak—but from the whole nature of the person concerned; so that art is not the product of a special part of the mind called the "aesthetic faculty," but each alike is the expression of the whole self.'" Graham Hough, *Image and Experience* (1960), p. 163.

2. After the war the exiled Spanish philosopher founded and lectured at an Institute of the Humanities, dedicated to the crisis of Western civilization. See especially *Man and Crisis* (1958).

3. Carefully researched studies of Nazi Germany reached the conclusion that Hitler's Reich never was as totalitarianized as he proclaimed; it remained in many basic ways a pluralistic society despite all the shouting and the agony. Perhaps this failure was part of the reason why he turned to foreign war.

4. Another example, chosen at random from a host of disciplines, is the not unimportant one of the law. Professor Grant Gilmore, in *The Death of Contract* (1974), notes the order-building process that went on in the nineteenth century—"the reduction of the basic fields of law to self-contained and logically consistent systems of rule and doctrine"—and the disintegration of these syntheses in recent years.

5. *Style and Stylistics* (1969), p. 110.

6. "The penetration of mathematics, mathematical methods, and above all the mathematical way of thinking, into areas which previously appeared to be closed to it seems to me to have occurred in many of the sciences in the last decades." Johannes Weissinger, in Thomas L. Saaty and F. Joachim Weyl, eds., *The Spirit and the Uses of the Mathematical Sciences* (1969). The hope that mathematics will "provide a unifying thread to our rapidly fragmenting education" (p. 199) because "what characterizes mathematics today is its universality, the power of its abstractions, and

its growing value and necessity in almost all fields of art and science" (p. 105) is expressed frequently throughout this symposium.

Some of the more important Structuralist statements in addition to Chomsky's *Syntactical Structures* and his *Language and Mind* (1972) are John Lyons, *Structural Semantics* (1963); John Lyons, ed., *New Horizons in Linguistics* (1970); Roland Barthès, *Mythologies* (1957, tr. 1972) as well as his *Elements of Semiology* (tr. 1968); Michael Foucalt, *The Order of Things: An Archaeology of the Human Sciences* (1970, a translation of *Les Mots et choses,* 1966) and also his *The Archaeology of Knowledge* (1970, tr. 1972).

9

Conclusion:
The Malaise of Our Age

We have thus come full circle, from the subject to the subject, and it is time to end, even though there is no end to the subtleties of contemporary thought. A recapitulation is in order.

Art moves toward its dissolution. Life and knowledge break apart. The age of books is over. The age of obscenity begins. Mere anarchy is loosed upon the world. The barbarians rise from the catacombs. Ancient authorities dissolve. Science and technology turn sour. Political reason decays. All is absurd.

But it is a remarkable age, too. Never have there been so many books, paintings, so much music. An explosion of knowledge and education occurs. Poetry is read to huge audiences. Incredible feats of the intellect abound: Wittgenstein, Sartre, Toynbee, Russell, Lévi-Strauss, Father Teilhard, the marvels of science and technology. There is a spiritual ferment, an uprising of youth. New frontiers of the mind are opened. Exciting syncretisms take place. New media appear for the arts and for knowledge.

But the very superabundance of achievements and novelties, pouring in as never before on the individual exposed to them, staggers the brain. And tremendous changes have clearly been underway. Apocalyptic feelings therefore abound. Any number of sages assure us that, somehow associated with the youth rebellion, with hippie drug-and-sex revolution, with the crisis of the machine age, with the end of art and of literature and of "society," we have reached the end of an era in Western civilization, or even in world civilization. Romano Guardini's book *The End of the Modern World* (1956) actually appeared on the eve of the explosion of the

1960s. "It's the end, Clov, we've come to the end," Samuel Beckett said in *Endgame*. Among innumerable others, Octavio Paz, the Mexican poet, voiced similar thoughts in *Conjunctions and Disjunctions* (1969), while the President of the French Republic speaking of a "crisis of civilization," singled out the family, religion, attitudes towards the nation, towards work, towards sex as areas where profound changes were at work. Particular nations have felt themselves to be in a state of crisis. (The crisis of a civilization is still likely to be felt within the national framework.) The British underwent a massive soul-searching about 1967, marked by a plethora of books about the survival of Britain, the anatomy of Britain, the future of British society, and the like. So did the Americans. Yet the malaise was clearly international. Student violence occurred in Germany, France, England, Mexico, Japan, Korea, the United States; a student riot in Yugoslavia followed the May Days of Paris, 1968; students behind the Iron Curtain tried as best they could to protest. Even under the special circumstances prevailing in Israel, Israeli youth in the sixties were more critical, less wholly dedicated to the national cause, than they were earlier.

If we think that our era is the first that thought itself the end, or experienced any of these pangs, we are of course mistaken. Apparently every generation since Adam's has declared itself to be in a state of degeneration. Thackeray, at the high noon of Victorian success (as it now seems to us), believed himself living in "a society in the last stages of corruption"; Balzac felt the same in Louis-Philippe's France. The 1890s are often thought of as the "belle époque" of insouciant happiness, but the serious writers then alive felt a sense of decadence and believed the *dies irae* to be near. "Mankind is in a state of sickness, now roused to feverish excitement, now inert, weary and discouraged. . . . We are at the end of an historical period"—or so thought Aasta Hansteen, Norwegian feminist, in 1894. In 1919, after the world had indeed come to an end, André Gide wrote that "Dada [the "After-Everything" gesture of its day] is the deluge, after which everything begins anew"—an ultimate "venture of negation" beyond which no one could possibly go. We ought at least to know that all this has been thought before, many times. The comparison of our epoch with the last days of the Roman Empire overlooks many factors, and among them is the fact that people in every century have been quite sure of their similar decadence.

Moreover, the particular forms our decadence takes are not original. Experiments with drugs for psychic effects apparently began with the cave men, were certainly known to the ancients, and were a nineteenth-century Romantic vogue. It is one of the more amusing notions of the recent young generation that they invented sex: for pornographic inspiration they have turned to *Fanny Hill* and the Marquis de Sade and the Other Victorians. Feminism, pacifism, and demands for extension of the vote were the stock in trade of early nineteenth-century radicals. We know that our revolutionists borrow what ideas they have from the earlier nineteenth century.

The Women's Liberation movement, which in its most recent manifestation believes itself to be so absolutely new that it dates the calendar from 1968 or some such year, actually existed in every generation at least since Mary Wollstonecraft wrote her *Vindication of the Rights of Women*—a book which seems to contain all the essential items of the women's creed—just after the French Revolution. The revolutions of 1848 harbored a prominent wing of libbers. Frau Hansteen lived in the midst of a most electrifying uprising of embattled women, by all appearances more energetic than the recent one. The emancipated woman, striding onto the Edwardian landscape just before 1914, announced her sexual freedom and demanded her political rights with acts of violence. The latest epiphany of feminism, like the sexual revolution, sometimes seems different only in its relative vulgarity, its extension to additional levels of the populace. The message has gradually percolated downward and will doubtless continue to do so, like other messages invented by and once reserved for an elite.

Life will surely go on. Ours is not likely to be the last generation, nor is it the only lost generation. Yet it has surely witnessed more novelties and oddities than most. It can readily be painted as the Age of Paradox.

There are dialogues between Communists and Catholics. While the age-old church cheerfully prepares to disband, the Communist society of Russia has become probably the most conservative in the world. A recent British book (*The Bogus Dilemma*) noted the utter irrelevance of old categories of political "Left" and "Right." The old formulae vanish. Sir Ivor Jennings is among those who have noted that "'the most common and least privileged of the people' have generally been conservative," while the upper class has frequently been quite radical. In Paris in 1968 the workers and the Communists defended the Gaullist state from the maddened (and privileged) students. We have seen manual workers defending the American flag in fights with revolutionaries from the affluent suburbs (the "radical chic"). The new theorists of the Left have themselves given up on the working class to place their hope in what Marx contemptuously called the *lumpenproletariat*—or, today, the *lumpenbourgeoisie*. What more dizzying changes could one imagine?

Historians no longer believe in history; novelists write antinovels; scientists become mystics; television personalities return to Jesus. It would seem passing strange, also, to all the radicals of the past two centuries that the conquest of poverty, where achieved, turns out to be grounds for fresh protest. According to a commentator (1966), the Swedish novel exhibits "an acute preoccupation with how to survive as a creative being in spite of material comforts and an atmosphere of smug contentment." The sad Swedes, who perfected the welfare state and were unhappy in it, became an international scandal. Jan Myrdal, in *Confessions of a Disloyal European* (1968), revealed so much assorted agony that it is difficult to know what his chief complaint was—in this respect, his is a typical document of our times. A son of the well-known Swedish socialist Gunnar Myrdal (he of so many impeccable Old Left causes), the younger Myrdal railed partly at the human condition, partly at the Romantic ego, but even more, being a Swede, at the welfare state, with which he was profoundly disillusioned. (He was disillusioned, too, with his parents, whose cause that state was, and who evidently spent so much time doing research on it that they had little to spare for parenthood. We are reminded of the character in one of Peter De Vries' comic novels who is so determined on a career in marriage counseling that she breaks up her marriage to pursue it.) The welfare state, so long and earnestly sought after by three generations of reformers, is now seen as a threat to men's souls, turning them into social security numbers. The smooth path from cradle to grave (provided one fills out the right forms) is intolerable, too; many people take to Asiatic highways as hobos to escape not poverty but affluence. The young militants do not really want socialism at all, whatever they may say, but the wildest individualism; not security but danger, not the rational organization of society but a regaining of mystery and adventure. If we now take social security and welfare checks for granted and cannot live without them, we nevertheless have little enthusiasm for them. Big government is as much an object of suspicion as big business. Some contemporary radicals sound like Adam Smith or even Herbert Spencer. They are anarchists at heart.

In 1972 the British commemorated the twenty-fifth anniversary of their welfare state in its present form, as outlined by the famous *Beveridge Report*. Many of the stock-taking reviews revealed profound disillusionment: thus *Spectator* said the great Beveridge experiment "must be rated a failure." A major British committee recommended wholesale reorganization of virtually the entire welfare apparatus (the *Seebohm Report*). While some complained of outrageous costs and the subsidizing of idleness, others demanded a much greater commitment of resources, a move that seemed unlikely. Statists debated with antistatists, who would rely on devices built into the market economy, such as a negative income tax, to avoid a huge bureaucracy. All agreed that the average person was no happier under the Beveridge system, that he was in fact more likely less happy than he had been before rescued by the benevolent state.

The loudest outcry about poverty seemed to come in the wealthiest country—by far—in the world. According to most calculations, through most of the 1945–1970 period the United States had a standard of living well above Europe's and many times above the world average.[1] Yet protests about grinding poverty, hunger, and dire need emanate more from the United States than from countries with one-fortieth of their living standard. (An annual per capita income of eighty dollars is typical of much of Africa and Asia and not a little of South America.) It would seem strange to these people (were they only aware of the fact) that American radicals demand a retreat from an American commitment to the far corners of the globe so that the money thus saved can be spent raising the standard of living of underprivileged Americans.

What this last point suggests is not so much that human wants are insatiable—though this is doubtless true, and the American suburbanite deprived of his second car and his color TV suffers just as acutely as an African farmer in need of a second cow and a screen door.[2] Rather, it suggests the extent of contemporary anomie, in Durkheim's famous term—the emancipation of the individual ego. People have learned that their wants are sacred and of right ought to be satisfied. They have learned to consider any obstacle to personal fulfillment an intolerable affront. They have greatly expanded the circle of ego awareness. They no longer accept sharp limitations on individual desires in the name of the group. Virginia Woolf once remarked that "nobody knows how many rebellions ferment in the masses of life which people earth." The amount of potential human discontent has always been infinite—misery, failure, misfitting, bitterness, hatred, envy beyond telling. It has usually failed of articulation, and in the past it was accepted passively as being beyond help.

Some eminent modern thinkers have feared this gradual release of the ego from inhibitions and silent social censorship. D. H. Law-rence hated, as the very epitome of Modernism, that situation "wherein each separate little ego is an independent little principality by itself." Product of social and cultural dissolution, honoring no religions, feeling no loyalties, no pieties, no ties to its fellows, the naked ego is a repulsive thing. As Saul Bellow's Mr. Sammler observes, "This liberation into individuality has not been a great success." Terrified of its own freedom, the ego easily becomes demoralized. How else can the widespread flight to mind-deranging drugs be explained? Though this habit is not new, its purpose is largely new today. In the nineteenth century, artists took drugs in the hope of stimulating their imaginations and creative powers. Today wretched, cultureless youths take them simply to wipe out a reality they cannot endure. Desperate and directionless souls unable to conceive what to do or what to think, they are terrorized by the reality of having to think and feel, form judgments and enter into social relationships. There is no authority able to tell them these things, as there was in the past. Thus Existentialism is no mere verbalization but a real condition; people do face the fearful freedom of gratuitous choice—and they cannot endure it.

The bitter little rebellions that break out today, assailing all authority, demanding more "rights," protesting all manner of "injustice" and "exploitation," and seemingly, often, so absurd (are not American students and women really less restrained than ever before in human history?) relate to this freeing of the ego from restraints previously accepted as beyond redress. And they relate also to the uneasiness that afflicts wholly emancipated people, adrift with only their vaguely understood desires to guide them. Such people must taste every forbidden fruit, for one of them might contain the magic ambrosia of happiness.

For the highest type of man or woman, able to cope with total freedom, the modern situation undoubtedly offers high rewards. For the others, it is dismaying, demoralizing. A substantial portion of significant intellectual history today takes place at that level where minds formerly not in the least "intellectual" are attempting to enter the realm of high intellectual culture previously reserved for the very few. These people would once have accepted the standard orthodoxies of a folk culture. They now feel released from all that, for it no longer has enough authority to command them; yet the other realm, the world of intellectual doctrine and formalized expression, of philosophy and literature and science and social thought, is so formidable that they are baffled by it. The in-between man, neither happy peasant nor high cleric, is the most significant creature of our times. It is he who chants slogans and pants after trends, who buys books that he cannot read, who thinks that he is being profound when he demands overnight perfection.

He also takes a strange delight in the nasty and macabre: how much of contemporary expression may be placed somewhere near the constellation embracing black humor and the literature of cruelty! (Again, neither is new; both are archetypal. *Ruthless Rhymes for Heartless Homes* was a Victorian favorite. These elements only seem to have bulked much larger in recent expression--and notably, like pornography, in expression regarded as artistically *significant*—than in other times.) There are a theater of cruelty; *pièces noires;* Godard's and Chabrol's cinema and Pinter's drama (surpassed by the post-Pinter British dramatists, Nichols, Wood, Bond, Orton); and innumerable novels, perhaps all owing some debt to the early Sartre and to Céline's novels of the 1930s, which deal in nausea and physical nastiness—a taint of all of this occurs in many other writings not entirely devoted to it. What fashionable novel or play or movie can do without some admixture of violence and horror? How many, indeed, might be described as one movie recently was: "The film is uniformly malevolent, unrelieved either by any spark of humor or by the presence of a coherent intelligence"—simply an incoherent cry of rage and disgust? Such a spirit goes with pornography, of course, incorporating in itself a sexual-sadistic impulse that is one aspect of the thoroughly liberated libido. But the essential black humor also takes a nihilistic delight in total breakdown—a form of *je me foutisme,* the *Catch-22* outlook—as it casts an eye on the hopeless bureaucratic confusions of mass society. It is childish, containing all the antisocial and destructive impulses found in the most immature fantasies. It is composed of pure despair, based on an outlook that sees no difference between good and bad, life and death, decency and indecency. This mood seeped even into popular music in the 1970s.

The paradoxes appear in cases of extreme ambivalence that mark our era. For example, ultrasophistication and extreme naiveté exist side by side. On the one hand, the modern intellect sees through every myth, plays with every idea, believes no truth. Its spirit is that expressed by Bertrand Russell when he wrote, "I have imagined myself in turn a Liberal, a Socialist, or a Pacifist, but I have never been any of these things in any profound sense. Always the sceptical intellect, when I have most wished it silent, has whispered doubts to me, has cut me off from the facile enthusiasms of others, and has transported me into a desolate solitude." There is no need to labor this point. On the other hand, the people who believe in witches, or become Jesus freaks, or follow a guru, or return to nakedness to celebrate human innocence provide examples of credulity and faith not equalled since the Reformation. "Believe what is impossible" is the existential watchword.

A similar contrast might be perceived between integrity and sham. One of the saving graces of the present age is a kind of integrity, even if an often despairing and wrong-headed one. People are seriously concerned and willing to try things. Martin Esslin, in an essay on Samuel Beckett, thought it reassuring that this author who never sought to gain fame or to court the public, who wrote in utter integrity to save his own soul—a fact of which one feels as sure as anyone can be of anything—nevertheless did win a wide following, did reach the public. Beckett's kind of honesty, which is the first virtue of the Existentialist ethic, can be found in the work of many other writers who have become modern masters: Orwell, Greene,

Camus, Hesse, Montherlant, Bernanos, Brecht, Grass, Bellow, and so on. Of these writers one can say many things in detraction, but they all are unflinchingly honest and never refrain from stating the truth as they see it to win popularity. And this quality is primarily what has won them admiration all over the world. Even more courageous, of course, are those brave writers who, when faced with totalitarian tyranny in Soviet Russia, kept faith with the spirit of man. And they too—Pasternak, Solzhenitsyn, Daniel—have become immortal.

And yet at the same time the phoniness of much that currently passes at all levels of the intellectual and spiritual life has never been more obvious. While academics inflate their bibliographies with trivia or create artificial empires of pseudoknowledge, the art world becomes an arena of meretricious hucksterism, as every weekly report confirms. Commercial television destroys serious theater and celebrates the death of the mind. Bureaucrats triumph over the creative soul of Russia and impose the most ludicrous cultural fare ever inflicted in the history of man upon a great and gifted people. The West, though it has the freedom to read what it likes, chooses to read, for the most part, not its great writings but trash. In France, most literate of Western countries, the best-selling hit of 1969 was the fraudulent memoirs of a small-time criminal. In the United States, recent best-sellers included the equally fraudulent life story of an American Indian, while public attention focussed on the story of an attempted literary hoax that duped one of the largest publishing houses in the world. Of a type of favorite reading in the English language, John Wain remarked that "such writing shows a basic contempt for humanity, exploiting its self-destructive impulses as one exploits a pig's greed by rattling his swill-bucket to call him into the sty." Wain specified those contemporary heroes James Bond and Mike Hammer, but his remarks would seem equally applicable to many others.[3]

The present age has its seriousness, as well as its triviality. The deadly, humorless seriousness of the leading prophets, Sartre and the rest, is familiar. And of our campus protesters no one could say—whatever else one might say—that they lacked seriousness. Their shining young faces upturned, they worshipped their god of Revolution or Instant Utopia with a solemnity unrivalled since the days of the Puritans. "The mercilessly idealistic young," as Harold

Perkin called them, with their penchant for tracts and propaganda, were anything but frivolous. We are driven to implore the gods of irony to visit upon them some small saving remnant of scepticism and laughter. As we earlier noted, their seriousness characterizes our age. Yet unimaginable depths of silliness are present, too, for all to see. Although it is no doubt chiefly in popular culture, there are intellectuals and serious artists these days who yearn to make art of broken-down refrigerators and music of automobile horns, to declaim their poetry before a mob, and in general to attune themselves to the beat of rock music, to "arse-creep youth," as one of Kingsley Amis' characters put it.

There are many other polarities. Reviewing the preceding chapters, we might list the essential elements in the contemporary cultural and intellectual situation as follows: (1) The closing out of past options: exhaustion of traditional faiths, whether ancestral Christianity or newer social utopias (disenchantment with Communism, for example); an inability to believe implicitly in any myth. *Yet:* anguished attempts to restore faith, assert belief (Existentialism, reaching out to Buddhism and other exotic religions, etc.). (2) An unmanageably huge intellectual heritage, topped by a contemporary explosion of knowledge, leading to extreme specialization, fragmentation of thought, collapse of unifying generalizations. *Yet:* determined attempts, against all the odds, to unify all knowledge (Toynbee, Teilhard, Lévi-Strauss); an obvious yearning for the restoration of wholeness, community. (3) The exhaustion of artistic modes, specifically the playing out of Modernism in a frenzy of bizarre fads: antiart, the dissolution of art forms, vast silences. *Yet:* a desperate need for art as an antidote to the bleak rationalizations of a mechanical and bureaucratic society ("our only refuge from a technological order where all can be calculated, formulated, regulated," Wylie Sypher writes); poetry readings, Pop art, innumerable "little magazines." (4) A cult of revolution, ecstatic belief in some future utopia. *Yet:* aimless violence, nihilism, "revolution for the hell of it." (5) Declining confidence in science and technology, antiscientific cults and ideologies, hatred of the "technological society." *Yet:* a renaissance of studies seeking to be scientific, such as sociology, behavioral studies, quantification methods, use of computers. (The Two Cultures battle results in a draw, with new bouts scheduled.)

"In history, as in nature," the historian Sir Lewis Namier has observed, "birth and decay are equally balanced." With all its despair, cynicism, insecurity, nastiness, confusion, the present age brings forth a creative profusion—thinking, writing, shaping more furiously than any previous age has done. If it is expiring, it is doing so not with a whimper but with a bang. Ours is an age much like that which fell between the high medieval civilization of the thirteenth century and the seventeenth-century dawn of modern times; a period when war, plague, belief in witchcraft, the downfall of the medieval church and philosophy, and other disasters led those then living to see nothing but harbingers of the Apocalypse, but one in which, as we now can see, powerfully creative forces were at work preparing a new order. Such comparisons can never be exact. Yet even the most pessimistic cannot deny that creation, as well as decay, is a feature of the present scene. And no one can be sure that after much torment a new, perhaps better civilization will not emerge. The materials for it are there, provided by the profuse modern genius.

For all that has been left out of this book, the author offers no apology but does owe an explanation. The totality of modern intellectual life is too vast to be digested. This applies especially to all the branches of the exact sciences. These have grown apace with the rest of the proliferating monster of knowledge. I am told by a friend in organic chemistry that his area of specialty doubles every few years in its content of knowledge. No chemist can now "know" more than a small part of this traditional subject. The same can be said of a dozen other branches of learning. From the physical and biological sciences, needless to say, has emerged a steady stream of discoveries that alter our lives. No general account of the world since 1945 could fail to deal with atomic energy, penicillin, a hundred other medical innovations; with the exciting work in genetics on the mechanism of heredity, space science and space exploration, lasers, masers, etc., etc. These are only the tip of the iceberg exposed to public view. Underneath is a huge body of research published in technical journals, destined to remain forever a mystery to all save the small band of specialists dedicated to each separate discipline. The situation is not very different in the social sciences. Synthesis has broken down in economics: no overarching theory such as Mill or even Keynes provided any longer exists, but rather a situation of "relativity," many zones of knowledge each with its own conceptual vocabulary. (There were some larger theoretical conceptions in the postwar years that gained fleeting fame, such as Game Theory and Systems Analysis, but none has lived up to its promise.) At the conclusion of his study, a leading historian of economic thought is driven to deplore its isolation and to ask its practitioners to "re-establish diplomatic relations with the other social and humanistic sciences, if it is to remain a culturally relevant discipline."[4] The last section of his book, covering the more recent period, is entitled "The Thrust toward Technique." As in many other branches of contemporary thought and expression, one finds here a formidable degree of technical competence, involving in this case a forbidding command of higher mathematics (which makes economics now about as intelligible to the layman as nuclear physics), but also a lack of practical content—and certainly no one large framework of meaning.

Yet in each of these disciplines much that is of interest goes on. Much has some significance for one cell or another of the social organism. It is part of contemporary intellectual history. So are many other things. The industry and ingenuity of scholars—as we have previously noted—create whole empires of highly technical expertise in areas where one would scarcely think it possible. How much is fraud and how much the super-wisdom of the future hardly any one can say, though we may have our suspicions.

It is scarcely possible, then, to encompass all these microspecialties in a short general account of Western thought. One would need an encyclopedia to do the job. And encyclopedias, one may urge, are something we do not need more of. There is a place for the encyclopedia, as there is for good histories of each of the various branches of knowledge—too few of the latter exist. But a work such as this, which attempts to draw the large-scale map of our intellectual world, can do no more than point to areas which the curious may explore, if he wishes to know them.

NOTES

1. Nevertheless, as measured in terms of per capita gross national product, some European countries had overtaken the United States by 1974. Some 1974 figures placed Switzerland as the world leader, followed by Sweden and West Germany, with

the United States no better than fourth. This represented an almost astonishing change from the 1945–1950 situation.

2. Or even more acutely. In *Relative Deprivation and Social Justice: A Study of Attitudes to Social Inequality in Twentieth Century England* (1966), W. G. Runciman, among others, noted that "steady poverty is the best guarantee of conservatism"; it is only when people observe others better off that discontent gnaws; the "revolution of rising expectations" works most in the most modern society.

3. A strange charlatanism that burgeoned internationally in the late 1960s was something called Scientology, which contained heavy borrowings from Eastern religions, Freudianism, theosophy, Dale Carnegie (how to win friends and influence people), the Jesuits, and Communism; it was equipped with a business corporation structure, and, though the creation of an obscure American science fiction writer, turned up most prominently in New Zealand.

4. Ben B. Seligman, *Main Currents in Modern Economics* (1962), p. 787.

Sources

The "bibliography" of all materials relevant to this subject is so vast as to defy description. The most relevant primary sources are the writings of the most important figures of thought, including their letters, diaries, and memoirs, where these are available, as well as their published works. One can only refer the reader, despairingly, to the library catalogues of the works of George Orwell, Jean-Paul Sartre, Ludwig Wittgenstein, C. P. Snow, C. S. Lewis, Claude Lévi-Strauss, Pierre Teilhard de Chardin, Arnold J. Toynbee, and others mentioned in the text. Still, there are some judicious selections from such authors that by bringing their main ideas into compressed editions offer good value to the harried student. A few examples may be given: Orwell's *Collected Essays, Journalism, Letters,* especially vol. IV (1968); Teilhard de Chardin, *Let Me Explain,* ed. J. P. Demoulin (1970); Robert D. Cumming, ed., *The Philosophy of Jean-Paul Sartre* (1965); Alden L. Fisher, ed., *The Essential Writings of Merleau-Ponty* (1969); C. S. Kilby, ed., *A Mind Awake: An Anthology of C. S. Lewis* (1968). One notes from Lewis's published *Letters* (1966) that he was sceptical of this enterprise, and no doubt it would be better to read all of Lewis, Orwell, Sartre, etc., but who can manage it?

Many will be more attracted to the letters and diaries as shedding light on authors' intentions. Aldous Huxley's (1969) and Malcolm Lowry's (1964) are among such interesting collections of letters. Sir Harold Nicolson's *Diaries and Letters,* vol. 3, *The Later Years, 1945–1962* (1968) were deservedly famous. So were Simone de Beauvoir's series of books about her life, shedding light on Sartre and his circle—among them *The Prime of Life* (tr. 1962) and *Force of Circumstance* (tr. 1965). Volume 3 of Bertrand Russell's absorbing autobiography covers the years 1944–1969. Other personal statements include John Wain, *Sprightly Running, Part of an Autobiography* (1962); C. S. Lewis, *Surprised by Joy: The Shape of My Early Life* (1955); Julian Huxley, *Memories* (vol. I, 1970; vol. II, 1974); and

Graham Greene, *A Sort of Life* (1971). Perhaps, like André Malraux, who wrote *Anti-Memoirs* (tr. 1968), writers these days "do not find themselves very interesting." Wives or mistresses (Clara Malraux, Françoise Gilot, Caitlin Thomas, Maeve Gilmore) seem more attracted to memoirs. Cited in the text for special purposes were Jan Myrdal, *Confessions of a Disloyal European* (1968) and Don McNeill, *Moving through Here* (1970). A memoir such as Wolfgang Leonhard, *Child of the Revolution* (tr. 1958) vividly realizes the setting of thought on the left. A unique commentary on the daily events of his times came from the veteran writer François Mauriac in the form of his *Bloc-Notes,* four volumes covering the years 1952-1967 (1958-1970). The alert student will easily be able to discover many more autobiographies.

One might also approach the field of contemporary intellectual history by a judicious selection of the great journals of opinion and expression. The London *Times Literary Supplement* has long held a unique place as a focus of international intellectual life. The French equivalent was perhaps *Figaro Litteraire.* Sartre's *Les Temps Modernes* occupied a unique station in postwar intellectual life. *Spectator* and *New Statesman* in Britain, also for its special contribution *New Left Review;* in the United States *Partisan Review,* for some of these years very distinguished indeed, *Dissent,* and *Commentary;* German periodicals such as *Die Zeit, Der Monat, Neue Rundschau, Merkur,* and, especially valuable for contemporary ideas, *Stimmen der Zeit*—such organs are but more obvious standouts in a crowd of worthy publications. *Revue des Deux Mondes* frequently discusses important intellectual movements in France, as do *Esprit* and *Tel Quel. Ideologie* was an Italian periodical devoted to Marxism-Leninism with a Maoist slant. The *World Marxist Review* (English edition published in Toronto) can be counted upon to dispense the Kremlin orthodoxy. By contrast, the Yugoslavian *Praxis* is an organ of Marxian revisionism, and *Marxism Today* is relatively undogmatic; *Studien über Marxismus* and *Studies in Soviet Thought* are scholarly. Guides to the numerous and ephemeral "little magazines" can be found from time to time in *TLS·* see, for example, the special issues of August and September 1964 on "The Changing Guard," and Patrick Bridgwater, "Little Magazines in German," July 3, 1969. See also *Index to Little Magazines,* in several volumes. Selected articles from leading periodicals are sometimes published in book form and as such constitute an interesting overview of the mind; see, for example, annual cullings from the *Times Literary Supplement* (*TLS 8,* the eighth annual anthology, was published in 1970 for the year 1969), or reprints of special *TLS* issues such as *The British Imagination* (1961). Other such volumes are Brian Inglis, ed., *Points of View,* selected from *Spectator* 1955-1961 (1962), followed by *Spectator's Choice 1962-1965* and others; Stephen Spender, Irving Kristol, and Melvin J. Lasky, eds., *Encounters: An*

Anthology from the First Ten Years of Encounter Magazine, (1963); William Phillips and Philip Rahv, eds., *The Partisan Review Anthology* (1962). Longer perspectives were those of Justin O'Brien, ed., *From the NRF* (1958), twentieth-century selections from the distinguished French journal *Nouvelle Revue Francaise;* and *The Cambridge Mind: 90 Years of the Cambridge Review 1879–1969,* edited by Eric Homberger and others in 1970. Still another approach to the journal world is via the collected articles of some notable commentator, of which an example is Kenneth Tynan, *Curtains* (1961) and *Tynan Right and Left* (mostly Left of course) (1967), reprinting the theater and cinema reviews of an outstanding critic.

Books of analysis and criticism that introduce the reader to individual thinkers of significance can be helpful. One series, the Fontana Modern Masters (published in the United States by Viking Press) undertakes to provide brief introductions to important contemporary minds; the list includes short books on McLuhan (by Jonathan Miller), Freud (Richard Wollheim), Russell (A. J. Ayer), Wilhelm Reich (Charles Rycroft), Marcuse (Alasdair MacIntyre), Wittgenstein (David Pears), Lévi-Strauss (Edmund Leach), and others. Though incomplete, this set could be used as the core of a course of study on recent thought. Needless to say, there are many other books dealing with individual writers and thinkers. The Crosscurrents series published by Southern Illinois University Press, general editor Harry T. Moore, is on twentieth-century authors, including Brecht, Camus, Kafka, Lorca, Malraux, Thomas Mann, Proust, Sartre, D. H. Lawrence, T. S. Eliot, Yeats, Dylan Thomas, Beckett, Orwell, Snow, Robbe-Grillet, Toynbee; also more general works such as Charles Glicksberg, *The Tragic Vision in Twentieth Century Literature* (1963).

Some broad-theme books seek to appraise the contemporary world of culture and ideas in general. Jacques Barzun, *The House of Intellect* (1959); George W. Morgan, *The Human Predicament: Dissolution or Wholeness* (1968); and Christopher Booker, *The Neophiliacs* (1969) are all significant statements on the fragmentation of culture and the need for reintegration. See also J. H. Plumb, ed., *Crisis in the Humanities* (1964). R. Buckminster Fuller, *Utopia or Oblivion: The Prospects for Humanity* (1969), awkwardly expressed though it often is, is a plea for the restoration of wholeness by a great contemporary designer. Irving Howe, *The Decline of the New* (1970) contains lively essays on a variety of modernisms, as does R. P. Blackmur, *A Primer of Ignorance* (1967). In addition to Yvor Winters' *In Defense of Reason* (1947, 1960), Richard M. Weaver's *Visions of Order: The Cultural Crisis of Our Time* (1964) is a notable plea for "the reunion of man into a being who will both know and desire what he knows." Also challenging large issues are George Steiner, *In Bluebeard's Castle: Some Notes Toward the Redefinition of Culture* (1971); Judith N. Shklar, *After Utopia: The Decline of Political Faith* (1957); Maurice Friedman, *To Deny Our*

Nothingness (1967), subtitled *Contemporary Images of Man;* Eric Kahler, *The Tower and the Abyss* (1967); and Hannah Arendt, *The Human Condition: A Study of the Central Dilemmas Facing Modern Man* (1958). Essays by Lionel Trilling, printed in *The Liberal Imagination* (1950) and *Beyond Culture* (1965), are valuable commentaries on the modern cultural scene. So are those of Geoffrey Gorer, *The Danger of Equality* (1966). Northrop Frye, *The Modern Century* (1967), lectures delivered for the Canadian centennial, offers far-ranging, if often rather slight and discursive, comment by a discerning literary critic. T. R. Fyvel, *Intellectuals Today; Problems in a Changing Society* (1968) is a devastating assault on "the intellectual aridity of the postwar years," as Auberon Waugh called it in a review. The *New Outline of Modern Knowledge,* edited by *TLS* editor Alan Pryce-Jones in 1956, bravely tries to sum everything up in one volume, an experiment perhaps significantly not repeated. Anthony Hartley, *A State of England* (1963) draws on English intellectuals for a rather alarming portrait of his country. Raymond Aron's *Eighteen Lectures on the Industrial Society* (tr. 1967) is the book that the young man in Georges Perec's novel read with such dismay; his *Progress and Disillusion: The Dialectics of Modern Society* (1968) and other works are among the most perceptive diagnoses of contemporary society. Compare Jacques Ellul, *The Technological Society* (1964) and his *The Political Illusion* (1967) with John Kenneth Galbraith's phrase-coining work, *The Affluent Society* (1958, 1969). Maurice Crouzet, *The European Renaissance since 1945* (1971) includes a chapter on "Intellectual and Cultural Life." Some rather more controversial construals of the modern era are R. Guardini, *The End of the Modern World; A Search for Orientation* (1956); José Ortega y Gasset, *The Modern Theme* (tr. 1961); Daniel Bell, *The End of Ideology; On the Exhaustion of Political Ideas in the Fifties* (1960); and Gabriel Marcel, *Man against Mass Society* (1952). The late Adrienne Koch selected a number of such statements in her *Philosophy for a Time of Crisis* (1959). C. B. Cox and A. E. Dyson, eds., *The Twentieth Century Mind,* vol. 3 (1972) covers the years 1945–1965 in Britain.

Literature and the Arts: Stephen Spender, *The Struggle of the Modern* (1963) stands out among attempts to get at the essence of Modernism. On the alienated artist of modern times, see Herbert Read, *Art and Alienation; the Role of the Artist in Society* (1969); Edgar Wind, *Art and Anarchy* (1963); Colin Wilson, *The Outsider* (1956). Maurice Nadeau, *The French Novel Since the War* (tr. 1967) may be supplemented by R. M. Albérès, *Le Roman d'aujourd'hui 1960–1970* (1970). H. M. Waidson, *The Modern German Novel 1945–1965* (1971); Henry Hatfield, *Crisis and Continuity in German Fiction: Ten Essays* (1969); and Peter Demetz, *Postwar German Literature* (1970) are among the relatively few books in English on this subject. Brian Keith-Smith edited *German Men of Letters: Essays on Contemporary German Literature,* vol. 4, in 1966. F. R. Karl, *The Contemporary English Novel* (1963); James Gindin, *Postwar British Fiction* (1962); and Bernard Bergonzi, *The Situation of the Novel* (1970) are useful; Rubin Rabinovitz, *The Reaction against Experiment in the English Novel 1950–1960* (1967) notes a significant aspect of the 1950s. In *Toward a New Novel* (tr. 1967), Alain Robbe-Grillet exposes his ideas about the *nouveau roman,* which he practiced so skillfully. Roland Barthès, *Le Degre zéro de l'écriture* (1st ed. 1953) is another critical landmark. Ihab Hassan, *Radical Innocence: The Contemporary American Novel* (1961); John Cruickshank, *The Novelist as Philosopher: Studies in French Fiction, 1935–1960* (1962); Stanley R. Hopper, ed., *Spiritual Problems in Contemporary Literature* (1957); and Marcus Klein, *After Alienation* (1964) have unusual interest for the student of ideas. J. Isaacs, *The Background of Modern Poetry* (1952); J. M. Cohen, *Poetry of This Age* (1959); and Michael Hamburger, *The Truth of Poetry: Tensions in Modern Poetry from Baudelaire to the 1960s* (1970) may be suggested for background in this area, along with John Press, *A Map of English Verse* (1969), a useful summary covering the twentieth century down through the 1950s; Press's more extensive work on the poets of the 1950s is titled *Rule and Energy* (1963). G. S. Fraser, in *Vision and Rhetoric* (1959) has two chapters on the poets of the 1950s. See also M. L. Rosenthal, *New Poets: American and British Poetry Since World War Two* (1967); Roy Fuller, *Owls and Artificers: Oxford Lectures on Poetry* (1971); and A. Alvarez, *Beyond All This Fiddle: Essays 1955–1967* (1968). Michael Hamburger and Christopher Middleton, *Modern German Poetry* (1962) is a sound guide. Martin Dodsworth, ed., *The Survival of Poetry: A Contemporary Survey by Donald Davie and Others* (1970) contains good essays on a number of recent major poets, including Philip Larkin and the Americans Sylvia Plath and Robert Lowell. Walter J. Bate, *The Burden of the Past and the English Poet* (1970) takes up the question of tradition and innovation. G. Manacorda, *Storia della letteratura italiana contemporanea 1940–1965* (1969) may be recommended as a starting place in its field.

The intriguing contemporary theater has inspired many books, such as Martin Esslin, *The Theater of the Absurd* (1961) and Eric Bentley, *The Theater of Commitment and Other Essays on Drama in Our Society* (1967). Others include Bamber Gascoigne, *Twentieth Century Drama* (1962); Joseph Chiari, *The Contemporary French Theater, The Flight from Naturalism* (1958); Leonard C. Pronko, *Avant-Garde: The Experimental Theater in France* (1962); and John Russell Taylor, *Anger and After: A Guide to the New British Drama* (new edition 1969). Tynan's writings, previously cited, may be compared with Eugene Ionesco's *Notes and Counter-Notes: Writings on the Theater* (1964). Taylor has added a report on *The Second Wave: British Drama for the '70s* (1971), while Frederick Lumley's *New Trends in Twentieth Century Drama: A Survey Since Ibsen and Shaw* reached a fourth edition in 1972. There is an annual *Jahrbuch* devoted to Bertolt Brecht. Hugh Kenner has authored *Samuel Beckett, A Critical Study* (1968). Ihab Hassan has compared Beckett with Henry Miller in *The Literature of Silence: Henry Miller and Samuel Beckett* (1967). *The Peopled Wound: The Work of Harold Pinter* (1970) is Martin Esslin's recent examination of Harold Pinter. Other examples of studies devoted to individual dramatists are Robert Cohen, *Giraudoux: Three Faces of Destiny* (1968), and Urs Jenny, *Dürrenmatt: A Study of His Plays* (tr. 1974). On a related art form, Roger Manvell, author with Heinrich Fraenkel of *The German Cinema* (1971), has also written *The New Cinema in Europe* (1966)—a rather bland but encyclopedic survey. Parker Tyler, *Underground Film: A Critical History* (1969) is suitably unreadable.

Morse Peckham's essay "The Current Crisis in the Arts" is printed in his *The Triumph of Romanticism: Collected Essays* (1970). Edward Lucie-Smith, *Movements in Art since 1945* (1969) attempts a difficult task. See also Gerald Woods, *Art without Boundaries 1950–1970* (1972), and John Russell Taylor and Brian Brooke, *The Art Dealers* (1969). H. H. Stuckenschmidt, *Twentieth Century Music* (1968) and Wilfrid Mellers, *Caliban Reborn: Renewal in Twentieth Century Music* (1968) provide some assistance in their area, as does Henry Barraud, *Pour comprendre les musiques d'aujourd'hui* (1968). John Cage, *Silence: Lectures and Writings* (1961) and *A Year from Monday: New Lectures and Writings* (1968) are the thoughts of an articulate contemporary composer. Aaron Copland, *The New Music 1900–1960* (1968) is also by a distinguished musician. In *The Voices of Silence* (1953) and *Museum without Walls* (tr. 1967), André Malraux perhaps comes close to creating a philosophy of art for modern man. Among much speculation about the future is Ihab Hassan. *The Dismemberment of Orpheus: Toward a Postmodern Literature* (1971).

Philosophy: Frederick Copleston, *Contemporary Philosophy, Studies of Logical Positivism and Existentialism* (1956) and I. M. Bochenski, *Contemporary European Philosophy* (1956) are able surveys of the era. See also vol. 5 of A. Caponigri's *A History of Western Philosophy* (1971). Mary Warnock, *Existentialism* (1970) is among a host of books on its subject, along with such earlier ones as F. H. Heinemann, *Existentialism and the Modern Predicament* (1953); Paul Roubiczek, *Existentialism: For and Against* (1964); and Fritz J. von Rintelen, *Beyond Existentialism* (1961). See also Frederick A. Olafson, *Principles and Persons: An Ethical Interpretation of Existentialism* (1974). Maurice Friedman, ed., *The Worlds of Existentialism* (1964) and N. Langiulli, ed., *The Existentialist Tradition: Selected Writings* (1971) are convenient anthologies. Selections from

Sartre and Merleau-Ponty were previously cited. Gabriel Marcel, *The Philosophy of Existence* (1949) was reprinted in 1969. Charles F. Wallraff, *Karl Jaspers: An Introduction to His Philosophy* (1970) is a good introduction to the celebrated philosopher whose own works have been often reprinted, for example, *Philosophy of Existence* (1971). John Cruickshank, *Albert Camus and the Literature of Revolt* (1960), and Philip Thody, *Albert Camus: A Study of His Work* (1957) are supplemented by Conor Cruise O'Brien's treatment for the Modern Masters series. On Sartre, see Thomas Molnar, *Sartre: Ideologue of Our Time* (1968); R. D. Laing and D. G. Cooper, eds., *Reason and Violence: A Decade of Sartre's Philosophy 1950–1960* (2nd ed., 1971); and Mary Warnock, ed., *Sartre: A Collection of Critical Essays* (1971). Germaine Bree, *Camus and Sartre* (1972) is lucid and discriminating. Paul Ilie has examined the Spanish philosopher *Unamuno: An Existential View of Self and Society* (1967). Edward N. Lee and Maurice Mandelbaum, eds., *Phenomenology and Existentialism* (1967) clarifies the connection between the two schools; among many books about the former, see Marvin Farber, *The Aims of Phenomenology; the Motives, Method, and Impact of Husserl's Thought* (1966), and *The Foundations of Phenomenology; Edmund Husserl and the Quest for a Rigorous Science of Philosophy* (1967). On Wittgenstein, see his own *Philosophical Investigations* (1953); Norman Malcolm and Georg J. Von Wright, *Ludwig Wittgenstein: A Memoir* (1958); David Pole, *The Later Philosophy of Wittgenstein* (1958); and Justus Harnack, *Wittgenstein and Modern Philosophy* (1965). Analytical philosophy may be sampled in the two volumes edited by R. J. Butler, *Analytical Philosophy* (1962, 1965), or in J. L. Austin, *Philosophical Papers* (2nd ed., 1970). Typical criticism may be found in Pratima Bowes, *Is Metaphysics Possible?* (1965); H. D. Lewis, ed., *Clarity Is Not Enough; Essays in Criticism of Linguistic Philosophy* (1963); and C. W. K. Mundle, *A Critique of Linguistic Philosophy* (1970). George L. Kline, ed., *European Philosophy Today* (1965) covers some lesser-known philosophers (Spanish, Italian, Polish) as well as Heidegger and Sartre. Colin Smith, *Contemporary French Philosophy* (1964) reveals some of the lesser peaks beneath the Existential giants Sartre and Marcel. Another useful collection is Richard Rorty, ed., *The Linguistic Turn: Recent Essays in Philosophical Method* (1967).

Religion and Theology: There are many editions of the classic twentieth-century religious thinkers; Martin Buber, Rudolf Bultmann, Karl Barth, Reinhold Niebuhr, Paul Tillich, Jacques Maritain. Thomas E. Bird, ed., *Modern Theologians, Christians and Jews* (1967), and Leonhard Reinisch, *Theologians of Our Time* (1964) offer selections. Expert commentary may be found in John Macquarrie, *Twentieth Century Religious Thought: The Frontiers of Philosophy and Theology 1900–1960* (1963), and his *Contem-*

porary Religions Thinkers (1968). Arnold J. Wolfe, ed., *Rediscovering Judaism: Reflections on a New Theology* (1965) may be compared to *New Theology,* a series of volumes edited by Martin E. Marty and Dean G. Peerman (6 vols., 1964–   ). Much of the so-called new theology stems from John A. Robinson, *Honest to God* (1963), and Paul M. Van Buren, *The Secular Meaning of the Gospel: An Original Inquiry* (1963); see also David L. Edwards, ed., *The Honest to God Debate* (1966). Compare the austere Pannenberg school, reviewed in Carl E. Braaten, *History and Hermeneutics* (1966), and James M. Robinson and John B. Cobb, Jr., eds., *Theology as History* (1967). The autobiography of an Anglican priest of the "swinging" variety who set out to modernize the church is Nicolas Stacey's *Who Cares* (1971). Thomas F. Torrance, *God and Rationality* (1971) protests against Existentialist irrationalism. William G. Cole, *The Restless Quest of Modern Man* (1966) is an example of a Christian critique of contemporary civilization along Niebuhr-Tillich lines, still quite common. Robert J. Reilly's study *Romantic Religion* (1971) treats the subject as represented by J. R. R. Tolkien, C. S. Lewis, Owen Barfield, and Charles Williams.

For examples of the Christian-Marxist detente, see Roger Garaudy, *From Anathema to Dialogue: The Challenge of Marxist-Christian Cooperation* (1967), by a leading French Communist; Garaudy and Quentin Lauer, *A Christian-Communist Dialogue* (1968); and Paul Oestreicher, ed., *The Christian-Marxist Dialogue: An International Symposium* (1969). A. J. Ayer, ed., *The Humanist Outlook* (1968) is mostly by those whom Kathleen Nott calls the non-Godists. Compare Julian Huxley, ed., *The Humanist Frame* (1961). Malcolm Muggeridge's *Jesus Rediscovered* (1969) is an interesting lay reaction toward the church. Augustin Cardinal Bea, *Unity in Freedom; Reflections on the Human Family* (1964) stands on the shelf with other "ecumenical" statements. E. L. Mascall, *Christian Theology and Natural Science: Some Questions on Their Relations* (1956, 1965) is one of the most intelligent statements of the issues in this long debate.

Political and Social Thought: H. Stuart Hughes, *The Obstructed Path* (1968) deals with French social thought between 1930 and 1960 and may be compared with Roy Pierce, *Contemporary French Political Thought* (1966). Such scholarly surveys seem less satisfactory for the tormented realm of politics than the steaming products of direct involvement, but here one runs into an immense quantity of ephemera. Statements from the embattled ranks of youth include Tariq Ali, ed., *The New Revolutionaries; A Handbook of the International Radical Left* (1969); Alexander Cockburn and Robin Blackburn, eds., *Student Power* (1969); and David Singer, *Prelude to Revolution* (1970), a rambling and jejune statement on the Parisian uprising of May, 1968. Reasonably judicious is R. Aya and N. Miller, eds., *The New American Revolution.* The turgid style and muddled thought of Peter Buckman, *The Limits of Protest* (1970) and Joseph Berke, ed., *Counter Culture* (1971) exemplify much of this sort of literature. More thoughtful and distinguished, and less uncritically revolutionary, statements come from Stephen Spender, *The Year of the Young Rebels* (1969), and Raymond Aron, *The Elusive Revolution* (1968), an account of those days in Paris in May 1968 that have inspired an incredible number of books, including J. Servan-Schreiber, *The Spirit of May* (tr. 1969)—the author of *The American Challenge* rather unconvincingly finding the source of the trouble in French technical and social "backwardness." Compare Max Heirich, *The Spiral of Conflict: Berkeley, 1964* (1971), and Christopher Driver, *The Exploding University* (1971). David Martin, ed., *Anarchy and Culture: The Problem of the Contemporary University* (1969) is a superior effort, which may be compared with George F. Kennan, *Democracy and the Student Left* (1968), and Hervé Bourges, ed., *Student Revolt: The Activists Speak* (1968). The veteran American philosopher Sidney Hook wrote *Academic Freedom and Academic Anarchy* (1971). An able summary exhibiting much sympathy for the young rebels is George Paloczi-Horvath, *Youth up in Arms* (1971). A witty comment on the "student stirs" at Oxford may be found in *The Letters of Mercurius* (1970), rumored to come from the pen of a well-known English historian.

Frantz Fanon, *The Wretched of the Earth* (tr. 1966) and *Toward the African Revolution* (tr. 1967); Regis Debray, *Blueprint for Revolution* (1968); and Daniel Cohn-Bendit, *Obsolete Communism: A Left-Wing Alternative* (1968) can represent revolutionary extremism. Herbert Marcuse's polemical works include *One-Dimensional Man* (1964), *Negations* (1969), and *Essay on Liberation* (1969). A polemic against him is *Contra Marcuse* (1971) by Eliseo Vivas. Richard King, *The Party of Eros: Radical Social Thought and the Realm of Freedom* (1972) is better than Paul A. Robinson, *The Freudian Left: Wilhelm Reich and Geza Roheim and Herbert Marcuse* (1969) at treating a group including Wilhelm Reich and Norman O. Brown, as well as Marcuse. Perry Anderson, ed., *Towards Socialism* (1965) was a New Leftish British symposium; compare Gerald Kaufman, ed., *The Left: A Symposium* (1966). Pauline Gregg, *The Welfare State: An Economic and Social History of Great Britain from 1945 to the Present Day* (1967) is excellent on its subject in Great Britain.

On Communism and Marxism since 1945, Raymond Aron, *Marxism and Existentialism* (1967) sums up the French debate involving Sartre and Merleau-Ponty, whose *Humanism and Terror: An Essay on the Communist Problem* was translated in 1969. Two convenient paperbacks (Doubleday Anchor) are Walter Odajnyk, *Marxism and Existentialism* (1965), and Wilfrid Desan, *The Marxism of Jean-Paul Sartre* (1971). Indispensable for the general topic of French Communism are Louis Aragon, *L'Homme communiste* (1953); Charles Micaud, *Communism and the French Left*

(1963); and Annie Kriegel, *Les Communistes français, essai d'ethnographie politique* (1969). Compare Henry Pelling, *The British Communist Party: A Historical Profile* (1958), and Milorad Drachkovitch, ed., *Marxist Ideology in the Contemporary World; Its Appeals and Paradoxes* (1966). The books of David Caute, *Communism and the French Intellectuals 1914–1960* (1964), and Neal Wood, *Communism and British Intellectuals* (1959), deal mostly with the prewar period. Examples of the post-1945 reaction against Communism are printed in Richard Crossman, ed., *The God That Failed* (1949), and are lucidly expressed in Raymond Aron, *The Opium of the Intellectuals* (1957). Among the many anniversary evaluations published in 1967 or 1968 are M. Drachkovitch, ed., *Fifty Years of Communism in Russia* and *Fifty Years of Soviet Power* published by *The Monthly Review*. J. D. B. Miller and T. H. Rigby, eds., *The Disintegrating Monolith: Pluralist Trends in the Communist World* (1967) pursues a fascinating theme, on which see Wolfgang Leonhard's *The Three Faces of Marxism* (tr. 1973). See his earlier *The Kremlin since Stalin* (1959). See also Richard Lowenthal, *World Communism: The Disintegration of a Secular Faith* (1964). Richard T. De George, *The New Marxism: Soviet and East European Marxism since 1956* (1968) treats an important subject, on which see also the chapter by George L. Kline on Kolakowski in *European Philosophy Today;* also Leopold Labedz, ed., *Revisionism: Essays on the History of Marxist Ideas* (1962). Leszek Kolakowski's *Toward a Marxist Humanism: Essays on the Left Today* was translated by Jane Z. Peel (1968). Compare Adam Schaff, *Marxism and the Human Individual* (1970). Martin Jay, *The Dialectical Imagination* (1973), a lengthy and very scholarly account of the "Frankfurt School" between 1923 and 1950, treats Marcuse, Adorno, Fromm, and others who began their experiments in a looser form of Marxism quite early in Weimar Germany. Professor Jay projects a continuation to cover the later years of this group, a work which should become the most scholarly treatment of Marcuse. Marcuse's *Soviet Marxism: A Critical Analysis* (1958) is pertinent here. Peter Demetz, in the last two chapters of his *Marx, Engels, and the Poets; Origins of Marxist Literary Criticism* (English ed., 1967), discusses recent neo-Marxist literary criticism (Lukács, Adorno). Lukács is treated in a volume of the Fontana Modern Masters series, by George Lichtheim. The same series offers short studies of Frantz Fanon and Ché Guevara. The revisionist books of Milovan Djilas, especially *The New Class: An Analysis of the Communist System* (1957), received much attention. An essay by George L. Kline in the previously cited *Phenomenology and Existentialism,* edited by Kline and Lee, adds to the literature on Communism and Existentialism. Erich Fromm, ed., *Socialist Humanism: An International Symposium* (1965), an Anchor paperback, reprints mostly eastern Europeans.

There is a large and interesting literature on dissent in the Soviet Union: Peter Reddaway, *Russia's Underground Intellectuals* (1970); Robert Conquest, *The Politics of Ideas in the USSR* (1967); Harold Swayze, *Political Control of Literature in the USSR 1946-1959* (1962); Abraham Rothberg, *The Heirs of Stalin: Dissidence and the Soviet Regime 1953-1970* (1972), an excellent monograph; Robert C. Tucker, *The Soviet Political Mind* (1972); and a chapter by Patricia Blake in Alexander Dallin and Alan F. Westin, eds., *Politics in the Soviet Union* (1966). Much has been reprinted from the dissenters: Pavel Litvinov, *The Demonstration in Pushkin Square: The Trial Records with Commentary and an Open Letter* (1969), tr. by Manya Harari; Karel von Het Reve, ed., *Dear Comrade: Pavel Litvinov and the Voices of Soviet Citizens in Dissent* (1969); Leopold Labedz, ed., *Solzhenitsyn: A Documentary Record* (1971); and the writings of Andrei Sakharov (*Progress, Coexistence, and Intellectual Freedom,* 1968), Solzhenitsyn (*Cancer Ward, First Circle, Gulag Archipelago*), and others, including R. A. Medvedev, *Let History Judge,* and Z. A. Medvedev, *A Question of Madness,* both translated in 1971. Some of the *Samizdat* have now been translated and reprinted. See also Alex Simirenko, ed., *Soviet Sociology* (1968); George L. Kline, *Religious and Anti-religious Thought in Russia* (1969); Richard T. De George, *Patterns of Soviet Thought* (1966) and, with others, *Science and Ideology in Soviet Society* (1967).

On political ideas farther to the right, C. Northcote Parkinson, in his *Left Luggage: A Caustic History of British Socialism from Marx to Wilson* (1967), displays considerable animus and considerable wit at the expense of socialism, British style. Compare Peregrine Worsthorne, *The Socialist Myth* (1971). Stephen Haseler, *The Gaitskellites: Revisionism in the British Labour Party 1951-1964* (1969) is a more serious study of a British socialism sobered not so much by power as by the loss of it. Compare John D. Hoffman, *The Conservative Party in Opposition, 1946-1952* (1964). Vernon Bogdanor and Robert Skidelsky, eds., *The Age of Affluence, 1951-1964* (1970) evaluates the Tory years from Churchill to Profumo. Harold K. Schellenger, *The SPD in the Bonn Republic: A Socialist Party Modernizes* (1968) relates an important transformation in German politics, similarly from mystique to politique. Conservative thought in the text is associated with Michael Oakeshott, *Rationalism in Politics and Other Essays* (1962) and Kingsley Amis, *Lucky Jim's Politics* (1968). W. H. Greenleaf has written a study of Oakeshott's thought (1967). The de Gaulle mystique is conveyed in the admiring work of a great French writer, François Mauriac, *Charles de Gaulle* (1964); de Gaulle's leading intellectual acolyte is examined by Janine Mossuz, *André Malraux et le Gaullisme* (1970). A representative manifesto of the free-market school is *Right Turn,* edited by Rhodes Boyson (1970). In *Left or Right: The Bogus Dilemma* (1968) Samuel Brittan suggests the irrelevancy of the old ideologies. C. K. Kaltenbrunner, ed., *Rekonstruktion des Konservatismus* (1972) indicates German interest.

For some discussion of utopias, see the stimulating *From Utopia to Nightmare* by Chad Walsh (1962); also George Kateb, *Utopia and Its Enemies* (1963); Thomas S. Molnar, *Utopia, the Perennial Heresy* (1967); and W. H. D. Armytage, *Yesterday's Tomorrows: A Historical Survey of Future Societies* (1968).

Pamela Hansford Johnson, *On Iniquity; Some Personal Reflections Arising Out of the Moors Murder Trial* (1967) was cited in the text in connection with a revolt against permissiveness. On pornography, Lawrence's own reflections were edited by Harry T. Moore as *Sex, Literature, and Censorship* (1953). Penguin Books published C. H. Rolph, ed., *The Trial of Lady Chatterley* (1961). There is an essay "The Problem of Pornography," in Herbert Read, *To Hell with Culture and Other Essays on Art and Society* (1963), and another by Geoffrey Gorer, "The New Pornography," in *The Danger of Equality* (1966). See also Read's *Does Pornography Matter?* (1966). John Sparrow's *Controversial Essays* (1966) includes two on the Lady Chatterley case and one on the Profumo affair. In addition to Anthony Burgess and David Holbrook, cited in the text, see Masud R. Khan, "The Politics of Subversion and Rage," *Times Literary Supplement*, February 4, 1972, and other articles in this series called The Abuses of Literacy. Ensuing letters to the editor in both *Spectator* and *TLS* may profitably be consulted. Other symposia are Douglas A. Hughes, ed., *Perspectives on Pornography* (1970) and Irving Buchen, ed., *The Perverse Imagination: Sexuality and Literary Culture* (1970). Edward M. Brecher, *The Sex Researchers* (1969) is informative. The French Kinsey or Masters-Johnson equivalent was Dr. Pierre Simon et al., *Rapport sur le comportement sexuel des français* (1972).

Science: In addition to C. P. Snow's *The Two Cultures and the Scientific Revolution* (1959), see his *The Two Cultures: And a Second Look* (1965). F. R. Leavis' reply is printed in Leavis and Michael Yudkin, *Two Cultures? The Significance of C. P. Snow* (1962). One of the best commentaries is Lionel Trilling's long essay in *The Liberal Imagination: Essays on Literature and Society* (1950). By way of interesting comparison as well as background, one might consult Walter M. Simon, "The Two Cultures in Nineteenth Century France," *Journal of the History of Ideas,* January–March, 1965. Charles Davy, *Towards a Third Culture* (1965); Jacques Barzun, *Science: The Glorious Entertainment* (1964); and George Levine and Owen Thomas, eds., *The Scientist vs. the Humanist* (1963) were among the many interventions in this debate. See also *TLS* special issue of October

25, 1963, "The Art of Science." Severe disenchantment is expressed in Lewis Mumford, *The Myth of the Machine* (1966, second volume 1970) and Montgomery Belgion, *The Worship of Quantity: A Study of Megalopolitics* (1969). Herbert J. Muller, *The Children of Frankenstein: A Primer on Modern Technology and Human Values* (1970), another fashionable attack on the technological society, may be compared to Jacques Ellul's work, *The Technology Society,* previously cited. In *A Runaway World?* (1968), the BBC Reith Lectures for 1967, Edmund Leach attempts to make science hip. Compare Bernard Dixon, *The Politics of Science* (1971). Snow's other nonfictional works include *Science and Government* (1961) and *Public Affairs* (1971), a collection of essays.

A book advocating that nonscientists get acquainted with more science is J. Bronowski, *The Common Sense of Science* (1953); see also his *Science and Human Values* (1965). Aldous Huxley, *Literature and Science* (1963), and Wylie Sypher, *Literature and Technology: The Alien Vision* (1968) explored the connection also treated in parts of the *TLS* "Crosscurrents" issue, September 28, 1967. Barry Commoner, *Science and Survival* (1966) is an expression of "environmental" concern by one of the more responsible ecologists, blaming science for contamination. Compare his 1971 book *The Closing Circle: Nature, Man, and Technology.* Arthur Koestler's gift for serious science popularization is further revealed in *The Roots of Coincidence* (1972). The book *Twentieth Century Sciences,* G. J. Holton, ed., is a reprint from the magazine *Daedalus* (1972).

The new obscurantism may be strikingly seen in John Michell, *The Flying Saucer Vision* (1967), in aspects of Theodore Roszak, *The Making of a Counter-Culture* (1970) with its preference for shamans over scientists, and in innumerable books about witchcraft, etc., to which a sound guide is Robert Galbreath, ed., *The Occult: Studies and Evaluations* (1972). Kathleen Nott, *A Soul in the Quad: The Uses of Language in Philosophy and Literature* (1969) contains some delightful forays against scientism invading the arts and philosophy. Morton Grodzins and Eugene Rabinowitch, eds., *The Atomic Age: Forty-Five Scientists and Scholars Speak* (1963) is a large book of readings from scientists on public issues involving science. Charles E. Raven, *Teilhard de Chardin: Scientist and Seer* (1962) ably appraises a figure who tried to unite disparate realms and earned the mistrust of both. Norbert Wiener, *God and Golem, Inc.* (1964) discusses the impact of cybernetics on man. Other serious philosophical explorations of science's status as knowledge are Karl Popper, *The Logic of Scientific Discovery* (1959); Norwood Hanson, *Patterns of Discovery: An Enquiry into the Conceptual Foundations of Science* (1965); George Boas, *The Challenge of Science* (1965); and Ernst Cassirer, *The Philosophy of Symbolic Forms* (3 vols., tr. 1953 1957). In *New Maps of Hell* (1960), Kingsley Amis wrote seriously about science fiction, on which theme also worth reading are essays by C. S. Lewis in *Of Other Worlds: Essays and Stories* (1966). An appreciation of J. R. R. Tolkien will be found in *Master of Middle-Earth: The Fiction of J. R. R. Tolkien* (1973) by Paul H. Kocher.

Possibly most significant of all was Edmund Husserl's last book, *The Crisis of European Sciences and Transcendental Phenomenology* (1970), edited by David Carr.

Sociology and Social Science: Robert A. Nisbet, *The Sociological Tradition* (1967), and Raymond Aron, *Main Currents of Sociological Thought* (2 vols., 1969) supply background. Thomas H. Marshall, *Sociology at the Crossroads* (1963); A. W. Gouldner, *The Coming Crisis of Western Sociology* (1971); and the *TLS* special issue, "What Is Sociology?" April 4, 1968, reflect currents of doubt and reappraisal among sociologists. Ralf Dahrendorf, *Essays in the Theory of Society* (1968) is by the *doyen* of present German sociologists, whose objectivity may be compared with the ideological commitment of the Marcuse school. See also Percy S. Cohen, *Modern Social Theory* (1968). A stimulating debate, *The Limits of Behavioralism in Political Science,* edited by James C. Charlesworth, was published by the American Academy of Political and Social Science in 1962. Harold D. Lasswell, *The Future of Political Science* (1963), intoxicated by visions of computerized exactitude, and Heinz Eulau, *The Behavioral Persuasion in Politics* (1963), may be compared with the deflating assaults on all social science of A. R. Louch, *Explanation and Human Action* (1965), and H. P. Rickman, *Understanding and the Human Studies* (1967). *The Study of Political Behaviour* (1958) was written by D. E. Butler, a leading English psephologist, whose works on British elections and the criticisms of their conclusions provide a good case study in the validity of the "scientific" approach to politics; but Dante Germino, *Beyond Ideology: The Revival of Political Theory* (1967), sees a reaction against scientific positivism, such as Eric Voegelin earlier expressed in *The New Science of Politics* (1952). W. G. Runciman, *Social Science and Political Theory* (2nd ed., 1969) is a sensible mediation. In *The Broken Image: Man, Science and Society* (1964), Floyd W. Matson accuses the social scientists of having a naive and obsolete set of scientific presuppositions. The most significant works on theory and philosophy of history published in the postwar years are probably R. G. Collingwood, *The Idea of History* (1946), and Karl Popper, *The Poverty of Historicism* (rev. ed., 1957). For a summation of recent theory of history, see Paul K. Conkin and Roland N. Stromberg, *The Heritage and Challenge of History* (1971). An excellent selection of readings may be found in Ronald H. Nash, ed., *Ideas of History,* vol. 2 (1969). In *Beyond Economics: Essays on Society, Religion, and Ethics* (1968), Kenneth E. Boulding brings the mind of an outstanding economist to bear on a variety of human issues. A good guide to some recent economic thought may be found in Part III of Ben B.

Seligman's *Main Currents in Modern Economics* (1962). Compare Claudio Napoleoni, *Economic Thought of the Twentieth Century* (1972). For an overview of the world of psychology, see Benjamin B. Wolman, *Contemporary Theories and Systems in Psychology* (1960); Daniel Hameline, *Anthologie des psychologues français contemporaines* (1969); Jean Chateau, *Le Malaise de la psychologie* (1972); Colin Wilson, *New Pathways in Psychology: Maslow and the Post-Freudian Revolution* (1972); Robert Boyers, ed., *R. D. Laing and Anti-Psychiatry* (1972); Rollo May, ed., *Existential Psychology* (1969); Medard Boss, *A Psychiatrist Discovers India* (1967).

Among introductions to Structuralism are Michael Lane, ed., *Structuralism: A Reader* (1970); Jean Piaget, *Structuralism* (1970); and Jacques Ehrmann, ed., *Structuralism* (paperback edition 1970). M. Leroy, *Main Trends in Modern Linguistics* (tr. 1967) is a useful guide, which can be supplemented by John Lyons, ed., *New Horizons in Linguistics* (1970). Serge Doubrovsky, *The New Criticism in France* (tr. 1973) reviews recent debates involving Structuralists. For an approach to the thought of another French master, see Octavio Paz, *Claude Lévi-Strauss, an Introduction* (1968), or Anthony Burgess, "Culture as a Hot Meal," a review of *The Raw and the Cooked, Spectator,* July 11, 1970. Much of Lévi-Strauss has been translated into English. There is a stunning review of *Mythologiques* in *TLS,* April 7, 1972. See also James A. Boon, *From Symbolism to Structuralism* (1972). Jacques Lacan, the structuralist psychologist and friend of Lévi-Strauss, had his *The Language of the Self* translated in 1968. Roland Barthès' *Elements of Semiology* was translated in the same year.

Raymond Rosenthal, ed., *McLuhan: Pro and Con* (1968), and G. E. Stearns, ed., *McLuhan: Hot and Cool* (1967) are interesting debates. Among McLuhan's books are *The Gutenberg Galaxy* (1962), *Understanding Media* (1964), and *War and Peace in the Global Village* (1968). William Kuhns, *The Post-Industrial Prophets* (1973) compares McLuhan with Fuller, Mumford, Ellul, and several other critics of technological society. On the theme of trendiness, there is an amusing Italian novel by P. M. Pasinetti, *Domani improvvisamente (Suddenly Tomorrow)* (1971). Henri Lefebvre, *La Fin de l'histoire* (1970) addresses itself to one of the themes of this book.

Index

Acton, Lord, 204
Adams, Henry, 90, 119, 120
Adams, John, 140
Adenauer, Konrad, 31–32
Adorno, Theodor W., 58, 64, 96, 185
Albérès, R. M., 100
Algren, Nelson, 133
Ali, Tariq, 82
Alvarez, A., 90, 93, 97–98
Amalrik, Andrei, 194
Amis, Kingsley, 84, 244
  as conservative, 53, 84, 113
  on educational explosion, 171
  as uncommitted, 37
  view of knowledge industry, 134–35
Anderson, Perry, 142
Anouilh, Jean, 38–39
Antschel, Paul, 97
Apollinaire, Guillaume, 98
Aquinas, St. Thomas, 168
Aragon, Louis, 35
Arendt, Hannah, 81
Arminius, 3
Arnold, Matthew, 14
  modern life and, 136
  scientific thought and, 148, 156, 157, 163, 164
Aron, Raymond, 38
  as conservative, 53
  on end of socialist myth, 82
  on Marxism and Existentialism, 8
  philosophy of, 126
  revolution as viewed by, 6
  scientific thought and, 185
  Weber and, 50
Auden, W. H., 49, 178
Austin, J. L., 24, 174
Ayer, A. J., 20–21, 150, 156

Bach, Johann Sebastian, 138
Bacon, Sir Francis, 121
Bagehot, Walter, 91
Bakunin, Mikhail, 69
Balzac, Honoré de, 236
Barraud, Henry, 96
Barrès, Maurice, 91, 221
Barth, John, 26, 207
  influences on, 28–29
  poll on reading of works of, 115 16
Barth, Karl, 4, 12, 15, 22, 202

Barthes, Roland, 231
Barzun, Jacques, 145, 151
Baudelaire, Charles, 87, 98, 139
Baynes, Ken, 99
Beardsley, Aubrey, 98
Beauvoir, Simone de, 11, 80, 84, 159
Beckett, Samuel, 29, 39, 41, 138, 236, 242
Beer, John, 146
Beethoven, Ludwig van, 96, 141
Behavioral sciences, 169–75
Belgion, Montgomery, 152
Bell, Daniel, 10
Belloc, Hilaire, 221
Bellow, Saul, 102, 131, 240, 243
Ben Bella, Ahmed, 75
Benn, Gottfried, 59, 134
Bennett, Arnold, 150
Bentham, Jeremy, 140, 150
Berdyaev, Nikolas, 15, 36, 190
Berenson, Bernard, 229
Bergson, Henri, 93, 156, 168, 219
Berlin, Isaiah, 142
  admired (1950s), 36
  on civilization, 146
  on Hitlerism, 4
Bernstein, Eduard, 197
Berryman, John, 97, 115
Besterman, Theodore, 140
Bevan, Edwyn, 10
Binswanger, Ludwig, 177
Bismarck, Otto von, 3, 4
Blackmur, R. P., 217
Blake, Robert, 140
Blake, William, 150
Bloch, Ernst, 48, 198
Blumer, Herbert, 175–76
Böll, Heinrich, 3, 28
Bolt, Robert, 104
Bonald, Louis G. A. de, 65
Bond, Edward, 104, 241
Bonhoeffer, Dietrich, 50, 203
Booker, Christopher, 87, 95
Boss, Medard, 177, 179
Boulez, Pierre, 96
Bowes, Pratima, 169
Boye, Karin, 10
Bradley, F. H., 92, 93
Brahms, Johannes, 96, 138
Braine, John, 43, 53, 83

Braque, Georges, 100
Braubach, Max, 140
Brecht, Bertolt, 3, 27, 243
  influence of, 59
  popularity of, 38
Breda, H. L. van, 19
Brée, Germaine, 27
Brezhnev, Leonid, 57
Brown, Norman O., 66, 176, 184
Browning, Robert, 89, 128, 199
Brunner, Emil, 26
Bryce, James Lord, 215
Buber, Martin, 15, 50, 207
Bukovsky, Vladimir, 193, 195
Bultmann, Rudolf, 15, 50, 203, 205, 207
Burckhardt, Jakob, 116, 117
Buckle, Henry Thomas, 124
Burgess, Anthony, 110, 115
Burke, Edmund, 164
  and conservatism, 44, 45
  scholars' interest in, 139, 140
Burlyuk, David, 92
Burne-Jones, Edward Coley, 116, 148
Burroughs, William, 110
Bury, J. T., 172
Butler, Samuel, 147, 148

Cage, John, 95, 138
Campbell, Roy, 221
Camus, Albert
  Communism and, 6, 35
  Existentialism and, 11, 13, 14, 17–18
  Marxism rejected by, 17
  Sartre and, 79, 81
  sees through myth of History, 9
  works of, 28, 100, 243
Capitalism, 10
  New Left hatred for, 59
  1950s, 45–48
  reaffirmation of free enterprise, 45–47
  rise of boredom and growth of, 55–56
Carlyle, Thomas, 91, 150, 164, 221
Carpenter, Edward, 107
Cary, Joyce, 52
Cassirer, Ernst, 159
Castro, Fidel, 58, 75, 83, 200
Celan, Louis (Paul Antschel), 97
Celaya, Gabriel, 11
Céline, Louis-Ferdinand, 241
Chabrol, Claude, 241
Chagall, Marc, 94
Charbonneau, Bernard, 219
Charteris, Hugo, 28

Chateaubriand, François René de, 56
Chesterton, G. K., 221
Chiari, Joseph, 38, 39
Chomsky, Noam, 213, 228–32
Christianity, 201–8
  Christian-Communist dialogue, 201–5
  secular, 205–8
Christie, Agatha, 196
Churchill, Sir Winston, 104, 213
Claudel, Paul, 221
Cleaver, Eldridge, 141
Clerk-Maxwell, James, 122
Cohen, Leonard, 101
Cohn, Norman, 190
Cohn-Bendit, Daniel, 63, 74
Coleridge, Samuel Taylor, 32, 150, 202
Collingwood, R. G., 49, 167
Communism
  ambivalence toward, 192
  art under, 195–96
  Christian-Communist dialogue, 201–5
  deproletarianization of, 70–71
  disenchantment with, 35, 43
  embracing (1930s), 2, 119–20
  evaluation of orthodox, 73–74
  irrational fear of (1950s), 32
  Marcuse and orthodox, 64
  New Left and orthodox, 50, 59
  rejection of, 5–10
  schism in, 76–77, 189–201
Comte, Auguste, 24, 91, 124, 198, 222
Conrad, Joseph, 132
Conservatism
  counterreaction of (1960s), 83–85
  of 1950s, 31–54
  varieties of (1950s), 52–54
Crane, Hart, 91, 98
Crawley, Harriet, 62
Croce, Benedetto, 67, 82, 134

Dahrendorf, Ralf, 185
Daiches, David, 6
Daniel, Yuri, 193, 195, 196, 243
Daniel-Rops, Henri, 51
Darwin, Charles, 122, 150, 182
Davidson, John, 93
Davie, Donald, 37, 53–54, 132
Debray, Régis, 84
De Kooning, Willem, 39, 103
Descartes, René, 15, 168, 222, 231
  revolt against, 121, 147
  Valéry and, 158
Devlin, Bernadette, 74

Dewey, John, 156
Dickens, Charles, 4, 164, 174
Djilas, Milovan, 197
Dodsworth, Martin, 102
Donne, John, 91
Dostoyevsky, Fydor, 15, 122
Dowson, Ernest, 92, 93, 116
Dumont, René, 75
Dunn, Nell, 172-73
Durkheim, Émile, 91, 240
Dürrenmatt, Friedrich, 51
Duverger, Maurice, 76
Dylan, Bob, 101

Eckstein, Harry, 214
Edel, Leon, 140
Einaudi, Luigi, 45
Einstein, Albert, 49, 92, 151, 168
Eisenhower, Dwight D., 32
Eliade, Mircea, 133
Eliot, George, 140, 155
Eliot, T. S.
    admired (1950s), 36
    Bradley and, 92
    Crane and, 91
    influence of, 128
    intellectual fragmentation and, 119
    Maurras' influence on, 53
    modern knowledge and, 131-32
    modern life and, 13, 136
    obscurity of, 89
    poetic resources of, 93
    as reactionary, 48, 221-23
    religion and, 50-51
    traditions and, 218
Ellis, Havelock, 93, 107
Ellison. Ralph, 102, 141
Ellul, Jacques, 154
Emerson, Ralph Waldo, 217
Empson, William, 37
Engels, Frederick, 8, 157-58
Enzenberger, Hans Magnus, 59, 75
Erhard, Ludwig, 45
Ernst, Morris, 111
Escriva de Balaguer, José Maria, 206
Esslin, Martin, 23, 242
Evans-Pritchard, E. E., 39-40
Euclid, 159
Existentialism, 10-20, 176
    apolitical element in, 35
    Christian, 50
    distrust of, 158
    Husserl and, 168

    as looking two ways, 37-38
    Marcuse and, 65
    New Left and, 63
    of novelists, 27-28
    radical dualism close to, 36
    reason and, 8

Fanon, Frantz, 70
Faguet, Émile, 90
Fascism, 213
    effects of, 2-3
    forerunner of, 222-25
    New Left affinities with, 71-72
    rise of, 69
    victims of, 67
Faulkner, William, 27
Ferlinghetti, Lawrence, 103
Feuerbach, Ludwig, 155
Fevre, Lucien, 229
Fisher, Marvin, 84
Flaubert, Gustave, 56, 91, 157
Fleming, Ian, 180
Ford, Henry, 67-68
Forster, E. M., 7, 213
Fourier, Charles, 91
Fragmentation
    assaults on heritage and intellectual,
        131-43
    consequences of intellectual, 128-31
    intellectual, 119-43
    synthesis and intellectual, 123-28
France, Anatole, 15
Franco, Generalissimo Francisco, 45-46
Frankel, Charles, 224
Frederick Barbarossa, 3
Frederick the Great, 3
Freud, Sigmund, 19
    influence of, 179-80
    Marcuse and, 64-66
    modern consciousness of, 93
    reductive strategy of, 141, 212
    science and, 155
    on sexual liberation and love, 114
    sexual repression and, 68
    trend in modern psychology and,
        176-78
Friedman, Milton, 45
Frohock, W. M., 100
Fromm, Erich, 64, 178

Galbraith, John Kenneth, 125, 152
Galileo, 123, 233
Galsworthy, John, 133

Gambetta, Léon, 156
Garaudy, Roger, 201, 219
Gaulle, Gen., Charles de
  Algerian conflict and, 55
  conservatism of, 31, 32, 48, 52
  cult around, 58
  on life, 48
  Malraux and, 35, 48, 164
  obscene publications under, 109
Gay, John, 174
Gellner, Ernest, 68
Genet, Jean, 80, 104, 110
Gentile, Giovanni, 134
George, Stefan, 139
Gheorghiu, Constantin, 149
Gibbon, Edward, 124
Gide, André, 27, 48, 93, 138, 175, 236
Ginsberg, Allen, 41
Ginzburg, Ralph, 109–10
Giraudoux, Jean, 39, 149
Gladstone, William Ewart, 164, 215
Godard, Jean-Luc, 78–80, 84, 211, 241
Godwin, William, 232
Goebbels, Joseph, 40
Goethe, Johann Wolfgang von, 4
Golding, William, 28, 166
Goldwater, Barry, 52
Gorbanevskaya, Natalia, 193
Gorer, Geoffrey, 39
Gramsci, Antonio, 67–68
Grass, Günther, 3, 26, 28, 110, 243
Graves, Robert, 22
Greene, Graham, 4, 28, 48, 242
Guardini, Romano, 236
Guevara, Ché, 58, 63, 75, 83, 84, 104
Guiton, Margaret, 27
Gunn, Thomas, 37, 225

Haight, Gordon, 140
Haldane, J. B. S., 148
Hallam, Henry, 124
Halle, Louis, 211
Hansteen, Aasta, 236
Hardy, Thomas, 37
Hartley, L. P., 52, 150
Hassan, Ihab, 102
Hawthorne, Nathaniel, 84
Hayek, Friedrich A., 45
Hefner, Hugh, 202
Hegel, G. W. F., 3, 8, 230
  Existentialism and, 11, 12
  Marcuse and, 65
  Teilhard de Chardin and, 219

Heidegger, Martin, 207
  Existentialism and, 11–14
  Laing and, 177
  Marcuse and, 64
  as rightist, 134
  on sameness of U.S. and Russia, 35–36
Heisenberg, Werner, 168
Heller, Erich, 125
Hemingway, Ernest, 27
Hempel, Carl G., 167
Hermann, Kai, 71
Hertz, Heinrich, 122
Hesse, Hermann, 27, 243
Hexter, J. H., 140
Hingley, Ronald, 196
Hitler, Adolf
  charisma of, 57
  conservative 1950s and, 33, 39
  effects of rule of, in postwar period, 28, 29
  effectual accomplices of, 156
  Frankfurt school and, 65
  humanistic culture not preventing, 134
  mass murder under, 34
  Mussolini compared with, 67
  New Left and, 142
  pacifism and, 62
  popular mythology exploited by, 212
  postwar mood toward, 2–5
  rage for order as characteristic of, 222
  subjectivism and condemnation of, 223
  Völkisch state of, 119
  as wild romanticist, 225
Hobbes, Thomas, 28, 62, 185
Hochhuth, Rolf, 3
Hoffman, Werner, 89, 90
Holbrook, David, 113
Honegger, Arthur, 96
Horn, D. B., 124
Hough, Graham, 84, 85, 231
Howard, Brian, 92
Hugo, Victor, 56, 156
Hume, David, 19
Husserl, Edmund, 12, 93, 168
  Marcuse and, 64
  Phenomenology of, 18–20
Huxley, Aldous
  on Christianity, 50
  on Freud, 180
  intellectual novels of, 133

on Lawrence, 148–49
as Romantic, 157
and sex as means of social control, 161
on thought and matter, 140
world view of, 10, 135
Huxley, Julian, 156
Huxley, Thomas, 148, 163
Hynes, Samuel, 106

Inglis, Fred, 222
Ionesco, Eugène, 59, 127, 137
Isaacs, Alan, 208

Jakobson, Roman, 228
James, Henry, 140
James, William, 19, 41, 93
Jameson, Storm, 111
Jarry, Alfred, 92, 106, 116, 158
Jaspers, Karl, 12–13, 16, 23, 50
Jefferson, Thomas, 140
Jennings, Ivor, 238
Joachim of Fiore, 190
Jonson, Ben, 223
Johnson, Samuel, 84, 147, 164, 224, 227
Jones, LeRoi, 141
Jouvenel, Bertrand de, 10, 45, 218
Joyce, James, 230
  as conservative, 48
  influence of, 52, 128
  Leavis and, 154
  as literary giant, 27, 89, 132
  on literature in modern world, 26
  poetic resources of, 92–93
  pornography and, 107, 108, 110
  scholars' interest in, 139
Jung, Carl
  academic trend in pscyhology and, 176
  influence of, 177
  later thought of, 179, 180, 232, 233
  scientific thought and, 156
  scholarship of, 19

Kafka, Franz, 10, 27
Kandinsky, Vasily, 94, 100
Kant, Immanuel, 4, 25, 166, 168, 230
Karol, K. S., 75
Kautsky, Karl, 64
Kennedy, John F., 32, 58, 211
Kepler, Johannes, 233
Kerouac, Jack, 41
Keynes, John Maynard, 45, 191, 245

Khan, Masud, R., 113
Khrushchev, Nikita, 32, 57, 58, 194
Kierkegaard, Sören, 8, 12, 38, 50, 203
Kinsey, Alfred, 161, 162, 174
Kissinger, Henry, 213
Klee, Paul, 94, 100
Koestler, Arthur, 6, 9, 33, 169
Kohl, Herbert R., 210
Kolakowski, Leszek, 197
Krutch, Joseph Wood, 1–2
Kubrick, Stanley, 115
Küng, Hans, 206

Lacan, Jacques, 232
Laing, R. D., 87, 177, 179
Laird, Melvin, 213
Larkin, Philip, 37, 41, 51, 132
Laski, Harold, 6, 9, 213
Lasswell, Harold D., 170
Lawrence, D. H.
  admired (1950s), 36
  as conservative, 48, 53
  on ego, 240
  A. Huxley on, 148–49
  Leavis and, 165
  literary reputation of, 27, 97, 223
  on modern life, 132
  on novel, 28, 218
  pornography and, 107–10
  scholars' interest in, 139
  scientific thought and, 156, 163
  ultimate value for, 11, 133
Leakey, Louis, 219
Lear, Elmer N., 212
Leary, Timothy, 77
Leavis, F. F., 40, 135, 150, 157, 163–65, 223
Le Corbusier, 158
Left, the, 45
  antiintellectualism of, 134
  decay of old non-Communist, 61
  Hungarian revolt (1956) and, 32
  kinds of Right and view of, 52
  Right extremism and extremism of, 226
  Swing to (1960s), 55–86
  See also New Left
Lenin, V. I., 104, 143
  betrayed, 82
  dogmatism of, 157–58
  Husserl compared with, 19
  left-wing infantilism and, 62–63
  Marxism and, 8, 64, 191–92, 197, 199

power sought by, 73
proletariat and, 69
Lessing, Doris, 37, 40
Levi, Albert W., 167
Lévi-Strauss, Claude, 133, 220, 228–31, 235
Lewis, C. S., 225
  classical temperament of, 157
  as conservative, 151, 220, 223
  followers of, 221
  on modern poetry, 88
  plunge into obscurity and, 89
  scientific thought and, 148
Lewis, Wyndham, 48, 119, 136, 182
Lichtenstein, Roy, 101
Lilar, Suzanne, 162
Lindop, Grevel, 101
Lindsay, Jack, 38
Litvinov, Pavel, 193
Lloyd, Trevor, 199
Lloyd-Jones, Hugh, 171
Locke, John, 19, 166
Logical Positivism, 20–22, 181
Logue, Christopher, 101
Lorca, Frederico Garcia, 132
Louch, A. R., 174–76
Lowell, Robert, 115
Lowry, Malcolm, 31, 97
Lucie-Smith, Edward, 100
Lukács, George, 58, 64, 69, 88, 198
Luther, Martin, 3, 4, 32
Lyell, Sir Charles, 123
Lysenko, Trofim, D., 198–99

McCarthy, Joseph, 32–34
McCarthy, Mary, 41
Macaulay, Thomas Babington, 124, 164
McCawley, James, 228
MacDonald, Dwight, 135
McDougall, William, 176
Machiavelli, Niccolò, 32, 62
McKuen, Rod, 101, 223
MacLeish, Archibald, 17, 29
McLuhan, Marshall, 64, 105, 135–37, 143, 222
Macmillan, Harold, 32, 60, 164
Mailer, Norman, 110, 112, 113
Malherbe, François de, 138–39
Malinowski, Bronislaw, 142
Mallarmé, Stéphane, 78, 89, 91, 139
Malraux, André, 27, 28, 100
  de Gaulle and, 35, 48, 164
  Russian Revolution and, 35
  on science, 151

Man, Henry de, 190
Mancini, Federico, 184, 209–10
Mann, Thomas, 27, 71
Mao Tse-tung, 58, 84, 200
  New Left and, 63, 64, 75
Marcel, Gabriel, 50
Marcus, Steven, 112
Marcuse, Herbert, 36, 185
  New Left and, 64
  Reich compared with, 68
  social and political views of, 64–66, 69, 71–73
  vulgarized permissiveness and, 111
Marinetti, Emilio, 92
Maritain, Jacques, 50
Markov, Vladimir, 92
Marquez, Pompeyo, 76
Martin, David, 62, 129, 171
Martin, Kingsley, 9
Martin du Gard, Roger, 133
Marx, Karl
  "alienation" and, 217
  crude evolutionary ethics of, 5
  early thought of, 66–67
  existentializing thought of, 198
  influence of, on modern world view, 122
  as Modernist, 91
  Nietzsche compared with, 45
  proletariat and, 73
  science and, 155
  working class and, 69
  youth and, 129
Marxism, 212
  abandoning dogmatic, 61
  antiintellectual aspects of popular, 141–42
  Camus rejects, 17
  Christianity and, 202, 204, 205
  congealed, 178, 179
  deproletarianizing, 69, 70
  dogmatic, 185
  Existentialism and, 9
  historians' view of, 190–91
  historical process and, 197
  as the ideology for contemporary man, 82–83
  Institute for Social Research and, 64
  Lenin and, 8, 64, 191–92, 197, 199
  Marcuse and, 65
  New Left and, 57, 59, 64, 76, 77, 82, 238
  reinterpretation of, 157–58
  rerevival of (1960s), 9

Sartre and, 6–8, 65, 67, 82, 158
Third World and, 199, 200
Toynbee on, 189–90
Mascall, Eric, 202
Maslow, Abraham, 179
Masters, William, 162
Matisse, Henri, 100
Mauriac, François, 4, 36, 48, 100
Maurras, Charles, 53, 221–25
Mauthner, Fritz, 22
Medawar, Peter, 219
Medvedev, Roy, 193
Melville, Herman, 223
Mercer, David, 74
Merleau-Ponty, Maurice, 7, 17, 24, 35, 176
Michelet, Jules, 121
Michell, John, 153
Micklem, Nathaniel, 25–26
Mill, John Stuart, 57, 122, 156, 164, 245
scholars' interest in, 139, 140
Miller, Henry, 29, 108, 113
Miller, Jonathan, 136–37
Millett, Kate, 113
Mills, C. Wright, 57, 175
Mills, James, 57
Milton, John, 164, 181
Minogue, Kenneth, 125
Mitchell, Adrian, 101
Modernism
beyond, 94–100
disease of, 87–118
modernist neurasthenia, 89–94
pornography as phase of, 106–15
recent themes in, 100–6
Moinot, Pierre, 132
Molière, 147
Mollett, Serge, 185
Molnar, Thomas, 159
Mondrian, Piet, 94, 100
Monod, Jacques, 182–83
Montesquieu, Baron de, 49, 185
Montherlant, Henry de, 26, 39, 100, 243
Moore, G. E., 21
Moreau, Marcel J., 72
Morgan, George W., 217
Morgenthau, Hans, 33
Morley, John, 141
Morris, William, 164
Mortimer, John, 112
Muggeridge, Malcolm, 160–61, 208
Mumford, Lewis, 151–52
Murdoch, Iris, 26, 28
Mussolini, Benito, 2, 67, 70, 222

Myrdal, Gunnar, 238
Myrdal, Jan, 238

Namier, Sir Lewis, 142, 245
Nationalism, 48
Nazism, 213
art under, 195
Christian resistance to, 50
cinema (in 1950s) and, 39
effects of, 2–3
New Left affinities with, 71–72
Nietzsche and, 4, 222
religion and, 203
rise of, 156
Neizvestny, Ernst, 194
Neoclassicism, 220–26
Neophilia, 87–89
consequences of, 115–17
defined, 87
Neruda, Pablo, 28
Neurasthenia, modernist, 89–94
Neville, Richard, 77
New Left
emergence of, 58–62
fragmentation and, 128–29
ideologists of, 62–73
ignoring whole segments of knowledge, 142
Marxism and, 57, 59, 64, 76, 77, 82, 238
Nihilism of, 200
Old Left and, 73–83
response of the arts to, 103–4
science and, 151, 153
Newby, P. H., 206
Newman, John Henry Cardinal, 222
Newton, Sir Isaac, 49
Nichols, Peter, 104, 241
Niebuhr, Reinhold, 7, 49–51, 53, 203, 213
Nietzsche, Friedrich
dissolution of art and, 93–94
dissolution of values and, 11
Existentialism and, 15
flight from civilization and, 132, 133, 139
fragmentation and, 217, 219
"God is dead" proclaimed by, 203
influence of, on modern world view, 122
Marx compared with, 45
Nazism and, 4, 222
science and, 147, 168
on truth, 64

Nkrumah, Kwame, 75
Nolte, Ernst, 224

Oakeshott, Michael J., 43–44, 53
Order
  neoclassicism and, 220–26
  rage for, 217–20
  structuralism as, 226–33
Ortega y Gasset, José, 121, 157, 218
Orton, Joe, 104, 241
Orwell, George, 6, 8–10, 18, 242
  Amalrik and, 194
  on life, 48–49
  obscene words and, 108
  as Romantic, 157
  science and, 149
  sexual repression and, 161
  view of utopias held by, 33
Osborne, John, 42, 53, 72, 83
Otto Rudolf, 18

Padilla, Heberto, 75
Paine, Tom, 45
Painter, George, 140
Pannenberg, W., 205
Pareto, Vilfredo, 6, 134
Parkes, Harry Bamford, 131
Parsons, Talcott, 173–75
Pascal, Blaise, 15, 147
Pasternak, Boris, 26, 193, 243
Pasteur, Louis, 122, 151
Patten, Brian, 101
Pattison, Mark, 122
Paz, Octavio, 236
Peckham, Morse, 90
Péguy, Charles, 203, 221
Penderecki, 96
Perec, Georges, 72
Perkin, Harold, 243–44
Perón, Juan, 204
Phenomenology, 18–20, 24, 63, 167–68, 176
Picasso, Pablo, 100
Pinter, Harold, 29, 104, 133, 241
Planck, Max, 49, 92, 168
Plath, Sylvia, 97, 115, 162
Plato, 45, 57, 168, 181, 233
Plomer, William, 52
Plumb, J. H., 140
Podhoretz, Norman, 85
Polanyi, Michael, 161
Pollock, Jackson, 39, 103
Ponge, M. Francis, 138–39
Popper, Karl R., 9, 142

Pornographic revolution, 106–15
Positivism, 167, 168, 172
Pound, Ezra, 1, 48, 93, 119, 132
  McLuhan compared with, 136
  as reactionary, 222–23
Powell, Anthony, 133
Propp, V. Y., 228
Proust, Marcel, 48, 128, 140
Psychology, 178–80
Puccini, Giacomo, 134
Pythagoras, 230, 233

Rabelais, 107, 161, 174
Ralegh, Sir Walter, 121
Rattigan, Terence, 104
Read, Herbert, 137
Reddaway, Peter, 193
Reich, Charles A., 69
Reich, Wilhelm, 68, 111
Religion, 1950s, 40, 49–51
Remond, René, 52
Renan, Ernest, 155
Rickman, H. P., 175, 176
Riefenstahl, Leni, 134
Riesman, David, 71
Right, the
  antiintellectualism of, 134
  French (1815–present), 52
  Left extremism and extremism of, 226
  science and, 152
Rimbaud, Arthur, 89, 98, 116
Robbe-Grillet, Alain, 41, 99, 110, 112–13
Robbins, Lionel, 45
Rockefeller, Nelson A., 52
Rolph, C. H., 109
Romains, Jules, 133
Röpke, Wilhelm, 45
Rossetti, Dante Gabriel, 116
Rostow, W. W., 47
Rousseau, Jean-Jacques, 133, 232
Rubin, Jerry, 143, 213
Rueff, Jacques, 45
Ruskin, John
  as conservative, 45, 65, 217, 221
  influence of, on modern world view, 122
  on literature, 108
  as social critic, 164
Russell, Bertrand
  change in political views of, 62, 125
  on himself, 242
  as intellectual leader, 126
  Marxism as viewed by, 190

philosophical endeavors of, 20, 21, 23, 41, 146, 230, 235
science and, 156, 163
Rycraft, Charles, 68
Ryle, Gilbert, 174

Sade, Marquis de, 109, 110, 237
Saint-Simon, Henri de, 120–21
Sakharov, A. D., 193, 196
Santayana, George, 44, 98
Sapir, Edward, 227
Sartori, Giovanni, 117
Sartre, Jean-Paul, 59
    Camus and, 79, 81
    Communism and, 7, 17, 192
    Existentialism of, 10–20, 58; see also Existentialism
    greatness of, 100, 220, 235, 243
    human condition transcends social order, 35
    influence of, 29, 241
    Marcuse compared with, 65, 66
    Marxism and, 6–8, 65, 67, 82, 158
    New Left and, 84
    1950s intellectuals dominated by, 34
    pornography and, 110
    reemergence of (1960s), 79–80
    revolutionist affinities of, 38
    as Romantic, 157
    works of, 28
Satie, Erik, 95
Saussure, Ferdinand de, 227
Sayers, Dorothy, 221
Schaff, Adam, 197
Schmidt, Michael, 101
Schopenhauer, Arthur, 32
Schweitzer, Albert, 51
Science
    attacks on, 148–55
    attempts at mediation between humanism and, 166–69
    attraction to, 155–60
    behavioral, 169–75
    clash of cultures and, 160–65
    computers, 180–83
    humanism vs., 145–48
    Positivistic, 49–50
    psychology, 175–80
    scientific reason, a case for, 183–85
Scrutton, Mary, 21
Shakespeare, William, 164
Shattuck, Roger, 92
Shaw, George Bernard, 69
Shklar, Judith, 9–10, 157
Sholokhov, Mikhail, 193

Shrewsbury, J. F. D., 159–60
Shute, Nevil, 34
Sik, Ota, 46
Sillitoe, Alan, 40, 42, 43
Silone, Ignazio, 6
Simirenko, Alex, 185
Sinclair, Upton, 133
Sinyavsky, Andrei, 193, 195, 196
Skinner, B. F., 176, 182
Smith, Adam, 45, 46, 76, 166, 239
Snow, C. P., 20, 40, 98, 127, 146, 157, 182
    science and, 161, 163, 164, 183
Solzhenitsyn, Alexander, 193–95, 243
Sorel, Georges, 69, 139, 190
Sparrow, John, 211
Spencer, Herbert, 126, 163, 239
Spender, Stephen, 29, 92, 164
    on modern innovations in art, 94
    on 1950s conservatism, 53
Spengler, Oswald, 1, 125
Stalin, Joseph, 5, 33, 35, 57, 62, 199
    crimes of, revealed, 58
    death of, 192, 198
    final years of, 34
    intellectuals and, 5, 6
    Lysenko and, 199
    Marxism and, 197
    New Left and, 142
    methods of, 194–95, 197
    Mussolini compared with, 67
    power sought by, 73
    Trotsky and, 82
Stalinism, 7
    as monstrous tyranny, 35
    relaxation of, 32
    resistance to, 134
Stein, Gertrude, 42
Steiner, George, 134, 137–38
Stoppard, Tom, 133
Strauss, Johann, 96
Strawson, P. F., 24–25
Structuralism, 226–33
Swift, Jonathan, 147
Sypher, Wylie, 41, 244

Talmon, J. L., 50
Teilhard de Chardin, Pierre
    attempts synthesis of knowledge, 126, 131, 218–20, 230, 244
    Freud compared with, 177
    greatness of, 235
    1950s and, 34
    religion and, 50

Teller, Edward, 162
Terson, Peter, 133
Thackeray, Henry, 236
Thody, Philip, 79, 80
Thomas, Dylan, 34
Thomas, Henri, 133
Thompson, Francis, 77
Tillich, Paul, 50, 207
Tito, Marshal, 199
Tocqueville, Alexis de, 139, 185
Togliatti, Palmiro, 58
Tolkien, J. R. R., 160, 221
Tolstoy, Leo, 23, 87–88, 193
Tönnies, Ferdinard, 71
Toscanini, Arturo, 134
Touré, Sékou, 75
Toynbee, Arnold J., 10, 165, 177, 235
  attempts synthesis of knowledge,
    123–26, 131, 218, 230, 244
  on Communism, 7
  Lévi-Strauss compared with, 230, 231
  on Marxism, 189–90
  1950s and, 34
  religion and, 50, 51
  "schism in the soul" in view of, 217
  Teilhard compared with, 218, 219
Trevor-Roper, H. R., 120, 123
Trilling, Lionel, 48, 161
Trotsky, Leon, 5, 82
Truman, Harry S., 32
Turner, Nat, 104
Tweedie, Jill, 112
Tynan, Kenneth, 59

Updike, John, 102, 110, 116, 133
Upward, Edward, 9

Valéry, Paul, 89, 105, 115, 119, 218
  Descartes and, 158
Van Buren, Paul, 202
Van Vogt, A. E., 178
Vico, Giambattista, 139, 147
Verdi, Giuseppe, 232
Victoria (Queen of England), 104
Vizetelly, Henry, 107
Voegelin, Eric, 50
Voltaire, 32, 93, 126, 140, 147, 158

Wagner, Richard, 139
Wain, John, 36–38, 54, 222, 243
Wallace, Edgar, 180
Walpole, Sir Horace, 15
Walsh, Chad, 149

Warhol, Andy, 101
Waugh, Auberon, 115, 117
Waugh, Evlyn, 36, 48
Weaver, Richard, 225
Webb, Beatrice, 155
Webb, Sidney, 155
Weber, Max
  influence of, 13, 50, 71, 79
  law of disenchantment of the world,
    192
  organization men and, 10
  scholarship of, 19, 185
  science and, 182
  world view of, 32–33, 72, 91
Weil, Simone, 6
Weizsaecker, Carl, 169
Welk, Lawrence, 84, 96, 223
Wells, H. G., 107, 126, 146, 150, 156
Wesker, Arnold, 58
Whitehead, Alfred North, 145, 230
Whyte, William H., 173
Wild, John, 19
Wilde, Oscar, 92, 93, 98, 107
Wiles, Peter, 129
Wilhelm II (German Kaiser), 3, 4
Williams, Raymond, 61
Willkie, Wendell, 62
Willmott, Peter, 172, 173
Wilson, Angus, 28, 52
Wilson, Charles, 212
Wilson, Colin, 28
Wilson, Harold, 58
Wilson, Woodrow, 62, 140
Winters, Yvor, 98, 222–25
Wittgenstein, Ludwig, 19, 21–23, 142,
    174, 220, 235
Wolfe, Thomas, 131
Wollstonecraft, Mary, 237
Wood, Charles, 104, 241
Woolf, Virginia, 40, 52, 150, 163, 240

Xenakis, 96

Yeats, William Butler, 6, 93, 94, 119, 203
  admired (1950s), 36
  on Christianity, 221
  as reactionary, 45, 48
  scholars' interest in, 139
Yevtushenko, Yevgeni, 193, 195
Young, Michael, 172, 173

Zhdanov, A. A., 40
Zola, Émile, 56, 107, 155